STABLE MONEY

A HISTORY OF THE MOVEMENT

BY

IRVING FISHER, LL.D.

Professor of Economics, Yale University

ASSISTED BY

HANS R. L. COHRSSEN

NEW YORK · ADELPHI COMPANY · PUBLISHERS

MANUFACTURED IN THE UNITED STATES OF AMERICA
BY THE VAIL-BALLOU PRESS, INC., BINGHAMTON, N. Y.

TO
PRESIDENT FRANKLIN DELANO ROOSEVELT

ACKNOWLEDGMENTS

I AM especially indebted to Mr. Cohrssen for his very efficient help. I wish also to express my thanks to several friends who have read the manuscript and offered many valuable suggestions as to form and substance. Among those who have helped me in this way are my wife, my brother Herbert W. Fisher, my son Irving N. Fisher, Norman Lombard, Arthur D. Gayer, Miss Alice Natt, and Miss Katherine Tracy. For important help on the two parts concerning Sweden I am indebted to Erik T. H. Kjellstrom, Per Wijkman, Baron Johan Liljencrants, and Anton Lindberger. To D. M. Dow my thanks are likewise due for help on the part concerning Australia.

I am also under obligations to the Committee for the Nation both for suggestions and for material assistance toward defraying the expenses of extensive library research.

And, finally, I wish to thank President Roosevelt for permission to dedicate the book to him. His avowed Monetary Policy represents the goal at which the stable money movement has aimed.

IRVING FISHER

August, 1934

CONTENTS

CHAPTER III. ACADEMIC STAGE (FROM 1914)

CHAPTER IV. POPULARIZING STAGE (FROM 1905)

CONTENTS

CHAPTER V.   LEGISLATIVE STAGE (TO 1932)

CHAPTER VI.   LEGISLATIVE STAGE (1932-1934)

CHAPTER IX. OFFICIAL RECOGNITION ABROAD
(FROM 1919)

APPENDIX I

APPENDIX II

APPENDIX III

APPENDIX IV

APPENDIX V

APPENDIX VI

INTRODUCTION

ABOUT ten years ago, when Owen D. Young was asked to take part in the stable money movement, he acceded to the request with alacrity, saying, "You need not try to 'sell' me on your proposition; for I think it is about the most important thing in the world—economically. What convinced me was my experience in Germany on the Dawes Commission. I found that the one great need was a stable mark. Even the workmen had come to see this. With the terrible inflation they complained that they had no way to lay by for a rainy day, even to provide the money needed for an expected addition to the family. The marks lost value faster than they could be saved."

Others who had, like Owen D. Young, observed inflation at first hand or who had read books on stabilization were equally easy to enlist in the stable money movement. But such people were few and far between. The great mass of people were "not interested," because they had never had their eyes opened either to the fact or the evils of unstable money.

There will, therefore, be two sorts of readers of this book: a few who had already studied stable money and know it to be "about the most important thing in the world—economically" and a large number who have not previously studied the subject and who will wonder what it is all about.

No one in the latter class can possibly appreciate the great importance of the subject of which this book treats until he has changed to the former class, that is has acquired a realizing sense of how, all his life, he has been the victim of the "money illusion." This illusion is the notion that the monetary unit is always

xvii

the same, so that it can serve as a measure of value of other things, but does not need to be measured itself.

We may cite two extreme examples of the money illusion—one in Germany, the other in the United States. In 1922 the present writer and another American economist, Professor Frederick W. Roman, visited Germany largely to find out if the ordinary German realized that the mark had fallen. Up to that time, the mark had, as a matter of fact, lost 98% of the purchasing power it possessed before the War. But we found that at least 19 out of 20 German men and women had no idea that anything had happened to their mark!

Of course, the Germans all knew that prices had risen, just as we all "know" that the sun "rises." But they thought this rise of prices had to do only with the supply and demand of commodities. Their reckonings were confused. A merchant who bought an article for 1 mark and later sold it for 3 marks thought he had made a profit, when actually he had made a loss because, between the buying and the selling, the mark had fallen so greatly. As to the real secret of the high prices—monetary inflation, causing a fall in the mark—they had no idea whatever.

A year later, in 1923, they woke up to the fact, almost overnight, that it was not so much that commodities had risen but that the mark had fallen, just as the school boy suddenly comes to realize that the sunrise or sunset which he thought he could "see" so plainly is an illusion and that really it is the earth which is turning. Thereafter they began to measure the mark not, however, in terms of commodities but in terms of the American dollar, that is, gold.

This experience gave the German public a vague notion of an unstable mark and a healthy fear of inflation, as well as of the "calamity boom" which goes with inflation. Unfortunately, however, this way of measuring the mark did not help the stable money movement but rather hurt it; for it fostered the myth

that *gold* is stable, simply because, in 1922–1923, gold was less unstable than the paper mark. It was quite natural that the German
people should thus measure the mark in terms of the nearest
thing for measuring money of which they could think—namely
some other sort of money. They could not be expected to know
of index numbers by which to measure the mark far better. Even
economists had only, a few years before, begun to make any
serious use of index numbers.

In the United States, we have had an object lesson the obverse
of Germany's. While in Germany, it required a *depreciation* of
over 99% in value of the mark to make any considerable number of Germans realize that it was the mark, rather than commodities, which had changed, in America, it required an *appreciation* of the purchasing power of the dollar of over 75% before
even a tiny minority of our citizens woke up. When, in July
1933, President Roosevelt cabled the London Economic Conference his insistence on controlling the purchasing power of the
dollar, the "experts" there were mostly bewildered, despite the
fact that Professor Cassel, Governor Rooth, and Mr. Per Wijkman (all of Sweden) were on hand ready and eager to show
that their country had already stabilized her krona in terms of
an index number representing cost of living. The only sort of
stabilization which the average delegate at that conference could
conceive of was stabilization relatively to gold, that is, stabilization in terms of the monetary units of other countries (stabilization of foreign exchange).

Yet no one could have spoken more plainly than President
Roosevelt when he radioed to the London Conference in favor
of "the kind of a dollar which a generation hence will have the
same purchasing and debt-paying power as the dollar we hope
to attain in the near future." Although the President has expressed the same thought many times, so that millions on millions of people must have heard it, and although his influence on

the average man's ideas is far greater than that of any one else in America and probably in the world, nevertheless the ordinary ear is still deaf even to the mere idea of stable money—all because, behind that ear is a brain in which, as a fixed part of its "mental furniture," is the almost ineradicable "money illusion."

Money and banking are so mysterious to the average person that the only popular concepts are those analogous to the ancient ideas of right and wrong—the "taboo." The popular notions, including those of the ordinary banker, are as primitive as the superstitions of a Russian peasant before the War. Such notions are: "It is a matter of honor to keep on gold" (instead of on a stable standard); "Inflation is always wrong" (even to correct deflation); "We must not tinker with the Currency" (even when it needs mending); "Irredeemable paper is unsound" (even when it is stable); "Money should be 'hard' money"; and so on. But of the fundamental principles, if any, behind such precepts, or even of the historical experiences which led to these precepts, he is blissfully unaware. And so, in Germany, the calamitous inflation merely left behind a precept: "Don't ever leave gold again." This was the "gold complex."

But fortunately, besides such naïve and unreasoning popular psychology, there are always a saving few who learn the lessons of history. Just as New York City got its health department seventy years ago from an epidemic, just as many cities get a good fire department after a bad fire, and just as safety at sea became a new object of solicitude after the Titanic disaster; so a stable dollar can come only after instability has worked enough havoc to cause some pivotal men to get emancipated from the money illusion. No banker like Governor Strong or Governor Rooth, and no President like President Roosevelt, would or could have achieved stabilization without some such antecedent catastrophies.

Besides emancipation of our leaders from the money illusion

and besides replacing crude taboos by some understanding of money, there is needed a greater appreciation of the evils wrought by unstable money—evils commonly attributed to the wrong causes.

Every period of inflation has tragic consequences to the creditor class and creditor-like class, including savings bank depositors, while every period of deflation has equally tragic consequences to the debtor and debtor-like classes, including farmers, business men, and stockholders. The wage earner loses at both times— during inflation through the high cost of living outdistancing wages, and during deflation through unemployment. Both inflation and deflation, in the end, do harm to all classes by throwing out of adjustment the whole economic mechanism. The inflation calamity boom exhausted Germany and the recent deflation exhausted America.

The present book is intended to be not so much a history of these catastrophies, due to unstable money and endured by unsuspecting millions subject to the money illusion, but rather a history of the efforts of a few to remedy or prevent such catastrophies. It is hoped, however, that some day a professional historian will write a history of the rôle of unstable money in history itself. A few of us who have looked over this field in a preliminary way are convinced that a rich harvest is ripe for the economic historian. He will find that other historians, subject to the money illusion, or entirely innocent of monetary economics, have repeatedly missed the point of outstanding events in history. Only a few even now realize that the waning of Hoover and the waxing of Roosevelt were little more than the political reaction to an enlargement of the dollar. If we can be so blind to our own times, we ought not to be surprised to find that historians have run blindfold over the many successive hills and dales of inflation and deflation from ancient to modern times.

Only occasionally does this "money question" come to the surface. Some historians do realize that deflation "made" Bryan politically and that subsequent inflation "unmade" him. A few economic historians have pointed out that war inflation causes a calamity boom after war, ending in a crisis,—for instance, after the Napoleonic Wars in 1818, after the Crimean War in 1857, after the Civil War in 1866, after the Franco-Prussian War in 1873, after the World War in 1920.

But history is also full of more hidden instances of the tremendous disturbances from unstable money. What at last broke the German morale but the fall of the mark, unrecognized as such but complained of under the cry of "profiteering"? What made "populism" but deflation, and unmade it but inflation? What finally led to bolshevism in Russia but a falling ruble? Lord D'Abernon, one of the keenest British students of money, went so far as to say that, in his opinion, 80% of the labor discontent in Europe after the War was due to this cause. What first brought the labor government to England? What caused the early agrarian discontent in Ireland, and what later precipitated that discontent into revolution? What has overturned governments and caused the many revolutions throughout Europe since the War?

It is not, of course, contended that unstable money is the sole economic determiner in history. It is only contended that its rôle is a big one and that it has been very generally overlooked— because of the money illusion; consequently the history of all important periods of rising and falling prices should be studied anew, with the historian's eyes open to the now known effects of inflation and deflation.

Nor is it contended that stable money is a panacea. But it will cure much and, to a large extent, clear our sight for whatever else is needed.

As the present writer stated in 1919 in *Stabilizing the Dollar*,

"It is not pretended that to stabilize the purchasing power of the dollar would banish all complaint in the financial, business, and industrial world, much less serve as a substitute for progressive economies. A stable monetary unit would be no more a substitute for the fertility of the soil than a stable bushel basket. Yet a reliable bushel will indirectly help even the tilling of the soil; and a reliable dollar would remove a heavy handicap now put on our productive energy and so indirectly help all production. Dependable weights, measures, and standards eliminate those enormous wastes which come from uncertainty, and, of all the possible wastes from uncertain units used in commerce, those from an uncertain dollar are by far the greatest and the gravest."

CHAPTER I

TO RICARDO (1816)

Section i. Meaning of Stable Money

*Stability in Terms of the Weight of Precious Metals, and
Stability in Terms of Foreign Exchange*

STABILIZATION, when this term is used in connection with money,
means in its most general sense keeping the value of money
stable according to some chosen standard. For centuries the precious metals have served as such standards, or measures of value.
The early advocates of stabilization, such as Oresme, Copernicus,
and Gresham, therefore, insisted upon the maintenance of a
fixed weight and fineness of the metal in circulating coins. When
paper had taken the place of coins, the stability of money became synonomous with the convertibility of paper money into
coin of constant weight and fineness.

As the precious metals, and particularly gold, came to be internationally accepted as the monetary standard of value, the
stability of the foreign exchanges, *i.e.* the ratio of exchange of
one gold currency to another became the criterion of monetary
stability, and this purely relative stability was automatically secured by gold shipments.

The supposed advantages of stable exchange rates in facilitating international trade, gradually made the maintenance of this
sort of stability the main object of monetary administration. Some
countries that had little or no monetary gold, even managed their
currencies so as to maintain stable exchange rates with gold

1

standard countries. In that manner their currencies became indirectly stabilized relatively to gold through the operation of
what is known as the "gold-exchange" standard.

If a currency is stabilized with regard to one commodity, such
as gold or silver, its purchasing power over all other commodities
consequently falls or rises with changes in the supply of and
demand for the chosen metal. Such fluctuations in the value of
money, that is, fluctuations in its purchasing power, have, in all
times, had a detrimental effect upon social conditions, and as a
result of this, there arose a demand for a kind of money which
would be stable, not in terms of a certain weight of gold or silver, but in terms of purchasing power over commodities.

Stability in Terms of Purchasing Power

Until recent times, the difficulty of measuring this purchasing
power of money over commodities prevented people from recognizing to what extent monetary fluctuations were responsible
for a great number of economic and social disorders. "Prices
rise," or "prices fall," people would say, when in reality the purchasing power of money had fallen or risen. "Too many goods,
overproduction," seemed to be the obvious explanation for low
prices; "scarcity of goods, and profiteering," were the reasons advanced for high prices. Yet, the trouble was really due to scarcity
of money (deflation) or oversupply of money (inflation). As already noted, the "money illusion" leads people to assume that
money is in itself stable, and they consequently look to the goods
for the cause of all price fluctuations.

Yet, each period of inflation and deflation has produced its
advocates of a currency which would have an invariable, or less
variable, purchasing power, and their number increased when
monetary fluctuations became more severe. But not until there
was a general recognition of the utility of index numbers in de-

termining the purchasing power of money could the demand for a money which would be stable in this respect, become articulate. At this writing, the movement which originated with the theoretical proposals of economists, has developed into the practical monetary policy of President Roosevelt.

It is primarily the development of this type of stabilization which the present book attempts to trace. The term "stabilization," whenever used, therefore, means only the stabilization of the purchasing power of money,—in other words, the complete absence of monetary inflation and deflation.

Besides stabilization relative to gold and stabilization relative to purchasing power, there have been numerous other plans for and efforts toward, monetary stabilization. There need here be mentioned only: bimetallism; symmetallism; the labor standard; and basing the value of money on a certain fraction of the national wealth. Sliding wage-scales, and similar attempts at overcoming the changing value of money, may also be called stabilization proposals. It would lead us too far afield, to describe all these attempts in detail. They will be mentioned only in so far as they have been of direct influence in evolving the idea of stabilization in terms of purchasing power, that is, stabilization relative to the general level of commodity prices.

The opponents of stabilization have frequently dismissed the entire problem of stable money as either non-existent or insoluble. The recent great deflation, however, was bitter proof of the fact that the problem exists, and President Roosevelt's aggressive action has demonstrated that he, for one, is not afraid of attempting a practical solution.

Essentially, monetary stabilization means the establishment of an invariable, or less variable, unit, or standard, of value. At present, economics is still in the position of a science without a dependable unit of measure with which to make its calculations.

Inaccuracy of the Standard of Value Compared with Other Standards

A "United Press" notice from London, May 2, 1932 [1] stated that because from 1852 to 1932, the imperial yardstick had shrunk in length by two ten-thousandths of an inch, and the imperial standard pound had lost one five-millionth of its weight, replicas of both standards were to be the subject of scientific observations extending over a period of nine months. The object of the observations was to be to discover substitutes which would be invariable.

The report further mentioned that tests for a light-wave yardstick had reached an accuracy of one four-millionth of an inch, and that more recent studies had substantiated the accuracy of the "light-wave" measure. The problem of obtaining an accurate measure of length is thus being solved progressively according to the discoveries of science. Similar scientific methods are used to determine a more accurate measure of weight, and even of time.

But with our measure of value the matter is different. One reason for this is undoubtedly that the problem of determining a measure of value is a very complicated one, and has been possible of solution only recently through the development of index numbers. A second reason is that the solution has been left to others than the monetary scientists. A third reason is that the general public has no idea that money varies in value at all.

How grossly this problem has been neglected can readily be seen if we translate the purchasing power of our dollar, which is our unit of value, into another term of measurement. Two ten-thousandths of an inch variation in the yardstick was sufficient to prompt research for a better standard of measure. If we express the purchasing power of the dollar over commodities dur-

---

[1] New York *Times*, May 3, 1932.

ing the year 1913 by the length of 36 inches, the length of this yardstick of value would have been as follows during 36 years:

1896	51	inches
1913	36	"
1920	19	"
1922	23	"
1929	20	"
1932	27	"

The above figures are taken from a book of Professor Edwin Walter Kemmerer.[2]

Section 2. Examples in Early History

Ancient Greece

One of the first laws for the management of currency was contained in the famous legislation of *Lycurgus,* about 840 B. C., banning gold and silver from the country, and making a certain iron disk the only legal tender. Whether the purpose of these laws was to prevent trade and intercourse with other countries, or to make Sparta independent of the gold and silver supply of other countries, may be difficult to ascertain. But the fact seems to be that, for several hundred years, the medium of exchange in Sparta was these iron disks, stamped on one side and intrinsically of little value.

In modern language, therefore, Sparta had an inconvertible currency, the soundness of which was based solely upon the limitation of its volume by the state, so as to maintain its purchasing power. Similar monetary systems are said to have been in use in the Greek republics of Ionia, and Athens, and in the Greek colony of Byzantium between 600 and 500 B. C.

[2] Edwin Walter Kemmerer, *Kemmerer on Money,* Philadelphia, The John Winston Company, 1934, p. 10.

Also in periods of financial stress, the use of almost worthless metal as money for domestic circulation was usually resorted to, in order to save the precious metals for foreign trade and for carrying on wars.

Plato, writing at about 350 B. C., described a legal tender money which would circulate only nationally, and which would have no value for transactions between different countries or their citizens, the precious metals to be reserved in the treasury to serve as "universal" currency for international use.[3] This practice was similar to the foreign exchange restrictions and the impounding of gold in the U.S. Treasury which became a part of the monetary policy of President Roosevelt.

There is even evidence that the early Greeks actually measured coins by commodities, *i.e.* determined the value of their money by its purchasing power over some other commodity or commodities than the one used for money. A certain gold coin, for many centuries, was always worth an ox; and Plutarch regarded the Drachma as worth a sheep, and also worth a "measure," probably of oil, or corn, or both.[4]

A number of students of monetary history believe that some of the most highly developed of the ancient peoples benefited, whether consciously or unconsciously, by systems of managed currency. Some even go so far as to declare that monetary management provided the basis for their culture, and that, with the abandonment of the principle of stabilization, the culture declined. The following quotation expresses this thought very well:

". . . there is at least some ground for supposing—and some profound students of monetary science are indeed convinced

[3] See: Alexander Del Mar, *A History of Money in Ancient Countries,* London, 1885; *The Science of Money,* New York, 1904.

Augustus Boeckh, *Public Economy of Athens,* translated from the German, London, 1828.

[4] Norman Angell, *The Story of Money,* New York, Frederick A. Stokes Co., 1929, pp. 60–61.

that it is the case—that some of these ancient people did for long periods live under a system of managed currency, and that it served their ends far better than the 'intrinsic value currencies' to which they lapsed. They achieved this—if they did—not by the elaboration of any intricate technique, but by the acceptance, almost accidental, certainly not very conscious or analyzed, of a single underlying principle, namely, that the value of money—should be a matter of social authority controlling its quantity; that it is a means of social bookkeeping, a piece of money being evidence that its holder is entitled to a certain amount of goods." [5]

Ancient China

Some of the early Chinese Philosophers also discussed the problem of monetary management for the purpose of arriving at a stable value, and it seems that their theories were tested by practical experience during various periods. *Kuan Tzu,* who died in 644 B. C., is said to have propounded the following principle of monetary management:

"The Government should control the ratio between money and commodities by issuing and redeeming money, . . ." [6]

In 524 B. C., the *Duke Mu of Shan* is said to have advocated the regulation of the purchasing power of money by the issuance of supplementary currency:

"In ancient time when there was any natural calamity, the Government coined money in accordance with its quantity and its value, for the relief of the people. If the people suffered from the cheapness of money, the government coined dear money and put it into circulation for them. Therefore, the dear money controlled the cheap money in the market, and all the people got

[5] *Ibid.,* p. 135.
[6] Quoted from: Chen Huan Chang, *The Economic Principles of Confucius and His School,* New York, Columbia University, Longmans, Green & Co., agents, 1911, p. 556.

the benefit. If they felt the money too dear, the Government coined more cheap money, and put it in circulation, but did not abolish the dear. Therefore, the cheap money controlled the dear money in the market, and all the people were also benefited." [7]

Several hundred years later, *Chia Yi* (200–168 B.C.) mentioned a similar principle of currency control when he said:

"The Government accumulates copper for the control of the value of money. When the value is low it lessens the quantity by some policy; and when it is high, it distributes the money by some policy. Hence, the price of commodities must be equalized." [8]

Banco-Money

Banco-money ("bank money"), or money of account is believed to have originated with the establishment of the Bank of Venice, about 1171.[9] It soon became the "stable money," not only of the Republic of Venice, but of the whole trading world during the Middle Ages. Its nature was as follows: People who deposited their money with the Bank, received credit measured by imaginary banco-coins of constant gold or silver weight. In Venice this imaginary coin was called the "zecchino d'oro." The Bank accepted all coins, good or bad, domestic or foreign, and credited the depositor with such a sum of bank money or "money of account" as corresponded to the gold or silver value of the deposit.

Banco-money not only permitted the merchants to change their foreign coins into current money; it also established a comparatively stable standard of payments between countries. Also it made the traders immune to the frequent currency debasements and changes, and furnished them with protection

---

[7] *Ibid.*, p. 436.
[8] *Ibid.*, p. 439.
[9] J. Schoenhof, *A History of Money and Prices,* New York and London, G. P. Putnam's Sons, 1897, p. 63.

against fraud. Later the same principle was successfully employed by a number of other banks, of which the Bank of Hamburgh and the Bank of Amsterdam were the most important. Adam Smith explained the functions of the Bank of Amsterdam in his "The Wealth of Nations." [10]

In general, these banks did not issue coins, but only accepted them. The Bank of Venice turned all of its receipts over to the government for the use in foreign wars, etc.[11] Meanwhile depositors of the coins received transferable credits, or money of account, and these credits were the chief means of payment in the large transactions of the depositors. Money of account thus unquestionably played an important part in the development of trade in Europe from the early Middle Ages down to the end of the 18th century.

Compared with the frequently varying value of coins, banco-money was stable and furnished a dependable standard of value which no sovereign or king could debase. One of the earliest advocates of stable money, Sir James Steuart even ranked the banco-money as preferable to gold or silver, because it was more stable:

"The terms of gold and silver should convey to us no other idea than that of pure physical substances. That of money of account represents an invariable scale for measuring value." [12]

The Bracteates

One of the most interesting examples of early monetary management, is to be found in the silver bracteates of central Europe between 1150 and 1350.[13] As a consequence of frequent

[10] Adam Smith, *The Wealth of Nations*, Bk. IV, Chap. III.
[11] See: Frank Parsons, *Rational Money*, Philadelphia, Pa., C. F. Taylor, 1898, p. 35.
[12] Sir James Steuart, *Works*, Vol. III, London, 1805, p. 63.
[13] See: Hans R. L. Cohrssen: *Fragile Money*, in "The New Outlook," September, 1933.

recoinage, involving debasement, when the rulers of the respective states usually retained some of the metal for profit, coins had gradually become so thin that they could be stamped on one side only, and were easily breakable. The latter fact no doubt accounted for their name—"bracteates." They were even, in some cases, provided with marks for breaking them into smaller pieces for the purpose of making change. In size they ranged from that of a dime to that of a half-a-dollar.[14]

The chief feature of these bracteates was, however, that their recoinage was periodical. On the average, a ruler would call in all outstanding coins twice to three times a year, and exchange them for new ones after deducting a seignorage fee of about 25%. The privilege of minting thus provided rulers and bishops with a steady and easily collectible income.

One advantage of the bracteates was that they provided, for the first time in the history of central Europe, a medium of exchange of small denomination. The current gold and silver pieces were of too high value to be of much use for general circulation. And for this reason, the bracteates also made possible an increased division of labor.

But this curious form of taxation through seignorage had one other important effect. Since the bracteates were subject to recoinage and a 25% seignorage after, say, five months, there was a loss of one fourth in the value of the coins; but this loss was spread over the entire five months, at the end of which period they were exchanged for new coins. The last holder, therefore, suffered, at the most, a loss of 5%, unless he had held his coins unnecessarily long. Thus the seignorage fee must have had a considerable influence upon the *velocity* of circulation of the

[14] See also: Dr. Wilhelm Jesse, *Quellenbuch zur Muenz-und Geldgeschichte des Mittelalters,* Halle, A. Riechman & Co., 1924.

J. Schoenhof, *op. cit.,* Footnote p. 93.

Fritz Schwarz, *Segen und Fluch des Geldes in der Geschichte der Voelker,* Bern, Verlag des Pestalozzi-Fellenburg-Hauses, 1931.

bracteates. No one would want to hold coins which on the average lost 5% every month. People preferred to change their coins immediately into goods. It is said that this period was a time of cash payment, and that trade, handicrafts and the arts received a stimulus from the eagerness of the people to get rid of their money. Yet, it is claimed that any great inflation of commodity prices was avoided, and the history of this period gives no account of that profiteering which is the usual consequence of inflation.

This first example of something akin to "velocity control" is of particular interest in a history of stabilization. After the bracteates had disappeared about 1350, this principle was forgotten, until it appeared more definitely in the writings of Silvio Gesell. After his death, velocity control was, in some instances, applied in the form of "stamp scrip," during 1931–1933, in Germany, Austria, and the United States.[15]

The Tabular Standard of Massachusetts [16]

A Tabular Standard of value consists of a chosen assortment of goods, in specified quantities, to be used as a test of the value of money, with a requirement that all money payments must be made according to the changes in the value of money in terms of this assortment of goods.

Long before any such explicit theory of "tabular standard" was developed, tithes were often levied in England "in kind"; in Scotland farms were rented in terms of grains; and as early as 1576 some of the foundation of land grants of Oxford University were rented in terms of "corn" (wheat).[17]

[15] See: Irving Fisher, *Stamp Scrip,* New York, Adelphi Co., 1933.

[16] For a full discussion see: Willard C. Fisher, *The Tabular Standard in Massachusetts History* in "The Quarterly Journal of Economics," Vol. XXVII, No. 3, pp. 417–451, 1913.

[17] Act 18, *Elizabeth.*

The Colony of Massachusetts Bay, in the 18th century, when suffering from a rapidly depreciating currency, put the principle of a tabular standard into practice. Previous to 1748, the Colony had made several attempts to stop the depreciation of its money and for that purpose had issued new currency.

As in every period of inflation, profiteering was blamed as the supposed cause of rising prices, and in 1777, the famous "Act to Prevent Monopoly and Oppression" was passed. This new law fixed and listed official prices of about 50 commodities, mainly foods and wearing apparel; but it did little good, for immediately complaints began to be heard that these listed prices did not apply to the costs of production. Prices continued to rise, and the Colony found it difficult to pay its soldiers. Therefore, to satisfy the demands of the soldiers, Massachusetts declared that it would make good their wages by "taking as a measure of their wages the prices set to the articles enumerated" in the above act.

Later, four commodities were selected to measure, during the years 1777 to 1780, the value of the money payments to the soldiers.

"It being calculated upon an Average of the Rates of Depreciation as computed by the prices of Beef, Indian Corn, Sheeps Wool and sole Leather they being the Articles agreed upon by this Court and the Committee of the Army to make the said calculations upon."

The soldiers and officers of the army consequently received their pay in special notes which had the following inscription, making them payable in more or less legal tender money according as the purchasing power of the latter became less or more.

". . . Both Principal and Interest to be paid in the then current Money of said State, in a greater or less Sum, according as Five Bushels of Corn, Sixty-eight Pounds and four-seventh Parts of a Pound of Beef, Ten Pounds of Sheeps Wool, and Sixteen Pounds of Sole Leather shall then cost, more or less than One Hundred and Thirty Pounds of Current Money, at the then current Prices of said Articles . . ."

The prices of commodities were ascertained by a special Committee of Citizens. Thus, a tabular standard was adopted and these "Soldier Depreciation Notes," or "Depreciation Notes," as they were called, were, or were intended to be, a stable standard for deferred payments.

Little is known of the practical working of this plan, but the usefulness of the "depreciation notes" seems to have been generally recognized, as several acts were passed after 1780, extending the issue of such notes to others than soldiers. For example, the President of Harvard College, on October 3, 1780, was voted the sum of £497.10s, "in the new money for & in consideration of his faithful Discharge of the office of President of Harvard College & to enable him to remove his Family & Effects." [18] However, as these notes were issued for only comparatively large amounts, it is hardly possible that they could have entered into general circulation.

SECTION 3. FIRST EXPRESSIONS OF THE IDEA BEFORE
THE BULLION REPORT (1810)

The value—that is, the purchasing power—of a gold or silver unit fluctuates. This has long been known. *Sir William Petty,* in 1691, expressed the thought clearly:

"Money is understood to be the uniform measure of value and rule for the value of all commodities. . . . And as things now stand, Silver only is the matter of money. . . . [Yet] The value of Silver rises and falls itself; for Men make Vessels of coyned Silver, if they can gain by the Workmanship enough to defray the Destruction of the Coynage, and withal, more than they could expect by employing the same Silver in a way of Trade. Now the Accidents of so doing make Silver rise and

[18] Willard C. Fisher, *op. cit.,* p. 448.

fall and consequently take from the perfect Aptitude for being an uniform, steady Rule and Measure of all other things." [19]

Another writer of that period, *Freiherr Samuel von Pufendorf*, (1632–1694), also called attention to this fluctuating value of the coins:

"For since metal as to its natural price may be, and often is, brought into commerce as well as other commodities, its value must rise and fall according to the scarcity and plenty of it. And the eminent price of money must necessarily follow the natural price of the metals; for it is unreasonable that a quantity of silver, considered as a commodity, should bear a different price from what it does when considered as money." [20]

The fluctuating value of the currency must have been inducive to speculation, much to the disadvantage of the ignorant public. Sir William Petty scornfully wrote that

". . . it becomes a Trade to study and make Advantage of these Irregularities, to the Prejudice of the good People, who are taught that whatever is called Money, is the same, and regular, and uniform, and a just Measure of all Commodities." [21]

The varying value of the coins was thus clearly seen, and in 1707, *Bishop Fleetwood* [22] estimated that the value of money during two and a half centuries had decreased in the ratio of 6 to 1, since the prices of corn, meat, drink and cloth had all increased about sixfold. The reason for this depreciation was presumably the huge imports of the precious metals from America.

G. R. Carli [23] in 1764, even made a specific investigation into

[19] Sir William Petty, *The Political Anatomy of Ireland*, London, 1691, p. 68.

[20] Samuel Pufendorf, *Law of Nature and Nations*, translated into English, Oxford, 1710.

[21] *Political Economy of Ireland, op. cit.*, p. 70.

[22] W. Fleetwood, *Chronicum preciosum*, or, an account . . . of the price of corn and other commodities . . . shewing from the decrease of the value of money . . . London, 1707.

[23] G. R. Carli, *Del Valore della Proporzione de' Metalli Monetati.* . . . Quoted from Wesley Clair Mitchell: "Index Numbers of Wholesale Prices in the United

the effect of the discovery of America upon the purchasing power of money. He made one of the first simple index numbers by comparing the prices paid for grain, wine and oil in 1500 and in 1750. In 1738, *Dutot* [24] had made a similar study for France.

The fact having been established that the purchasing power of money fluctuates, *Bishop Berkeley* [25] in 1737 asked the question, whether it might not be possible to make money itself a stable measure of value:

"Question 23. Whether Money is to be considered as having an intrinsic Value, or as being a Commodity, a Standard, a Measure, or a Pledge, as is variously suggested by Writers? And whether the true Idea of Money, as such, be not altogether that of a Ticket or a Counter?

"Question 24. Whether the Value or Price of Things, be not a compounded Proportion, directly as the Demand, and reciprocally as the Plenty?

"Question 37. Whether Power to command the Industry of others be not real Wealth? And whether Money be not in Truth, Tickets or Tokens for conveying and recording such Power, and whether it be of great Consequence what Materials the Tickets are made of?"

David Hume was also concerned with the stability of money; but he attacked the problem from the credit side when, in 1752, he proposed the establishment of a National Bank for the purpose of controlling credit and the price level.

"If the public provide not a bank, private bankers will take advantage of this circumstance; . . . And therefore 'tis better, it may be thought, that a public company should enjoy the

States and Foreign Countries," Bulletin of the U.S. Bureau of Labor Statistics, No. 173, July, 1915, p. 6.

[24] Charles De Ferrare Dutot, *Reflexions Politiques sur les Finances et le Commerce*, La Haye, 1738.

[25] George Berkeley, *On Several Queries Proposed to the Public*, in "A Reprint of Economic Tracts," edited by Jacob H. Hollander, Baltimore, The John Hopkins Press, 1910, pp. 17 ff.

benefit of that paper credit, which always will have place in every opulent kingdom. But to endeavor artificially to increase such credit, can never be to the interest of any trading nation; but must lay them under disadvantages, by encreasing money beyond its natural proportion to labour and commodities, and thereby heightening their price to the merchant and manufacturer." [26]

Sir James Steuart (1767) called attention to the inadequacy of the precious metals to serve as a standard of value:

"Question IV. Is the preserving of the pound sterling at the mean value of a determinate weight of fine gold, and fine silver, a sure method of realizing the unit of money of accompt, so as to preserve it at all times invariable?

"Answer. I apprehend it is not; although it seems to be the best that can be devised, upon supposition that the metals are to be made use of, as the most proper substance for realizing the scale." [27]

Not many writers have since then presented the "case against the gold (or silver) standard" with more clarity. Although there have been numerous other expressions since that time, Sir James Steuart has laid down the fundamental principles so well that his statement of them may be used even today.

"Since gold and silver, then, are commodities like every other thing, the invariable scale of value must measure *them* as well as every other commodity, and money of account must be considered in no other light, than a scale for expressing the proportional value of grains of metals, yards of stuffs, pounds of wares, bushels of grain, or gallons of liquors. In this view, when we mention a hundred pounds, it is just as proper to consider this

[26] David Hume, *Political Discourses,* Edinburgh, 1752. Discourse III, "Of Money," p. 44.
[27] Sir James Steuart of Coltness Bart, *Works,* Collected by Sir James Steuart, Bart. His Son, Vol. III, London, 1805, p. 74.

value relatively to the measures of any merchandize, as to the metallic measure of the coin." [28]

Sir James Steuart's conclusion was that falling and rising prices represent the fluctuating purchasing power of the metals which serve as money. He said:

"To conclude; no material money, let it be contrived as it will, is exempted from vicissitudes in its value as a metal. This is proved by the universal risings and sinkings in the price of commodities, in consequence of circumstances peculiar to the coin. These risings and sinkings of prices, I say, are properly the risings and sinkings of the value of the coin, and this fluctuation again in the value of the coin, is a lengthening and contracting of the equal parts of the scale of value which is attached to it. Now there is no such thing as any vicissitudes in the prices *of all commodities* with respect to bank money, although nothing is more common than fluctuations in agio, with respect to current money; consequently, bank money has a property and a stability in it, which no material money is capable of acquiring, and for this reason it is preferable to it, and is properly considered the thing fixed." [29]

Another well-known writer of that period, *Count v. Soden,*[30] suggested that, in order to prevent confusion between money as a medium of exchange and money as a measure of value, the two should be called by two different names: the one "money" (measure of value), and the other "coin" (medium of exchange). There is little difference between Professor Warren's statement, in 1933, that a gold dollar must be rubber with regard either to weight, or to value and the following statement of Count v. Soden:

[28] *Ibid.,* p. 3.
[29] *Ibid.,* p. 78.
[30] Julius Gr. v. Soden, *Die Nazionale Oekonomie,* 2. Bd. Leipzig, 1806, pp. 304 ff.

"Metal coins, like all commodities are subject to the laws of value and price. This seems to make it impossible to have a stable and constant coin-weight, and a sound coin system."

SECTION 4. THE REPORT OF THE BULLION COMMITTEE (1810)

The High Price of Gold Bullion

One of the most important mile-stones on the road to currency reform, is the investigation and report in 1810, of Britain's "Select Committee on the High Price of Gold Bullion." [31] This report was perhaps the first really penetrating attempt by any governmental agency to make an economic analysis of changes in the general level of prices and rates of exchange.

As early as 1797 the Bank of England suspended specie payment because of depletion of its gold reserves. The House of Commons had become alarmed, because in the period 1806–1808 the price of gold bullion which, by regulation, was £3.17.10½ per ounce of standard fineness, had risen in the open market, in terms of Britain's own paper money, to £4. and in 1810, to £4.10 and £4.12. At the same time, foreign monetary units had risen in terms of English money.

"So extraordinary a rise in the Market price of gold in this country, coupled with so remarkable a depression of our Exchanges with the Continent very clearly . . . pointed to something in the state of our own domestic currency as the cause of both appearances." [32]

Statements of the Directors of the Bank of England

English currency was in a state of inflation, but few people, even among the bankers, knew what inflation was. Most of the

---

[31] See: *Report together with Minutes of Evidence and Accounts,* from The Select Committee on the High Price of Gold Bullion, London, 1810.
[32] *Ibid.,* p. 2.

witnesses examined by the Bullion Committee ascribed this high price of gold to an extraordinary demand for it in Europe for the payment of the Napoleonic armies, "though increased also by that state of alarm and failure of confidence, which leads to the practice of hoarding." Mr. Whitmore, the Governor of the Bank of England, explained that the high price which was paid for gold outside England had even drawn gold out of the country.

But some of the merchant-witnesses stated that the price of gold had not changed materially in Europe in the period when its price rose in England, and that the difference of the gold price in England as compared with that in other European countries was expressed in the rate of exchange. Mr. Harman, a director of the Bank of England, suggested that an excess of imports accounted for the state of the exchanges. But the Committee found that, on the contrary, the balance of trade was in the opposite direction and that the excess of exports had risen from £5,456,781 in 1805 to £14,170,758 in 1809. At this point, the blindness of the bankers to inflation became evident. Asked whether the excessive issue of inconvertible paper money had not something to do with the rate of the exchange, Mr. Harman replied:

"I must very materially alter my opinions, before I can suppose that the Exchanges will be influenced by any modifications of our paper currency." [33]

The Governor of the Bank of England was under the same illusion. He stated that

"My opinion is (I do not know whether it is that of the Bank) that the amount of our paper circulation has no reference at all to the State of the Exchange."

And Mr. Pearse, the Deputy Governor and later Governor of the Bank of England, testified that he did not believe the

[33] *Ibid.,* p. 144.

volume of bank notes had any relation to the price of gold bullion or the rate of exchange. He said:

"I cannot see how the amount of Bank notes issued can operate upon the price of Bullion, or the State of the Exchange and therefore I am individually of opinion that the price of Bullion or the state of the Exchanges, can never be a reason for lessening the amount of Bank notes to be issued."

Mr. Whitmore, the Governor of the bank, enforced this statement by saying:

"I am so much of the same opinion that I never think it necessary to advert to the price of gold, or the state of the Exchanges on days on which we make our advances. . . ."

He offered as the explanation for the high price of gold that there was a scarcity of it in the country.

The Bullion Committee also asked Mr. Pearse about the relation of the volume of circulating medium to its purchasing power:

"Do you conceive that a very considerable reduction of the amount of the circulating medium would not tend in any degree to increase its relative value compared with commodities, and that a considerable increase of it would have no tendency whatever to augment the price of commodities in exchange for such circulating medium?" [34]

Mr. Pearse's answer indicates that he was not at all clear whether such a relation existed:

"It is a subject on which such a variety of opinions are entertained, I do not feel myself competent to give a decided answer."

Thus it is an interesting fact that the men who represented the Bank of England, and who had the most intimate knowledge of the process of inflation which was going on, actually did not see that the state of affairs was due to their own actions. They blamed everything else but themselves for conditions with which

[34] *Ibid.* p. 127.

they were by no means satisfied. And, as they could not realize their part in these developments, they opposed any attempts to change their policies.

Conclusions of the Bullion Committee

Finally, however, the Bullion Committee gave the right explanation of the matter based on exhaustive data and statistics. Beginning in 1797, the Bank of England had suspended cash payments of her notes and increased the amount of inconvertible paper notes in circulation progressively from £13,334,752 in 1798, to £19,001,890 in 1809. The Committee, therefore reasoned that the change in the price of gold bullion was caused by the excess circulation of paper currency and that this must be so,

". . . So long as the suspension of Cash Payment is permitted to subsist, the price of Gold Bullion, and the general Course of the Exchange with Foreign Countries, taken for any considerable period of time, form the best criterion from which any inference can be drawn, as to the sufficiency or excess of paper currency in circulation; and that the Bank of England cannot safely regulate the amount of its issues, without having reference to the criterion presented by these two circumstances."

The Committee believed that because of the suspension of cash payments, the Bank of England, through its note issue, had become solely responsible for the adequacy of the country's circulating medium.

"The suspension of Cash payment has had the effect of committing into the hands of the Directors of the Bank of England, to be exercised by their sole discretion, the important charge of supplying the country with that quantity of circulating medium which is exactly proportioned to the wants and occasions of the Public. . . ." [35]

[35] *Ibid.*, pp. 21 and 24.

The Committee believed, however, that the Bank had not acted from selfish motives although its profits grew with the increase of its note issue; but that "their recent policy involves great practical errors, which it is of the greatest public importance to correct." [36]

The Committee, accordingly, recommended the resumption of cash, or specie, payments at the earliest possible time.

The Report of the Bullion Committee gave rise to a bitter controversy for and against the principles laid down in it. Those who were against the resumption of cash payment contended that the proposed measure was "more desirable than practicable." [37] The consequence of such policy would, they believed, be a contraction of the circulating medium, resulting in falling prices and injustice to all classes of society, except the owners of money.

Ricardo

A leader in the fight for a return to the gold standard was David Ricardo who was chiefly responsible for formulating the Bullion Report.

His great contribution to the question of currency control was his advocacy of a paper money, convertible into gold bullion (not coins) at the option of the holder,—a standard similar to that gold bullion standard which was eventually adopted by England in 1925. Ricardo advocated a constant price of gold bullion as the criterion of monetary policy:

"The issuers of paper money should regulate their issues solely by the price of bullion, and never by the quantity of their paper in circulation. The quantity can never be too great or too

---

[36] *Ibid.*, p. 24.

[37] John Hill, *An Inquiry into the Causes of the Present High Price of Gold Bullion in England with Observations on the Report of the Gold Bullion Committee*, London, 1810.

little, while it preserves the same value as the standard." [38]

Ricardo's proposal was a considerable advance over the inconvertible, depreciated paper money which was current at that time and over the gold coin circulation. Undoubtedly, he recognized also the importance of the stability of the currency in terms of something other than a single commodity.

But apparently he held little hope of realizing such a standard. He said:

"No plan can possibly be devised which will maintain money at an absolutely uniform value, because it will always be subject to those variations to which the commodity itself is subject, which has been fixed upon as a standard."

In this statement he was mistaken, though he was correct when he said:

"While the precious metals continue to be the standard of our currency, money must necessarily undergo the same variations in value as those metals." [39]

Up to this point in the history of money, two conceptions had developed among the experts:

(1) gold was a more stable standard than paper

(2) but gold was not perfectly stable.

[38] *Proposals for an Economical and Secure Currency*, London, 1816, p. 22.
[39] *Ibid.*, p. 7.

CHAPTER II

TO THE WORLD WAR (1914)

SECTION 1. THE FIRST DEFINITE PROPOSALS (1822–1853)

Lowe

IN 1822, six years after Ricardo had made his statement that a stable standard was impossible, Joseph Lowe, a Scotch merchant, proposed a plan to overcome the effects of unstable money by the use of a tabular standard. He analysed the causes of the fluctuations in the value of money in an admirable manner. For a rise of prices he gave the following causes:

"The contingency of war;

"The probable increase of the produce of the mines, from the application of steam engines and other improved machinery;

"The farther substitution of bank paper for metallic currency; a substitution, in its general (though not in its local) effect, operates like the increased productiveness of a mine."[1]

The causes leading to a decline of prices, he listed as follows:

"The tendency of all improvements in productive industry, whether in agriculture, manufacture, mechanics, or navigation, to produce cheapness.

"The increasing demand for the precious metals, from the increasing population of the civilized world."

Lowe explained in detail the "Injurious effect of fluctuation in the value of money," and then described a tabular standard, or, as we would say today, an index number of consumption,

---

[1] Joseph Lowe, *On the Present State of England,* London (Second Edition, 1823), pp. 320 ff.

which was to serve as basis for long term contracts. He called it a

"Table comprising articles of general consumption to each of which is affixed the probable amount of money expended on it by the public . . .

". . . the object is to show that contracts for a series of years ought to be made with a reference to the power of money in purchasing the necessaries and comforts of life." [2]

Lowe then proceeded to enumerate the benefits of such a measure:

"In what would the benefits of it consist? In ascertaining, on grounds that would admit of no doubt or dispute, the power in purchase of any given sum in one year, compared to its power of purchase in another.

"And what would be the practical application of this knowledge? The correction of a long list of anomalies in regard to rents, salaries, wages etc., arising out of unforeseen fluctuations in our currency. . . ."

He mentioned particularly the effect of this measure on labor,

"At a time when reduction of wages became expedient, it would relieve the inferior from the humiliation attendant on such a step; and, in the case of a rise of prices, it would guide the employer to a fair advance of wages. . . ." [3]

Lowe enumerated with equal pains the benefits that would accrue to agriculture, the advantages with respect to tithes, leases, and other contracts, and the application of the plan to the Public Fund.

He is thus the first advocate of a "Tabular Standard"—its use, however, to be optional with all contracting parties:

"It would be in itself merely a table of reference, and all contracts, whether relative to loans, leases or bequests, might, at

[2] *Ibid.*, p. 333 and appendix, pp. 94–96.
[3] *Ibid.*, p. 335.

the will of the parties, be made payable, either according to the proposed standard, or in money of undefined value." [4]

Rooke

In 1824, two years after Lowe, John Rooke,[5] contrary to Ricardo, suggested that money itself could be made a stable measure of value. As he expressed it, the government ought ". . . to regulate the quantity of money kept in circulation in such a manner that its amount shall never be either deficient or excessive, and cause equal medium prices to present equal values at all times." [6]

Rooke proposed the following rules:

"1. The annual price of farm labour, on the average of the United Kingdom, shall remain as nearly as possible the same from one year to another.

"2. The market price of land, if the value of that land be equal, shall have a constant tendency to produce equal prices at all times.

"3. Equal rents and equal annuities shall have a tendency to purchase equal means of living.

"4. The rental of land or buildings, while such land or buildings continue to be of the same value, shall uniformly remain worth an equal amount of money. . . ."

Rooke then mentioned the technique by which such stabilization of the price level could be accomplished. This was analogous to the "compensated dollar" plan, proposed many years later. What Rooke advocated was to make the British currency convertible into a varying number of grains of gold, so managed, as (in this case) to keep the level of farm wages stable. Rooke said: "To accomplish the ends here contemplated it is proposed,

---

[4] *Ibid.*, p. 345.
[5] John Rooke, *Inquiry into the Principles of National Wealth*, Edinburgh, 1824.
[6] *Ibid.*, p. 225.

"1. To vary the market rate of standard gold, by the forcible circulation of more or fewer bank notes in proportion as an equal amount of gold coin shall purchase either more or less farm labour annually. Therefore, if farm labour had a tendency to rise in price, or to produce a corresponding fall in the price of an ounce of standard gold, it would cause the annual price of farm labour to remain stationary; and by a reverse operation, prevent the price of farm labour from falling whenever it had the tendency to do so." [7]

Rooke saw the difficulties in the way of putting his plan into effect. "First, the price of labour," he said, "cannot be ascertained with perfect accuracy." He further pointed out that some silver and copper coins would have to remain in circulation for small change, which might create confusion. But he insisted that the introduction of his plan would make the management of the national currency no more difficult and complicated than it already was.

Rooke also seems to have conceived of what would now be called an index number of commodities to represent the measure of value.

"The market price of every commodity, except the metals of coinage, or the instrument of exchange, furnishes the rule to which the measurement even of value itself is subjected. . . ." [8]

But he thought that, because commodities were subject to various influences in addition to those from the money side, a stable price of labor would be more satisfactory as a test of money, and would, in the end, help to keep even the prices of commodities stable. He seems not to have been familiar with Lowe's tabular standard and his tables.

Rooke appears to have been the first to suggest putting the correction in the monetary *unit* used for payment instead of in

[7] *Ibid.*, p. 226.
[8] *Ibid.*, p. 228.

the *number* of units paid. After his contribution to the subject, both kinds of corrections found advocates among the proponents of a stable standard of value.

Scrope

In 1833, independent of Lowe and Rooke, another Englishman, G. Poulett Scrope,[9] investigated the possibilities of improving the standard of value. Scrope, who also made a reputation as an outstanding geologist, was one of the most active members of Parliament during 1833 to 1868, where he fought incessantly for currency reform. His first monetary proposals were published at the time when the charter of the Bank of England was about to terminate.[10] To him the fluctuations of the value of money were more than theoretical. He saw the definite dislocations in the money system as the causes of intense human suffering, wholly preventable.

". . . And what a farce it surely is," he said, "to talk of property being effectively protected in a country in which an unseen and secret cause may, within a few years, transfer property to the amount of 1500 millions from one set of people to another, contrary to the intentions and understanding of the parties?—may covertly despoil of value to this enormous extent the classes whose industry or property is embarked in productive operations, for the benefit of those who own monied obligations payable out of the proceeds of the produce of the former?"[11]

Scrope thus appears to be the first to have, in effect, noted the prevalence of "the money illusion." He continues:

". . . had the secret causes been known which brought about

[9] Redvers Opie, *A Neglected English Economist: George Poulett Scrope,* in "Quarterly Journal of Economics," November, 1929, pp. 101–137.
[10] G. Poulett Scrope, *An Examination in the Bank Charter Question with an Inquiry into the Nature of a Just Standard of Value and Suggestions for the Improvement of Our Monetary System,* London, 1833. See also: *Principles of Political Economy.*
[11] *Ibid.,* p. 24.

changes in the wealth of people, which brought ruin to the struggling manufacturers, idleness to labour, . . . the demand for monetary reform—the fixation of the money standard, would have become irresistible." [12]

Scrope traced the fluctuations in the value of money to the fact that only one single commodity was employed as the standard of value, and like Lowe recommended instead the tabular standard plan.

"But must a standard necessarily consist of a single commodity? . . . Why then cannot a standard be formed by taking an average of the mass of commodities, or, at least, of so considerable and varied a list of them as may with sufficient correctness represent that mass? Even though not employed as the legal standard, it may serve to determine and correct the variations of the legal standard. . . . The table need only be sufficiently extended to afford, in the mean price of the whole number of articles contained in it . . . a standard of value (in its true sense of general purchasing power) as near to complete invariability as can be desirable for any practical purposes." [13]

Scrope wanted to do away with the "monopoly" of the Bank of England, in which he saw the power to control the prices of goods and the life of commerce. Asking to whom such a power should be given, he answered: to any one, except to "a company of Money Dealers associated for private profit and, like all mercantile societies, naturally looking to that object only, with a pardonable disregard of the interest of every other party." [14]

Porter; Wade; and Walsh

In 1843, *G. R. Porter,* one of the most highly esteemed economists of his times, recommended that "Tables of prices be made

[12] *Ibid.,* p. 16.
[13] *Ibid.,* p. 25.
[14] *Ibid.,* p. 36.

and recorded at short intervals." [15] He explained this proposal in detail, as follows:

"It is not meant by this to recommend a mere record of prices of goods such as would be afforded by a collection of prices current, but a calculation conducted upon the plan already described, or some other that should be equivalent to it, and which would afford, on inspection, a correct comparative view of the average fluctuations that should occur.

"Such tables would not be without benefit, even when they had been continued for only a few years; but when they should have been carried over a considerable period of time, and the results which they present could be studied in conjunction with actual occurrences, we might be enabled to read the signs they would present, so as to secure ourselves with certainty, from those alternations which now so frequently bring alarm and ruin to commercial men."

In an accompanying table, Porter showed "the amount of bank notes in circulation; the Rate of Exchange with Hamburg and Paris; the comparative prices of Wheat, and of fifty articles of commerce (including Wheat), at the beginning of each month, from January 1833, to December 1837."

During the forties and fifties, in England, there was keen interest in the matter of money and banking, as evidenced by a long list of books.

John Wade, in his "Principles of Money" [16] also wrote of the importance of stability. He said that money

". . . should possess stability of value; as money is the standard by which the worth of all other commodities is estimated, it is as necessary that its own value should be invariable as that a yard measure or a pound weight should be invariable; with-

[15] G. R. Porter, *The Progress of the Nation,* London, 1836–43. Sec. III, pp. 235–6.
[16] John Wade, *Principles of Money with their Application to the Reform of the Currency and of Banking,* London, 1842, pp. 20 ff.

out the essential requisite of stability, it in fact ceases to be money, and introduces the greatest confusion in the value of property and mercantile transactions."

Yet, like many similar writers, Wade presented no definite plan for maintaining the stability of the value of money which he desired so much. He merely recommended a paper currency, convertible into gold at the will of the holder.

Richard Hussey Walsh in 1853 [17] referred with approval to Scrope's proposal of a tabular standard. He also said:

"In determining the commodities to be employed in a tabular standard, considerable care should be taken to select those which experience and general principle might concur in indicating to be calculated to remain as constant as possible in their capacity of furnishing, either directly or indirectly by means of exchange, the means of satisfying the different wants and desires of mankind. . . . It is not to be pretended that any such perfect standard of value could be arrived at, but this should not prevent us from endeavouring to obtain, as far as we can, the useful end which it would serve to accomplish." [18]

SECTION 2. IMPROVEMENTS THROUGH INDEX NUMBERS (1876–1889)

Jevons

The famous English economist, W. Stanley Jevons, was an ardent advocate of the tabular standard. In 1865 he impeached a fixed weight of gold as standard of value, and in 1875, he proposed the substitution of a tabular standard. First he enumerated the functions of money as follows: [19]

[17] Richard Hussey Walsh, *Elementary Treatise on Metallic Currency*, Dublin, 1853, p. 94.
[18] *Ibid.*, pp. 95–96.
[19] W. Stanley Jevons, *Money and the Mechanism of Exchange*, London, 1876, p. 16. See also: *Investigations in Currency and Finance*, London, Macmillan & Co., 1884.

(1) medium of exchange; (2) measure of value; (3) standard of value; (4) store of value. For greater efficiency he wanted these functions separated, and cited historical examples to show that something of the sort had been done during Queen Elizabeth's reign, when

"Silver was the common measure of value; gold was employed in large payments, in quantities depending upon its current value in silver, while corn was required by the Act 18th Elizabeth, c. VI (1576), to be the standard of value in drawing the leases of certain college lands." [20]

Jevons weighed the possibility of a "legal tender note, which should be convertible, not into any single commodity, but into an aggregate of small quantities of various commodities, the quantity and quality of each being rigorously defined." [21] However, he dismissed this idea as impractical, and advocated instead the tabular (or multiple) standard proposal of Lowe and Scrope. The following quotation gives an excellent description of the technique which he proposed for this tabular standard system. He even went so far as to recommend making the use of the tabular standard compulsory, once its usefulness had been proven:

"Such schemes for a tabular or average standard of value appear to be perfectly sound and highly valuable in a theoretical point of view, and the practical difficulties are not of a serious character. To carry Lowe's and Scrope's plan into effect a permanent Government commission would have to be created and endowed with a kind of judicial power. The officers of the department would collect the current prices of commodities in all the principal markets of the kingdom, and, by a well-defined system of calculations, would compute from these data the average variations in the purchasing power of gold. The decisions

[20] *Ibid.*, p. 17.
[21] *Ibid.*, p. 327.

of this commission would be published monthly, and payments would be adjusted in accordance with them.

"At first the use of this national tabular standard might be permissive, so that it could be enforced only where the parties to the contract had inserted a clause to that effect in their contract. After the practicability and utility of the plan had become sufficiently demonstrated, it might be made compulsory, in the sense that every money debt of say more than three months' standing, would be varied according to the tabular standard, in the absence of an express provision to the contrary." [22]

". . . the work of the Commission, when once established and directed by Act of Parliament would be little more than that of accountants acting according to fixed rules. . . ."

Gold would be retained as a basis of the paper currency, and for international settlements. Jevons realized the difficulty of arriving at the best method of calculation, and of selecting a representative list of commodities. But he said, "Whatever method were adopted, . . . the results would be better than if we continued to accept a single metal for the standard as we do at present." [23]

Jevons urged the definite abandonment of gold as a standard of value, in his "Investigations in Currency and Finance."

". . . Now that gold has actually lost its stability," he said, "all pretence for retaining it as the standard of value might seem to be gone. The country may be said to be calmly looking on while every contract, including that of the National Debt, is being violated against the intentions of the contracting parties." [24]

Giffen

In January 1879, Robert Giffen, the Chief Statistician of the London Board of Trade, in a paper read before the Statistical

[22] *Ibid.*, pp. 330–1.
[23] *Ibid.*, p. 332.
[24] *Investigations in Currency and Finance, op. cit.*, p. 101.

Society,[25] called attention to the declining production of gold
which must inevitably result in the contraction of the currencies
of all gold standard countries. Eight years later, he presided at
the famous meetings of the British Association for the Advancement of Science, at which "Methods of Ascertaining and
Measuring Variations in the Monetary Standard" were discussed.[26]

A year later, in 1888, Giffen spoke before the Royal Statistical
Society on "Recent Changes in Prices and Incomes Compared,"
and definitely recommended either a stable money, or a plan by
which the effect of the instability of money upon long term
contracts could be counteracted. To this effect he said:

". . . All these difficulties seem to me to suggest the expediency
of further scientific study, by those interested in the theory and
practice of index numbers, which supply a means for providing
for deferred payments by substituting a different currency for
money, as is done by the corn averages for tithe and by corn
rents generally. If we cannot invent a money which will itself
be stable over generations, may it not be possible to devise a
substitute by which the deferred payments will themselves
change with the changing value measured by some other standard, and in that way the redistribution of wealth will in some
degree be lessened?" [27]

A few years later, however, Giffen attacked, in the following
words, a practical proposal for such a standard made by Aneurin
Williams, M. P., [28]

"I cannot help thinking that our standard for money in the
last twenty years has answered social necessities generally much

[25] "On the Fall of Prices of Commodities in Recent Years," in Robert Giffen,
Essays in Finance, London, 1880, pp. 333 ff.
[26] *The Currency Question before the British Association for the Advancement
of Science,* 57th Meeting, 1887, Manchester, September 1, 2, 6, 7th.
[27] Journal of the Royal Statistical Society, Vol. LI, December, 1888, pp. 713–805.
[28] Robert Giffen, *Fancy Monetary Standards,* "The Economic Journal," September, 1892, pp. 463–471.

better than a standard which would have varied with the average of commodities. . . ."

Royal Commission on Gold and Silver; J. Barr Robertson

In 1885, the English Parliament appointed the "Royal Commission to inquire into the Recent Changes in the Relative Values of the Precious Metals." The Commission held extensive hearings from 1886 to 1888. At these hearings the champion of the cause of "stable money" was *Mr. J. Barr Robertson,* who, after stating that there was not enough gold and silver in the world to correspond with the increasing demand from business, recommended the use of an index number, as a basis for the issuance of inconvertible paper currency. Such a measure, he believed, would have prevented the fall of prices with all its evil consequences.

"If we could have adopted some means," he said, "by which, during the last 12 years we could have added to the quantity of money in circulation enough to have kept our standard average prices up to 100, then it is unnecessary to say that this standard of average prices, would not have fallen to 69, both present and future payments would have been justly dealt with on the basis of 100, and no mediatization of wealth could have gone on, at least not to any material extent. This would have been a tabular standard perpetually rectified in the interests of justice by the actual rectification of the standard itself, namely, of the amount of money in circulation." [29]

The Royal Commission in its Final Report, referred to this proposal as follows:

"There are indeed some who think that in an ideally perfect system of currency, whatever may have been the cause of an alteration in the relation of the standard to commodities, the

[29] *Second Report of the Royal Commission on Gold and Silver,* 1887, pp. 25–26.

standard ought to adjust itself to this variation, so that prices should remain constant. . . ." [30]

But their decision was negative:

"In our opinion, therefore, we must dismiss this theory from consideration, and devote our attention exclusively to the question how far the fall in the price of commodities is due to currency changes."

The Commission suggested the issuance of small notes which were to be based on silver bullion, in order to relieve the existing scarcity of circulating medium; but it could not decide on any changes in the currency system. The concluding paragraph of the Report was as follows:

"Under these circumstances we have felt that the wiser course is to abstain from recommending any fundamental change in a system of currency under which the commerce of Great Britain has attained its present development." [31]

Whitelaw; Marshall; Edgeworth

Thomas Newton Whitelaw [32] in 1886, referred to the close relationship between the value of the currency and the supply of precious metals. He gave a short, but excellent, description of the effects of monetary fluctuations, the gist of which was as follows:

Cause	Effects
Rising Money	Falling prices for goods; falling interest; contracting commerce; currency stagnant; probable loss from all commercial enterprise.

[30] *Final Report of the Royal Commission on Gold and Silver*, 1888, Part II, pp. 64–65.
[31] *Ibid.*, p. 92.
[32] Thomas Newton Whitelaw, *Just Money*, Glasgow, 1886.

Cause	Effects
Stable Money	Prices of goods constant or rising; interest constant; commerce expanding; probable profit from all commercial enterprise; true mobile currency.
Falling Money	Prices of goods rising; interest rising; over-production; speculation in goods; probable crisis.

Whitelaw recommended a form of paper money which "can be so issued as to influence the whole commerce of a country, and direct it steadily into the safest channels." [33]

In an article on "Remedies for Fluctuations of General Prices," 1887, *Professor Alfred Marshall,* of Cambridge University, "the Dean of English economists" said:

"The want of a proper standard of purchasing power is the chief cause of the survival of the monstrous fallacy that there can be too much produced of everything. . . ." [34]

Marshall also mentioned the possibilities of maintaining the value of the currency itself by varying the metallic content of coins—now known as the "compensated dollar" plan. He also suggested what are now called "open market operations" by which the Government or Central Bank puts money into circulation in purchase of securities, or takes money out of circulation by selling securities.

"The Economist" magazine criticized Marshall's proposal, calling it "impossible" and adding, "to say more of it would be superfluous." [35]

To this criticism Marshall replied in a letter to "The Econo-

---

[33] *Ibid.,* p. 66.
[34] Alfred Marshall, *Remedies for Fluctuations of General Prices,* in "Contemporary Review," March, 1887, pp. 355–375.
[35] "The Economist," March 5, 1887.

mist" saying "It is enough that even in its simplest and most easily workable form the Unit [as he called an invariable monetary unit] gives a tenfold better standard of value than that afforded by the precious metals." [36]

He even suggested that "The Economist's" own index number could readily be taken as the basis for the new standard. In 1888 he suggested symmetallism as standard of value.

During 1887–1889, *Professor F. Y. Edgeworth,* distinguished English economist, editor of "The Economic Forunal" from 1891 to his death in 1926, acted as Secretary to the above mentioned Committee of the British Associations for the Advancement of Science on the Monetary Standard. In this capacity, he presented to the Committee three memoranda on the subject on which the Committee functioned, namely the investigation of the best methods of ascertaining and measuring variations in the value of the monetary standard.

The object of Edgeworth's first memorandum was to "define the meaning and measure the magnitude, of variations in the value of money." [37]

"The advantages," he continued, "of rendering money a steady measure of value-in-use would be considerable wherever there may be violent fluctuations of general retail prices. Such oscillation in the purchasing power of money intensifies the ups and downs of Fortune—so trying both to the sentient and the moral nature of men. The disturbance superadded by a bad currency might be annulled by a corrected standard." [38]

The subject of Edgeworth's second memorandum was "Tests of Accurate Measurement," in which he discussed several methods for calculating index numbers, as well as the several proposals for determining the purchasing power of money.

[36] "The Economist," March 12, 1887.
[37] F. Y. Edgeworth, *Papers Relating to Political Economy,* London, Macmillan & Co. Limited, 1925, Vol. I, Section III, "Money," p. 199.
[38] *Ibid.,* p. 200.

In his third memorandum, he gave an analysis of the proposals of economists for measuring variations in the purchasing power of money. The "Conclusion" of this latter paper lists the principal "Standards" which had been mentioned in his former papers. In this list we find all standards which had until then been proposed in place of the gold or silver standards. He classified these standards according to the method of "weighting" employed: [39]

1.) *The Capital Standard* takes for measuring changes in the value of money the changes which occur in the monetary value of "a certain set of articles," comprising "all purchasable things in existence in the community." Edgeworth mentions Professor Nicholson [40] as the authority for this standard.

2.) *The Consumption Standard* also measures monetary fluctuations by the changes in the value of a list of goods, consisting, however, "of all the commodities consumed yearly by the community." As the main proponent for this standard, Edgeworth mentions Professor Marshall.[41]

3.) *The Currency Standard* measures variations in the value of money by the change in the monetary value which changes hands in the average sales of all commodities that are bought and sold in the course of a year. This standard was proposed by Professor Foxwell, who was a member of the above mentioned Committee of the British Association for the Advancement of Science.

4.) *The Income Standard* takes as the measure of changes in the value of currency "the average consumption, or the income per head." This was Mr. Bourne's proposal, who was also a member of the Committee.

5.) *The Indefinite Standard* takes as the measure of the

[39] *Ibid.*, pp. 295 ff.
[40] J. Shield Nicholson, *A Treatise on Money and Essays on Present Monetary Problems*, London, 1888.
[41] See: Alfred Marshall, *op. cit.*

changes in the monetary unit "a simple unweighted average of the ratios formed by dividing the price of each commodity at the later period by the price of the same commodity at the earlier period." As the authorities for this proposal, Edgeworth mentioned Cournot, Soetbeer, Jevons, and himself.

6.) *The Production Standard* "takes as the measure of appreciation or depreciation the change in the pecuniary remunerations of a certain set of services, namely, all (or the principal) which are rendered in the course of production throughout the community during a year. . . ." This and similar methods, Edgeworth said, had been proposed by Ricardo, Marshall, Giffen, and Newcomb.

Edgeworth made other valuable, and highly technical, contributions to the science of index numbers which is the essential foundation of the demand for a stable money. Like Marshall, he became a proponent of symmetallism.

SECTION 3. OTHER EUROPEAN PLANS (BEFORE 1900)

Walras; Lawes; Zuckerkandl

Professor Léon Walras of Lausanne (Switzerland) has frequently been quoted as to his plan (1885) for a gold standard with a "silver regulator." [42] Under this plan, gold coins would be used as the basis of the currency, but would be supplemented by silver, coins with 15½ times as many grains of silver in a silver coin as of gold in a corresponding gold coin. The supplementary, or regulatory, silver coinage would then be so manipulated as to maintain a stable value of the currency in terms of commodities. Thus if gold became scarce, silver coins would be added to the currency; and if gold became abundant, silver

[42] Léon Walras, *D'une Méthode de Régularisation de la Variation de Valeur de la Monnaie*, Lausanne, 1885.

coins would be withdrawn from the currency. But although Walras thus proposed to forestall the *contraction* of the currency through the scarcity of gold, he did not consider the possibility of such an *over-supply of gold* as would require the withdrawal of all silver and thereafter cause a gold inflation.

Professor Theodor Lawes (1890), in his "Warenwaehrung," [43] after tracing the fluctuations in the value of money to the changing supply of gold, advocated the tabular standard, which he called "money of account."

In 1893, *Robert Zuckerkandl* also recommended the tabular standard for all contracts.[44]

Williams; Price; Wallace

Aneurin Williams, an Englishman and member of Parliament, in 1892, and apparently independently of Rooke and others, proposed a paper currency, to be convertible into a varying amount of gold (or silver) so that each paper unit would continuously buy an invariable amount of commodities. This plan he expressed as follows:

"In a country, having circulation—apart from small change—of token money—, wholly made up of paper, and where the Government was always prepared to buy or sell bullion for notes at a price, the standard of value might be kept constant by varying from time to time this price, since this would be in effect to vary the number of grains of gold . . . which could be got for a note representing that standard unit, and which would instantly procure such a note on demand. If gold appreciated, the number of grains given or taken for a unit of paper money

[43] Dr. Theodor Lawes, *Die Warenwaehrung als Ergaenzung der Edelmetallwaehrung,* in "Jahrbuch fuer Gesetzgebung, Verwaltung und Volkswirtschaft im Deutschen Reich" 14. Jahrgang. Gustav Schmoller, Leipzig, 1890.

[44] Robert Zuckerkandl, *Die Statistische Bestimmung des Preisniveaus,* in "Handwoerterbuch der Staatswissenschaften" 5. Band, Jena, 1893.

would be reduced: the mint price of gold raised. If gold depreciated, the number of grains given or taken for the note would be increased: the mint price of gold bullion lowered." [45] Williams' plan differed from that of Rooke in that it provided for the redemption by the Government of its notes. He would have the commodity index checked every night, and the adjustments made immediately. From a rising price of gold he expected a huge profit to accumulate to the Government, which he wanted to be set aside as a special fund for the purchase of securities which were to be bought and sold as a further means towards achieving stability of the currency. Gold bullion would be used for international payments only, and would not circulate.

In 1896, an excellent book on "Money and Its Relation to Prices" was published by L. L. Price.[46] In a chapter on "The Measurement of Changes in Prices," the author spoke of index numbers as one of the most revolutionary discoveries in economic science.[47]

In 1898, another well-known Englishman, *Alfred Russel Wallace,* the naturalist, advocated the use of an index number in order to arrive at a stable money, which, as he explained, could very well be in the form of an inconvertible paper currency. In the opinion of this man of science, the index, representative of the necessaries of life, should include: "Food, clothing, houses, fuel and literature." [48]

There remain two Europeans, whose activities for stabilization extended well into the twentieth century: Knut Wicksell, a Swede, and Silvio Gesell, a German.

[45] Aneurin Williams, *A Fixed Value of Bullion Standard,* in "Economic Journal," London, June, 1892, Vol. II, pp. 280–89.
[46] London, Swan Sonnenschein & Co., Ltd., 1896.
[47] See also: L. L. Price, *Reconstruction and Monetary Reform,* in the "Economic Journal," Vol. XXXII, March, 1922, pp. 48–52.
[48] Alfred Russel Wallace, *Paper Money as a Standard of Value,* in "The Academy," December 31, 1898.

Wicksell; Gesell

Dr. Knut Wicksell, a Swedish economist, was one of the first to advocate (in 1898) the maintenance of a stable price level through the manipulation of the discount rate by Central Banks. That is, he wanted to have stable foreign exchange rates replaced by a stable domestic price level. As he expressed it:

". . . the regulation of the discount rate for the purpose of maintaining the foreign exchanges . . . should be replaced by a more important discount policy for the purpose of maintaining the average price level invariable." [49]

Wicksell believed that if the central banks of the leading nations put this plan into effect by agreement, the remaining countries would find it advantageous to follow a similar policy. A stable world-price level would then be adopted by an international commission. As soon as a deviation from that level occurred, all central banks would immediately take concerted action to correct it. Wicksell's proposal has been endorsed by almost all later proponents of stabilization.[50]

Silvio Gesell,[51] was a German business man who, in the nineties, lived in Argentina and became interested in the money problem partly to protect his own business from the dangers of fluctuating currencies. Beginning his study of the problem without the benefit—or disadvantage, as he said—of previous study of economic literature, Gesell arrived at some original conclusions.

"All controversies about the currency," he said, "can only be questions of the price of money;—that means, whether it should be cheap, dear, or stable." [52]

[49] Dr. Knut Wicksell, *Geldzins und Gueterpreise,* Jena, 1898, p. 175.

[50] For a discussion of the more recent activities of Knut Wicksell, see Chapter 3, Section 4.

[51] For a review of Gesell's part in the German Stable Money Movement, see Chapter 4, Section 5.

[52] Silvio Gesell, *Die Anpassung des Geldes und seiner Verwaltung an die*

In his effort to find a practical solution, Gesell concluded that not only the quantity of money, but also its velocity of circulation should be controlled.

"The Government has the duty to prevent the money from fluctuating, and, if necessary, to enforce this stability. As the regularity in the actual circulation of money is the basic condition for its stable value, the circulation of money must be freed from the whims of individuals, and the greed of speculators, and must be enforced."

Gesell claimed that goods deteriorate and must therefore be offered for sale, while money could be hoarded without damage, and its circulation was therefore not subject to the pressure which forces goods on the markets. He therefore suggested that money be made, by taxation, subject to the same deterioration which most goods suffer. He proposed a currency, ". . . the price of which suffers, just like that of goods, at the expense of its holder." That is, he would have a dollar in terms of goods remain constant but decrease in value as if it were a commodity.

Calculating the average deterioration of all commodities at 5% per annum, Gesell proposed a currency which should be taxed 5% per annum, or $\frac{1}{10}$ of 1% weekly, in order to make it equal to goods.

Gesell condemned gold and silver, because they were objects of speculation. He would judge money not by its chemical analysis, but by the number of unemployed and by the unsold inventories. These he regarded as the real tests of monetary efficiency. With regard to the compilation of an index number, he would have the relative importance of each commodity determined according to the number of men employed in its production.

Gesell's work is mentioned here because he seems to have been

Beduerfnisse des Modernen Verkehrs, Buenos Aires, 1897, p. 6. See also: Die Reformation im Muenzwesen als Bruecke zum Sozialen Staat, Buenos Aires, 1891.

the first who considered the problem of controlling the velocity of circulation for the purpose of influencing the value of money.

SECTION 4. THE IDEA IN AMERICA (1877–1895)

Horton; Walker; Newcomb; Mills; Andrews

One of the first American advocates of a stable standard of value was *S. Dana Horton*, who was a prominent bimetallist in his time. Discussing Jevons' chapter on the tabular standard, Horton said in 1877: "It is in fact the key to the entire theory of money." [53] He judged writers on the subject of money by their knowledge of monetary fluctuations. The tabular standard, which he called "Standard of Desiderata," should in his opinion be stipulated in long-term contracts. He also thought that bimetallism would make money itself more secure against fluctuations in value.

Francis A. Walker was Professor of Economics at Yale, and later President of the Massachusetts Institute of Technology. He was also a prominent international bimetallist, and one of the outstanding economists of his period. Many times in his writings he mentioned the problem of a stable standard for deferred payments. In 1877 he wrote concerning the tabular standard:

"Certainly, as Professor Jevons says, 'such a standard would add a wholly new degree of stability to social relations, securing the fixed income of individuals and public institutions from the depreciation which they have often suffered.' " [53a] In 1886 Walker showed how beneficial the tabular standard would be to the many classes and interests of society:

"To . . . all who have definitely retired from active life, carrying away with them all they will ever have to support old age and provide for their children; to . . . trustees and guardians, under

[53] S. Dana Horton, *Silver and Gold in their Relation to the Problem of Resumption*, Cincinnati, 1877, p. 40.
[53a] *Money*, New York, Henry Holt & Co., 1878, p. 161.

a solemn responsibility in the care of estates, where loss is more
to be dreaded than gain to be desired; to . . . institutions whose
funds are sequestered from the stock of active capital, for pious
and charitable uses. The funds of Savings Banks," he said, "might
be put under the same safeguard, and government loans might
also be issued in terms of the multiple tender." [54]

The distinguished astronomer, *Simon Newcomb*,[55] in an article, published in 1879, offered as the solution for the problem of
monetary stability the "compensated dollar" plan:

". . . if we could, from time to time, increase or diminish the
amount of the metal in the dollar, so that it would always exactly
fulfill the required condition, we should have all that we want.
We conceive that a little careful consideration will show that a result equivalent to this can be attained much more easily than
would appear at first sight. The first and most obvious method of
attaining the object is to issue a paper currency which shall be redeemable, not in gold dollars of fixed weight, but in such
quantities of gold and silver bullion as shall suffice to make the
required purchases. We have already shown that the determination of this quantity does not offer the slightest difficulty, when
once a system is carefully devised."

Complaining of what has since been called the "money illusion," which prevents people from seeing clearly the problem of
monetary stability, Newcomb said:

"The great cause of the stationary condition of society with
respect to the standard of value is undoubtedly the absence of a
clear appreciation of the nature of the subject on the part of the
public. Our whole education from infancy upward leads us to
look upon the dollar, the pound, the franc, or other unit of value
to which we have been accustomed, as something equally ab-

[54] Francis A. Walker, *Political Economy,* New York, Henry Holt & Co., 1888,
p. 375.
[55] Simon Newcomb, *The Standard of Value,* in "The North American Review,"
September, 1879, pp. 223–237.

solute and invariable with the ground on which we tread."
Carlton H. Mills, in a booklet published in 1879,[56] suggested
that the government set up a commission for the purpose of determining the fluctuations in commerce and in the price level.
Money should then be issued and withdrawn with the object of
maintaining a stable price level.

In a small book, published 1889,[57] *E. Benjamin Andrews,* once
President of Brown University, criticized even men like Walker
and Jevons for not realizing the full extent of the evils of unstable money. His plan followed the outlines of Professor Walras'
plan to supplement the gold basis of currency with silver; but he
was in favor of limiting the coinage of gold, should its supply
become so abundant that it would create inflation. Andrews, in
those days, seemed so radical in matters of currency that he was
ousted from his position at Brown. Monetary heresy or public
advocacy of it in those days was held inconsistent with the position of a University President.

The Silver Controversy

America had at this time entered the great free-silver controversy. The Greenback inflation of the Civil War had been
followed by deflation and in 1879 by the return to specie payments. Silver had been demonetized in 1873 although we were
then on a paper basis. At the same time, other deflationary measures which had previously been adopted, began to make themselves felt. But the public associated the falling price level with
the fact that silver was demonetized and that accordingly the
currency had become contracted. Many, therefore, put the entire
blame for the deflation on the demonetization of silver.

From 1873 to 1896 the price level fell about 50%, paralyzing in-

---

[56] Carlton H. Mills, *Honest Money,* The Barometer of Commerce, Detroit, 1879.
[57] E. Benjamin Andrews, *An Honest Dollar,* Baltimore, Guggenheimer, Weil
& Co., 1889.

dustry and trade. During 1896, when the "free-silverites" denounced the contracted currency as the root of all the evil, the adherents of the gold standard maintained that the gold basis had become more than adequate for the existing price level. Nevertheless there was a declining gold supply which aggravated the deflation; and the bimetallists demanded that the price level be raised somewhat, to repair the drastic fall. They were universally in favor of eventual stability; but they demanded that silver, freely coined like gold, be made part of the metallic basis of money in order to prevent the recurrence of deflation. The "gold-bugs," on the other hand, insisted that the "free-silverites" wanted inflation, and nothing else.

It would take us too far afield to attempt mentioning all those who favored monetary stability during the silver-controversy (and down to the year 1900). Without being exhaustive, the following list contains the names of some of the outstanding advocates of stabilization of that time.

Del Mar; Frost; Fonda; Winn; Kitson

Alexander Del Mar, formerly a Director of the U.S. Bureau of Labor Statistics, Member of the United States Monetary Commission of 1876 and the author of a number of books on the history of money,[58] although a great defender of bimetallism, was also an advocate of what he called "numerical" money—money so limited in amount as to be of invariable purchasing power. In 1880–1885 in his studies of ancient moneys, Del Mar showed that the precious metals have not always served as the only money. Iron disks, leather pieces, and similar, intrinsically worthless tokens were, he said, used when no gold or silver was available, and were given "numerical" value. He went into many

---

[58] Alexander Del Mar, *The Science of Money,* London, 1885.
   A History of Money in Ancient Countries, London, 1885.
   A History of the Precious Metals, London, 1880, etc.

detailed studies of ancient cultures to show that, on the whole, such numerical money has served the purpose far better than the precious metals ever did. In spite of his advocacy of silver, Del Mar regarded paper money as still better; in fact, ideal. He thought that eventually it would be the only remedy for violent fluctuations in value, that is, for unstable prices.

O. J. Frost [59] suggested that an index of 100 leading commodities be compiled by an authorized commission to serve as an index for the issuance of paper money which was to be convertible into gold or silver bullion.

In a number of highly theoretical papers, the problem of a stable "standard of deferred payments" was discussed by outstanding economists.[60]

In 1895, in a clearly written book called "Honest Money," Arthur I. Fonda [61] advocated inconvertible paper currency to be issued so as to keep the purchasing power of money stable, as registered by an index number, properly weighted. He proposed that through a government commission and with the aid of statisticians, "the average price of each of the commodities selected . . . should be ascertained and tabulated. . . . In addition to the average prices of each commodity, the approximate amount or value annually consumed in this country should be ascertained. From these data a table should be prepared showing the amount one dollar would have purchased.

[59] *Vice-Presidential Address,* delivered before the Colorado Scientific Society, Denver, December 8, 1893.

[60] Lucius S. Merriam, *The Theory of Final Utility in its Relation to Money and Standard of Deferred Payments,* in Annals of the American Academy, Vol. III, No. 4, January, 1893.

Edward Alsworth Ross, *The Standard of Deferred Payments,* in Annals of the American Academy, Vol. III, No. 3, November, 1892.

Frank Fetter, *The Exploration of Theories of Value in the Discussion of the Standard of Deferred Payments,* in Annals of the American Academy, Vol. V, No. 6, May, 1895.

John B. Clark, *The Gold Standard Currency in the Light of Recent Theory,* in Political Science Quarterly, Vol. X, No. 3, September, 1895.

[61] Arthur I. Fonda, *Honest Money,* New York, Macmillan & Co., 1895, pp. 159 ff.

"This would evidently provide a standard that would closely represent the average purchasing power of one dollar for the time selected."

Fonda wanted to have the volume of money in circulation controlled by the purchase and sale of Government securities, and by variations in the "interest rate." Gold would not be legal tender, but would still be used for international payments.

Henry Winn, (who in 1891 was the People's Party candidate for Governor of Massachusetts) in 1895, wrote an admirable article on "The Multiple Standard" (in other words, the Tabular Standard). The following sentences are quoted because of their clarity and the administrative knowledge they show.

"The test of good money comes when it is used as a standard for deferred payments,—when men incur debts to be paid in money. . . ."

"The security against over- or under-issues of paper would lie, first, in the positive mandate of the law making it the duty of the executive officers to maintain as nearly as possible the same average of prices. Second, in publicity. The commission would hang out a barometer of monetary value whereby all men could see, not only what the government ought to do, but what it was actually doing, and whether it was acting honestly. . . ."

"The multiple standard plan is to check prices promptly after they begin to move. Out of it, however, would grow a higher system under which the causes which produce the price change would be met before they could act. . . . The money department would become in time a sort of financial weather bureau and the great statesman would be he who could keep the index finger stillest on the dial of prices." [62]

[62] Henry Winn, *The Multiple Standard,* in "The American Magazine of Civics," December, 1895.

In 1895 *Arthur Kitson,* an English business man who then lived in America, published his first book on the money problem.[63]

Instead of a standard of value he recommended a numerical relationship which could not be affected by changes from the side of money: ". . . The numerical relationship being once established, our monetary system should be such that prices can be affected only by changes in the demand for and supply of commodities themselves, and not by reason of any change in money." [64]

In order to eliminate the fluctuations in the purchasing power of money, Kitson advocated "the adoption of an invariable value denominator," [65] representing units of purchasing power, not tied to any one commodity and free from the control of governments as well as of individuals.

SECTION 5. THE IDEA IN AMERICA CONTINUED (1896–1903)

In 1896, *George H. Shibley,* who was apparently the first to use the term "Stable Money," published his book, "The Money Question." [66] He was then an advocate of bimetallism, but is also one of the veterans of the movement for stabilization in America. To demonstrate the need for stabilization and to get the political parties to adopt a stable money platform, he prepared, in 1900–1901, with the help of Professor *John R. Commons,* an index number which he published through the Bureau of Economic Research.

In 1900, Shibley succeeded in having introduced in the platform of the People's Party (at the National Convention in

[63] Arthur Kitson, *A Scientific Solution of the Money Question,* Boston Arena Publishing Company, 1895.
[64] *Ibid.,* p. 179.
[65] *Ibid.,* p. 212.
[66] George H. Shibley, *The Money Question,* Chicago, 1896.

Suffolk, N. Dak.) a clause providing for the withdrawal of Bank
Notes if prices should rise above a certain level. In a later booklet [67] he listed the requirements for a stable currency, which included: Repeal of the right of banks to issue money; and the
replacing of bank money by non-interest bearing National Money.
This was to be issued by a Currency Commission consisting of
the Secretary of the Treasury, the Director of the Mint, and five
appointees of the Senate. The Commission, by selling and buying
securities in the open market, would so regulate the volume of
money as to maintain a stable price level. The price level was to
be computed daily and based on 100 commodities, weighted as
to their importance. The adjustments of the volume of money
would also be made daily.

In a later article, Shibley asserted that such a system of monetary management would inevitably have to come:

"When such a system is adopted, the money question will be
removed from politics, just as is to-day the number of pecks in a
bushel. That such a monetary system is to be established is as
certain as was the discarding of the stage-coach after the discovery of the improved modes of travel. . . ." [68]

One of the clearest expositions of the problem was given in
an article on "The Multiple Standard," by Professor *J. Allen
Smith* in 1896.[69] Without taking sides in the silver-controversy,
he nevertheless expressed his belief that the bimetallists had a
clearer conception of the function of money than their opponents.
The maintenance of the stability of the general price level he
held essential to industrial activity. He believed that money, instead of helping the exchange of goods, frequently prevented such
exchange:

[67] George H. Shibley, *Currency Reform,* 1900.
[68] George H. Shibley, *Who Shall Control the Price Level?,* "The Arena," January, 1900.
[69] J. Allen Smith, *A Multiple Money Standard,* in "Annals of the American
Academy of Political and Social Science," March, 1896, pp. 1-60.

"If goods were exchanged directly for other goods, without the intervention of money, there could be no such economic disturbances as panics and industrial depressions. . . ." [70]

He criticized the tabular standard, however, as impractical, and suggested instead that the standard of value itself be made stable:

"What we need is to make the standard itself stable, and not rely on some outside measure to find how our standard fluctuates. The inconvenient feature of this scheme is that the real standard is not incorporated in the monetary system." [71]

He therefore advocated a "compensated dollar" plan such as Aneurin Williams had proposed, but, to make it more simple, he would have only one metal, gold, as the backing for the paper currency.

William Hope Harvey ("Coin" Harvey) had more readers among the general public than any other writer on monetary questions. It is claimed that a million copies of his book, "Coin's Financial School," were distributed. He was, however, one of those who advocated the remonetization of silver at 16 to 1.

"The purchasing power of 23 grains of gold is about as well defined and as stable as the location of a tract of land once described by Rufus Choate, as follows to wit: 'Beginning at a certain rotten stump, thence North to a swarm of bees, thence East to a cat that has a fit, thence South to a can, tied to a dog's tail, and thence West to the place of beginning.'"

In these terms of ridicule two popular writers of that period, *R. B. McCluer* and *J. S. Konkel*,[72] described the gold standard. They talked of the "overproduction-humbug," and they suggested a "Money Meter," for measuring the purchasing power of money, advocating the application of a tabular standard to long-term contracts.

[70] *Ibid.*, p. 6.
[71] *Ibid.*, p. 25.
[72] R. B. McCluer and J. S. Konkel, *Money Meter*, 1896, p. 28.

In 1896, *Wm. A. Whittick* published a book [73] in which he pleaded for an "ideal" standard, not based upon commodities, but simply upon an imaginary scale. While he would have this standard remain stable, he would permit prices of commodities, as measured by it, to decline in accordance with the increasing efficiency of industry.

Also in 1896, the late *Dana J. Tinnes* proposed for the first time his "Market Gauge Dollar" [74] which he afterwards persistently brought to the attention of economists and of Congress. His proposal was, in brief, to establish an index number, which he called the Market Gauge, calculated from the wholesale prices of the most important commodities. To keep this index number stable, a Government agency would calculate the index every night, and immediately adjust the gold weight of the dollar,—such adjustments to be supplemented by changes in the volume of currency in circulation.

William Jennings Bryan, the Presidential Nominee of the Democratic Party in 1896, stated on many occasions his adherence to the principle of a stable purchasing power of money. In his speech accepting the presidential nomination, on August 12, 1896, at Madison Square Garden, New York, he said:

"What is the test of honest money? It must certainly be found in the purchasing power of the dollar. An absolutely honest money would not vary in its purchasing power; it would be absolutely stable, when measured by average prices. A dollar which increases in purchasing power is just as dishonest as a dollar which decreases in purchasing power."

Of course, however, such stability could not be attained by his 16 to 1 proposal—much, if any better than by the gold standard.

---

[73] Wm. A. Whittick, *Value and an Invariable Unit of Value,* Philadelphia, 1896.
[74] Dana J. Tinnes, *An Ideal Measure of Value,* "The Adrian (Minn.) Guardian," November 16, 1896.

Eltweed Pomeroy, in 1897,[75] suggested that a Government agency construct an index number, to be kept invariable by the increase and decrease of the volume of the circulating medium. Inconvertible paper currency would be the only legal tender.

Frank Parsons, the author of a number of books opposing monopolies, wrote in 1898 an able book on the money question.[76] He suggested the establishment of a Government Commission for the regulation of the currency, similar to that mentioned by Shibley. Parsons was a special critic of the bankers, whom he not only blamed for money panics, but even accused of manipulating the Government's gold holdings. The bankers, he said, by constantly depleting the Government's gold stocks, forced the issuance of new bonds, which brought the bankers a high profit. He explained the procedure as follows:

The U.S. Government had to borrow repeatedly in order to gain gold. The scheme was, he said, invented by the bankers: To present Treasury notes and bills for redemption, which the Government had to redeem in gold, and then had to issue bonds to get back the gold. According to Parsons, the bond record stood as follows:

"December 1891, 50 millions of bonds were issued to get gold for the Treasury, and in two months the gold thus obtained was gone from the Treasury again.

"March, 1894, 50 millions of bonds, and in three months the gold was gone.

"February, 1895, 62½ millions of bonds, and by 1896 the gold had vanished again.

"January, 1896, a new issue of bonds brought 116 millions of gold, nearly the whole of which departed within six months." [77]

Such statements added much bitterness to the silver-controversy.

[75] Eltweed Pomeroy, *The Multiple Standard for Money,* "The Arena," September, 1897.
[76] Frank Parsons, *Rational Money,* Philadelphia, Pa., C. F. Taylor, 1898.
[77] *Ibid.,* p. 50.

Worthy P. Stern, in 1898,[78] proposed the regulation of the value of money through the issuance of legal tender bills by the Comptroller of the Currency. These notes would be convertible at Government warehouses into a variety of standard commodities at fixed prices. Further, he would force all commercial or check-deposit banks to join a system which would be under Federal control, through which all deposits would be guaranteed. The Comptroller of the Currency, in whom the control over this system would be lodged, would also have the power of raising or lowering the price of gold or silver, and of changing the reserve requirements of all banks in the system. The object of all these regulations would be the maintenance of the purchasing power of the currency.

Correa Moylan Walsh was, perhaps, the first American who investigated the problem of index numbers in a truly scholarly fashion.[79] His work published in 1901 has remained one of the most fundamental studies of the subject, and has helped greatly to build up the science of measuring the purchasing power of money. Walsh maintained, with Dana Horton, that the theory of a multiple standard was the "key to the entire theory of money." He cited previous proposals for such a multiple standard and discussed the various methods by which currency regulation was being attempted. The bibliography attached to his book, listing 141 books "dealing with the measurement of the exchange value of money by comparing many prices," has been exceedingly helpful to the students of the stabilization problem, in general and of index numbers in particular.

In a second book, published two years later (1903), Walsh dealt exclusively with the stabilization of the monetary standard, which for him had become "The Fundamental Problem in Mone-

---

[78] Worthy P. Stern, *A New Standard and a New Currency,* in "The Journal of Political Economy," No. 4, Vol. VI, September, 1898, pp. 523–535.
[79] Correa Moylan Walsh, *The Measurement of General Exchange Value,* New York, Macmillan Co., 1901.

tary Science." [80] Without proposing any specific plan of his own, he reviewed the principles of the proposals of others, viz., the commodity-standard; the wages-standard; the prices- and wages-standard; the cost-standard; the income-standard. He pleaded that the problem be attacked from a scientific point of view and that economists should not rest until they had found its correct solution.

Section 6. The "High Cost of Living" Problem (1905–1914)

Gold Inflation

Bryan's defeat, in 1896, and the consequent return of confidence would never have sufficed to overcome the depression of that period. Had not the increased supply of gold, beginning in 1896, broadened the basis of the currency, the bimetallists would have had a better chance of winning the next election in 1900. But rich gold mine discoveries in South Africa in 1889, the opening of the Klondike and Alaskan Mines, the discovery of the cyanide process of extracting gold from formerly unusable residues, soon quadrupled the annual gold production.[81]

Largely as a consequence of this increased gold supply, the average wholesale price level began to rise, from a low of 78 in 1896, to 117 in 1913.[82] The price movement was now reversed, but the general public was again the victim. Fixed incomes bought less and less goods. The "profiteer" took the place of the "bloated bondholder." A financial paper, in 1912, published a symposium of the views of 32 leading economists on the high cost of living. The concensus of these men was summarized as follows:

[80] Correa Moylan Walsh, *The Fundamental Problem in Monetary Science*, New York, Macmillan Co., 1903.

[81] See: Lionel D. Edie, *Gold Production and Prices before and after the War*, Indiana University Studies, Vol. XI, March, 1928.

[82] 1880–1914 = 100; G. F. Warren and Frank A. Pearson, *Money and Prices*, Farm Economics, No. 74, pp. 1689–90, February, 1932, Cornell University.

"That the gold supply is the basic cause, or at least one of the chief causes of the present high price level.

"That the present price level is practically certain to continue to advance in the future." [83]

Interest in the Cost-of-Living Problem

Thus the problem of the high cost of living again brought the attention of the public to the money question. The advocates of a stable standard of value explained that a high cost of living in reality meant a low value of money. A list of publications in the Library of Congress shows how interest in the matter grew. During the five-year period 1896–1900 there were 7 publications on the high cost of living; in 1901–1905 the number had increased to 36; and during 1906–1910, it became 121.

Official reports on this problem were made in the following countries: France in 1900 and 1910; Austria, 1903; Germany, 1909; United States, 1910; Australia, 1911; Canada, 1911; Italy, 1911; Great Britain, 1911 and 1912; New Zealand, 1912; India, 1914. Many other investigations were planned, but the War interferred with carrying them through. One of such plans was that for an International Conference on the High Cost of Living. This was the subject of a special message to Congress by President Taft in 1912. A bill for the purpose passed the Senate and was reported favorably by the House Committee on Foreign Affairs, but did not reach the House Calendar before adjournment, and was not revived by the next Congress.

The present writer's plan for a "Compensated Dollar," first published in 1911,[84] began at this time to be discussed as a remedy for the varying price level. The reader is referred to the Appendix for details.

[83] "Securities Review," Scranton, Pa., April, 1912.
[84] Irving Fisher, *The Purchasing Power of Money,* New York, Macmillan Co., 1911.

CHAPTER III

ACADEMIC STAGE (FROM 1914)

SECTION 1. IN THE UNITED STATES

The Stage Set for a Movement

BEFORE the World War, the so-called "high cost of living" had brought with it a new realization of some of the evils of unstable money, and this was intensified by the rising price level during and after the War. It was then that the plan for a "Compensated Dollar" began to attract special attention and favorable comment.[1]

In the War itself (1914–1918)—particularly after the United States had entered it—the use of index numbers became common in many industries, as well as in departments of the Government. To meet the constant demands for higher wages and to settle numerous strikes, the National War Labor Board made wide use of an index of the cost of living.[2] The Shipbuilding Labor Adjustment Board, which was then under the jurisdiction of Franklin D. Roosevelt, as Assistant Secretary of the Navy, also recognized this use of index numbers and adopted a plan of making half-yearly adjustments of wages (April 1 and October 1) in all shipbuilding centers, using for these adjustments the cost

---

[1] See Irving Fisher, *Stabilizing the Dollar,* New York, Macmillan Co., 1920, pp. 274–277.

[2] For an exhaustive study of the use of a cost of living index during the postwar period see: Elma B. Carr, *The Use of Cost-of-Living Figures in Wage Adjustments,* U.S. Department of Labor. Bulletin of the Bureau of Labor Statistics, No. 369. May, 1925.

of living index as determined by the U.S. Bureau of Labor Statistics.

During 1919–1921, a number of organizations were induced to pass resolutions in favor of legislation for stabilizing the purchasing power of the dollar. The following resolution, passed on March 8, 1920, by the Rochester Chamber of Commerce (in which George Eastman was very influential) is a good example of such efforts:

"Resolved, That the Rochester Chamber of Commerce urges upon the President, Senate and House of Representatives, the earnest and immediate consideration through the agency of a national or international commission, or otherwise, of the stabilizing of the American dollar, by adjusting its gold content or by any other means, if available, which will effectively safeguard its purchasing power against further fluctuations."

A "Committee on the Purchasing Power of Money in War Time" was formed by the American Economic Association. It consisted of economists whose chief interest was in the field of currency and banking (B. M. Anderson, Jr.; E. W. Kemmerer; Royal Meeker; C. W. Mitchell; Warren M. Persons; and the present writer as chairman). The Committee did not conclude that stabilization in war time could always be accomplished but expressed the following opinion, which was unanimous:

"The Committee regards the stabilization of the value of monetary units under international agreement as desirable and economically feasible. The details of the plan, the time of its introduction, and the question whether international agreement is indispensable, should receive the immediate attention of the statesmen and economists."

Those who were most interested recognized that only organized effort of some sort could advance the cause. The problem of creating an organized movement was one of educating the public, that is, to be specific, it was the problem of showing

business men, industrialists and bankers the evils of an unstable
currency and the need of definite and determined action to overcome these evils. Once business men and industrialists should see
this need, they might exert pressure upon politicians and legislators to take the next step, that of introducing the principle of
monetary stabilization into the law.

But the very first stage in the movement was that of educating
the educators themselves—those to whom the public would
naturally turn for enlightenment. If we call this effort the "Academic Stage," the following stage may be called the "Popularizing Stage." The "Legislative Stage" would then be the concluding one.

In the actual history of the movement, these three stages cannot be clearly separated. They overlap. In fact, all three are going
on at the present time; but our study will gain in clarity by
looking at each separately.

The "Academic Stage" involved chiefly those economists who
either propounded specific plans for stabilizing the currency, or
who became the supporters of the general purpose of stable
money. Within the space of this book it would be impossible
to mention all who have thus identified themselves with the
movement. Some of the outstanding leaders of stabilization in
this country and abroad will be mentioned in the text, and
others will be listed in a selected bibliography in the appendix.

Warren; Pearson; Rogers; Commons

Ever since President Roosevelt asked Professor *George F. Warren* to advise the administration on steps towards re-flation and
stabilization, the public has come to know of Mr. Warren as one
of the foremost proponents of stable money in this country. As
a professor of Agricultural Economics at Cornell University, he
had become interested in the price problems of the farmer; but

the close relation between the problem of prices and that of the so-called business cycle, led him to study these fluctuations, and their effect not only upon agriculture but upon business generally. Warren realized that the inflated price-level of post-war years could not be supported by the available gold supply and, as early as 1918, he predicted the drop in farm prices which actually occurred in 1920–1921.

By means of a table of index numbers, covering 130 years, he traced and explained the monetary changes which have usually occurred after a war:

"After each of the previous wars a very violent drop in prices occurred, followed by partial recovery and somewhat stable prices for a year or more, then again followed by a longer but less violent drop and again followed by a period of somewhat stable prices. . . ." [3]

Warren thus predicted a long decline of the prices of farm products, and perceived that the danger was increased by the uncertainty of America's monetary policy and the monetary policies of the other countries of the world. He therefore warned the farmers against incurring long term debts. He also became a strong advocate of a stable price level, and especially of the "compensated dollar" plan as a means to that end.

He was one of the few American economists who saw before the event that a general return of the world to the gold standard would produce a scramble for gold, with a consequent rise in its value. In fact, he predicted the 1929 collapse, and the subsequent deflation, long before they occurred. In books [4] written by himself and his colleague, Frank A. Pearson, a realistic and vivid picture is presented of the effects of price changes upon the in-

[3] George F. Warren, *Prices of Farm Products in the United States*, Bulletin of the U.S. Department of Agriculture No. 999, August, 1921, p. 2.
[4] George F. Warren and Frank A. Pearson, *The Agricultural Situation*, New York, John Wiley & Sons, Inc., 1924; also: *Prices*, New York, John Wiley & Sons, Inc., 1933.

terests of the farmer and the business man. In a heart-to-heart talk with the reader the authors explain how conditions must develop under the economic system as it is, and give practical advice for correcting the system.

For years, Warren has been intimately in contact with the American farmers. He has talked to them from Cornell by radio and made frequent trips to their meetings, constantly advising his listeners as to the effects of price changes. The organized farm population of the country has become the most outspoken advocate of stabilization and this fact is largely due to the untiring efforts of Professor Warren.

Professor James Harvey Rogers, co-worker with Warren in advising the Roosevelt administration, had been for many years during his early life a student of the present writer's. During the war he became particularly interested in the price problem and participated in the work of the War Industries Board.[5] In a book about the French Inflation [6] and also in a later work, "America Weighs Her Gold," [7] which aroused much attention, Rogers explained the workings of the post-war gold standard and warned us of the dangers it involved—dangers to the economic conditions of the entire world. His interest in the stabilization of the dollar made him a supporter of the various stabilization bills for which he testified before Congressional Committees as early as 1923.

Professor John R. Commons of the University of Wisconsin, who is mentioned before, is one of the veterans of the stabilization movement. As early as 1900, he worked out index numbers [8] for the purpose of showing the public the need of a stable money.

[5] James Harvey Rogers, *Prices of Cotton and Cotton Products,* W.I.B., Price Bulletin, No. 23, Washington, 1919.

[6] James H. Rogers, *The Process of Inflation in France,* 1914–1927, New York, Columbia University Press, 1929.

[7] New Haven, Yale University Press, 1931.

[8] In collaboration with Mr. George H. Shibley, *Quarterly Bulletin of the Bureau of Economic Research,* July and October, 1900.

He also contributed to the movement largely by testifying before
Congressional Committees on pending stabilization bills, and in
preparing and analysing such measures. His suggestions to these
committees, his analysis of Federal Reserve credit policies, and
the data he gave in proof of the fact that the Federal Reserve System had actually succeeded in stabilizing the American price
level to some extent, have been used as foundations for many
later discussions of this question.[9]

Snyder; Meeker

Carl Snyder, head of the Statistical Department of the New
York Federal Reserve Bank, has long been an advocate of stable
money. During the War, huge quantities of gold had come to the
United States, and continued to flow in afterwards in the partial
liquidation of the war debts; so that in 1923, this country held
more than double the amount of gold necessary as legal reserve
for the dollar. In an article, "The Stabilization of Gold: A
Plan," [10] Mr. Snyder proposed a practical measure to prevent the
imminent danger of a gold inflation. His proposal was that the
issuance of the country's currency be regulated on the basis of
the available statistics of prices, production and so forth. He
said:

"In the quite astonishing array of index numbers which we
now possess, of wholesale and retail prices, wages, production,
employment, wholesale and retail trade, volume of goods trans-
ported, etc., coupled with most exhaustive bank statements for
the whole country, we now have a far more accurate and reliable
guide for automatic determination of the currency issue than the
foreign exchanges could possibly be; so accurate, indeed, that we
now know definitely when and at what rate our currency is de-

[9] See John R. Commons, *Farm Prices and the Value of Gold,* in "The North
American Review," January-February, 1928; *Price Stabilization and the Federal
Reserve System,* in "The Annalist," April 1, 1927.
[10] In "American Economic Review," Vol. XIII, No. 2, June 1923, pp. 276–285.

preciating or appreciating, and have little or no need to refer, for this, to the foreign exchanges, as in Ricardo's time." [11]

This important statement, showing as it did, the practical means already at the disposal of the monetary administration for maintaining the value of the dollar, was one of the first of its kind to come from anyone intimately connected with the Federal Reserve System. Snyder's proposal was for a stabilized dollar fully redeemable in gold; but gold itself to be stabilized as to its purchasing power over American commodities, thereby, to some extent, stabilizing the purchasing power of the currencies of all other gold standard countries. In order to effect this stability of gold, Snyder proposed,

"To control or restrict the total issue of this gold standard currency by means of an index number of prices, checked by other index numbers of production, employment and trade . . ." [12] Mr. Snyder showed how the wholesale commodity price index of the Bureau of Labor Statistics could be used as the basis for such calculations, and suggested that the central banks regulate the discount rates with reference to the price level:

"Control of the note issue to be through the medium of the Federal reserve banks, which should be required by law on a change in the price level of, let us say, 3 per cent (or whatever figure might be decided upon) to raise or lower the rate of rediscount by 1 per cent, or, in the same way, to raise or lower their holdings of securities and acceptances by, let us say, some conventional figure like 100 million dollars, as might be agreed upon; or both. The changes in the bank rate and securities holdings might be at a mildly progressive rate, as for example, a change of 1 per cent in the rate for the first 3 per cent change in the price index, another 1 per cent for the next two points change in the price index, etc. . . ."

[11] Carl Snyder, *The Stabilization of Gold, A Plan, op. cit.,* p. 279.
[12] *Ibid.,* p. 283.

"It seems clear that this control must be automatic and free from the possible intervention by any kind of influence, political, financial or otherwise. It seems evident, from our experience, that this is the one possible means of obtaining such control." [13]

Finally, Mr. Snyder suggested that all exports and imports of gold or currency be required by law to be registered and certified, and that when a given amount of gold or currency had left the country, the Federal reserve banks increase their holdings of securities by a corresponding amount. In the case of gold or currency imports, the operation would be reversed.

"The idea, in sum," he said, "is to keep the amount of currency and credit in balance with the price level and maintain the latter at as nearly a constant figure as is practically possible."

One of Mr. Snyder's most important discoveries, which was apparently new, was the fact that, as to short periods, the velocity of money, and the activity of business are correlated. From this, and the "equation of exchange," it follows that variations in the price level have a strong correspondence with variations in the quantity of the circulating medium—except for a secular change.[14] This discovery has reinforced the economic theory that the quantity of money, including bank deposits, can be used to influence the price level, and that the annual growth of trade, calculated to be about 2 to 4 per cent, should be accompanied by a corresponding increase in the volume of the circulating medium.

Another of Mr. Snyder's achievements is his construction of a "General Price Level," which, besides wholesale prices includes retail prices; rents; transportation costs; realty prices; prices of securities (bonds and stocks); and wages. This General Index is less sensitive than the wholesale commodity index of the Bureau of Labor Statistics which has often been proposed as a basis for stabilizing the dollar. Mr. Snyder prefers his general index for

[13] *Ibid.*, p. 284.
[14] See Carl Snyder, *New Measures in the Equation of Exchange,* in "American Economic Review," December, 1924, pp. 699–713.

stabilization purposes as more representative of the purchasing power of the dollar than the wholesale price index. It is designed to fit into the equation of exchange, being the "P" in "MV = PT."

Mr. Snyder has enriched our knowledge of the actual working of the monetary system. As he put it, he wanted economics "to escape from the endless logomachy, or battle of words and definitions of the schools, and take its place beside the inductive and experimental sciences," [15] and he has helped materially to forward that consummation.

Professor Royal Meeker, formerly of Princeton University, who was the U.S. Commissioner of Labor under President Wilson, was also an early advocate of monetary stabilization. He was the first economist after the appearance of "Stabilizing the Dollar" to become an enthusiast for the compensated dollar plan. It was mainly due to his efforts that, during and after the War, the U.S. Bureau of Labor Statistics constructed its "Cost of Living Index" which he hoped might some day be used as a basis for the stabilization of the dollar. Dr. Meeker has contributed many articles to periodicals and newspapers in the cause of stabilization.

King; Mitchell; Hastings; Hansen; Edie

Most economists have become interested in the problem of stabilizing the dollar through a study of index numbers, prices, and similar statistical researches, and particularly through the study of business cycles. Such activities have, therefore, become an important factor in the stable money movement, and credit is due to those economists who, although sometimes not actively engaged in this movement, have, through their efforts in these fields, advanced the cause.

One of the most prominent in this group is *Professor Willford*

[15] Carl Snyder, *New Measures of the Relations of Credit and Trade,* an address before the Academy of Political Science, November 22, 1929.

I. King,[16] of New York University. He has long been an enthusiastic advocate of stabilization.

Professor Wesley Clair Mitchell in 1915 wrote an interesting and exhaustive history of index numbers.[17] Under his direction, during and immediately after the War, a series of important price studies were carried on for the War Industries Board in Washington.[18]

In 1923, *Professor Hudson B. Hastings* prepared an excellent paper on the "Analysis of the Problem of Controlling the Price Level" [19] in which the various stabilization proposals were subjected to a searching analysis and constructive criticism. He came to the conclusion that short-term fluctuations were more difficult to avoid than long-term or secular price changes. For the control of the latter, and, in a limited way also for controlling the former, he recommended the adoption of either one of the following methods: (1) Carl Snyder's plan of controlling the issuance of the circulating medium according to a price index, to be checked by trade, production and employment indexes; (2) impounding the country's gold stock as a reserve, and issuing against it paper currency, so controlled as to maintain the price level; either plan to be supplemented, however, by open-market operations and changes in the discount rate.

At the time he presented it, Professor Hastings' paper was one of the most inclusive and up-to-date studies of the subject.

[16] See: Willford Isbell King: *The Elements of Statistical Method,* New York, Macmillan Co., 1912.

The Wealth and Income of the People of the United States, New York, Macmillan Co., 1915.

The National Income and its Purchasing Power, New York, National Bureau of Economic Research, Inc., 1930.

Index Numbers Elucidated, Longmans, Green and Co., New York, 1930.

[17] Wesley Clair Mitchell, *Index Numbers of Wholesale Prices in the United States and Foreign Countries,* U.S. Department of Labor, Bureau of Labor Statistics, Bulletin No. 173, July, 1915.

[18] See *History of Prices During the War,* War Industries Price Bulletin, No. 96, 1919. *International Price Comparisons,* dto. No. 2, 1919.

[19] Presented on June 7, 1923, at a Session of the National Monetary Association.

Professors Alvin Hansen, Lionel D. Edie, and others have also
made valuable contributions to the subject, which will be mentioned in the Appendix.

From January 27 to 31, 1932, the *University of Chicago* held
Round Table Conferences on "Gold and Monetary Stabilization"
during which many phases of the stabilization problem were
discussed.

SECTION 2. IN THE UNITED STATES, CONTINUED

(*The Report of the Columbia University Commission*)

In May 1934, there was published the report of the Columbia
University Commission on "Economic Reconstruction." [20] This
volume contains the most thorough discussion of the stabilization
problem which has thus far been issued by an American academic
group.

The Commission, appointed in December 1932 by President
Nicholas Murray Butler of Columbia University, included Professors of Columbia, and of other Universities, as well as outstanding men not directly connected with any University.

The Commission originally consisted of sixteen members, of
whom two resigned because of pressure of work; [21] three because
of having become active in Government service; [22] one because
of absence from the United States; [23] and one apparently because
of disagreement.[24]

On January 31, 1934, the Chairman of the Commission, Professor
R. M. MacIver, submitted the Report to President Butler. It was
signed by the following:

[20] Columbia University Press, 1934.
[21] Edmund E. Day and Walter Lippmann.
[22] Adolf A. Berle; James H. Rogers; Leo Wolman.
[23] Jacob Viner.
[24] Benjamin M. Anderson, Jr.

Robert M. MacIver	Arthur D. Gayer	Harlow S. Person
James W. Angell	Alvin H. Hansen	George H. Soule
Joseph W. Barker	Alvin Johnson	Josef A. Schumpeter
John M. Clark	Wesley C. Mitchell	

A partially dissenting opinion as regards the broad principles of monetary stabilization laid down in the Report is appended by Professor James W. Angell and subscribed to by Professor Josef A. Schumpeter. In a separate statement, the former says that he recommends a "definite return (of the United States) to the full international gold standard at the earliest possible moment, without regard to the action of other nations. . . ." [25] Professor Joseph W. Barker, an engineer, while in agreement "with the general tenor and conclusions of the report," can not "subscribe to that part of the report dealing with currency reforms."

Observations on Unstable Money and the Gold Standard

The report places great emphasis upon the importance of monetary stability in terms of purchasing power, which is even considered fundamental to the attainment of recovery and ultimate economic equilibrium.

"So long, for example," the report says [26] "as general prices move violently up and down, arbitrarily altering the relation between price and cost factors or between creditor and debtor, any calculated policy aiming at a higher level of productivity is bound to be distorted and continually interrupted."

In another connection the report mentions the effect of violent price fluctuations not only on production and the distribution of income, but upon national and international political conditions:

[25] Columbia University Commission, *Economic Reconstruction, op. cit.*, p. 77 and pp. 239-40.
[26] *Ibid.*, p. 20.

"The confusion introduced into economic life and the cruel injuries and injustices inflicted upon society by price chaos have often been described in detail. The evil has a twofold aspect. Rapid changes in the price level not only have a calamitous effect upon *productive activity;* but they also arbitrarily alter the *distribution* of national income between different classes of society. In addition they play havoc with smooth economic, and consequently with political relations, not only between classes but also between nations." [27]

A stronger condemnation of our past system of uncontrolled and fluctuating price levels can hardly be conceived. In similar terms America's adherence to the gold standard for eighteen months after Great Britain had abandoned it, is criticized:

"Great Britain and the other countries which followed her off gold in 1931 were spared the long and agonizing process of devastating deflation to which the United States was subject during the next eighteen months by her desperate attempt to cling to gold at all costs. By this course America precluded any measures directed to the deliberate encouragement of business recovery and to the deliverance, otherwise than by wholesale bankruptcy, of the nation from the morass of unpayable debt which extended further the more the process of deflation advanced." [28]

Objectives of American Monetary Policy

Regarding the practical policy to be followed by the United States, the report is quite definite in its recommendation of a "managed" currency. It says:

"The choice before us, under existing conditions, does not lie between an automatic regulator of money and a managed currency, with or without a gold basis. We cannot, even if we would, avoid the necessity of control. The only choice concerns the form of control we adopt and the objective we deem most essential for the determination of its policy." [29]

[27] *Ibid.,* p. 38.
[28] *Ibid.,* p. 29.
[29] *Ibid.,* p. 29.

The Commission finds the continuation of a system of private initiative and profits to be dependent upon the immediate establishment of a stable standard of value. Under the old order of stable exchanges and unstable price levels, severe economic crises have brought revolutions and drastic changes in the political conditions of nations. The elimination of violent price level fluctuations which are considered a basic cause of economic crises appears, therefore, a fundamental requirement for preventing the destruction of our political and economic order. In regard to this, the report says:

"Of the permanent desiderata, we regard as paramount the establishment of a standard of value which is not subject to violent fluctuations. Since the War the world has witnessed a series of violent price movements which cannot continue if the economic order we know is to survive in any form at all.

"We therefore give priority to internal economic stability over stability of the exchange rate for foreign currencies. The latter is at the same time a genuine desideratum . . ."[30]

The Commission's recommendations in the monetary field are summarized in the following statement, confirming, on the whole, the reflation-stabilization policy as enunciated by President Roosevelt:

". . . Our primary, immediate need, so far as the monetary system is concerned, is a rising price level reflecting an increased volume of business and increased employment, and associated with general confidence in the price-raising methods or impulses. Our primary permanent need is a price system maintaining an approximately steady purchasing power of the dollar over goods. This requirement still leaves open the question whether a *slow* secular trend of prices upward or downward may not be preferable to an *absolutely* stationary equilibrium. The concomitant non-monetary conditions necessary to ensure the preservation of economic balance under such a price policy are indicated below

[30] *Ibid.*, p. 32.

Of secondary importance, though well worth striving for, if it is compatible with the main desideratum, is some such stability in exchange as the traditional gold standard assured." [31]

The Commission answers those who have been clamoring for an immediate return to the international gold standard, and who have so violently attacked President Roosevelt's policies because he disregarded the importance of stable exchange rates in favor of purchasing power stability. The report says:

"While the advantages derived from concerted international action are enormous, while they are of great importance even apart from their direct economic benefits, they can in large measure be achieved only through patient, thorough, and probably slow deliberations, and there is still no guarantee that the necessary agreement will be forthcoming. It would therefore be foolish to wait for international price-stability until it can be achieved by means largely beyond our control. There is good reason to believe that a preliminary equilibrium can be achieved without the return to an international standard. After this is achieved it will be easier to plan for a return to what should be a greatly reformed and internationally managed gold standard.

". . . Fortunately, while international stability could not be attained under the traditional gold standard, this end can be pursued in its absence, while we are waiting for some better international system. It is an entirely fallacious notion that paper standards are uncontrollable. It is strange that such statements should still be made by monetary authorities in the light of the experience with paper currencies in the past few years. During the periods when England has been off gold, from 1797 to 1821, from 1914 to 1925, and again since 1931, the paper currency was never abused by inflationary excesses. In fact, in terms of their internal purchasing power, paper currencies have shown themselves far more stable than gold currencies during the last two years, despite the critical difficulties of the times and the grave temptations they offered to governments to indulge in inflationary finance.

[31] *Ibid.*, p. 33.

"Between September, 1931, and the banking panic of 1933 it was not the pound sterling, the Canadian dollar, the Scandinavian currencies, etc. which were unstable, but the American dollar, the franc, the mark, and other gold currencies. The paper money of the 'sterling area' retained a remarkably steady purchasing power—altogether too steady in the opinion of those who would like to have seen a deliberate expansionist policy adopted to correct the previously deflationary trend of prices—while gold underwent an outrageous appreciation in value." [32]

In its "Specific Recommendations," the Commission also stresses the need for adequate provision to secure purchasing power stability before an international standard is again adopted. It says:

"(2) The return of the United States to an international gold standard should be conditional on the assurance of a number of important reforms in the working of that standard, including an agreement by central banks to maintain a reasonable stability of gold itself." [33]

The Commission, however, also emphasizes that it regards price stability as important merely as a means to an end, and expresses this as follows:

"First, however, we wish to warn against the mistake of regarding price-stability as an absolutely inflexible principle in the realization of which the dollar would become as fixed and undeviating a measure of value as the yardstick is a measure of length. Even were this attainable, it is more than doubtful whether such an ideal would be desirable. There are considerations that favor a secularly rising price level, other considerations that favor a moderate secular decline. These slow, or long-run movements are here not in question. What is without doubt desirable is to prevent the constant and often severe short-period fluctuations of the standard of value. . . .

"There is no especial virtue in any particular price level in itself and for its own sake. The best price level will be the one which best facilitates that mutual adjustment of costs and prices,

[32] *Ibid.,* p. 40.
[33] *Ibid.,* p. 73.

promptly and with least friction, which is continually necessary in a progressive economy." [34]

The suggestion is also made that under a stable price level, the gains of increased efficiency which normally should find expression in a slightly declining price level, ought to be paid out in the form of higher wages and salaries. Regarding this point, the report continues as follows:

"Such regulated wage and salary increases would mean a constant increase in effective demand for goods in the degree in which industrial advance occurred. The essential problem is to adjust wages upward in line with increased productivity lest windfall and excessive profits destroy the economic balance." [35]

The stand on monetary policy taken by the Columbia University Commission seems to be of great importance in several respects. First, it sustains the basic objectives of President Roosevelt's monetary policy of reflating the domestic price level, and then stabilizing it. This view is in sharp contrast to that of those who favor stabilization of foreign exchange rates.

The Commission exhibits signs of impatience, implying a criticism of the administration's hesitant manner in which it has pursued its chosen policy and the uncertainty thus created.

In a third respect, the report is important: This is the first time that the advocates of monetary stabilization, on the one hand, and of industrial planning, on the other, have come to agree on and subscribe to, a common program.

From the "Special Report" which the members of the Columbia Commission have prepared, it appears that certain members had been especially active in drawing up the monetary proposals. Professor Arthur D. Gayer, of Columbia University, the Executive Secretary of the Commission is the author of four separate

[34] *Ibid.*, p. 45.
[35] *Ibid.*, p. 48.

special reports [36] from which almost all of the above mentioned statements in the General Report are drawn. Professor Alvin Hansen of the University of Minnesota; [37] and third, the Chairman, Professor Robert M. MacIver of Columbia, have also been particularly active in the work of the Commission on the monetary problem.

Criticism of Contradictory Recovery Measures

In addition to the above proposal for a constructive monetary policy, the Columbia Commission criticizes some features of the "New Deal," particularly the attempt to raise prices by restricting production. Such a rise of prices is sharply distinguished from a rise of prices effected by monetary means.

"In fact," the report says, "many of the devices to which recourse is had under the stress of bad times are intrinsically wasteful. Such devices range from the raising of new tariff barriers and other impediments in the way of trade between countries, to the deliberate limitation of production and even the physical destruction of goods and crops in order to raise the price of the remainder. These devices are in effect a confession of failure in respect of our present ability to deal with the major problem." [38]

And in dealing with the minimum-price requirements of the codes under the National Recovery Act, the report says:

"There should be no illusion with regard to the fact that a general rise in prices through such measures is not a sign of increasing prosperity. It is the rise of prices reflective of increased demand and increased purchasing power which alone can be

[36] Arthur D. Gayer: *The Nature and Functioning of the Post-War Gold Standard, ibid.,* pp. 127–145.

Non-Monetary Factors Affecting the Functioning of the Post-War Gold Standard., ibid., pp. 146–159.

Monetary Policy and Public Works., ibid., pp. 160–169.

Monetary Policy and the Monetary Standard., ibid., pp. 177–209.

These reports are excerpts of the author's forthcoming book on "Monetary Policy and Economic Stabilization."

[37] Alvin Hansen, *The Flow of Purchasing Power, ibid.,* pp. 210–237.

[38] *Ibid.,* p. 12.

associated with the process of recovery. The concomitant illusion that a *deliberate* limitation of output, because it raises prices, helps toward recovery is a still more dangerous fallacy. It is more dangerous because the limitation of output of an individual commodity may be for the advantage of its producers if they can thereby control its price. The abnormal situation of agriculture may justify special and temporary measures along such lines, but it should be fully recognized that they involve a tax on the rest of the community, and above all that an all-round application of this policy would make for general impoverishment and would solve the problem of 'poverty in the midst of plenty' by removing the plenty." [39]

The report thus condemns those of the recovery measures of the "New Deal" which, in the opinion of the advocates of stable money, have retarded, rather than promoted recovery.

SECTION 3. IN ENGLAND

Pigou

Professor A. C. Pigou, of Cambridge University although currency and banking were somewhat removed from his immediate interests, early recognized the connection of monetary fluctuations with unemployment and similar social problems. As early as 1905 [39a] he referred to the need for automatic adjustments of wages to meet fluctuations in the price level. In his "Wealth and Welfare," he mentioned the need for eliminating, by means of stabilization, the monetary cause of industrial depressions, citing the proposals of Professor Marshall's and of the present writer. In every one of his later works,[40] Pigou devoted much attention

[39] *Ibid.*, p. 17.
[39a] A. C. Pigou, *Principles and Methods of Industrial Peace*, London, Macmillan & Co., Ltd., 1905.
[40] See: *Wealth and Welfare*, London, Macmillan & Co., Ltd., 1912.
Unemployment, London, Home University Library, 1913.
Economics of Welfare, London, Macmillan & Co., Ltd., 1920.
Essays in Applied Economics, London, P. S. King & Son, Ltd., 1923.
Industrial Fluctuations, London, Macmillan & Co., Ltd., 1927.
The Theory of Unemployment, London, Macmillan & Co., Ltd., 1933.

to the stabilization question, and though he advanced no new plan for it, he weighed carefully the practicability of the proposals made by others. In a word, he brought the question of currency and credit management into the proper relation to "welfare economics," of which he is one of the foremost exponents.

Stamp

Sir Josiah Stamp, economist and chairman of the Midland Railways and Director of the Bank of England, in several articles and in a readable biographical book,[41] has told the story of his interest in monetary stability and of his efforts to arouse a similar interest in others. In 1909–1910 he realized that increased land values which were due to changes in the purchasing power of money might attract unjust taxation. He said:

"My first serious concern with the long range effect of price levels arose in dealing with the new Land Taxes of 1909–1910, for it was obvious that increments in money value, where no real increment in real or comparable goods existed, might attract taxation in the long run, and real increment might be obscured by decrement in money value." [42]

In 1917, also with reference to taxation, Sir Josiah wrote about the Excess Profit Duty which throve on fictitious increases in profits, due entirely to price changes.[43] After the War, Sir Josiah foresaw the danger which a fall in prices would bring about in reducing income, while maintaining the debt structure. He therefore made the first calculation of the real weight of the national debt in order to make possible an adjustment of debts in accordance with a changed purchasing power of money.

[41] Sir Josiah Stamp, *Papers on Gold and the Price Level,* London, P.S., King & Son, Ltd., 1931, pp. 81 ff.
[42] From *Local Government Review,* 1912.
[43] In "Economic Journal," March, 1917.

In 1919–1920, Sir Josiah anticipated the end of inflation and the consequent fall in prices.[44]

His next reference to changing prices was made in his New-march Lecture, February 1921, his subject being "The Effect of Changing Price Levels on Profits and Wages."

He wrote, "In July 1923 the higher bank rate, the continued fall in the dollar-sterling exchange, and the Government's declaration that it was our policy to do all in our power to keep prices steady, made me ask the question: 'Are we Deflating Too Much?'" [45]

When, in 1923, Mr. Keynes' "Tract on Monetary Reform" first appeared, Sir Josiah Stamp reviewed the book in the "Statistical Journal" and declared himself as favorable to the principles of the proposed reform. This did not mean, however, that he accepted Mr. Keynes' "Managed Currency" without reservations. In an article,[46] in 1924, he summarized his objections and doubts to such a managed currency as follows:

"Inability to discern at all clearly the technique and criteria of day-to-day management.

"Wonder whether the occupants of the institutions which manage will always be masters of that technique.

"The probable absence of general popular confidence in the managed standard. . . .

"The possible existence of political influences (or the prevalence of popular notions that such influences do exist).

"The complications of foreign exchange for a country with large foreign trade and investments."

But Sir Josiah indicated that, even though he was in favor of the gold standard, he believed that it should result in a stable price level:

"Having said that I prefer a gold standard does not mean I am

---

[44] See his *Evidence before the Select Committee on Increase of War Wealth,* April, 1920.
[45] In "Weekly Dispatch," July 8, 1923.
[46] "Wall Street Journal," February, 1924.

satisfied with it. The fine measurements and complex relations of
modern times demand something less rough and wayward. . . .

"For we must manage our standard or it will mismanage
us. The price level must be controlled and we must control it by
a golden handle."

Further articles by Sir Josiah give evidence of his growing fear
of the future of the gold standard, because gold continued to
accumulate in the United States so that Europe was faced by the
dangerous prospect of falling prices at home due to a scarcity of
gold.

In 1925, when troubles had begun in the British coal-mining
industry, Sir Josiah was appointed on a committee of three to
report on the causes. As his colleagues did not agree with his
diagnosis that the main causes were deflation and the return of
England to gold, he expressed his views separately in a special
addendum to the report.[47]

In an article, in 1928, on "Public Opinion and the Price Level" [48]
he wrote as follows about the stabilization problem:

"When I have said quite seriously, as I have done on a number
of occasions, that the problem of the price level is the most important single problem of our age, I have been accused either of
exaggeration or of flippancy. 'What about trade depressions in the
basic industries, unemployment, labour unrest, class hatred, high
taxation, and the rest?' My answer is that the problem of the
price level is fundamental to a solution of them all."

In an address, delivered before the Stable Money Association,
whose Vice-President he had become, Sir Josiah Stamp closed
with the following words, which emphasized the great economic
importance of the purchasing power of money: [49]

"We are just in the stone age in economic thinking compared

[47] *Report by a Court of Inquiry Concerning the Coal Mining Industry Dispute,*
1925. Addendum to Paragraph 14 by Sir Josiah Stamp, July 28th, 1925.
[48] In "Spectator," November, 1928.
[49] June 6th, 1930, at the Harvard Club, New York.

with that immense advance that we have made in other directions, and it is the task of this Association to make every man, when he is looking for the cause of things, to ask *first,* and not *last,* the question: What is the price level? What is it doing to me? What is it doing to the wage earner? What is it doing to the profit margin, to the whole balance-sheet and profit and loss account? In that way, upon the world will some day dawn what we now mean by Stable Money."

One of Sir Josiah's achievements in the cause of stable money occurred when he was British Representative on the Dawes Reparation Commission. He succeeded in introducing into the Dawes Plan a provision that in case of a change in the price level of 10% or more, the whole annuity was to be changed correspondingly in order that the proposed burden on the debtor nations might not be unjustly altered.

Hawtrey

R. G. Hawtrey, Director of Financial Studies in the British Treasury has for many years advocated co-operation among Central Banks in order to achieve an invariable value of money. As early as 1913, regarding the possibility of credit control by the central banking institutions, he said:

"If the great Central Banks of the world, in whose hands this control [of the money market] rests, could agree together to draw the reins a little tighter at times when an expansion of trade is in progress, they might prevent the inflation of credit money reaching the danger point. . . . And on the other hand, when the supply of credit money is being diminished, the banks ought to be in a position to release a sufficient amount of cash. . . . In practice this would mean that the banks would maintain a larger proportion of reserves to liabilities than the average when trade is good and a smaller proportion when trade is bad." [50]

[50] R. G. Hawtrey, *Good and Bad Trade,* An Inquiry into the Causes of Trade Fluctuations, London, Constable & Co., Ltd., 1913, p. 263.

In 1919 Hawtrey suggested [51] the adoption of the gold-exchange standard by a group of countries, including England, which had abandoned gold during the War. The national currencies of these countries, he said, should be limited in volume by the international agreement of central banks, the common object being the maintenance of a stable index number of prices.

In his "Currency and Credit," he expressed the belief that the gold standard could very well be maintained if the central banks of large nations would agree to maintain the purchasing power of gold.

"What is desirable is not the indiscriminate abandonment of the old gold reserve conventions," he said, "but the regulation of gold reserves by international agreement with the express object of preventing either a rise or a fall in the wealth value of gold. . . ." [51a]

Hawtrey pointed out that the ability of central banks to influence the value of the currency imposes upon them a grave responsibility, which they could fulfill only through wise administration:

"In view of the serious evils arising from the credit cycle, the responsibility is a heavy one" he said. "Whoever has control over credit does in fact determine the fluctuations of prices, and the magnitude and frequency of the alternations of inflation and depression. Legislation can do but little. Everything depends on administration. . . ." [52]

The authorities of our American Federal Reserve System had also frequently stated that automatic regulation would be in-

---

[51] *The Gold Standard*, read to the Economic Section of the British Association, September, 1919. Chapter III, of *Monetary Reconstruction*, Longmans, Green & Co., Ltd., London, 1922.

[51a] R. G. Hawtrey, *Currency and Credit*, London, Longmans, Green and Co., first edition 1919; third edition, 1928, p. 106.

[52] R. G. Hawtrey, *Trade and Credit*, London, Longmans, Green and Co., 1928, pp. 16–17.

effective. But while the argument by the Federal Reserve was in opposition to stabilization, Hawtrey, on the other hand, believed that this fact only showed the need of an "Art of Central Banking" [53] which the central bankers had not yet mastered. The one man whom he excepted from this impeachment was Governor Strong, of the New York Federal Reserve Bank, of whom he said, "It was a disaster for the world that Governor Strong died. . . ." [54]

In the men who decided the financial destiny of Great Britain (the directors of the Bank of England) Hawtrey had little confidence:

"A technical understanding of the art of central banking is not required as a qualification. If occasionally an economist or financier who enters the circle has made a study of the art, that is not regarded as a recommendation. Probably it adds little or no weight to his opinion in the eyes of his colleagues." [55]

The abandonment of the gold standard by England, in 1931, may have brought to Hawtrey the unpleasant conviction that his insistent warnings had been correct; but he now urged that England make the best of the situation, and restore the equilibrium in the price level through currency reflation:

"But the essential advantage of abandoning the gold standard" he said, "is that the value of the currency can be adjusted to the point at which *prices and costs are in equilibrium*. Here is the key to the unemployment problem. . . .

"This policy does not threaten a *competitive* depreciation among the countries pursuing it. The relief each country gets is not derived from over-reaching the others; it is derived from the country's industry becoming remunerative at the world price level." [56]

[53] *The Art of Central Banking,* London, Longmans, Green and Co., 1932.
[54] *Ibid.,* p. 209.
[55] *Ibid.,* p. 246.
[56] R. G. Hawtrey, *The Gold Standard in Theory and Practice,* London, Longmans, Green and Co., 1933, p. 208.

Besides asking for a price level adjusted to the costs of industry, he asked that it be such as to enable industry to re-absorb most of the unemployed, and said the money required was to be tested not by gold but by goods.

"We are thus supplied with a very definite objective in the regulation of an inconvertible paper currency," he said, "the maintenance of the currency unit at that value which will just secure equilibrium between prices and wages. The 'value' so determined is not itself a value in *gold* but a value in *goods*. If the advantage of equilibrium, that is to say of industry being remunerative and fully employed, are to be obtained, the value of the unit in gold must be varied whenever the value of gold in goods varies, so that the value of the unit in goods may be kept stable."

And he added, "This is precisely the plan advocated by Mr. Keynes." [57]

That is, Hawtrey had come to see the advantage of an inconvertible currency which could be managed nationally without waiting for an international agreement.

Contrary to some students of this subject in both Britain and the United States, Hawtrey believed that the so-called "Business Cycle" was due mainly to changes in the purchasing power of money. He said:

"The trade cycle is essentially a cycle in the purchasing power of money, that is to say, in the price level. . . ." [58] On the basis of the Federal Reserve policies under Governor Strong (1922–1927) he was encouraged to state that stabilization (*i.e.* avoidance of business cycles) by means of central bank credit control was feasible. He said:

"The American experiment in stabilization from 1922 to 1928 showed that an early treatment could check a tendency either to inflation or to depression, before any serious damage had been

[57] *Ibid.*, p. 209.
[58] *Trade and Credit, op. cit.*, p. 16.

done. And even that practice can undoubtedly be improved upon. . . .

"The American experiment was a great advance upon the practice of the nineteenth century. In the nineteenth century and up to 1914 the trade cycle was accepted in a spirit of fatalism. Economists, unwilling to admit that it could be merely a monetary disease, surrounded it with an atmosphere of mystery." [59]

It is regarded by those who have been close to the stabilization movement, as an open secret that the famous resolutions on stabilization of the Genoa Conference were due largely to the efforts of Hawtrey.

Section 4. In England continued

Bellerby

J. R. Bellerby in 1923, in a study submitted to the International Association on Unemployment, of which he was a member, traced the problem of unemployment directly to the problem of monetary stabilization which he held essential for stable industrial activity. Bellerby believed that a great part of the responsibility for such stability rested with the banks.

"The various links in the chain of reasoning," he said, "are as follows: Unemployment will be reduced if industry can be stabilized at a comparatively high level of activity. Greater stability in industry can be secured by greater stability of the price level. The movement of the price level is determined largely by the volume of money, or 'purchasing power' made available to the community. Control over the contraction or expansion of the purchasing power of the community rests partly with the banks." [60]

Bellerby's book on "Monetary Stability," [61] published in 1925,

---

[59] The Art of Central Banking, op. cit., p. 300.
[60] J. R. Bellerby, Control of Credit as a Remedy for Unemployment, P. S. King & Son, Ltd., 1923, p. 10.
[61] J. R. Bellerby, Monetary Stability, London, Macmillan Co., 1925.

contained a proposal for an international agreement under which the Federal Reserve System would adhere to a "normal" price level, and all European central banks would maintain the parity of their exchanges with the money of the United States—the Reserve System itself to keep its price level stable through a wise discount and credit policy.

Lehfeldt

Professor R. A. Lehfeldt, although he lived in South Africa, may perhaps best be classed among the English economists. His books were published in London and he wrote mainly for an English public. His stabilization plan, first proposed in 1923, was that of controlling the production of gold by the several governments.[62] This plan he later described more in detail in his "Controlling the Output of Gold" (1926).[63]

The plan was that England and the United States, possessing already four-fifths of the world's gold resources, should organize a syndicate of nations to regulate the production of gold with the primary object of adapting the supply to the requirements of trade. This syndicate of nations should operate, not for profit but in the public interest. It should encourage gold production in case of need for additional supply, and discourage such production whenever the gold output exceeded the monetary requirements.

Under the Lehfeldt plan, gold mines would not necessarily have to be nationalized. Even if they were left under private ownership, the governments could stimulate production by granting subsidies to the gold producers, and curb production by levying a special tax. Lehfeldt believed that the individual governments were not trustworthy in matters of currency, and that,

---

[62] R. A. Lehfeldt, *Restoration of the World's Currencies,* London, P. S. King & Son, Ltd., 1925.
[63] London, General Press, 1926.

therefore, the other stabilization proposals, such as the compensated dollar plan and managed, inconvertible currency were not advisable. The advocates of these plans, on the other hand, accused Lehfeldt who came from the richest gold mining section of the world, of being prejudiced in favor of the gold producers. At the same time, Lehfeldt actually made enemies among his gold mining neighbors for they were opposed to plans of governmental regulation.

Keynes

One of the best known English advocates of stabilization is John Maynard Keynes who is credited with having coined the expression "Managed Currency." He established a reputation not only as a brilliant writer, but also as an economist of great foresight by the warnings contained in his "The Economic Consequences of the Peace." [64] When later he advised against England's return to the gold standard, he was looked upon as a monetary heretic. But developments have again proven the soundness of his proposals, and his "managed currency" has become an essential point in recent discussions on currency reform.

In 1923 he stated [65] that the value of gold was no longer due chiefly to gold discoveries, nor to new chemical methods of extracting the metal but to the policies of the most important central banks. The United States, for instance, by rendering ineffective its huge hoard of gold, had started a new method of gold control, as a result of which the gold standard had become, to a certain extent, a managed standard. Keynes took the position that whatever standard we finally decide upon, it must be "managed." No automatic control is possible:

"We have no ready-made standard," he said. "Experience has

[64] John Maynard Keynes, *The Economic Consequences of the Peace*, New York, Harcourt, Brace and Howe, 1920.
[65] John Maynard Keynes, *Monetary Reform*, New York, Harcourt, Brace and Company, 1924, pp. 180–82.

shown that, in emergencies, Ministers of Finance cannot be strapped down. And—most important of all—in the modern world of paper currency and bank credit there is no escape from a 'managed' currency, whether we wish it or not;—convertibility into gold will not alter the fact that the value of gold itself depends on the policy of the Central Banks." [66]

For this reason Keynes criticized the Genoa resolutions. The plan proposed in those resolutions was too dependent on gold. ". . . why drag in gold at all?" he asked; and he found the reason in, ". . . the force of sentiment and tradition, and the preference of Englishmen for shearing a monarch of his powers rather than of his head." [67]

Keynes now advanced his proposals for the regulation of money. His plan deals with both the domestic price level and international exchange:

"A sound constructive scheme" he says, "must provide—if it is to satisfy the arguments and the analysis of this book:

"I. A method for regulating the supply of currency and credit with a view to maintaining, so far as possible, the stability of the internal price level; and

"II. A method for regulating the supply of foreign exchange so as to avoid purely temporary fluctuations, caused by seasonal or other influences and not due to a lasting disturbance in the relation between the internal and the external price level." [68]

The technique of such stabilization includes the use of all available index numbers, dealing with employment, production, interest rates, etc., but merely for the purpose of maintaining a stable price level:

". . . Actual price movements must of course provide the most important datum; but the state of employment, the volume of production, the effective demand for credit as felt by the banks,

[66] *Ibid.*, p. 184.
[67] *Ibid.*, p. 188.
[68] *Ibid.*, p. 192.

the rate of interest on investments of various types, the volume of new issues, the flow of cash into circulation, the statistics of foreign trade and the level of exchanges must all be taken into account. The main point is that the *objective* of the authorities, pursued with such means as are at their command, should be the stability of prices." [69]

The Bank of England should effect stability of exchange by regulating the price of gold, which would retain its usefulness for the settlement of international payments, and as a war-chest in emergencies. The Bank would have a buying and a selling price for gold, just as before the War. This price might remain unchanged for considerable periods, but it would be no more fixed than the bank rate. But there would remain no logical reason for employing gold as a reserve for paper currency, which would be regulated with the sole object of maintaining internal stability of prices, trade and employment.

"Therefore I make the proposal . . . of separating entirely the gold reserve from the note issue. Once this principle is adopted, the regulations are matters of detail. The gold reserves of the country should be concentrated in the hands of the Bank of England, to be used for the purpose of avoiding short-term fluctuations in the exchange. . . ." [70]

Keynes' final conclusion, however, regarding the practical adoption of his plan, sounded somewhat pessimistic, and he suggested that, as he did not believe one country alone could stabilize, England and the United States should begin such currency management in unison:

"We have now reached a stage in the evolution of money when a 'managed' currency is inevitable, but we have not yet reached the point when the management can be entrusted to a single authority. The best we can do, therefore, is to have *two* managed

[69] *Ibid.*, p. 204.
[70] *Ibid.*, p. 212.

currencies, sterling and dollar, with as close a collaboration as possible between the aims and methods of the managements." [71]

But later, having become more familiar with the actual technique of price level control by central banks, Mr. Keynes made less drastic demands upon them. He referred particularly to the testimony of the Federal Reserve officials before a Congressional Committee:

". . . But when all is said and done," he wrote, "does it lie within the power of a Central Bank in actual practice to pursue a policy which will have the effect of fixing the value of money at any prescribed level?

". . . I have more sympathy to-day than I had a few years ago with some of the doubts and hesitations such as were expressed in 1927 by Governor Strong and other witnesses before the Committee of the U.S. Congress on Stabilization." [72]

"These are reasonable doubts expressed by persons of great experience. They cannot be expelled merely by pointing to the truism of a Quantity Equation. In a sense they can only be dispelled by the prolonged success of an actual attempt at scientific control. But I should like a try to show that the prospects of such an attempt are sufficiently promising for it to be worth a trial." [73]

In his final conclusions he listed five causes which limit the power of central banks to stabilize money, and which have been confirmed, to some extent, by the Swedish experience. [74]

"a) It is much easier to preserve stability than to restore it quickly, after a serious state of disequilibrium has been allowed to set in. . . .

"b) . . . non-monetary causes of instability may sometimes

---

[71] *Ibid.,* p. 221.
[72] *A Treatise on Money,* New York, Harcourt, Brace & Co., 1930, Vol. II, pp. 339–40.
[73] *Ibid.,* p. 345.
[74] See: The Swedish Experiment, Chapter 9, Section 5.

arise so suddenly that it is impossible to counteract them in time. In this event it may be inevitable that an interval should elapse before stability can be restored.

"c) If there are strong social and political forces causing spontaneous changes in the money-rates of efficiency-wages, the control of the price-level may pass beyond the power of the banking system. . . .

"d) If a country adheres to an international standard and that standard is itself unstable, it is, of course, impossible to preserve the stability of the domestic price-level in face of this. . . .

"e) Even where the banking system is strong enough to preserve the *stability* of the price-level, it does not follow that it is strong enough both to *alter* the price-level and to establish equilibrium at the new level without long delays and frictions."[75]

Mr. Keynes was appointed a member of the Macmillan Committee during 1930–1931,[76] and later became an enthusiastic supporter of President Roosevelt's monetary policy.[77]

Salter

Another important English economist who became an advocate of stabilization is *Sir Arthur Salter*. For a number of years he was the Director of the Economic Division of the League of Nations. In his "Recovery, The Second Effort"[78] he proposed that the Bank for International Settlement become the "Bank of Central Banks"; that is a central point from which to manage the gold standard for the purpose of maintaining both stable exchange rates and stable purchasing powers of the several currencies. In his Halley Stewart Lecture, 1931,[79] he also suggested

[75] *Ibid.*, p. 351.
[76] See Chapter 9, Section 4.
[77] See Chapter 10, Sec. 2.
[78] Sir Arthur Salter, *Recovery The Second Effort,* New York, The Century Company, 1932.
[79] Halley Stewart Lecture, 1932: *The World's Economic Crisis and the Way of Escape,* London, George Allen & Unwin, Ltd., 1931.

that England, being then off gold, put the objective of an internally stable price level above any other objective of her monetary policy.

SECTION 5. OTHER EUROPEAN LEADERS

Sweden: Wicksell; Cassel; Ohlin [80]

More than any other Scandinavian economist, *Knut Wicksell* has influenced economic thinking and interest in stabilization in his country. We have already mentioned briefly his first important contribution to the problem of controlling the price level,[81] namely the proposal of raising or lowering the central bank's discount rates so as to influence the price of credit, and thus arrive at a regulation of the credit volume. In 1906 he read a paper before the Economic Section of the British Association on "The Influence of the Rate of Interest on Prices" [82] in which he repeated the theoretical principles of his proposal.

In 1913,[83] Wicksell predicted that if the increase of the cost of living which (caused by gold inflation) was then going on, was permitted to continue, or even if prices were to decline again due to gold scarcity, the need for monetary reform would become so evident as to be unavoidable. "The practical means for this purpose" he said, "will become obvious, even though they may not be perfect in the beginning." [84]

During 1917–1918 Wicksell proposed that the Riksbank (the Swedish Central Bank) be permitted to pay interest on its deposits, the idea being that this measure might help to counter-

---

[80] For a better appreciation of the wide-spread interest in stabilization among Swedish economists, see the part on the Swedish Stabilization Experiment, Chapter 9, Section 5, also Appendix II on the Controversy over the Swedish Stabilization.

[81] See Chapter 2, section 3 on *Geldzins und Gueterprise* (1898).

[82] Printed in "The Economic Journal," Vol. XVII, pp. 213–220, London, 1907.

[83] Knut Wicksell, *Vorlesungen ueber Nationaloekonomie*, Zweiter Band, *Geld und Kredit*, Jena, Verlag von Gustav Fischer, 1922.

[84] *Ibid.*, p. 256.

act, to some extent, the drastic war-inflation. That is, he hoped that by this measure the Riksbank would be able to retire notes, decreasing the volume of outstanding currency, an effect similar to that obtained through the sale of Government securities. Not until 1920 was such a law adopted by the Swedish Government, but it was then too late to use it for an orderly contraction of the currency.

In 1919, in an article on "The Riksbank and the Commercial Banks; Proposal for the Reform of the Swedish Currency and Credit System" [85] the essence of his proposal was as follows:

1) Riksbank notes are to be the only legal tender currency (small change to be convertible into notes); gold coin and bullion are to be accepted by the Riksbank at rates to be determined by it and announced monthly.

2) All legal provisions for reserves of precious metals are to be abolished, and the Riksbank may dispose over its reserves as it deems best.

3) The issuance of notes to be so regulated as to attain, as far as possible, an invariable price level.

Through such reorganization of the Swedish monetary system Wicksell hoped to bring about the united action of all Scandinavian central banks. He even believed that eventually the discount rates of these countries could be determined by an Inter-scandinavian Commission on Currency.

In the opinion of Wicksell, a modern central bank should not only be a state institution, but it should function solely with regard to the public welfare, and without consideration of profit. In this manner, the administration of the monetary system should become equal to that of the judicial or educational systems.

---

[85] In Swedish in "Ekonomisk Tidskrift II" (1919); this and the greatest part of the following data on Wicksell are taken from an excellent article by Emil Sommarin, *Knut Wicksell's Auffassung der Entwicklung des Preisniveaus und die Krise der Schwedischen Waehrung*, in "Archiv fuer Sozialwissenschaft und Sozialpolitik," 67. Band 3. Heft. Mai, 1932, pp. 257-282.

In 1918 Wicksell had been appointed one of seven members of the Swedish "Valuta Committee" which was to report to the Government on monetary policy. In his report he wrote that "if there should be a general tendency to return to the pre-war gold standard, there is no doubt but that the value of gold would also gradually rise to its pre-war level." He was however opposed to Sweden's return to gold and advocated that instead she retain her inconvertible currency. He also suggested that Sweden return to the pre-war price level by way of the partial retirement of circulating notes—simultaneously with the revision of all contracts that had been entered into during the inflation period. In 1920, when Wicksell made this proposal, Sweden's price level had risen to 360, as compared with 100 in the summer of 1914. Three years later, in 1923, the price level had fallen to 163 with tremendous losses to industry and trade.[86] Now adjustments of contracts had to be made to prevent bankruptcy; but much of the suffering and waste could have been prevented had Wicksell's proposal been adopted.

In 1922 [87] Wicksell made the return to gold conditional upon the possibility of regulating the value of gold—"to give gold a stability which, when left to itself, it does not possess." He proposed again to leave the stabilization of the purchasing power of money entirely in the hands of the central banks, but free them of their obligation to redeem their notes in gold. "In other words," he said, "it would be best to demonetize gold,—retain it at a status which silver has had during the last fifty years—as metal of variable value." Paper currency, *i.e.* the Riksbank's notes, would constitute the only legal tender currency. "Each country" he continued, "would seek to maintain its price level stable through adequate adjustments of its interest rates. This would,

---

[86] The losses to the Swedish banks during 1920–1924 were estimated to have been about 1200 million kronor, plus a shrinkage of loans also amounting to about 1200 million kronor.

[87] In the Foreword to his *Geld und Kredit, op. cit.*

at the same time, keep the fluctuations of the foreign exchange rates within narrow limits, without, however, re-establishing their complete pre-war stability." Such national monetary regulation he believed would open the way for far-reaching international co-operation.

Wicksell died in 1926 and was therefore not permitted to see his predictions come true; as he had said, Sweden was eventually again forced off gold, and now she took the inevitable step towards the regulation of her price level. But he is now called the "Father of the Swedish Monetary Experiment." [88]

As early as 1903, Professor *Gustav Cassel* laid down the basic principles of his stabilization proposal, to which he has adhered ever since, namely that the price level is to be controlled through the regulation of credit and the manipulation of the discount rate, as first explained by Wicksell. Cassel put it thus:

"Hence we see that the problem of securing stability to the money scale is essentially a question of the regulation of credit.

"It is conceivable that the bank might keep the proper middle course and lend just so much as not to influence prices in one direction or the other. This is exactly what the bank should do; and, if it could be trusted always to follow such a policy, no special regulations would be necessary. We may say, too, that the present fixing of certain limits for the gold price, and other similar regulations, have no other purpose than to compel the bank to observe a credit policy which will insure stability of prices; and certainly the possibility must be admitted that a higher degree of stability might be attained without such regulations."

"Now it is universally accepted that credit can be regulated efficiently by the single expedient of the rate of interest, and, indeed, that it should not be interfered with in any other manner. Hence all schemes for securing stability of money, though they

[88] See Bertil Ohlin, *Knut Wicksell, Father of the Swedish Monetary Experiment,* in "Economic Forum," June–July, 1934, pp. 159–168.

differ considerably in the means they propose to use, ultimately depend on the same expedient,—a wise administration of the bank rate." [90]

However, the real rate of interest changes with fluctuations in the purchasing power of money; that is, when prices fall, the real interest rate rises, and vice versa. Cassel therefore declared that a stable price level was prerequisite to a discussion of interest rates. He said:

". . . the true problem of interest can be studied only where a stable money standard has been established . . ." and further,

". . . that the true rate of interest, for any form of loan is that which is necessary in order to prevent variations of the general price level, or, in other words, of the money standard."

Cassel's efforts, after the War, to get stabilization adopted internationally, are among the outstanding contributions to the stable money movement. He prepared for the International Financial Conference in Brussels [91] a memorandum in which he attempted to show the importance of stabilization for all countries. He explained that the stabilization of the internal purchasing power of each currency should be accomplished first. The exchange rates between countries which would thus have stabilized their price level would then also be stable.

"The stabilization of the internal value of money, *i.e.* of its buying capacity against commodities, is by far the most urgent object to be pursued by the monetary policy which the different countries now have to enter upon. Between two nations which have attained this end a new normal rate of exchange will establish itself, this rate being determined by the quotient of the purchasing power of money in the respective countries." [92]

---

[90] Gustav Cassel, *The Nature and Necessity of Interest,* London, Macmillan & Co., Ltd., 1903, pp. 162 ff.

[91] See also Chapter 9, Sec. 1.

[92] League of Nations Publications: *Memorandum on the World's Monetary Problems,* Paper No. XIII, Brussels Conference, 1920, p. 30.

In Cassel's opinion, the introduction of an international monetary unit would greatly complicate the problem, as there would be no certainty that the new standard itself would be kept stable. He had given much thought to the problem of a probable gold scarcity. On the basis of statistical evidence he calculated the annually increased demand for gold, for which there is no corresponding increase in its annual production. He therefore recommended that the Brussels Conference adopt among other proposals the following: Stabilizing each country's currency at its present purchasing power over commodities; and arrive at some international agreement to prevent a rise in the value of gold. These recommendations read as follows:

"5. That the internal value of the money of every country be stabilized in relation to commodities; that Utopian ideas of a restoration of a pre-war value of the monetary unit be abandoned, and that the future monetary policy of the country be fixed as soon as possible, and publicly announced.

"6. That this stabilization of the monetary standards be recognized as a common interest of all nations.

"11. That it be recognized to be a common interest for the world to prevent gold from rising in value; and that, therefore, international agreements be entered upon in order to keep back the monetary demand for gold within due limits." [93]

In September, 1921 a number of nations were planning to restore their currencies to their pre-war parities with gold. Cassel saw that such a policy must result in disastrous deflations. He therefore proposed stabilization at the current post-war purchasing power, expressing it as follows in a paper submitted to the Financial Committee of the League of Nations:

"The level at which we wish to stabilize wholesale prices should

[93] League of Nations Publications: *Memorandum on the World's Monetary Problems*, Supplement to Paper No. XIII, Summary of Recommendations, Brussels Conference, 1920.

be chosen so that the necessary equilibrium between the price of products and the cost of their production is established with the least disturbance to wages and other prices entering into the cost of production. . . ." [94]

At the First Congress of the International Chamber of Commerce in London, 1921, he again urged the adoption of this proposal.[95]

In 1923, he spoke before the Second Congress of the International Chamber of Commerce and urged again that the domestic purchasing powers of currencies be stabilized first, in order that a true international stability might result.[96]

The Congress however did not adopt these recommendations.

In 1928, Cassel lectured in the United States, and also appeared before a Congressional Committee to testify in favor of a pending stabilization bill.[97] In the course of the lectures, he explained the workings of the gold standard, really a gold-exchange standard, which was based on the value of the dollar.

The dollar itself was not being managed by the Federal Reserve System with regard to the rules of the gold standard, that is, the dollars was managed independently of gold reserves. Other countries, which could not afford such independence in their monetary policies, had to adopt their policies to that of the United States, to prevent a serious loss in their gold reserves.[98]

His conclusion was that the dependence of the entire world upon the monetary policy of the United States could be turned to advantage if the Federal Reserve System would itself adhere to a principle of purchasing power stabilization:

[94] Gustav Cassel, *The World's Monetary Problems*, London, Constable & Co., 1921, p. 137.

[95] *International Chamber of Commerce, Brochure No. 18*, Proceedings of the First Congress (London), June 27–July 1, 1921.

[96] *International Chamber of Commerce, Brochure No. 32*, Proceedings of the Second Congress (Rome), March 18–24, 1923.

[97] See Chapter 5, Section 5.

[98] Gustav Cassel, *Post War Monetary Stabilization*, New York, Columbia University Press, 1928, p. 75.

"If all the gold currencies of the world are regulated so as to be kept at the same value as the dollar," he said, "the stabilization of the world's monetary system is ultimately dependent upon the stabilization of the dollar. A stable dollar is therefore no longer merely a matter of internal American interest, but becomes a question of primary importance for the whole world. Thus the leaders of the monetary policy of the United States have a great responsibility." [99]

In a later book, Cassel also gave an exposition of his views on the typical business-cycle theory, and criticized the failure of that theory to give adequate consideration to the fluctuations in the monetary unit.[100]

Another Swedish economist, *Bertil Ohlin,* has also for many years been an advocate of stabilization. In 1927, he stated rather dogmatically that ". . . The value of gold is a question of the organization of the monetary system, and nothing else." [101]

Like Cassel, he came to the conclusion that the future of the world price level depended largely upon the policy of the Federal Reserve System. He said:

". . . The development of the world price level during the next decade is a question of American monetary policy. The decision regarding its stabilization lies in the hands of the leaders of that policy. It is a tremendous responsibility. . . ." [102]

[99] *Ibid.,* p. 77.

[100] Gustav Cassel, *The Crisis in the World's Monetary System,* Being the Rhodes Memorial Lectures delivered in Trinity Term, 1932, Oxford, Clarendon Press, 1932, p. 40.

[101] Bertil Ohlin, *The Future of the World Price Level,* in "Index" of Svenska Handelsbanken, Stockholm, No. 18, June, 1927.

[102] See also: Bertil Ohlin, *The Course and Phases of the World Economic Depression.* Published by the Secretariat of the League of Nations, Geneva, 1931.

Bertil Ohlin, *Interregional and International Trade,* Cambridge, Harvard University Press, 1933.

Austria: Eisler

Dr. Robert Eisler's "Stable Money" [103] is one of the most recent contributions to the stabilization movement. His proposal is based on the principle of the ancient "Banco-Money," [104] and aims at a double currency: (1) bank-money which retains its purchasing power; and (2) cash, the circulating currency which depreciates slowly. Eisler described the operation of his scheme as follows:

"Under the new system there would be two sorts of money: (1) legal tender, called a pound, or a U.S. dollar of *'current money,'* or money proper, and (2) bank or contract money of account, called a pound, or a dollar *banco.* Money banco would be obtained by concluding a contract about a future payment of money proper, or by depositing 'current money' with a bank or similar institution. Current money would be exclusively used for small transactions between persons not well known to each other, or not in possession of a bank account, especially for the payment of wages, transport fares and occasional retail purchases.

"All other payments would be effected by means of bank-money, that is, by cheques or traveller's cheques or transfers of money *banco.* All prices in catalogues of shops selling goods of which the price does not vary much . . . would be marked in money *banco.* The index-multiplicator of the week would be affixed to the desk of the cashier, who would calculate by means of simple multiplication or conversion tables published in the Sunday papers, the sum due in 'current money.' " [105]

Eisler would have his "current money" depreciate slowly [106] through deliberate credit and currency expansion, a process similar

[103] Robert Eisler, *Stable Money,* London, The Search Publishing Co., Ltd., 1932. See also: *Das Geld,* Muenchen, Diatypie G.m.b.H., 1924.
    La Monnaie, Paris, Valois, 1932.
[104] See Chapter 1, section 2.
[105] *Ibid.,* p. 234.
[106] *Ibid.,* p. 238 ff.

to that of reflation, except that the holders of bank deposits, insurance, bonds, and other monetary claims such as salaries, wages, etc., would be protected from loss by receiving payments on the basis of stable banco-currency which would maintain its purchasing power as measured by a cost-of-living index. This process he calls "compensated inflation."

This constant depreciation of the current money would, he says, most effectively prevent its being hoarded, and would speed up its circulation. People would either immediately convert their current money into goods, or deposit it, thus converting it into stable bank-money. Eisler contends that this system would give us all the advantages of a controlled inflation,—that is, it would stimulate the demand for goods up to the capacity of manufacturers to produce—without the disadvantage of such inflation as involves loss of the purchasing power of wages, salaries, and so forth. In addition, he believes his plan would maintain the velocity of currency at the maximum, eliminating one of the most baffling causes of monetary instability.

Eisler also believes that the Central Banks of the different countries could expand their several currencies, and keep the foreign exchange rates unaltered, with the same efficiency with which they had previously diminished credits, following the lead of the main creditor countries.[107]

In fact, the plan is not intended for national operation. Eisler also suggests maintaining the stability of the foreign exchanges through a mechanism which since the war has kept the English and Egyptian exchange rates absolutely stable. Egypt maintains a large Currency Guarantee Fund in London through which drafts on Egypt are paid at the determined rate; and England maintains a similar account in Egypt for reverse transactions. By similar means, Eisler believes, the exchange rate of any two countries may be kept stable.

[107] *Ibid.*, p. 194.

Based on the studies of *Georges Guillaume*,[108] Eisler presented a new theory of the gold problem.[109] According to this theory the annual increase of about 3% in the demand for monetary gold is not due to a corresponding increase in the annual production of goods, as Cassel, Kitchin, Strakosch and others believe, but to the demand for gold arising from the payment of compound interest on the credits extended by the Central Banks. As the annual increase in the gold supply is generally smaller than the amount needed for such interest payments, the difference must be taken from the current gold stock, which results inevitably in a contraction of the volume of currency and credit, and is the main cause of periodic crises. Eisler advances this theory partly to reinforce his proposal for a currency which is free from the influence of gold.

Netherlands: Verrijn Stuart

The Dutch economist *C. A. Verrijn Stuart*, in 1923, called attention to the importance of stability of the monetary unit in the following words:

"Since time is so important a factor in economic life, I presume it will generally be admitted that a currency is sound only if it can offer the best possible guarantee that the purchasing power of the unit of money shall not be affected by lapse of time or change of place. As soon as money ceases to be a purely passive connecting link in trade transactions, analogous to the kilogram, the metre, or the hectoliter, it begins, despite its undoubted utility as a medium of exchange, to display mischievous propensities." [110]

His son, *G. M. Verrijn Stuart*, in 1919 published a book, "In

[108] Georges Guillaume, *Sur les Fondements de l'Economique Rationelle*, Paris, Gauthier-Villars et Cie., Editeurs, 1932.

[109] Robert Eisler, *The Case Against the Gold Standard*. "The Manchester Guardian Commercial" June 10 and 17, 1933.

[110] C. A. Verrijn Stuart, *Metallic and Non-Metallic Standards*, in the "Economic Journal," 1923, June, pp. 143–154.

troduction to the Theory of the Stability of the Value of Money" [111] the theme of which is that the medium of exchange should not interfere with the natural movement of prices and incomes. This book also gives an interesting account of the development of the idea of stabilization and the various proposals for realizing it.[112]

[111] Dr. G. M. Verrijn Stuart, *Inleidung tot der leer der Waardevasteheid Van het geld,* 's-Gravenhage, Martinus Nijhoff, 1919.
[112] See also: Dr. G. M. Verrijn Stuart, *Geld en Crediet,* 's-Gravenhage, N. V. Uitgevers-Maatschappij v/h, G. Delwel, 1932.

CHAPTER IV

POPULARIZING STAGE (FROM 1905)

SECTION I. IN THE UNITED STATES (FROM 1921)

The Stable Money League and The National Monetary Association

As early as 1921, at the suggestion of the present writer, a small group of economists and business men who had become interested in the problem of a stable money met in Washington to discuss the preliminary steps necessary to create a popular stabilization movement. The result of this gathering was the formation of the "Stable Money League," an association pledged to the development of the stabilization idea.

The formation of this league marks the first organized effort toward eventually realizing the dream of stable money. As has been seen, the archives of history contain many records of such a dream in many minds. But each was promptly forgotten soon afterward. The flame had invariably gone out.

The Stable Money League had as its first President Jeremiah W. Jenks, Professor of Economics and business man, and as its first Vice-Presidents Robert D. Kent, bank President, and Henry A. Wallace, editor of *Wallace's Farmer,* later under President Franklin D. Roosevelt, Secretary of Agriculture.[1]

---

[1] Ralph W. Wescott, now Collector of Customs in Philadelphia, kindly took the laboring oar as Secretary. The Treasurer was Eugene C. Pomeroy, another enthusiast. The Executive Committee included Leonard P. Ayres; Malcolm C. Rorty; Henry M. Waite, later Deputy Administrator of the Federal Emergency Administration of Public Works; and J. G. Winant, later Governor of New Hampshire.

Its Research Council included William T. Foster, David Friday, E. W. Kem-

The second President of the Stable Money League was Professor John R. Commons of the University of Wisconsin. The Vice-Presidents were W. F. Gephart, Vice-President of the First National Bank of St. Louis, and Henry A. Wallace.[2]

In 1923 there were rumblings of an inflation movement in the West, and Paul Warburg, wishing to forestall this, suggested to his friend Waddill Catchings that the Stable Money League might become an useful instrumentality for heading off this movement. But one condition was that it should change its name in order not to have any association with other monetary proposals. Waddill Catchings was made Chairman of the Executive Committee.

As this suggestion seemed to offer an opportunity to enlist in the cause of preventing inflation (which is half of the cause of Stable Money) a great number of business men who feared inflation, and as the Stable Money League stood for opposition to both inflation and deflation, the offer was accepted, and a new organization, the "National Monetary Association," was formed to take over the old League.

The first and only President of *The National Monetary Association* was Professor John R. Commons, Vice-Presidents were W. F. Gephart of St. Louis, and Henry A. Wallace. The Research Council included those who held corresponding positions in the Stable Money League, and also John E. Rovensky, Execu-

merer, Wesley Clair Mitchell, Warren M. Persons, Carl Snyder, H. Parker Willis, Allyn A. Young, John Hays Hammond, Thomas R. Marshall, George Foster Peabody.

[2] Among the Honorary Vice-Presidents were Arthur T. Hadley, President of Yale University; Thornton Cooke, President of the Columbia National Bank of Kansas City; George Eastman of Rochester; John V. Farwell of Chicago; John P. Frey, labor leader; Lyman J. Gage, ex-Secretary of the Treasury; Frederick H. Goff, President of the Cleveland Trust Company; Samuel Gompers, President of the American Federation of Labor; Honorable Carter Glass, now Senator; John Hays Hammond; Edmund D. Hulbert of the Chicago Merchants Loan and Trust Company; John B. Larner, President of the Washington Loan and Trust Company of Washington, D. C.; Thomas R. Marshall, former Vice-President of the United States; George H. Woodruff, of the Merchants National Bank of Los Angeles; and Congressman Oscar W. Underwood.

tive Vice-President of the Bank of America in Wall Street.

The National Monetary Association, however, had a short life for the simple reason that the inflation movement which it was designed to meet failed to develop, so that the conservative business men whose interest was confined to that emergency, did not continue to support the Association. In fact, it became evident that some of them were well satisfied to have, apparently, side-tracked the Stable Money Movement.

The result was in 1925 a third transmigration of the stabilization soul, through founding of the "Stable Money Association" to take up the work anew.

The Stable Money Association

The first President of the Stable Money Association was H. Parker Willis, former Secretary of the Federal Reserve Board. The other officers were largely the same as those who had been associated with the two former organizations, besides Professor Willford I. King and Professor Frederick W. Roman. The following is a list of the succeeding Presidents of the Stable Money Association:

John E. Rovensky (1927)

Edwin W. Kemmerer (1928)

Frederic A. Delano (1929–1933), uncle of President Roosevelt, formerly member of the Federal Reserve Board.[3]

Under the active and enterprising leadership of *Mr. Norman Lombard,* its Executive Director, and Mr. Charles W. Birtwell, Executive Secretary, the new Association obtained the support of some of the most prominent leaders of American business and finance, who for five years made possible this work through their moral and financial support. Mr. Lombard had become interested

[3] See Appendix III for a list of Honorary Vice-Presidents of the Stable Money Association.

in stabilization through the effect of monetary fluctuations upon his business. As early as 1920, he lectured on the subject in California, and (as stated in the "Autobiographical" Appendix) later came East to prepare himself for this work with the Stable Money Association which he began in 1926. Mr. Lombard has recently published an interesting treatise on the stabilization question [4] in which he reveals the vast knowledge of the subject he accumulated through his work for the Stable Money Association. Besides discussing the historical, theoretical and practical aspects of the problem of stabilization, Mr. Lombard outlines his conception of the future objectives of American monetary policy. An interesting feature of this readable book is the large number of extensive citations of expressions by prominent men on stabilization, monetary and banking questions.

In pursuit of its educational purposes, the Association distributed reprints of articles and speeches. Its newspaper service supplied the press with releases on stabilization; the officers of the Association spoke at conventions of business men, bankers, farmers, and other conventions. Special representatives travelled over the country, enlisting the support of the most prominent men in the several communities; it appointed special committees of professional organizations which tried to stimulate study of the stabilization problem.

For instance, Sir Josiah Stamp spoke at one of the Association's dinners,[5] and Hjalmar Schacht, the President of the Reichsbank, was its guest and speaker on a similar occasion. In January, 1931, Mr. Lombard submitted to Mr. Roosevelt, then Governor of the State of New York, a Memorandum on the Relationship between Unemployment, Business Depression, and Monetary and Credit Policies, to be presented at a conference of Governors at Albany. In August, 1931, Mr. Delano suggested to President Hoover that

[4] Norman Lombard, *Monetary Statesmanship*, New York, Harper & Brothers, 1934, 203 p.
[5] June 6, 1930.

the Stable Money Association be represented in the membership of a Commission to study the statistics of unemployment.

The following statement of the Stable Money Association is one of the first that was circulated, and gives a comprehensive expression of the task this Association had undertaken:

"Purpose: The Stable Money Association was organized in 1925 to promote stabilization of the purchasing power of money by spreading of understanding of: (1) the serious evils attending wide fluctuations in the general price level; (2) the preventability of such fluctuations; (3) the methods proposed for stabilization.

"Policy: We do not advocate any plan for stabilization, but encourage discussion of all plans. We feel that, before it can competently discuss plans or legislation, public opinion must be educated to the policy of stabilization. It must come to realize that a stable dollar is as necessary to stable business and social conditions as a stable yard, a stable bushel, or a stable watt, . . .

"Methods: Our methods are educational and we utilize existing machinery so far as possible. Our speakers address meetings called by Rotary Clubs, Kiwanis Clubs, Chambers of Commerce, and other organizations in social welfare problems, . . . Articles are prepared under our auspices by outstanding authorities for submission to leading periodicals. Reprints of these articles are frequently circulated."

The termination of the activities of the Stable Money Association was one of the ironies of fate. Unstable money sapped its finances and thereby destroyed it as it destroyed so many other organizations dependent on philanthropic contributions!—just at a time when a Stable Money advocate was most needed.

Fortunately, however, there had come into existence, independently of the Stable Money Association, the "Committee for the Nation," largely through the activities of Frank A. Vanderlip formerly President of the National City Bank of New York, and James H. Rand, Jr., President of the Remington Rand Company. It is devoted to reflation as a preliminary to stabilization.

It consists of leading business men who had become convinced of the important rôle of money in the depression.

Although reflation had never been included in the studies of the Stable Money Association, founded as it was during a period of relatively stable money, the Stable Money Association donated its assets, liabilities and good will to the Committee for the Nation in the expectation that as soon as reflation was completed, the Committee would take up the project of stabilization as its major objective.[6]

The effect of these activities may perhaps best be judged by a review of the growing public sentiment in behalf of stabilization. Naturally, the increasing demand for stabilization was not solely due to the efforts of the Stable Money Association, but chiefly to the evil effects of monetary fluctuations.

Response of the Public

The response of the public to the stabilization idea was not always favorable. Indeed, strong opposition arose due to three different sets of motives:

(1) *Conservatism and fear of change:* This was the motive of many men and women who were comfortably situated—whose personal economic problems were solved. They were able to live without too much discomfort through the booms and depressions, for the elimination of which the stable money proposals were intended. Of course, such people are always against change of almost any sort, but once a change has occurred, they become the staunchest defenders of the new system.

(2) *Ignorance and lack of understanding:* For most people, problems of money and credit are too technical to be easily understood. The average person looks to an authority for guidance in these matters, and who could be better equipped as a guide in

---

[6] For a more detailed description of the activities of the Committee for the Nation, see this chapter, section 2.

monetary questions, than those in class (1) above, especially bankers? And even the average banker looks to the big banker for an opinion; and the big banker, who had had personal success under the monetary system as it always existed, too often assumes that this system is sound and good. He is apt to suspect the proponents of monetary reform of being monetary cranks; and some bankers have been known to place a personal construction upon criticisms levelled only at the system.

(3) *Selfish interest:* It is at least possible that some speculators who benefit from monetary fluctuations are interested in increasing such fluctuations rather than eliminating them.

Nevertheless, a few bankers, and perhaps a still larger proportion of business men, definitely joined the movement. They knew what they had suffered from the unstable dollar. In 1921, the Congressional Committee on Civil Service held hearings to consider the Reclassification of Salaries; and, somewhat later, the judges of the United States Courts presented their case for higher salaries on the basis of the decreased purchasing power of the dollar.[7]

Business Men

In 1922, *Carl Strover,* a Chicago lawyer, published a book on "Monetary Reconstruction,"[8] in which he put forth, in telling language, the demand for a stable dollar.

He was also one of the first who raised the demand for reflation after the recent depression had set in, urging as early as in 1930 the restoration of the 1926 price level.[9] Mr. Strover's efforts were directed particularly toward educating the farmers of the Middle West as to the part played in their troubles by falling prices. Early in 1931, he gave a series of radio talks which were

---

[7] Senate Committee Print, 69th Congress, First Section; Letters from Judges of U.S. Courts.

[8] Published by the author, 133 West Washington Street, Chicago, Ill.

[9] *Hard Times Can Be Ended,* in "The Prairie Farmer," August, 1930.

doubtless an influence in bringing about a demand for reflation and stabilization on the part of the several Farmers' Organizations. Carl Strover was thus one of the first advocates of the policy which was incorporated in the Goldsborough bill that passed the House of Representatives in 1932.[10]

In 1922, *Mr. M. K. Graham,* a business man of Graham, Texas, published a book on "Gold," [11] in which he expressed his "Stable Money Creed" as follows:

"We believe that all currencies should be on a gold basis and parity, with the stabilized general price level as the ultimate standard of value; and that, in order to avoid confusion of thought, such a standard should be termed 'The Stabilized Gold Standard.' " [12]

In 1924, the *Philadelphia Rapid Transit Company* decided to adjust wage payments to changes in the purchasing power of the dollar, according to a Philadelphia cost-of-living index. It called its unit of pay a "Market Basket Dollar."

In 1922–1923, *Henry Ford* and *Thomas Edison* presented their proposal for a "commodity dollar." They let loose a barrage of magazine and newspaper articles which did much to make people money-conscious. Their plan, although designed in a general way to create stable conditions, did not provide for an index number as the guide. Edison, to whom Ford looked to formulate the plan, suggested the issue of money upon the delivery of basic commodities to Federal Warehouses. Under this plan the goods thus deposited would remain the property of the depositors for the period of one year; and if, within that time, these goods were not reclaimed, the Government would proceed to sell them.[13]

[10] See Chapter 6, Sec. 1.

[11] M. K. Graham, *An Essay on Gold,* Dallas, Texas, Hargreaves Printing Co., 1922.

[12] *Ibid.,* p. 160.

See also, by the same author: *Continuous Prosperity,* Nashville, The Parthenon Press, 1932.

[13] See William T. Foster, *Edison Ford Commodity Money,* in "Proceedings of the Academy of Political Science," January, 1923, Vol. X, No. 2, pp. 57–75.

In 1925, the *Rand Kardex Company* of Buffalo, N. Y. offered the public the first "Stabilized Bond" in history. This bond provided that, as the index of commodity prices rose, the Company would pay more dollars by way of principal and interest; and if the index number fell, the Company would pay fewer dollars. Fluctuations of less than 10% were to be disregarded.

This unique form of security attracted much attention from lawyers and lawschools, because it was so difficult to classify. After the Rand Kardex Co. was merged in a larger organization (the Remington Rand Inc.) this issue was converted into ordinary preferred stock and bonds to gain a wider market than was possible for an infamiliar form of security.

Alvan T. Simonds, President of the Simonds Saw and Steel Company, was another prominent business man who helped spread stabilization ideas at that time. For a number of years he offered a cash prize of $1000 for the best essay on the stable money problem.

On May 24, 1927, *Mr. Paul M. Warburg,* formerly a member of the Federal Reserve Board, as the Chairman of the Committee on Banking and Currency of the Merchants' Association of New York, submitted a report from which the following is an extract:

"The Association shares the view universally held that the interest of the country is served best by the greatest possible stability of price levels, and believes that, in fashioning their discount and open market investment policy, the Federal Reserve Board and the Federal Reserve Banks should ever be mindful of this aim."

On January 20, 1929, *Owen D. Young,* speaking at the Park Avenue Baptist Church in New York, with reference to observations he had made in Germany during the post-war inflation, said

"Never before had I realized how the stability of money goes to the very basis of life, and that, when any sudden change affects the purchasing power of money, it touches every kind of moral question and every kind of obligation."

On a later occasion, speaking on the subject of the Bank for International Settlements, he said: [14]

"The proper handling of price stability is one of the most important matters facing the capitalistic system today. In it will be found the roots of those maladjustments which result in the unequal and unfair distribution of wealth, in unemployment, and other serious problems."

SECTION 2. IN THE UNITED STATES (CONTINUED)

Farmers

By bitter experience American Farmers, as a class, have become remarkably well instructed in the subject of monetary fluctuations. For many years, the leaders of farmers' organizations have been fighting for monetary reform and stabilization. Besides Professor Warren already mentioned, *Henry A. Wallace,* who became Secretary of Agriculture in the Roosevelt administration, has been of great influence in stimulating the farm sentiment for stabilization. Ever since 1913 he had been interested in this problem. As the editor of *Wallace's Farmer,* Des Moines, Iowa and the *Iowa Homestead,* he was in constant touch with a large number of Middle West farmers whose interests he frequently represented at hearings on stabilization bills.

Clarence Poe who, through a chain of Farmers' Newspapers,[15] reaches about one million homes in the South, and who is an enthusiastic advocate of stabilization, has also been influential in stimulating the farmers' demand for a stable dollar.

For many years, the different Farmers' organizations, the National Grange, Farmers' Union, American Farm Bureau Federation, etc., have sent representatives to hearings before Congressional committees, to testify in favor of stabilization bills; and

[14] Address at the University of California, 1930.
[15] *The Progressive Farmer and Southern Ruralist,* Raleigh, N. C.

many resolutions favoring stabilization have been passed at Farmers' Meetings and Conventions. The following are examples:

"Resolution, unanimously adopted at the 31st Meeting, Illinois Farmers' Institute, Quincy, February, 1926.

"We favor the stabilization of the dollar in purchasing power and urge our legislative representatives in Congress to consider what measures may best be adopted to bring about such stabilization."

"Resolution adopted at the 9th Annual Meeting, American Farm Bureau Federation, December, 1927.

"We endorse the effort now being made in Congress to effect a stabilized price level and stable purchasing power of money through additional instructions to the Federal Reserve Board." [16]

After the collapse of the general price level in 1929, such resolutions for stabilization usually included a demand for reflation, to be followed by stabilization. And naturally, with the increasing severity of the depression, the farmers' demands for stable money became more insistent and more frequent. In 1932, the stabilization hearings brought a rather complete representation of American organized farmers to Washington, pleading for this reflation-stabilization program.

On April 14–16, 1934 the *National Agricultural Conference* which met in Washington, D. C. adopted three resolutions [17] which may serve as more recent examples of the farmer's demand for reflation and stabilization. The first of these resolutions demanded a further increase in the price of gold (to $41.34 an ounce, the highest point permitted by law); the second asked

---

[16] Similar resolutions were adopted by:
   Kansas Committee of Farm Organizations (at Topeka, October 25, 1927).
   Kansas State Board of Agriculture (on January 11, 1928).
   Kansas Live Stock Association (at Wichita, March 9, 1928).
[17] Signed by: Louis J. Taber, Master National Grange.
   Edward A. O'Neal, President American Farm Bureau Federation.
   W. M. Thatcher, alternate for C. E. Huff, President Farmers National Grain Corporation.
   John D. Miller, President National Cooperative Council.

for the establishment of a "Federal Monetary Authority" [18] with adequate powers to carry out a policy of reflation and stabilization; the third called for joint action between these farmer groups and the Committee for the Nation in promoting the realization of the above demands.

Bankers

Bankers have always been looked upon as opponents of a stable dollar. By the very selection which makes them bankers, they are conservative. They think in terms of money and find little occasion in their daily business to measure money in terms of commodities. They naturally rebel against being asked to run their business so as to stabilize the price level, instead of so as to make money; and they rebel still more strongly against being directed by law to accomplish such a task, which most of them sincerely believe is beyond their powers. But their opposition is much less now than it was when the stable money movement began.

Two outstanding American bankers have long been advocates of stabilization: Frank A. Vanderlip, formerly President of the National City Bank of New York, and George LeBlanc, formerly Vice-President of the Equitable Trust Company of New York.

As early as 1921, Robert D. Kent, President of the Merchants' Bank of Passaic, N. J. gave an address on "The Second Function of Money" [19] emphasizing the fact that money, besides being a medium of exchange, must also serve as the standard of value. Like Ford and Edison he suggested that the value of money be based on the value of a few basic commodities which should be deposited in Federal Warehouses.

Many bankers, especially country bankers who were particularly

[18] See also the *Goldsborough-Vanderlip Bill* for a Federal Monetary Authority, Chapter 6, Section 3.
[19] At the organization meeting of the Stable Money League, May 28, 1921, at Washington, D. C.

familiar with the plight of the farmers, came to approve of the efforts for obtaining a stable dollar. The following resolution, adopted by the Convention of the *Iowa Bankers' Association,* in 1923, represents their point of view:

"It is the self-evident duty of the Federal Reserve Board to administer the Federal Reserve Act in such a manner as will safeguard the Nation from inflation and deflation in the future, and we heartily approve all sincere efforts being made to find and apply the best legislative methods for safeguarding the purchasing power of money."

The Bankers' Associations of South Carolina and Missouri appointed special committees on stabilization, and these committees made extensive reports to their respective organizations on the progress being made in the movement for a stable dollar.[20]

The late *Benjamin Strong,* the most outstanding central banker America ever had, expressed himself in favor of a stable price level as follows:

"Labor disputes are rarely very serious, long extended or disorderly, except when they have to do with compensation, and compensation disputes almost always arise when prices are rising.

"Periods of falling prices give rise to demands for fiat money and Government subsidies of this industry or that.

"Therefore, is not the fundamental condition of industrial and national tranquillity that of reasonable stability of prices, as from 1909 till toward the close of 1915?

"I believe, with Mr. Henry Ford, that what the great body of our workingmen most desire is security of employment and an adequate wage that represents a fairly even and stable purchasing power." [21]

[20] *Report* of the Committee on stabilization of the Money Standard, E. H. Zimmerman, Chairman; Missouri Bankers Association Annual Meeting, Excelsior Springs, Mo., May 15–16, 1929.
Report of the Committee on Stabilization of the Money Standard, South Carolina Bankers Association; South Carolina Bankers Convention, 1930.
[21] In "Collier's Weekly," 1923; quoted from a publication of the Stable Money

To a specific group of bankers, namely the Investment Bankers, the fluctuating value of money presented a real and practical problem. In periods of falling prices and declining profits, a bond yielding a fixed income is, no doubt, the best form of investment. On the other hand, when prices rise, profits also rise, and stocks become preferable. Investment Bankers had to make a study of these conditions, and their advice was but another factor which helped to educate the public on the effects of fluctuations in the value of money.[22]

E. C. Neill, Vice-President and Managing Director of the Royal Bank of Canada, the largest bank in that country, gave an example of Canadian banking sentiment towards stabilization, in his address to the shareholders at the Annual Meeting, January 8, 1931. From this statement we see that Mr. Neill understood not only the social effects of violent price changes, but also the fact that such fluctuations in the price level are caused by changes in the purchasing power of money. He said:

"For the future it is absolutely essential that means should be devised to prevent the drastic changes in the price level which have been characteristic of the period since the close of the war. Such changes in their effect are not much less damaging to civilization than those produced by war. . . .

"These wide fluctuations in the money value of output are clearly a monetary phenomenon which, if properly understood, could be prevented. Over-supply of individual commodities could explain the decline in the value of one commodity in relation to another. Overproduction of agricultural products in relation to manufactured articles would justify a decline in the price of

Association. For additional expressions of Governor Strong see chapters on Stabilization Hearings and on the Federal Reserve System.

[22] See: Kenneth S. Van Strum, *Investing in Purchasing Power*, Series of Articles in "Barron's Weekly," Vol. V, March, 1925 and ff.; also in book form.

Edgar Lawrence Smith, *Common Stocks as Long Term Investments*, New York, Macmillan Co., 1924.

farm products as compared with the products of industry, but
when the average of all prices declines this can only be explained
by an under-supply of that in which prices are expressed, *i.e.*,
money, and it would seem that, if the effective supply of money
is kept in the right relation to production of commodities, the
phenomenon of a declining price level will not occur."

The following quotation indicates that Mr. Neill knew that the
Federal Reserve System was opposed to stabilization, but that he
did not approve of their laissez-faire attitude, and, on the contrary, urged a positive stabilization policy.

"I am well aware that the question of central bank policy and
its influence on prices is a much debated one; even in recent
times, for example, many bankers in the United States have expressed the opinion that the Federal Reserve System exercises no
dominant influence in the price field. Followed to their logical
conclusion on a world-wide basis, these opinions indicate a belief
that the stability of the world's medium of exchange is practically
at the mercy of the elements; that man is incapable of controlling
an instrument of his own devising; and that the instability, which
for generations has caused untold losses to business and suffering
to workers, must continue to exert its evil influence as chance
dictates. I cannot subscribe to any such views. The situation can
be remedied. It must be remedied."

In 1931, an American Banker, *Paul M. Mazur,* published a
book [23] in which he recommended the stabilization of the price
level through the agency of the Federal Reserve System, even if
the system must get new and larger powers for the purpose.

The Committee for the Nation

In the summer of 1932 some industrialists began to see the
need for monetary thinking. Vincent Bendix and General Robert

[23] Paul M. Mazur, *New Roads to Prosperity,* The Crisis and Some Ways Out,
New York, Viking Press, 1913, scc pp. 158–161.

E. Wood initiated investigations as to the causes of the depression. In September they were assured of the cooperation of Frank A. Vanderlip, and of Magnus W. Alexander of the National Industrial Conference Board. James H. Rand, Jr., who for some time had been carrying on independent efforts to trace the monetary forces causing the depression and to overcome unemployment, joined the group. Fred H. Sexauer, representing the five major farm organizations, and Frederic H. Frazier, Chairman of the General Baking Company, as well as E. L. Cord, subsequently joined in carrying forward investigations.

In January, 1933, these and other industrialists formally organized under the name "COMMITTEE FOR THE NATION to Rebuild Prices and Purchasing Power." Edward A. Rumely, who had been cooperating with the organizers, became Executive Secretary. Mr. Vanderlip was Chairman of a Planning Committee and Mr. Rand was, from the beginning, Chairman of the group's Directing Committee. The other members are Messrs. Bendix, Sexauer, Frazier and Lessing J. Rosenwald.

The National Industrial Conference Board was engaged to make statistical studies for this group. Bankers, industrialists and economists were invited to private hearings in New York. Among those called in frequent consultation were Professors Warren and Pearson of Cornell.

In February, 1933, the Committee's first survey of conditions, in the form of an "Interim Report," formulated by Mr. Vanderlip as the concensus of the group, was circulated privately among government, business and agricultural leaders.

The Committee recommended immediate suspension of the gold standard, emergency guarantee of bank deposits, and legislation to raise and stabilize the price level.

Discussing the need for a new monetary standard, this "Interim Report" said:

"The world has been so long accustomed to metallic money and then to a metallic base for redemption of currencies into metallic money that it is extremely difficult for the practical commercial mind to contemplate a change. To think in terms of an ultimate standard other than a fixed amount of gold or of gold and silver is so remote from experience that any plan contemplating such a change is usually rejected at once as dangerously theoretical and wholly impractical. There is a growing recognition, however, of the inadequacies of the metal standard in terms of a fixed number of grains of gold or of gold and silver.

"The distress which follows a general change of commodity price level as measured in the fixed metallic standard is finding lodgment in the common mind. The distress of such change is by no means confined to debtors although at the present time the emphasis is all on that side. Both creditors and debtors are equally concerned with the problem of securing a currency which at some future date will have the same buying power for purchasing commodities as it had when the obligation was made. Injury and injustice fall on both classes with the fluctuating command over commodities that changes in the metallic values engender.

"If a future contract could be made based not on a given number of grains of precious metal but upon this [Bureau of Labor Statistics] weighted price index, so that we have a currency which will always purchase the same average amount of commodities, it will be far more scientific and desirable. Such an aspiration would not be a foolish and impossible one, but instead a highly practical and desirable aim.

"We believe that this subject of a change of standard from a definite number of grains of metal to a definite relation to the value of all commodities is practical and desirable. It would mean that our dollar, instead of calling for redemption in a fixed number of grains of gold might call for a varying number of grains, so calculated as always to keep the price index at a practically fixed level. We would not suggest that this should mean a constantly changing weight of gold coins. The actual coining of gold would probably cease and the redemption would be in bullion, but the number of grains of bullion would vary up or down so as to hold the commodity price index level."

There followed in April, 1933 the Committee's public proposal of "Five Steps for Recovery." These included the repricing of gold and the creation of a Federal Monetary Board to stabilize the purchasing power of the dollar once it had been restored to its 1926 level.

These five steps were endorsed by several hundred industrial and agricultural leaders. Within a year the Committee for the Nation expanded its advisory and auxiliary membership to over 2,000, and continued its educational work in behalf of price level restoration and stable money.

An idea of the magnitude of the Committee's efforts may be obtained by inspecting its list of publications, speeches, radio addresses, articles and studies.[24] The first year and a half's activities were listed as follows in July, 1934:

"Numerous network and electrical transcription broadcasts over 381 radio stations.

Printed matter distributed (pieces)	750,202
Multigraphed bulletins and reports (pages)	1,318,421
Photolith reproductions (pages)	2,438,350
Letters	412,564
National Ind. Conf. Bd. Reports (copies)	14,150
Warren & Pearson Economic Papers	17,700
Total	4,951,387"

The following sequences, whether or not they represent cause and effect, are, to say the least, striking and must be gratifying to the Committee. The statement of them is taken from one of the Committee's publications:

"In February, 1933 the *Committee for the Nation* recommended embargo of gold exports and suspension of specie payments as prerequisite to restoration of the American price level. These two steps became accomplished facts early in March.

"April 6th, the Committee pointed out that the effect experienced in other countries of suspending specie payments could

24 See Appendix IV.

not be realized in the United States so long as the Government continued to peg the dollar in international exchange. April 19th the dollar was cut loose from gold.

"May 18th the Committee made the establishment of a free gold market in New York one of its objectives as a means to increase the price of gold and raise commodity prices. August 29th free exportation of newly mined American gold was permitted.

"Through May and June the Committee vigorously opposed currency stabilization (in the sense of foreign exchange stabilization) at the World Economic Conference. July 3rd the President rejected stabilization."

The Committee's first proposal for creation of a Board to control the purchasing power of the dollar was incorporated in H.R. 5073, introduced by Congressman T. Alan Goldsborough of Maryland, in April, 1933. This was superseded in the regular session by the Federal Monetary Authority Bill, drafted in its original form by Mr. Vanderlip, endorsed by the Committee for the Nation, and sponsored by Congressman Goldsborough.

Hearings on this Bill before the House sub-Committee on Banking and Currency, under the Chairmanship of Mr. Goldsborough, January 30–March 8, 1934, fill a printed volume of 514 pages. The essential parts of these hearings will be found in Chapter 6, Section 3.

Section 3. In England (from 1905)

Kitson

One of the most active and persistent advocates of stabilization in England has been Mr. Arthur Kitson, whose first book has already been mentioned.[25] An engineer, inventor and manufacturer, Mr. Kitson lived in the United States during the silver controversy. This had brought the money problem vividly to his

[25] See Chapter 2, Sec. 3.

attention and upon his return to England, he worked for monetary reform through the writing of articles, books and pamphlets, and by lecturing to business and professional groups.

The following data are taken from a recent book of his in which a short account of his stabilization efforts is given.[26]

In 1905, he started the first English league for monetary and banking reform, and published a small book on "The Industrial Depression." [27] Two years later he began the publication of a monthly magazine, "The Open Review," devoted mainly to his ideas of monetary and banking reform. Financed as well as edited by Kitson, the magazine appeared for a number of years. In 1911, he wrote a 76-page letter to the Chancellor of the Exchequer, Lloyd George, warning him of the dangers of the gold standard, and submitting a rather complete statement of his monetary ideas.

In 1917, he published a book on the "Fraudulent Standard" [28] in which he referred to the stabilization problem as follows:

". . . the main problem in monetary science is not the selection of a suitable commodity possessing value, stability, ductility, divisibility and other physical qualities which economists assert are essential in a standard. The fundamental problem is to discover— not a commodity, but—a method which will enable us to (1) accurately express at all times the exchange-values of commodities in terms of some common denominator regardless of why such values exist or how they have arisen, and (2) to issue tokens as evidences of debt and credit, in terms of some invariable unit representing some proportional part of the general wealth of the community at a given time."

Thus Mr. Kitson did not recommend a standard of value based

[26] See Arthur Kitson, *The Bankers' Conspiracy!*, London, Elliot Stock, 1933, pp. 25–44.
[27] London, T. Fisher Unwin, 1905.
[28] Arthur Kitson, *A Fraudulent Standard*, London, P. S. King & Son, Ltd., 1917, p. 113.

upon the index number of wholesale commodity prices, but seemed to prefer a unit representing a fixed proportion of the national wealth. In some of his later writings, however, he mentioned the stabilization of the price level as the aim of monetary policy. As to the mechanism for carrying out the proposal, he believed the nationalization of the banking system to be an essential part of a practical stabilization plan.

During 1917, in conjunction with some Midland Manufacturers, Mr. Kitson formed the Banking and Currency Reform League of Birmingham. As its President he published a criticism of the famous Cunliffe Report in 1919.[29] In 1920, he re-published in book form a series of articles in a book called "Money Problems"; [30] and in 1921, he published a book on "Unemployment." [30a] During the following year the "Economic Freedom League" was formed, with Mr. Kitson as President. In 1930, the "Monetary Reform Association" was inaugurated of which he became the Chairman. On July 4th, 1931, Kitson addressed a public "Letter to the Prince of Wales on the World Crisis." [31] The "New Europe Group" which was formed in that year made him its President, and in 1932, he was on the Executive Committee of the "National Money Service." All of these organizations made the reform and stabilization of the currency a part of their respective programs.

Mr. Kitson had appeared as a witness before the Cunliffe Committee, in 1918; and in 1930–1931 he was called upon to testify before the Macmillan Committee. Due partly to the fact that eventually conditions developed much as he had predicted, Mr. Kitson's influence kept increasing, and he was the subject of some favorable comments in the English press.

[29] See Chapter 9, Sec. 1.
[30] Stamford, Dolby Brothers.
[30a] *Unemployment*, The Cause and a Remedy, London, C. Palmer, 1921.
[31] *A Letter to H.R.H. The Prince of Wales on the World Crisis*, Oxford, The Alden Press, Ltd., 1931.

Although not directly devoted to the cause of monetary stabilization, the "Social Credit" movement deserves mention here, because the evils of an unstable money were discussed in many of its publications.[32]

Pethick-Lawrence

Another enthusiastic advocate of stabilization is F. W. Pethick-Lawrence, in 1929–1931, Financial Secretary to the British Treasury; he is also a prominent Labour Leader in Parliament. In 1920, he published a booklet on "Why Prices Rise and Fall" [33] and in 1922 a book in which he held such fluctuations to be the main cause of unemployment.[34]

In a still later book, he stated again: [35]

"I am convinced . . . that unemployment as it exists today is not an economic but a monetary phenomenon," and he concluded "A stabilized price level with neither inflation nor deflation is the only workable solution." [36]

In another book, "The Money Muddle and the Way Out," Pethick-Lawrence proposed the following six practical steps to be taken by the British Government in order to carry out successfully a new monetary policy of stabilization: [37]

[32] See: C. H. Douglas, *Economic Democracy,* New York, Harcourt, Brace and Howe, 1920.
    Social Credit, London (Third Edition), Eyre and Spottiswoode, 1933.
    J. Taylor Peddie, *The Producer's Case for Monetary Reform,* London, The British Economic Federation, Ltd., 1927.
    The Invariable Standard and Measure of Value, London, P. S. King & Son, Ltd., 1928.
    The Dual System of Stabilization, London, Macmillan and Co., Ltd., 1931.
    See also: P. W. Martin, *The Flaw in the Price System,* London, P. S. King & Son, Ltd., 1924.
    The Problem of Maintaining Purchasing Power, London, P. S. King & Son, Ltd., 1931.
[33] Oxford, Humphrey Milford, Oxford University Press, 1920.
[34] *Unemployment,* Oxford, Humphrey Milford, Oxford University Press, 1922.
[35] *This Gold Crisis,* London, Victor Gollancz, Ltd., 1931, p. 136.
[36] *Ibid.,* p. 211.
[37] F. W. Pethick-Lawrence, *The Money Muddle and the Way Out,* London, George Allen & Unwin, Ltd., 1933, pp. 71 ff.

(1) A declaration that the Government makes the stability of the wholesale price level the main object of its policies, and does not decide to return to the gold standard at the old level.

(2) The Government should revise its economy program, and instead launch a program of public expenditures to re-distribute purchasing power.

(3) The Government should get repealed the present limitation on its fiduciary issues of notes.

(4) Setting up of an official domestic and international price level which is representative of the most important commodities after adequate survey.

(5) The preparation of a proposal to be placed before the World Economic Conference at London with the object of linking the several nations to an international commodity index standard.

(6) If the other nations show no desire to co-operate, the British Government should go ahead on its own with the stabilization of wholesale commodity prices.

Soddy

Professor Frederick Soddy, Nobel Laureate for Chemistry in 1921, is another important representative of the stable money movement in England. The failure of mankind to reap the benefits of the marvellous discoveries of science led him to investigate the operation of our modern distributive system; and, partly under the inspiration of Arthur Kitson, he made a close study also of currency and banking. In one of his first publications on monetary reform he applies his scientific methods to the solution of the monetary problem and suggests a number of fundamental measures with which he would begin the reform. The outstanding proposals are: Avoiding the danger of inflation by a repeal of the present power of banks to create money; using an index number as criterion of monetary policy; the Government to convert its outstanding bonds into a new issue with the option of premature redemption; compensating the banks for the loss sustained by them through the inauguration of the new system; nationalizing the banking system; the national stock of gold to be acquired by the Government; the taxation of minimum bank balances (in order to prevent hoarding).[38]

In a small booklet, "Poverty, Old and New," Professor Soddy showed the wide divergence between what he held to be orthodox economics, and his own views:

". . . If you want a true conception of the real nature of wealth, you should not consult Professors of Economics, least of all those of the London School of Economics, or that of any other great Metropolis. Any starving and destitute man you would find sleeping at night on the London Embankment has naturally, without having been to college to acquire it, far more accurate ideas of the real nature of wealth than a whole College of Professors of Economics." [39]

In a later book, Soddy declared dogmatically his demand for the nationalization of the banking system:

"The only way banking can today be made safe for the banker and for the nation is for the nation to be the banker." [40]

He further explained that the banks only pretend to lend money. He calls them "money-lender-pretenders," saying that in reality they create money and then extract toll for its use. This power of creating imaginary wealth, Soddy maintains, makes the

[38] Frederick Soddy, *The Inversion of Science* And a Scheme of Scientific Reformation, London, Henderson, 1924, pp. 48 ff. See also *Money versus Man*, London, Elkin Mathews & Marrot, 1931.
[39] *Poverty, Old and New*, London, Search Publishing Company, Ltd., 1932, p. 5.
[40] Frederick Soddy, *Wealth, Virtual Wealth and Debt*, New York, E. P. Dutton & Co., 1933, p. 1.

banks the supreme rulers. The following quotations from his "Summary of Practical Conclusions" are characteristic.

First, there is his demand for a constant purchasing power of money:

"(9) It is recognized that the invariable standard of value proposed is a debtor-creditor standard to facilitate long-term business engagements and remove the speculative element introduced into them by the change in the value of money. . . . But no social progress can be secure until the purchasing power of money is made invariable."

Regarding a monetary policy to be pursued with the aim of increasing production, while maintaining a stable price level, Soddy recommends the use of employment and production indexes along with the price index.

". . . In practice the issue would be determined" he says, "by the price level as indicator, with the returns of unemployment and the condition of industry as guiding indications." [41]

In dealing with the problem of technological unemployment and social unrest, Soddy considers the reform of our system of money and banking as unavoidable, if we want our present individualistic society to survive:

"It is claimed that these suggested reforms, whilst they do not entirely meet the deeper economic causes of social unrest, are necessary if an individualistic society is to continue and the nation in the future is to be in a position to deal with a further displacement of men by machinery and the methods of mass production, and to distribute monetary titles to consume in proportion to the quantity of wealth capable of being produced, rather than to the number of workers employed in production."

[41] *Ibid.*, pp. 297–301.

Section 4. In England (continued)

Industrial and Business Leaders

Viscount D'Abernon, formerly a prominent banker, and after the War the British Ambassador to Germany, has long been a strong advocate of stabilization. During the War he made many addresses on the subject of unstable money before the House of Lords. In 1930 he delivered a lecture to the Liverpool Chamber of Commerce, denouncing the laissez-faire attitude towards the price level and urging stabilization.[42]

Speaking over the radio to America, on March 29, 1931, he said: "It is too much the custom to act as though prices were born and not made—as though they were sent down by Providence independently of human action, and as if they had to be accepted like the gentle rain from Heaven. Such a view is, in my judgement, a profound mistake. The price level is determined in the main by human action and by wise or unwise decisions. A stable price level is an achievement of intelligence and not an accident of Nature." [43]

Lord Vernon, a prominent leader of the Coal Industry, in 1927 wrote a brochure on "Coal and Industrial Peace," [44] in which he gave a very excellent analysis of the difficulties in his industry, and proposed practical measures for overcoming them. In the following passage he summarizes the main causes of the conflict between capital and labor, tracing it to the instability of the monetary unit:

"1) Movements to change wages and hours of labour up or down are the main cause of industrial strife.

[42] Viscount D'Abernon, *The Economic Crisis: Its Causes and the Cure,* London, Hodder & Stoughton, Ltd., 1930.
[43] Viscount D'Abernon, *The Path To Recovery,* London, Hodder & Stoughton, 1931, p. 26.
[44] London, Ernest Benn, Limited, 1927.

"2) These movements are largely due to changes in the value of money, which is expressed by the average level of prices.

"3) Changes in the value of money further aggravate the trouble by opening out a gap between wholesale prices and the cost of living.

"4) For these reasons it is urgently necessary that the value of money should be stabilized in the interests of industrial peace.

"5) Changes which are not due to alterations in the value of money are due to changes special to individual industries, and can be dealt with only as they arise, by frankness and co-operation within each industry." [45]

Lord Vernon suggested that a more flexible banking system be instituted with the object of international control of the value of gold, as outlined at the Genoa Conference. If international agreement cannot be obtained, he concluded,[46] Britain should modify her gold standard policy, even if the fixed foreign exchanges have to be sacrificed, by controlling her money with the sole object of a stable price level.

A letter signed by *One Hundred Prominent British Leaders* connected with the productive industries, and sent to Prime Minister Baldwin, in May, 1928, contained the following strong demand for a stable price level as a prerequisite for the restoration of prosperity:

"We believe that a more stable system of currency credit and a means of stabilizing the price level are pre-requisite to the restoration of prosperity of the great basic industries of this country. It would do far more than the expedients which the Government has been compelled to adopt." [47]

On April 18, 1928, a Memorandum was sent to the Chancellor of the Exchequer by a joint conference of the *British Trades*

[45] Lord Vernon, *Coal and Industrial Peace, op. cit.*, p. 16.
[46] *Ibid.*, p. 36.
[47] From New York *Times*, May 27, 1928.

Union Congress, and the *Employers Group,* headed by *Lord Melchett (Sir Alfred Mond).*[48] This letter contained the following resolutions, demanding that an inquiry be made into the best form of credit policy for the country so that a method could be found by which the Bank of England was able to maintain a stable price of gold in cooperation with other central banks.

"(a) That under the special conditions in which the gold standard operates at the present time we are not convinced that it is either practicable or desirable that the credit policy of the country should be determined more or less automatically by gold movements as in pre-war days.

"(b) That it is highly undesirable that the Bank of England should be so tied down by the provisions of a gold reserve law as to be unable fully and freely to co-operate in the plans adopted by this country and the rest of Europe at Genoa, 1922, for International Co-operation in economising the use of gold, regulating its distribution, and preventing undue fluctuations in its value in terms of wealth.

"(c) That it is therefore essential to hold a full inquiry into the best form of credit policy for this country before decisive steps are taken by the Government."[49]

Sir Henry Strakosch, the Chairman of one of the world's largest gold mining companies, Member of the Council of India, and a member of the Financial Committee of the League of Nations, has taken particular interest in the problem of stabilizing the value of gold. Supporting the views held by Gustav Cassel and others, he and *Mr. Joseph Kitchin* pointed to the dangers arising from the maldistribution of gold; the necessity of economizing the monetary use of gold; and the need for international co-

[48] Lord Melchett's interest in stable money is explained in his books:
Why the Crisis, London, Victor Golancz, Ltd., 1931.
Modern Money, London, Martin Secker, 1932.
[49] Quoted from *Bulletin of the Stable Money Association,* Vol. I, No. 2, November, 1928.

operation, as outlined at the Genoa Economic Conference.[50]

Sir Henry made exceedingly interesting investigations into the problem of the distribution of the national income. He came to the conclusion that the yearly increase of income due to increased production should accrue to the large mass of consumers, so that this additional wealth could be immediately spent for consumption. Only thus, he said, could production and stability be maintained.

The *London Chamber of Commerce,* on November 10, 1931, appointed a committee, "to consider the means necessary to provide the currency required for the maintenance and development of British Trade, while avoiding those evils which are invariably attendant upon inflation and deflation alike." The Committee subsequently recommended an invariable measure of value, based not upon one commodity, such as gold, but on a large number of commodities. These recommendations read in part as follows:

"1) . . . in order to have a just measure of value, subject neither to inflation nor deflation, the currency should rise and fall automatically with business activity: it should not be 'managed.'

"2) The currency must be backed 100 per cent. by real wealth, *i.e.* commodities with a market value: that backing must not be one commodity the value of which, in terms of other commodities, can be made to fluctuate widely, either through scarcity from natural causes, or through being 'cornered'. . . ."

On June 20, 1932, a special meeting of the Council of the Chamber was called to consider further action on the above report. A resolution was adopted on this occasion which called special attention to the necessity of arresting deflation. The British Government was urged to bring about agreement among the other members of the British Empire at the forthcoming Ottawa Con-

---

[50] See: *Gold and the Price Level,* in "Supplement to the London Economist," July 5, 1930.
   The Crisis, a memorandum, in "Supplement to the London Economist," January 9, 1932.

ference, upon a "constructive Monetary Policy," and "to give a lead to the other nations of the world and invite their cooperation." The above monetary report of the Chamber was submitted to the British Government "as a contribution to the reform of the Monetary System, and as a basis of discussion at Ottawa on the subject."

The man who supplied the principal driving power behind the activities of the London Chamber of Commerce in behalf of stabilization is its Secretary, *Mr. A. de V. Leigh,* who continuously stimulated the above and similar activities. He has also contributed a number of articles in periodicals to the cause of stable money.[51]

Organized Labor

The English organized Labor groups have ever been awake to the problem of monetary stabilization. At the hearings of the Macmillan Committee, in June, 1930, the *Trades Union Congress General Council* submitted a written statement which included the following sentences on the importance of a stable level of prices:

"Our own view is that stabilization of the general price level is extremely desirable, if it can be attained without resulting in worse evils than those it seeks to rectify. If these great fluctuations in the level of general prices were obviated, the entire industrial system would in our view benefit. Whether the general price level can be stabilized or not is a highly technical problem upon which we offer no opinion at this stage. We raise the matter for the Committee to consider because we feel it is one of the most important questions that remain to be determined." [52]

[51] See for instance: *New Monetary Policy. London Chamber's Proposal,* in "The Times, Trade and Engineering Supplement," December 17, 1932 and December 24, 1932.
The Monetary System and Means to Consumption, in "The Times, Trade and Engineering Supplement," March 25, 1933.
[52] *Minutes of Evidence* taken before the *Committee on Finance and Industry,* London, 1931, by H. M. Stationary, Vol. I, p. 312.

A statement submitted on the same occasion by the *Independent
Labour Party* also referred to stabilization, and, in particular, to
the Genoa proposal of international cooperation for maintaining
the price of gold. In part this statement read:

". . . a nationalized Bank of England would reverse the policy
of deflation on its international side by co-operation with other
Central Banks to stabilize world gold prices on lines propounded
at the Genoa Conference. No doubt, the Bank of International
Settlements will at last bring such action within the range of early
possibility." [53]

In 1931, in Parliament, an emergency policy was proposed by
Sir Oswald Mosley and sixteen other labor leaders. Currency
management was advocated by them as a means of establishing a
stable price level. This part of the proposed policy was thus expressed:

"We believe that no economic proposals will in the end succeed
unless they include the rational planning of currency so that the
present disastrous fall in the general price level is arrested, and
producers are given a firm expectation of a reasonably stable general price level in the future." [54]

Although a stable price level was not looked upon as a cure-all,
it was believed to be fundamental to all other national economic
planning:

". . . We are not, however, amongst those who believe that a
stable general price level would solve every problem. The disastrous tendency of undirected economic forces to disproportion-
ate production—to produce too much of one thing and not
enough of another—would remain. That can only be met by
national planning. But we readily agree that such national planning is impossible without a relatively stable general price
level." [55]

[53] *Ibid.*, Vol. II, p. 135, M. 6.
[54] *A National Policy,* An Account of the Emergency Programme Advanced by
Sir Oswald Mosley, M.P., as drafted by: Allen Young, John Strachey, M.P., and
Aneurin Bevan, M.P., London, Macmillan and Co., Ltd., 1931, p. 41.
[55] *Ibid.*, p. 44.

The desire for a stable currency had become so universal that in 1932 two great political parties of England, though opposed to each other in most things, adopted almost identical resolutions concerning monetary policy:

The *Labor* Platform said:

"The aim of British monetary policy should be to stabilise wholesale prices at a suitable level in this country and to seek by international agreement the largest practical measure of stability in the rates of foreign exchange." [56]

The *Conservative* Platform said:

"That this Conference would deprecate any attempt to return to the gold standard in the near future, and urges that His Majesty's Government should consult with the Dominions with a view to stabilising the purchasing power of money, within the Empire, on the basis of an index-scale of wholesale commodity prices." [57]

Bankers

Reginald McKenna, formerly Chancellor of the British Exchequer, and afterwards the Chairman of the Midland Bank, has for many years been an enthusiastic and untiring advocate of stable money. At the annual meeting of shareholders of any large English bank it is customary for the Chairman of the Board of Directors to state his views not only on the condition of his bank, but also on the general economic situation of the country. For years at the annual meetings of his own bank Mr. McKenna has emphasized the advantages of a stable currency. In 1922 he gave the proof of his interest in stabilization, when he said:

"The truth is, of course, that both [inflation and deflation] are

[56] Extract from Resolution carried unanimously by the Labour Party in its National Conference at Leicester, October, 1932.

[57] Resolution carried unanimously by the Conservative Party in its National Conference at Blackpool, October, 1932.

Both quoted from F. W. Pethick-Lawrence, *The Money Muddle and The Way Out, op. cit.,* p. 7.

bad. What is needed is stability, the point from which both alike proceed in opposite directions. When we have stability of prices we have a basis upon which trade can be carried on with confidence."

At the Ordinary General Meeting, January 25, 1924, he was more specific as to the possibility of avoiding the extremes of booms and depressions by wise monetary policy:

"Ups and downs in trade we are bound to have, but wise monetary policy can always prevent the cyclical movement from going to extremes. The speculative excesses of an inflationary boom and the cruel impoverishment of a prolonged slump can both be avoided. They are not necessary evils to which we must submit as things without understandable or preventable cause."

The "Monthly Review" of the Midland Bank for 1927 is a veritable textbook on stabilization, critical but constructive. In the January–February issue, dealing with "American Prosperity and British Depression," Reginald McKenna contrasts the rigidity of the Bank of England with the elasticity of the Federal Reserve System, and urges an inquiry into the principles of central banking with a view to safeguarding prosperity in the future. "The vital need of the future" he said, "is to insure that the maintenance of prosperity, with a growing population and an ever improving standard of living, both requiring an expansion in the volume of trade, shall not be hampered by false restrictions on the quantity of money."

The May–June, 1927 issue of this review is entitled "The Course of Gold Values." It contains a study of gold movements and prices during the past century, showing the close relationship between the two. The danger of a shortage in monetary gold is pointed out, and the estimates of gold production by Mr. Kitchin are cited.

The next issue, that of June–July, 1927, is entitled "The Problem of Gold Values." It reviews the various proposals for the stabilization of the value of gold, and contains one of the strongest appeals for stabilization that has ever been made by a man of Mr. McKenna's importance:

"History has shown that, apart perhaps from wars and religious intolerance, no single factor has been more productive of misery and misfortune than the high degree of variability in the general price level. This may sound like an extravagant statement, but so far from being of the nature of a demagogic outburst it is clearly demonstrable from the course of events in various countries ever since money became an important element in the life of civilized communities. A stable price level is a thing to be desired, second only to international and domestic peace."

The issue for August–September, 1927 is entitled "Stabilizing the Value of Gold." Mr. McKenna here gives warning that the dissipation of the gold stock justifies "the worst fears of the prophets" regarding the future of the price level. He advocates concerted action by the Federal Reserve System and the Bank of England in order to arrive at a stable world price level, chiefly through wise control of the discount rate.

His book, "Post War Banking Policy" which contains all his addresses during 1921–1928, is essentially the story of the lost opportunity of England and America as to monetary policy.[58]

Let us now look at the Opposition in England at this time and see what the adherents of the "good old gold standard" had to say.

The *Sound Currency Association,* at its annual meeting, April 1, 1927, credited itself with having been instrumental in bringing about England's return to gold in 1925. The President of that Association, the Rt. Hon. Earl Beauchamp, in opening this meeting, proudly stated:

". . . we have been gradually able to bring our influence to bear upon Governments and institutions already anxious to be a

[58] See Reginald McKenna, *Post War Banking Policy,* London, William Heinemann, Ltd., 1928.

little bit stimulated in our direction. We are glad to think and proud to think that we have succeeded in successive years to bring back the currency to a sound foundation. . . ."

Mr. Mason, an officer of the Association, then went into the details of these achievements, and particularly attacked Mr. Mc-Kenna for his advocacy of monetary reform:

"Mr. McKenna . . . as you probably remember, in his address to the shareholders of the Midland Bank, . . . was of the opinion that the Federal Reserve System of the United States of America was much more suitable for the attainment of prosperity as compared with what he termed the more rigid system which we have in this country under the Bank of England. But in looking at his speech there are a number of points which I think might be of interest to you if I referred to them.

"The first is that when he supported his argument by the fact that the deposits of the American Banks during the last five years show a considerable increase, whereas the deposits of the British Banks show a decrease, he omitted, in pointing that out, to take into account the very important point that in that period we resumed the gold standard; and that therefore the deposits which we now have are re-valorized pounds, and much more valuable pounds. That is a very important point to bear in mind.

"When you commence this comparison in 1922, this country was then experiencing a considerable amount of inflation. It should be remembered that we resumed and restored the gold standard in 1925, and that those deposits held by our great banks are re-valorized pounds; *and when you saw as you saw the other day, that coal had come down five shillings a ton, you got some idea of what a pound is if it is a good pound. . . .*" [59]

Mr. Mason then dealt with Mr. McKenna's assertion that for three years, 1922–1923–1924, the country had been exposed to rigorous deflation.

[59] Italics mine.

"During these years to which Mr. McKenna refers, . . . there was little or no change in the amount of currency in circulation in this country. I have taken out the figures. . . . Now it is time, I think, that this nonsense, for it is nonsense, that there was a hasty and premature and drastic deflation during those years, as a preliminary to the restoration of the gold standard—it is time that this should be exposed. There was no such drastic deflation. . . . So I hope we shall hear now no more about the intensity of deflation or the hasty return to the gold standard during those years previous to the restoration."

In spite of what Mr. Mason said, if a pound is a good pound when it buys more of everything, this "improvement" is undoubtedly due to deflation—and the British "Sound Currency Policy" unfortunately resulted in just those conditions which the advocates of stable (*i.e.* really sound) money had predicted.

Mr. McKenna, although for a number of years he stood almost alone as an English banker with progressive monetary ideas, was presently joined by three directors of the Bank of England. The first was Sir Josiah Stamp; the second, Sir Basil Blackett, who was also chairman and director of some of the most important British industrial corporations, and had been the representative of the British Treasury in the United States during the War; and the third, Sir Charles Stewart Addis, who was also Vice-Chairman of the Bank of International Settlements and Chairman of the Hongkong & Shanghai Bank.

Sir Basil Blackett, in his Halley Stewart Lecture in 1931, said: "If I put stable money in the forefront of what is needed for a successful national reconstruction, it is because national planning ahead is so difficult as to be almost impossible without reasonable stability of prices." [60]

In a book on "Planned Money" [61] he pleaded for a currency

[60] Halley Stewart Lecture, 1931, *The World Economic Crisis and the Way of Escape,* London, George Allen & Unwin, Ltd., 1931, p. 109.
[61] London, Constable and Company, Ltd., 1932.

the purchasing power of which would always remain constant and which was to be managed with regard to the internal price level only. The control of this he would assign to the Bank of England, whose inconvertible notes would be the only legal tender. According to Sir Basil, the management of a Central Bank would become considerably simplified under a stabilization policy, under which the bank would disregard reserve requirements and seek instead to maintain the price level.

"If the Central Bank has been given the task of maintaining a constant level of prices, it should not be hampered by any restrictions on the amount of notes it may issue, and it would be wise to leave it wide, if not complete, discretion as to the nature of the cover which it will hold against its notes. . . . The community's interest is not to prevent the Bank's issuing currency beyond a practical limit, but to enjoy the benefits of a stable measure of value, and the criterion by which the Bank should be judged ought to be its success in maintaining a Constant Price Level." [62]

Sir Basil believed that, "The main difficulties of the Central Bank's task arise, not in using effectively the wide powers it possesses for raising or lowering the price level, but in knowing when to act." [63] He further thought that the Bank would need only ". . . reasonably accurate and up-to-date information as to the course of production. . . ."

In concluding his chapter on the "Control of the Price Level," he stated that he regarded stabilization as feasible. ". . . There is no reason," he said, "to regard it as a super-human task. It is not, in essence, so formidable as the maintenance of the currency on a parity with gold in conditions of economic instability. . . . If immediate success cannot be guaranteed for a new experiment, there is every reason for believing that, even allowing for initial

[62] Basil Blackett, *Planned Money*, London, Constable and Company, Ltd., 1932, p. 106.
[63] *Ibid.*, p. 110.

disappointments, in due course true stability of prices would be assured." [64]

The third Director of the Bank of England, referred to above, *Sir Charles Stewart Addis,* speaking before the Bond Club of New York in 1930, urged the stabilization of the world price level, as a means of ending the depression, and said that the Bank for International Settlements would be the natural instrument to accomplish this. He pleaded for the support of public opinion, without which the Directors of the Bank for International Settlements would be quite unable to act. He concluded:

"It is simply unthinkable that we shall continue to sit with folded hands while industry and trade throughout the world are becoming the sport of our ineffectual monetary systems. We must be masters in our own house, the rulers and not the slaves of money." [65]

Section 5. Germany—Austria—Switzerland (from 1900)

Gesell

The popular movement for a stable currency which developed in Germany, Austria and Switzerland was due largely to the efforts of Silvio Gesell whose proposal of monetary reform we have already reviewed.[66] Gesell was successful in business, as he claimed, because of his insight into the workings of monetary laws. He retired about 1900, and settled in Switzerland as a gentleman-farmer and devoted himself to spreading his ideas. But in spite of numerous articles and other publications, which he financed himself, Gesell, in six years of effort, found only one man whom he had been able to convince of the merits of his theories.

[64] *Ibid.,* p. 114.
[65] The New York *Times,* November 25, 1930.
[66] See Chapter 2, Section 3. I may note here that the only part of Gesell's program which I have endorsed is his stamped currency proposal—and that without accepting his belief that it would lead to the abolition of interest.

When the death of his brother had forced Gesell to return to Argentina, in 1907, this disciple, *Ernst Frankfurth* by name, followed him, and together they published a summary of their monetary-reform proposals.[67] They distributed 3000 copies of this book, sending it to economists, financial editors, politicians, business men, and other prominent persons, and received no replies, reviews, nor even acknowledgments. But later, by some accident, a high officer of the German army got hold of the book, and wrote Gesell an enthusiastic letter. So happy was Gesell that he made the trip from Argentina to Germany in order to meet his new found friend; but when he arrived, the man was dead. In Switzerland, during the War, he published his "Natural Economic Order"[68] describing his proposed monetary reform to which he had added a land reform somewhat like the single-tax.

Bavarian Revolution (1919)

After the War Gesell's socialist friends[69] became the masters of revolutionary Bavaria and called him to Munich to organize the monetary system and the finances of that state. Through his indefatigable efforts and his many writings, he had, by this time, acquired a number of friends, and he was now able to secure the assistance of two outstanding men, Professor Polenske of Berlin, and the late Dr. Theophil Christen of Zurich.[70]

[67] *Aktive Waehrungspolitik*, 1909.
[68] *Die Natuerliche Wirtschaftsordnung durch Freiland und Freigeld*, Hans Timm Verlag, Leipzig (First edition, 1916), translated into English, *The Natural Economic Order*, 1929, Free Economy Publishing Co., 312 Madison Street, San Antonio, Texas.
[69] Particularly Gustav Laudauer who became Minister of Education in this revolutionary Government (the 2. Räte-Regierung).
[70] Dr. Christen is the author of *Free-Economy*, a small, but comprehensive book on Gesell's monetary theories, published by the Free-Economy Publishing Co., San Antonio, Texas.

Silvio Gesell, as the new Bavarian Minister of Finance, moved into his Executive Offices, at Munich on April 8, 1919, and immediately set to work to restore and reform the currency. The money system was in a deplorable condition, and as Bavaria had no currency of its own, it was dependent upon Reichsbank notes, which were already considerably overissued, with high prices as a result. Gesell immediately ordered the printing of his "stamp currency." At the same time he began an educational campaign. On April 13, 1919, the revolutionary Government was driven out of power. Gesell and Dr. Christen were arrested, accused of high treason and put in jail. After a few weeks Christen was released, mainly through the intervention of the Swiss Government. Gesell, however, was held for several months, and finally, after a dramatic trial, in which he defended himself with great eloquence, he was acquitted.[71]

Free Economy

This episode gave Gesell some influence and the *Free-Economy* movement, which, before the war, had included only Gesell and a few friends in Switzerland and Berlin, suddenly grew to a membership of many thousands. The disaster of German inflation further helped the movement grow. But as it was mainly a labor movement, which had no political representation and was opposed by the Socialist (Marxist) labor parties, it became disorganized after 1924, when the Reichsmark had returned to the gold standard. Three distinct political groups of Gesell's followers remained, of which two survive at this writing.[72]

A number of weekly and monthly papers continued the propa-

[71] See *Die Freiwirtschaft vor Gericht,* compiled by Richard Hoffmann, Erfurt, Freiland-Freigeld-Verlag, 1920, 70 pp.
[72] December, 1933. The Hitler Government has since suppressed these two.

ganda which Gesell had started shortly before the war in his own publications.[73]

A monthly magazine dealing with Gesell's ideas has recently appeared in the United States.[74]

There are now groups of "Free Economists" in a number of other countries, such as France, Canada, Australia, Argentina, Mexico, Roumania, Latvia.

A number of prominent men in various countries have openly espoused Gesell's ideas.[75]

Stamp Scrip

Hans Timm was the first disciple of Gesell to bring stamp scrip into actual use as an unofficial, supplementary currency. This was in Germany in the small mining community of Schwanenkirchen, in 1930–1931, where the owner of a coal mine, Hebecker, by means of stamp scrip (called "Wära"), not only succeeded in reopening his mine but kept it open from 1931 on, in spite of increasing deflation.[76] This experiment aroused much interest, and the Austrian town of Woergl, in 1932, began to issue similar stamp certificates in order to relieve unemployment and promote public works. In Germany, at the instigation of the Reichsbank, the issuance of Wära was stopped, and later a similar prohibition was decreed in Austria, at the instigation of the Austrian National

[73] *Freiwirtschaftliche Zeitung* (weekly), Bern, Switzerland (Schwarztorstrasse, 76), edited by *Fritz Schwarz* who in 1926 won a prize offered by the "Economic Guild" for an essay on stabilization.
Geld und Arbeit (monthly, illustrated), edit. by Mr. Rödelsberger, Bern, Switzerland.
Der Neue Tag (monthly), Niederlindewiese, Czechoslovakia.
[74] *The Way Out,* edited by Dr. Hugo Fack, 312 Madison Street, San Antonio, Texas.
[75] Among them were the late Dr. Forel of Switzerland; the late Prof. Bunge of Germany; Prof. Bernoulli of Basel; Dr. Uhde of Graz. Peter Westen, a prominent industrialist, has done much to spread Gesell's ideas in Central Europe.
[76] See Hans R. L. Cohrssen, *Wara,* in "The New Republic," August 10, 1932.

Bank. Nevertheless, both experiments had been successful.[77] But Gesell had already died in 1930.

[77] For more about Stamp Scrip see Irving Fisher, *Stamp Scrip,* New York, During 1933–1934, Mason City, Iowa successfully used $10,000 of the dated stamp scrip. At this writing (August, 1934) Winfield H. Caslow is issuing dated stamp scrip in Chicago, Ill. in co-operation with the Merchants' Scrip Exchange. In June, 1934, Reval, in Estonia, is said to have issued 200,000 kronor of the dated Stamp Scrip. (Freiwirtschaftliche Zeitung, Bern, July 7, 1934.)

CHAPTER V

LEGISLATIVE STAGE (TO 1932)

Section 1. Some Legal Aspects

The American Constitution, in Article I, Section 8, Clause 5, provides that Congress shall have power,

"to coin money, regulate the value thereof, and of foreign coin, and fix the standard of weights and measures."

Dr. Frank Wolff, formerly with the U.S. Bureau of Standards, said in 1928 that Congress had at first ignored its obligation of fixing the standard of weights and measures by delegating it informally as a Federal bureau. Testifying before a Congressional Committee on Stabilization,[1] he mentioned a few pieces of legislation, permissive and otherwise, which Congress had passed pursuant to this constitutional provision:

"In 1828 a certain troy pound was adopted as a standard for coinage.

"In 1836, by joint resolution, Congress directed the Secretary of the Treasury to deliver to the governor of each state,

'a complete set of weights and measures adopted as standards 'and now either made or in process of manufacture for the use 'of the several customhouses.'

"In 1866 the metric system was legalized for permissive use throughout the United States.

"In 1911 Congress provided that the standard troy pound of the Bureau of Standards should be the standard troy pound for the regulation of coinage, thus repealing the previous act of 1828.

"In 1915 a mandatory standard barrel was adopted for the sale

---

[1] From *Hearings* before the Banking and Currency Committee of the House on H.R. 7895, March to April, 1926, pp. 149 ff.

of dry commodities, whether in intrastate or interstate commerce. "A standard lime barrel and standard baskets have also been legalized for use in interstate commerce.

"In addition to that, in 1894, Congress legalized standards for electrical measurement suggested by the International Electrical Congress held at Chicago in 1893. These, I am frank to state, were disregarded by the Bureau of Standards, because that action has been superseded by the decisions of subsequent Congresses."

Dr. Wolff then related that Congress had largely avoided its responsibility by delegating to the Bureau of Standards the regulation of standard weights and measures. He said:

"In effect the regulation or fixing of standard weights and measures has been informally delegated to the Bureau of Standards. The standards in customary use are actually those which have been adopted by the Bureau of Standards. They pass by general sanction without any strict legalization."

With regard to the regulation of the value of the currency, Dr. Wolff explained (on another occasion), that Congress merely determined certain metal weights for our coins, but had done nothing to determine the value of our money in terms of goods:

"Congress has practically limited itself . . . to fixing the weight and fineness of composition of coins, whether gold, silver, nickel or copper. It did not recognize that this merely fixed the value of such coin in terms of the number of grains of gold in the dollar, which is not an expression of real value in terms of commodities." [2]

And yet, in spite of the above provision in the Constitution, experts now maintain that new legislation will be necessary in order to standardize the measure of value, i.e., to stabilize the dollar!

[2] *Hearings* before the Banking and Currency Committee of the House, 67th Congress, 4th session, on H.R. 11788, December 20, 1922, p. 81.

SECTION 2. FEDERAL RESERVE ACT—1913

Stable Money Provision in the Senate's Bill

Though the Federal Reserve System of 1913 was not expressly dedicated to price level stabilization, as defined in this book, yet the sponsors of it hoped that it would put an end to the periodic money panics which had always plagued us, and that thus the severe fluctuations in the value of money would automatically be eliminated. These hopes have been only partly justified. The Federal Reserve System has provided an "elastic" currency, but the fluctuations in the purchasing power of money have not only continued—they have become worse.

The original draft of the bill contained a distinct provision that the system should promote a stable price level. This was inserted by Senator Owen, then Chairman of the Senate Banking and Currency Committee, at the suggestion of Mr. George H. Shibley.[3] The paragraph read as follows:

"Every Federal Reserve Bank shall have the power . . . (d) to establish each week, or much oftener, as required, subject to review and determination of the Federal Reserve Board, a minimum rate of discount to be charged by such banks for each class of paper, which shall be made with a view to accommodating the commerce of the country, *and promoting a stable price level.*" [4]

This stabilization provision, which was incorporated in the Senate bill, was, however, stricken out by the House Committee on Banking and Currency, of which Congressman Carter Glass was the Chairman.

Mr. Shibley's Testimony

Mr. Shibley, at the Senate Hearings, protested earnestly that the elimination of this provision from the bill would leave the con-

[3] For Mr. Shibley's previous interest in stabilization, see Chapter 2, Section 5.
[4] *Hearings* before the Committee on Banking and Currency, U.S. Senate, 63rd Congress, 1st session, on S. 2639, 1913, vol. 2, p. 1730, sec. 15 of the bill. Italics mine.

trol of the price level still in the hands of the bankers. He insisted that the insertion of the stabilization clause in the Federal Reserve Act would not only avoid giving the Board discretionary power in this respect, it would in effect be the beginning of the scientific solution of the money problem:

"If the law shall declare that stability in the purchasing power of money shall be the aim toward which the national Board shall work, then the said board will have no discretionary power in the matter. . . ."

"The fact is, monetary science has reached a point where the money question can be settled in this country, if Congress will restore in the bill the four or five words in the administration bill that the interest shall be so controlled as to promote stability in the price level." [5]

And *Senator Owen* added to Mr. Shibley's statement this explanation of his own interest in the stabilization provision:

"I took a good deal of pains to have that put into the bill. I was very much interested in it, because I thought the great thing we needed in this country, both for the creditor class and for the debtor class, was stability, that they might know their relations to each other, and so that they might know there would be no change of contract by a change in the purchasing value of the dollar. For that reason I insisted upon its going into the original draft of the bill."

At that time, an increased supply of gold was making itself felt, and Mr. Shibley suggested a way to keep this supply from developing into a serious depreciation of the currency. He proposed that the United States Government communicate with the Governments of other gold-standard countries for the purpose of raising, by agreement, the mint price of gold. He further suggested a provision for the prevention of inflation through the retirement of bank notes.

[5] *Ibid.*, pp. 1724–1860.

The following quotation, which reveals how little understanding of index numbers and price levels there was at that time, perhaps explains the fate of this stabilization provision:

"*Senator Nelson:* 'Your figures are of no earthly value. You might as well take one of those calendars they had 2000 years ago and tender those dates.'

"*Mr. Shibley:* 'I am afraid you have not looked at them carefully."

"*Senator Nelson:* 'I do not intend to look at them, because they go against my own sense and good judgement, no more than I intend to read Professor Fisher's book. (Laughter) . . . Don't try to fool us with such things.'

"*Mr. Shibley:* 'I just wish to state in the record the prices of farm products go into the general index number and are given a proper proportion.'

"*Senator Nelson:* 'Oh, index numbers! Old Mother Hubbard!' (Laughter.)"

Yet, Mr. Shibley was not the only witness who appeared in favor of stabilization. Among others, the present writer, who stated (testifying in favor of an "elastic" currency):

"My definition of a perfectly elastic currency would be one which varied with the demands of trade in such a manner as to maintain the price level constant." [6]

SECTION 3. FIRST STABLE MONEY BILLS (1919–1924)

Husted Resolution (1919); Dallinger Bill (1920)

The War interrupted any further attempts at getting legislation for a stable dollar. The next effort was made on September 3, 1919, when Congressman *James W. Husted* of New York introduced a resolution, proposing an investigation into the stabilization problem: [7]

"To provide for a special committee to inquire into plans for

[6] *Ibid.*, p. 1157.
[7] H. Res. 287.

stabilizing the purchasing power of the American gold dollar, and to report such measures as it may deem advisable to effect such stabilization."

This resolution was referred to the Committee on Rules, but nothing further was heard about it.

On April 30, 1920, Congressman *Frederic W. Dallinger* of Massachusetts, introduced the first definite Stabilization bill in the House of Representatives.[8]

"To stabilize the purchasing power of the dollar."
This bill was referred to the Committee on Coinage, Weights and Measures, but no action was taken.

First Goldsborough Bill (1922)

On May 23, 1922, *Congressman T. Alan Goldsborough* of Maryland introduced his bill [9] for "Stabilizing the Purchasing Power of Money" and addressed the House of Representatives explaining his interest in stabilization:

". . . For a great many years, in fact, ever since I have been old enough to think very much, I have wondered about the gradual expansion and contraction of general price levels through long periods of years, but never until I became a member of Congress did it seem that I had time enough to even attempt any sort of a real analysis.

"Last summer, on the occasion of a dinner, at which former Vice-President Marshall and I were guests, I brought up the subject and found that he had given the matter a great deal of consideration, and he made several luminous suggestions based upon his study and supported by his splendid common sense. I am profoundly convinced that the problem of stabilizing the purchasing power of money is soluble. I believe it is the second problem of economic importance confronting the people of the world at this

[8] H.R. 13875.
[9] H.R. 11788 (67th Congress, 2nd Session).

time, and I believe this to be the psychological time to bring the matter up for serious consideration. . . ."

From December 18, 1922 to January 29, 1923, hearings were held on the Goldsborough bill before the Committee on Banking and Currency. This bill was practically in the form suggested by the present writer in "Stabilizing the Dollar." [10] In fact it was essentially the "Compensated Dollar" plan and provided, in part, as follows:

"Beginning January 8, 1924, the Gold Dollar of the United States shall cease to be a constant quantity of gold of variable purchasing power, and thereafter be a variable quantity of standard gold bullion of approximately constant computed purchasing power.

"Said quantity of standard gold bullion, constituting a gold dollar at any given time, shall be ascertained and fixed from time to time by the computation and use of index numbers of wholesale prices as hereinafter set forth. . . ."

The wholesale commodity index of the Bureau of Labor Statistics was to be used as a basis, and every two months the gold value of the dollar was to be determined by this index. A "brassage" charge of one per cent was provided for; that is, the mint was to pay less for gold bullion than it asked for it. Gold coin would cease to circulate. Instead, the Government would issue Gold Bullion Certificates, convertible into gold bullion at the current ratio and backed by a 50 per cent gold bullion reserve.

Hearings on First Goldsborough Bill

The present writer appeared as the first witness at these hearings. Mr. Wingo, a member of the Banking and Currency Committee, asked, "If you stabilize gold, will it stabilize currency?" The answer was that the cooperation of the Federal Reserve

[10] See Irving Fisher, *Stabilizing the Dollar, op. cit.,* pp. 205 ff.

System was necessary to carry out the purposes of the bill, as credit control as an essential part of stabilization:

". . . in order to stabilize the dollar most perfectly and to keep it stable, we should not only adopt this bill, but have the good will and the cooperation of the Federal Reserve Board not to adopt a policy inconsistent with the purpose of this bill. . . .

"For the most perfect stabilization these things are sufficient: First, to pass this bill substantially as it is; and the other is to control credit. . . .

"Many people think I am purely confined to gold in this proposition, and that I have taken no account of the credit superstructure on gold. Now, if your superstructure is kept within reasonable proportion to your base, all you need is to stabilize the base. I firmly believe that the Federal Reserve Board, the minute this bill is passed, would not require any other hint, but would at once try to co-operate; it would readjust the rate of discount from time to time; it would watch the price level too, and if the price level seemed to rise at any time it would raise the rate of discount and check inflation; if it seemed to fall, it would lower the rate of discount and check deflation. . . ." [11]

Professor James H. Rogers was the next witness. He warmly endorsed the bill and cited particularly its advantages for the farming population. He had, however, an interesting objection to make: If prices should fall very rapidly, and the possible correction in the gold weight of the dollar should not amount to more than 1% every two months, this adjustment might be insufficient, and a difference might arise between the price level, representing the actual purchasing power of the dollar, and the weight of the dollar in gold, representing the purchasing power of gold. This would undoubtedly give rise to speculation.

The answer was made that this could be remedied by a provision for changing the weight of the gold dollar sufficiently to correspond to the actual price changes. Without actual experience no one could say with certainty how frequently, and to what extent, adjustments would be necessary.

Professor Willford I. King, the next witness, asked that a different index number be used, namely that of retail instead of wholesale prices. He explained that he preferred a consumption index because, first, retail prices did not fluctuate as widely as wholesale prices, and second, people were interested in the stability of the prices of things they actually used. As he expressed it:

"The reason I would rather favor retail prices for the basis for the index is because they do not fluctuate so widely, and I think that the ultimate things that people can use are the final determinants of prices. I feel that it is important that we stabilize in terms of the commodities that the people use rather than in the terms of the commodities that are dealt in at wholesale. . . ." [12]

He also suggested a 100 per cent reserve for the gold bullion notes and that, to prevent speculation, the brassage charge should always be larger than any change in the gold weight of the dollar.

Professor King also stated that in 1920–1921 deflation had transferred forty billion dollars of value from one part of the population to another,—a "robbery of considerable size" as he said.

Mr. Robert D. Kent, President of the Merchants' Bank of Passaic, N. J.[13] testified next in favor of the bill, and made the following statement:

"I feel in my business (which is dealing in money and credit) something like the dry-goods merchant would, who was selling to his customers yards of cloth every day measured by the yardstick that was elastic in its nature; I feel that I have been doing that so long and to the detriment of the community in which I deal, and other bankers are doing it in their communities, that as

[12] *Ibid.,* p. 61.
[13] See also about him Chapter 4, Section 2.

a matter of fair dealing we should have a fixed yardstick for measuring money and credit which we have not now." [14]

Dr. Frank A. Wolff (whose statements on the legal status of our monetary and other standards have been mentioned) also appeared on behalf of the bill. He stressed the difficulty of Government departments in budgeting their expenditures so long as the price level was permitted to fluctuate.

Mr. George H. Shibley, who, as the next witness, explained his efforts to get a stabilization provision into the Federal Reserve Act, was rather doubtful as to the possibility of stabilizing the dollar by the provisions of this bill, without any added provision for credit control. He suggested that an amendment be made to the Federal Reserve Act, adding the words "promote a stable price level."

Mr. Goldsborough then introduced a number of letters which he had received from prominent men endorsing his bill. Thus, former Vice-President of the United States, *Thos. R. Marshall*, wrote that the problem was only half solved by the establishment of the Federal Reserve System which supplied a flexible currency but not stability.

Professor *E. W. Kemmerer*, of Princeton, afterward known as "the international money doctor," wrote (among other things) a strong endorsement of the "Compensated Dollar" plan:

"The most promising plan for attaining a stable unit of value with which I am acquainted is the so-called Fisher plan for stabilizing the purchasing power of money, which is the basis of H.R. 11788. I believe that this plan is essentially sound, and, while it will probably be modified in certain particulars in the light of experience, I believe it offers a good basis upon which to begin." [15]

However, the bill was not reported out of Committee. Significant of the state of mind of those who opposed it were the

[14] *Hearings* on H.R. 11788, *op. cit.*, p. 66.
[15] *Ibid.*, p. 116.

following statements of Mr. Wingo. Answering the present writer, he said:

". . . It is the most vicious form of socialism to say that a governmental agency will undertake to control the volume of credit." [16]

Answering Professor Rogers, Mr. Wingo expressed the thought that the time was not yet ripe for stabilization legislation, as popular understanding of the evils of a fluctuating money standard had not yet progressed far enough. He said:

"If all men knew what you and Professor Fisher know, that would change the situation. Professor Fisher has just called attention to the fact that the great mass of the people do not understand the underlying philosophy of price movements, and the average man in the street would say, 'I want something definite and certain; I want so many grains of gold on a specific date.' If all people had the vision and recognition of the underlying philosophy of price movements as affected by the instability of our present currency, it is true they might do like you would do. Don't you think the average man in the street would be like myself and say, 'I want something definite, fixed and certain'?" [16a]

Second Goldsborough Bill (1924)

At the next session of Congress, Mr. Goldsborough promptly reintroduced his bill [17] with minor changes, such as the elimination of the provision for a 50% reserve as backing for Gold Bullion Certificates. Hearings on this revised bill were held on February 26, 1924. Dr. Wolff, Professor Rogers and the present writer repeated essentially the statements they had made before.

Mr. M. K. Graham of Texas [18] was a new witness. He thought that the time was ideal for stabilization, as on the average, the out-

[16] *Ibid.*, p. 49.
[16a] *Ibid.*, p. 32.
[17] As H.R. 494 (68th Congress, 1st Session).
[18] See also: Chapter 4, Section 1.

standing debts had been incurred on about the price level which then existed.

Congressman *Olger B. Burtness* of North Dakota, who had introduced a stabilization bill of his own,[19] presented a written statement by the late *Dana J. Tinnes* who was the author of his bill.[20] Mr. Burtness consistently re-introduced his bill "To stabilize the buying power of money" during every session of Congress, and also on several occasions impressively addressed the House of Representatives on the subject of stabilization.[21]

The second Goldsborough Bill was again "shelved" in the Banking and Currency Committee.

SECTION 4. FIRST STRONG BILL HEARINGS (1926–1927)

The Bill

On January 18, 1926, Congressman *James G. Strong* of Kansas, urged by Mr. George H. Shibley, introduced a bill in Congress to amend the Federal Reserve Act so as to make the Federal Reserve System responsible for the maintenance of monetary stability. The hearings on this Bill before the House Banking and Currency Committee began on March 24, 1926, and extended until February 4, 1927.

In introducing his bill, Mr. Strong explained that its form was meant to be tentative. He hoped to arrive at a more suitable wording after the hearings had shown just what amendments were desirable, so as to make the bill both effective, and acceptable to the Federal Reserve authorities.

This Bill,[22] read as follows:

"A Bill to amend paragraph (d) of section 14 of the Federal Reserve Act, as amended, to provide for the stability of the price level for commodities in general,

---

[19] H.R. 433 (68th Congress).
[20] See Chapter 2, Section 9, for a review of Mr. Tinnes' proposal.
[21] See, for instance, *Congressional Record* of March 3, 1925.
[22] H.R. 7895 (69th Congress, 1st Session).

"(d) To establish from time to time, subject to review and determination of the Federal Reserve Board, a mimimum rate of discount to be charged by such bank for each class of paper, which shall be made with a view to accommodating commerce and promoting a stable price level for commodities in general. All the powers of the Federal Reserve System shall be used for promoting stability in the price level."

Supporting Testimony

Mr. *Shibley* was the first witness. He explained the purpose of the bill and said that, if necessary, it could be enlarged, and that other stabilization features could be added to it. If necessary, more power could be delegated to the Federal Reserve Board so as to enable it to carry out the provisions of the bill. He insisted that the Federal Reserve already possessed the power of price-level control, but that they had used it badly, deferring to the passing will of the party in power. This tendency could be corrected by a mandate to adhere to an index number. Such a mandate would remove the Federal Reserve System from politics.

The present writer, as the next witness, did not share Mr. Shibley's distrust of the Federal Reserve System. He then suggested that the bill be amended so as to supplement the credit control with gold control.

As to the general purpose of the measure, he emphasized particularly that *stabilization is not price fixing,* saying:

"I am prejudiced against price fixing, just as much as anybody is. . . . I dislike these farm relief measures which involve the matter of price fixing, much as I sympathize with the farmer. That is my personal attitude, and I want to emphasize it. This bill is not price fixing, it is one step towards stabilization of the general level of all prices—which is a very different thing. . . . It is an attempt to control credit, an attempt to fix the general price level, but not to fix specific prices. It does not fix the price of wheat or of beef or any other commodity. It merely fixes the general average price level, and I would like to emphasize the fact that it will leave the law of supply and demand just as free as it is today as regards individual commodities; in fact, freer." [23]

Mr. Norman Lombard, Executive Director of the Stable Money Association, speaking as an individual, was next on the witness stand. He cited an imposing array of prominent persons who had expressed themselves as recognizing the need of stable money. He also presented a large number of quotations from economists, bankers and business men who advocated stabilization.

Dr. Frank A. Wolff, who followed Mr. Lombard, again expounded the legal aspect of the stabilization question, as he had done at previous hearings.

Dr. William T. Foster, Director of the Pollak Foundation for Economic Research, was also heard. Asked whether he believed that the Federal Reserve Board had the power to affect the price level, Dr. Foster answered: "Undoubtedly it has the power to affect the general price level, and it has used that power." [24]

Although he believed that eventually the Federal Reserve System would have difficulty in maintaining the stability of the economic system, unless the distribution of income were changed, Dr. Foster expressed himself in favor of having the Federal Reserve Board use all its powers for monetary stabilization, and that this should be an avowed and conscious policy, known to everybody. [25]

Professor James H. Rogers, who followed Dr. Foster, repeated the points of his previous statements in favor of stabilization. Again he emphasized how helpful this measure would be to the farmer, pointing out that, of all classes, the farmers are the worst hit when the price level falls, since the fall begins with the prices of raw materials and affects these prices most severely. He also

[23] *Hearings* before the Committee on Banking and Currency, of the House of Representatives, 69th Congress, 1st Session, on H.R. 7895, p. 67.

[24] *Ibid.,* p. 193.

[25] *Ibid.,* p. 211.

suggested that the control of gold would still have to be provided for; but that such need for additional legislation ought not to interfere with the immediate passage of the bill. He said:

"If we need something else, I should say by all means, pass something else in addition; something similar to the Goldsborough Bill. But this bill consists of a simple provision which I think can be made with little opposition from anyone, and will nevertheless bring us pretty nearly the stability we need in ordinary times." [26]

Western Starr, representing the National Committee of the Farmer-Labor Party, was the next witness. He suggested the introduction of an entirely new bill, to provide for:

A separate Board, established for the purpose of stabilizing the price level by the control of interest and rediscount rates which the Federal Reserve Banks are to charge. The Board to consist of five members, appointed by the President. Its first duty was to ascertain the average purchasing power of the dollar during the past 10 years on the basis of the prices of 300–400 commodities. The index thus calculated was to constitute the "standard dollar."

Under Mr. Starr's plan, the Secretary of the Treasury was to be charged with the duty of maintaining this index number stable through the sale and purchase of Government securities in the open market. A newly established Government bank was to execute all operations of the Secretary of the Treasury for the stabilization of the price level. For the purpose of bringing about international stabilization, the Secretary of the Treasury was to be authorized to negotiate with foreign countries. [27]

Professor Robert A. Lehfeldt of South Africa (since deceased) then explained his proposal for controlling the output of gold. [28] He stated why he thought the gold problem would have to be handled separately. He said that the short-period fluctuations

[26] *Ibid.,* p. 219.
[27] *Ibid.,* pp. 246–247.
[28] See also Chapter 3, Section 3.

could be controlled by banking policy; but that long-term trends must be controlled through gold.[29]

Major J. R. Bellerby, of Great Britain, testified in favor of the bill. He suggested, however, that action be delayed until international accord could be reached as to the method of stabilization. He was in favor of changing the proposed amendment to the following form:

". . . to maintain the gold standard and the value of gold, and to promote business stability." [30]

Opposing Testimony: Professor Sprague

The following statements came from men who were more or less opposed to the stabilization provision.

Professor O. W. M. Sprague, who later became the special adviser to the U.S. Treasury under the Roosevelt administration, was of opinion that the Federal Reserve System might do better without this provision as the problem of stabilization was largely one of administration:

"I much prefer the simple statute, so far as these matters go, to that under which the Bank of England operates. I feel that you are bound to rely primarily on management in the conduct of this Reserve System; that you can not expect to accomplish any one thing surely by its operation and, therefore, I am inclined to feel that it would be better to leave the system alone, so far as this particular legislation is concerned." [31]

Dr. Sprague, three years later (1929), advocated the stabilization provision on the very ground that the conduct of the Reserve System depended upon management.

Here follow additional reasons which prompted him in 1926 to advise against the Strong bill:

[29] *Ibid.,* pp. 1045–1065.
[30] *Ibid.,* pp. 935 ff. See also Chapter 3, Section 3.
[31] *Ibid.,* p. 410.

"I confess" he said, "that I am unable to decide in my own mind what the advantage or result of inserting this provision in the Reserve act would be. I am very certain in my own mind that it is not possible to handle the ordinary oscillations of prices effectively by means of the Reserve bank operations." [32]

"I should not suppose that the Reserve bank people would be compelled to give any more attention to price changes in the determination of their discount policy if this provision were inserted in the act. I am sort of fearful it might give rise to misunderstandings as to what they are expected to accomplish." [33]

Dr. Sprague summarized his views in the following sentences: "I think they can prevent extreme advances in prices, and thereby avoid sharp, sudden declines. I do not think that they can serviceably attempt to meet sliding oscillations in credit, whether in an upward or downward direction; and I am not certain as to just when they should endeavor to apply the brakes. I do not think that the price index furnishes a definite enough guide. . . ." [34]

"So that for the immediate future and until perhaps there has been more discussion of this problem by the public, I should be disinclined to see this measure upon the statute books. . . ." [35]

Governor Strong

But the chief witness at these hearings was *Governor Strong* of the Federal Reserve Bank of New York. His testimony covered almost every phase of the activities of the Federal Reserve System. He showed much sympathy with the general purpose of the bill, but did not wish to see the Federal Reserve System under legal compulsion to accomplish any prescribed result; nor did he think the bill would really change any of the powers of the

[32] *Hearings* on H.R. 7895, *op. cit.*, p. 408.
[33] *Ibid.*, p. 410.
[34] *Ibid.*, p. 415.
[35] *Ibid.*, p. 418.

System to control the price level, and that such control was essentially a matter of administration:

"Well, there is no magic formula" he said, "that can be introduced into the Federal Reserve Act to control prices. You cannot eliminate human judgment in the administration of these matters. . . . Our examination of the past produces the most accurate knowledge of past action and reaction but when it comes to a decision as to what we are going to do for the future, then just human judgment has got to govern. There is no mathematical formula for the administration of the Federal Reserve System or the regulation of prices." [36]

He feared that, once such a bill had passed, the public might infer that now the Federal Reserve System actually controlled the price level. This, he said, might create a wrong impression:

"I have in mind the possibility especially that the farming community of the country might be led to believe—they might assume at once—that this would provide a remedy for their difficulties and if they were disappointed and disillusioned later, and a sharp revulsion of feeling took place as to the position of the Federal Reserve System in that matter, and what it could accomplish, it might do us very great injury. It might do the system great injury, and I think it would do the country injury." [37]

This statement was due, apparently, to Governor Strong's fear that the public at large would be subject to a confusion of the price *level* with individual prices, as can be gathered from the following:

"Mr. Chairman, I do not understand that anybody claims —that is, intelligent people—that the Federal Reserve System can, by some manipulation of credit, deal with the price of wheat, or any other particular commodity, or even 404 commodities appearing in the index number of the Department of Labor."

[36] *Ibid.*, p. 302.
[37] *Ibid.*, p. 301.

"Mr. Goldsborough: 'Governor Strong, is it your idea that this proposed legislation is intended as a legislative direction to the Federal Reserve Board to control the normal operations of the law of supply and demand as it affects any particular commodity?'

"Governor Strong: 'By implication I think it would be so interpreted.'

"Mr. Goldsborough: 'You think so?'

"Governor Strong: 'Yes.' " [38]

But presently Governor Strong withdrew this statement:

". . . I do not think that would necessarily be read into the act; no. In a general way, I think the possible interpretation of the amendment would be by farmers who are not students of economics, that this is a way of fixing up their troubles, and that now this matter of price adjustments is in the hands of the Federal Reserve System." [39]

The question whether the Federal Reserve System had consciously stabilized the price level under Governor Strong, has been a much disputed one. The opponents of stabilization usually held and declared that this stability had just happened—in spite of much evidence to the contrary. Governor Strong's viewpoint appeared in the following discussion:

"Mr. Williamson: 'Do you think that the Federal Reserve Board could, as a matter of fact, stabilize the price level to a greater extent than they have in the past by giving greater expansion to market operations and restriction or extension of credit facilities?'

"Governor Strong: 'I personally think that the administration of the Federal Reserve System since the reaction of 1921 has been just as nearly directed as reasonable human wisdom could direct it toward that very object.'

"Mr. Williamson: 'Of course, there has always been a very material stabilization of price level since that time, and do you think

[38] *Ibid.,* p. 304.
[39] *Ibid.,* p. 305.

the Federal Reserve Board has been a considerable factor in accomplishing that end?'

"*Governor Strong:* 'I think they have made their contribution
in the administration of credit with some success.' " [40]

Governor Strong admitted that the system had a reasonable
control over the volume and cost of credit. But in case there
should be a gradual decline in prices, and if then business were
unwilling to borrow, he doubted whether the system could do
anything to raise the price level by forcing business men to use
more credit. He believed that a declaration favoring the return
of all former gold-standard countries to gold might be incorporated into the Federal Reserve Act, and in his opinion this
would be more conducive to stabilization than the proposed
bill.[41] Towards the end of his long statement, however, he appeared to be more reconciled to the idea of having a stabilization
provision in the Federal Reserve Act. He even offered his assistance in revising the present bill so that it might no longer be
objectionable to the Federal Reserve authorities:

"If I could find it possible to frame language which would accomplish the very desirable purpose that you have described, and
which I stated at the first hearing by saying I thoroughly agreed
with, I would not hesitate to do it, and with the approval of my
associates, because I am simply one small element in the system
—one bank—I would not hesitate to do it, and I do not know but
what it may be possible to devise some language. Frankly, I would
avoid the use of the words 'inflation' and 'deflation.' 'Stability' is
a less objectionable word from my point of view. We all want
stability of prices and conditions of all kinds, and I wish I might
be able to write the words. I will try to if you would like to
have me." [42]

Carl Snyder of the New York Federal Reserve Bank, and

[40] *Ibid.,* p. 307.
[41] See also Governor Strong's opinions as mentioned in Chapter 7, Section 2.
[42] *Hearings* on H.R. 7895, *op. cit.,* p. 553.

Ethelbert Stewart, the U.S. Commissioner of Labor Statistics, also appeared at these hearings. Their testimony was mainly intended to inform the members of the Banking and Currency Committee about the nature and use of index numbers. Mr. Snyder, for instance, pointed out that the wholesale commodity index of the Bureau of Labor Statistics was not fully representative of the purchasing power of money, and not practical for the purpose of stabilization. He wanted to have wages specifically included as an important element of the index. Mr. Stewart, on the other hand, said that wages, since they are a part of wholesale prices, are already included, and to add them again would be duplication.

Governor Norris

The testimony of *Governor Norris* of the Federal Reserve Bank of Philadelphia contained several interesting points. He noted the difference between a price and a price level.

"Now, it seems to me that the first question involved in this bill is whether it is desirable that the Federal Reserve System, let us say, or any other agency, should undertake the task of stabilizing prices, and by prices I presume that it is not meant the price of any particular commodity, but the general price level. . . ." [43]

Yet, almost immediately afterwards, he said:

"Prices, be they either of particular commodities or even the price level, are the result, in the first instance, of the constant struggle between the producer for high prices, and the consumer for low prices. In that continuing struggle there are ebbs and flows as various cross currents intervene. . . ."

Mr. Norris illustrated this point of view by the practical example of an individual merchant who cannot be expected to consider more than his particular commodity:

"When the movement of prices is under way, it seems to me

[43] *Ibid.,* p. 381.

that it is always a doubtful and generally a dangerous thing for any outside agency to interfere with and attempt to alter that current. It is to my mind, very much like erecting a dam to stop the flow of the natural current. To give a homely illustration of that, several years ago, when the price of wool was dropping almost out of sight, the largest wool merchant in Philadelphia came into my office and said, in the course of the conversation, that he made his money when wool was going up and when wool was going down he was pretty nearly sure to lose money. 'But,' he said, 'I would not give anybody 5 cents to try to stop this downward movement in the price of wool. I would much rather have it go down as low as it wants to go, because if it does that, then I know that I can start in to buy and do business with perfect confidence, whereas, if anybody attempts to put a peg in it, I do not know whether the peg will hold or not and I can not deal with the same confidence.' . . .

"I am personally prepared to agree that stabilization of the price level is a desirable thing . . . but when we consider the enormous number of elements that enter into the price of a single commodity or the price index, is it wise, is it safe to undertake to stabilize an existing price level?" [44]

". . . the stabilization of prices is a doubtful, not to say dangerous experiment," [45] Mr. Norris concluded, and suggested that the Department of Commerce, or the Bureau of Labor Statistics be commissioned to take care of the disagreeable task. But he added that the Federal Reserve System should consult the price level, and that it had already prevented violent changes in the price level:

"In stating those conclusions I do not mean to say that the Federal Reserve System cannot or that it ought not—I do not say it ought not give any consideration to the price level, nor do I mean to say it is powerless to affect the price level. If stabilization

[44] *Ibid.*, p. 382.
[45] *Ibid.*, p. 395.

is limited to what I would rather call mitigating or minimizing price movements, so as to make the movements slower and to cut off the peaks and smooth out the extreme hollows, then I will go along with the proponents of this or any other bill and say that I think that not only can be done, but it has been done for the last three years." [46]

Dr. Miller

Dr. Adolph C. Miller,[47] who had been a member of the Federal Reserve Board since its establishment, acted as the unofficial spokesman of the Board during these hearings. Like Governor Strong, he made extended statements touching upon almost every phase of the System's activities. He explained, among other things, that the price level alone was considered inadequate as a guide to the System's credit policy, and that the checking of other data was equally important, if not even more so. In this connection he referred to the report of the Federal Reserve Board for 1923, in which the development of a new technique of statistical measurement and procedure was announced, which the Board hoped would make its decisions more reliable than if guided only by the price level.[48]

But Dr. Miller also clearly indicated that the very composition of the Board was a serious handicap to efficient action, and that whatever decisions were made, were not necessarily the best that could have been made at the moment:

"Neither the Federal Reserve Board nor the Federal Reserve banks are composed of men who are economists or financial statesmen in the sense that they have had much training that qualifies them to develop systematically and long in advance of an actual urgent situation methods of dealing with it. For the most part, what is done, is done because some one feels uncomfortable

[46] *Hearings* on H.R. 7895, *op. cit.*, p. 395.
[47] See also his statements in Chapter 7, Section 2.
[48] See also Chapter 7, Section 3.

about what is transpiring and what he thinks may develop." [49]

Regarding his own part, he later indicated that he did not expect to do better than his colleagues, if the stabilization provision should become law:

". . . Candidly, I do not know just how I would proceed if I undertook, in the event this bill became law, to try to meet what this amendment to the act might seem to contemplate. I think the disposition of a good many in the Federal Reserve would be to get out or else to try something different from what has been done. . . . I think we should construe it—I at least should construe it, particularly after what I have said in the course of these hearings—as implying that Congress did not have much faith in the procedure we have been setting up and trying to make effective in guiding our credit policies." [50]

The development of the succeeding years showed that Dr. Miller's statement was prophetic. But at that time Congress, as well as Dr. Miller, were under the impression that the Federal Reserve System would function best if it had the widest possible discretionary powers, and that it could be expected to develop eventually a satisfactory policy.

"If I were a member of this Committee with the knowledge I have of the internal workings of the Federal Reserve System, of its capacity and limitations, I should be very chary myself of changing the laws; certainly in this particular. I think we have given in practice to the conveniently vague phrase (of the Federal Reserve Act) 'accommodating commerce and business' a meaning, a content, that is about as good a promise as can be had that the Federal Reserve System will be operated so as to conduce to economic stability. What you want after all is a result and not a formula, and if you find that a Government agency is in process of working out a procedure that holds a fair prospect of obtaining

[49] *Hearings* on H.R. 7895, *op. cit.*, p. 647.
[50] *Ibid.*, p. 835.

the result I should say you are much more likely to get that result in a high degree if you let that process go on, than if you try to impose a formula that does not carry with it a self-interpreting or self-operating system of procedure, or, even though it might lead eventually to the establishment of such procedure, might in the interim defeat the purpose you are after. . . ." [51]

The statements of *Mr. W. W. Stewart,* formerly the Statistician of the Federal Reserve Board in Washington, and afterward adviser to the Bank of England, and of *Mr. W. R. Burgess,* then the Assistant Federal Reserve Agent of the New York Federal Reserve Bank, in general supported Governor Strong's and Dr. Miller's statements.

Professor Commons' Summary

Professor John R. Commons had been called to Washington by Congressman Strong. His concluding statement summarized the claims that had been made for and against the bill. He had made a detailed study to demonstrate that the Federal Reserve had learned by actual experience to use its powers for the stabilization of the price level. These powers he identified as the control over the rediscount rate; open-market operations; and the power of "moral suasion" which the Federal Reserve Board exerts over the member banks.

Commons also expressed his belief that America by reason of its being the world's chief creditor, and its possessing such a large hoard of gold, already largely controlled the world price level.

Professor Commons remained in Washington for five months to help Congressman Strong in re-drafting the bill which was to be re-introduced in the next session of Congress. Governor Strong also helped, as he had offered to do when testifying. The final draft of the bill was made by the two Strongs at Atlantic City

[51] *Ibid.,* p. 836.

where Congressman Strong visited Governor Strong who was ill. Governor Strong reserved official approval of this final draft in order first to confer with his associates. As soon as he was able to come to Washington, he conferred with the Federal Reserve Board in company of Congressman Strong and Professor Commons. The Board disapproved of the bill and Governor Strong felt bound by their action.

This account of the facts concerning Governor Strong's attitude may help clear away the obscurity which has enveloped the controversy on this subject. Professor Commons writes of Governor Strong, "I admired him both for his open-minded help to us on the bill and his reservation that he must go along with his associates."

Section 5. Second Strong Bill Hearings (1928)

The Second Strong Bill

Hearings on the second Strong Bill [52] began on March 19, 1928 and lasted to May 29, 1928. The revised bill added four distinct purposes to the Federal Reserve Act: 1) stabilization; 2) cooperation between the Federal Reserve and foreign banks of issue; 3) publicity with regard to changes in policy; 4) investigation as to how its present methods of credit regulation could be improved.

The new bill read in part as follows:

"(h) The Federal Reserve System shall use all the powers and authority now or hereafter possessed by it to maintain a stable gold standard; to promote the stability of commerce, industry, agriculture and employment; and a more stable purchasing power of the dollar, so far as such purposes may be accomplished by monetary and credit policy. Relations and transactions with foreign banks shall not be inconsistent with the purposes expressed in this amendment.

"(i) Whenever any decision as to policies is made or whenever

[52] H.R. 11806 (70th Congress, 1st Session).

any action is taken by the Federal Reserve System tending to affect the aforesaid purposes of this amendment, such decision or action and reasons therefor shall be thereafter published by the governor of the Federal Reserve Board at such time, place, and in such detail as may be deemed by him to be most effective in furthering such purposes, and at least once each year in the Annual Report of the Federal Reserve Board to the Congress.

"Sec. 28 A. The Federal Reserve Board and the Federal Reserve banks are hereby authorized and directed to make and to continue investigations and studies for the guidance of the system's policies . . . namely

"1) Of the manner and extent to which operations of the Federal Reserve System affect, a) the volume of credit and currency, b) the purchasing power of the dollar, c) the general level of commodity prices and of other relevant prices, d) the prices of stocks and bonds, and e) business activity; through changes of rates of discount, purchases and sales of securities in the open market, relation and transactions with other banks of issue, or through any other means."

2) Of the various influences not under control of the Federal Reserve System.

"3) Of the effect upon the purchasing power of the dollar of changes in the supply of and demand for gold, either actual or prospective.

"4) Of existing means and proposed plans, both national and international, having for their aim the stabilization of agriculture, industry, commerce, employment, and the purchasing power of money.

"5) Of existing or proposed index numbers of prices or other measures of the purchasing power of money, which are used or might be used, singly or in combination, by the Federal Reserve System as a guide in executing its policies.

"Sec. 28 B. The Federal Reserve Board shall report to the Congress from time to time, and at least annually, the methods pursued and the conclusions reached, either final or otherwise, resulting from the aforesaid investigations and any legislation which will, in its judgment, best promote the purposes of this amendment to the Federal Reserve Act."

Congressman Strong, in introducing this bill, explained that he and Professor Commons had had many conferences not only with Governor Strong, but also with members of the Federal Reserve Board. He also stated that a general questionnaire had been sent to the members of the Federal Reserve Board who were to appear as witnesses at subsequent hearings.

Mr. Young, the Governor of the Federal Reserve Board was present on this occasion, and mentioned that the Board wanted to be represented by Dr. Goldenweiser, Dr. Miller, and Mr. Wyatt. Asked by Mr. Wingo, whether the Board approved this bill, Governor Young answered:

"No; the Board is opposed to the Bill." [53]

Governor Strong was the first witness to be heard. In view of what Governor Young had just said, he made it clear that he had no authority to speak either for the Federal Reserve System, nor for his Bank, but that he merely would state his own personal opinion. Summarizing what he had said at the previous hearings, he declared:

"I do not believe and I have never believed, that any method of fixing the general level of commodity prices can be devised which would enable a monetary and credit policy by a bank of issue to accomplish that object. That is, the theory that the volume of credit and money in circulation alone controls the price level, I think is not altogether to be accepted. There are other theories of price changes which obviously can not be dealt with by legislation at all." [54]

He further pointed out that he was not so certain whether the public would not still be under the impression that the Federal Reserve System was in fact able to maintain a stable price level,

[53] *Hearings* before the Committee on Banking and Currency, House of Representatives, 70th Congress, 1st Session on H.R. 11806 (superseding H.R. 7895— 69th Congress), p. 11. Italics mine.
[54] *Ibid.*, p. 12.

which, he held, could not be accomplished by monetary policy alone. He repeated, what he had said in the previous hearings, that the "scientific application of the well-known principles of the gold standard" would be a better way of bringing about a stable price level, than this bill.

Governor Strong felt that the publicity clause was good. He said:

"The language employed which seems to me conservative, makes feasible a procedure under which I feel much good can be accomplished in educating the public and the Congress as to why the Federal Reserve System undertakes certain policies, and at the same time escapes the danger of publicity in advance of, or simultaneous with, the adoption of policies." [55]

Governor Strong also believed that the purpose of the bill could be accomplished by the Federal Reserve System, provided the System were properly managed and provided the international gold standard were restored:

"Now, I think it is only fair—and I am trying to give a judicial opinion, if that is possible on such a matter—to say this: That I very firmly believe that everything sought to be accomplished by this amendment to the Federal reserve act can be accomplished, and, in fact will be accomplished, provided you have two things. First, good management in the System, honest, intelligent management; and, second, a general restoration of the full gold standard in the world. . . . I mean the full and free payment of gold in redemption of notes circulated in the nations." [56]

This was Governor Strong's last public appearance.[57] He died in the Fall of 1928.

[55] *Ibid.*, pp. 13–14.
[56] *Ibid.*, p. 17.
[57] For additional statements by Governor Strong see Chapter 7, Section 2.

Dr. Goldenweiser's Testimony

Dr. E. A. Goldenweiser, the Director of Research and Statistics of the Federal Reserve Board followed Governor Strong as a witness. Some of the important points he brought out in his testimony may be summarized as follows:

Only the short-term fluctuations in the price level are felt by the public, and not the long trends. It would be difficult, however, to determine what type of trend is developing at any given moment.[58]

If prices were declining at a time when bank credit was growing rapidly and when money rates were so low that the decline of prices could not be imputed to a shortage of credit, the Federal Reserve System could do nothing to stop this decline. "I think that you cannot make people use credit when they do not wish to, and that the price of credit determines the volume only at certain times."[59]

An uncontrollable decline in prices might be due to increased efficiency of production:

". . . the price index could go down entirely as the result of the increased efficiency and economy of production and distribution, and could be reflected in larger consumption rather than in compensating rise in some other price."[60]

On the other hand, he did think that an aggressive inflation could be arrested by the System.

Dr. Goldenweiser did not draw any sharp distinction between the general price level and individual prices or the prices of groups of commodities:

"The advance in price in one group of commodities makes a larger group of individuals go into that particular industry, with the consequence that there is a boom in it and ultimately the

[58] *Hearings* on H.R. 11806, *op. cit.*, p. 32.
[59] *Ibid.*, p. 37.
[60] *Ibid.*, p. 44.

prices decline somewhat; and the low price of another commodity makes industry move out of the production of that commodity, with the consequence that there ultimately is a shortage and a rise in that price. In other words, price movements are to a certain extent business stabilizers, and price stability and business stability are in that sense not entirely consistent." [61]

Thus the "price stability" which Dr Goldenweiser referred to (and found objectionable), would mean stability in the relation of one commodity, or of one group of commodities to others, an effect not involved in price *level* stabilization. Such an effect could be produced only if we could successfully interfere with the law of supply and demand as affecting separate commodities; and interference with the law of supply and demand was condemned, both by Dr. Goldenweiser and the advocates of stabilization.

Dr. Miller's attitude was very different. He would guard the particular prices as related to each other but seemed to disregard the general price level. He said:

"The important thing from the point of view of good functioning of the economic system either of this country or of the world is that there shall be stability in the price structure, *in the relationships of prices to one another*. Whether the average of prices goes up or goes down is of little consequence to the good functioning of an economic structure and the maintenance of economic stability. That is something that concerns long-term creditor and debtor." [62]

Dr. Goldenweiser wanted it clearly understood, however, that the price level was one of the indicators of business conditions:

"I think nothing that I have said was intended to mean that the price index is no good. I merely want to point out its limita-

---

[61] *Ibid.*, p. 45.
[62] *Hearings* before the Committee on Banking and Currency, U.S. Senate, 72nd Congress, 1st Session on H.R. 11499 and S. 4429, May 18, 1932, p. 243. Italics mine.

tions at times as sole guide to credit policy or as the determining guide of credit policy." [63]

His objection to the stabilization provision was that it would not work when applied to slight fluctuations—it could influence only those violent changes which occur rarely.

"The only objection I have to writing that into the law" he said, "is that I feel the powers of the system in the matter are applicable only at times when the rise or decline is extremely violent. That is the only time when the system could be pretty certain to exert an influence, and those times occur rarely. The fluctuations in prices ordinarily are very much milder and are not directly influenced." [64]

Professor John R. Commons then made an extended and carefully prepared statement, in which he showed that, in spite of the opinions of Dr. Goldenweiser and Mr. Stewart, the Federal Reserve System had actually influenced the price level by wise action, and kept it somewhat stable. He denounced the gold standard as being deflationary in its ultimate consequences, and then attacked Dr. Goldenweiser's statement that prices might fall as a consequence of increased efficiency. Such fall in prices Mr. Commons held to be unnecessary and preventable:

"It is the argument of the Federal Reserve Bulletin" he said, "that with an increase in efficiency prices will fall, and they put that forth as a justification for the fall of prices since 1925 of about 10 per cent. They make an estimate that the increased efficiency of man power in this country owing to machinery and the rapidity of communication and so on, has increased output 10 per cent, just about equal to the fall in prices.

"The question then arises, Is a fall of prices necessary along with increased efficiency? I say no; because you have to take into

[63] *Hearings* on H.R. 11806, *op. cit.*, p. 45.
[64] *Ibid.*, p. 47.

account that on one side is money and credit, and on the other side is the output of this increased efficiency. Now, if money and credit keep up relatively to the output, there is no reason why prices should fall on account of increased efficiency." [65]

Dr. Miller's Opposition

Dr. Miller testified again. He expressed himself in favor of the investigations which this bill contemplated, but unlike Governor Strong, he did not approve of the provision for publicity. Also he objected to the stabilization provision (paragraph h), because he found such legislation premature. He expressed this opposition in the following words:

"I think legislation of the character contemplated in paragraph (h) is inadvisable. When I say that, I am putting it more mildly than I feel it. I would say that it is perhaps objectionable, and mainly objectionable because it is premature and not founded on any solid basis. . . ." [66]

His main reason for this objection to stabilization was the expected restoration of the international gold standard which he felt would eliminate the need for legislation regarding credit control.

". . . we are very close in the Western world to a position where the beneficial results of the gold standard as a kind of banking and credit regulator in gold standard countries are likely to be realized. My position, therefore, is to wait and see what the results of the operation of the restored gold standard are before entering upon any such striking innovations in reserve banking as contemplated in paragraph (h) of this bill." [67]

When asked what there was injurious in this paragraph (h), and how it could harm the Federal Reserve System, Dr. Miller answered:

[65] *Ibid.*, p. 81.
[66] *Ibid.*, p. 105.
[67] *Ibid.*, p. 107.

"Let me say first and foremost that it uses language that really means nothing definite or tangible.

". . . In other words, the whole conception of paragraph (h) is built upon the theory that whatever controls credit in the United States—and it assumes that such control of credit resides in the Federal Reserve System—has it within its power to do what?—to stabilize commerce, industry, agriculture and employment as well as prices and the gold standard. The theory is untenable; the thing can not be done. Let me say it right here—and let me say it dogmatically in order to be brief—that I think the whole of this paragraph (h) proceeds on two assumptions; and I use the word 'assumptions' advisedly. One of those assumptions is that changes in the level of prices are caused by changes in the volume of credit and currency; the other is that changes in the volume of credit and currency are caused by Federal Reserve policy. Neither of these assumptions is true to the facts or the realities. They are both in some degree figments—figments of scholastic invention—that have never found any substantial foundation in economic reality, and less to-day in the United States than in other times. . . ." [68]

". . . The proposal contained in paragraph (h) of this bill rests on no secure economic foundation. It must be regarded as a notion, an academic proposal." [69]

But Dr. Miller thought the advocates of stabilization used "vague" and "magnificent phrases" which were of no practical value in determining the policy of the Federal Reserve System:

"I don't think," he said, "they are proceeding in the right way. If they did I should be for this bill. To be frank—but I hope not offensive—these phrases in paragraph (h) are very magnificent phrases. They will do in oratory, they are suitable in Chamber of Commerce resolutions, etc. but they are vague and do not translate

[68] *Ibid.*, p. 109.
[69] *Ibid.*, p. 111.

themselves into a thing sufficiently concrete for handling the problems of credit administration. . . ." [69a]

Perhaps a part of Dr. Miller's opposition had to do with the fact that Governor Strong had helped to draft the bill. At any rate, there was much friction between the New York Bank and the Board.[70] Dr. Miller seemed to have this in mind when he said:

"I venture to say that some of the men you have consulted do not know what it is all about. These are high sounding and captivating words you are using for your proposed amendment.

"I do not question that you may have gotten the impression that this or that group of officers of the Federal Reserve Board or of the Federal Reserve System may agree with you, and I do not say that these men are not able, very able men, but on this particular subject I do not know that they understand just what they are about. . . ." [71]

Dr. Miller, however, did seem to think that Federal Reserve policies could be made to influence the stock market. The System was of the opinion that some of the credit it had created was apparently leaking into the speculative field. To find a way of preventing such leakage he held to be the most important problem confronting the Board at that moment.

"I wish to avail myself of this opportunity to say that when that 'something' is done, you will find me very much more sympathetically inclined toward your major proposal. . . . I should say, then, hold off, until it is demonstrated that the Federal Reserve has found a way." [72]

This was the second instance in which Dr. Miller advised waiting for the outcome of other movements.[73] Yet in 1932, when both the gold standard and the stock market problems were no longer

[69a] *Ibid.*, p. 114.
[70] See also Chapter 8, Section 4.
[71] *Hearings* on H.R. 11806, *op. cit.*, pp. 213–214.
[72] *Ibid.*, p. 363.
[73] The first was with regard to the gold standard.

in the foreground, Dr. Miller was even less sympathetic towards stabilization than before.

Supporting Testimony

Mr. Henry A. Wallace again testified in the interest of the farmers. He declared that they were fearful of deflation; that they had a great debt to carry and that a declining price level would increase the burden of this debt. The farmers were also distrustful of the monetary administration. It was in the hands of men who, they thought, might not object to deflating the currency gradually, over an extended period, back to the pre-war price level.[74]

Mr. Andrew Shearer, representing several influential farm organizations, testified to the same effect:

"Our fear is for deflation and consequent price reduction, and I want to repeat what Mr. Wallace said, in a little different way, that our business of farming is a long-time business. . . . We are very much interested in stability. All we are asking is stability, a stable price level so that we may know when we engage in stock raising that at the end of four or five years, when those cattle are fattened and ready to go on the market, we will not be ruined by a sudden fall in the general level." [75]

Professor O. M. W. Sprague, although he was less dissatisfied with the present bill, than with its predecessor, nevertheless feared that the public was not yet sufficiently interested in stabilization, and also that such stabilization was impossible as long as the officials of the Federal Reserve System were hostile to it.

"In the first place" he said, "the business community is not as yet converted to the proposition. . . . I am not sure but there should be some years of further successful missionary work before it would be advisable to amend the Federal Reserve act along the lines suggested by this measure.

[74] *Hearings* on H.R. 11806, *op. cit.,* pp. 193 ff.
[75] *Ibid.,* p. 204.

"In the second place I am impressed by the conspicuous lack of belief in this measure on the part of those entrusted with the management of the Federal Reserve System. . . . When . . . you come to a provision directing the promotion of a stable value of the dollar, you are requiring the management of the Reserve banks to do something that cannot be done except by the exercise of judgment in a succession of situations." [76]

In Dr. Sprague's opinion, the measure would not inconvenience the Federal Reserve. He also thought that the powers of the system were already sufficient to effect what the bill intended. But he agreed that there would be a definite advantage if, as a consequence of the bill, the Federal Reserve should adjust its policy more quickly to the needs of the community. His objections were directed to the propaganda for effecting the passage of the bill, because it might arouse false expectations in the public.

Professor Gustav Cassel of Sweden also appeared before the Committee to testify in favor of the bill. Among other things he said:

"I want to emphasize that the Federal Reserve System has no other function than to give the country a stable money." [77] Asked whether non-monetary causes did not also affect the price level, he answered: "No; the general level of prices is exclusively a monetary question." In Cassel's opinion the Federal Reserve had all the powers necessary to maintain a stable value of money. "How can they keep the gold standard," he asked, "if they do not keep the purchasing power of the dollar exactly like the purchasing power of the weight of gold comprised within the dollar?" From this he concluded that they might as well keep the purchasing power of the dollar stable, which would stabilize the value of gold.

Mr. Charles S. Hamlin, another member of the Federal Reserve

[76] *Ibid.,* p. 130.
[77] *Ibid.,* pp. 382 ff.

Board, was one of the last witnesses to be heard. He did not approve of the bill as it stood, and he had therefore prepared a substitute for paragraph (h) which read as follows:

"The Federal Reserve System shall use all the powers and authority now or hereafter possessed by it to maintain a stable gold standard and shall furnish credit facilities commensurate with the requirements of credit stability, of agriculture, industry employment, and of the purchasing power of the dollar, so far as such purposes can be accomplished by monetary and credit policy. To this end the Federal Reserve System is authorized to enter into relations with foreign central banks not inconsistent with the purposes of this amendment." [78]

Mr. Hamlin explained that he had prepared this substitute in order that the price level might decrease slightly to match the increase in efficiency of production, so long as there was such increase in efficiency, and stability was maintained.

Mr. Hamlin's statement seems to have been the only instance in which a member of the Federal Reserve Board testified in favor of stabilization, and also furnished a constructive proposal of his own. Although he specifically stated that he was speaking only in a private capacity, he nevertheless gave his opinion in spite of Dr. Miller's apparent belief that those members of the Federal Reserve System who seemed to be in favor of the bill did not "understand what they are about."

The Strong Bill, however, was not reported out of the Banking and Currency Committee.

LEGISLATIVE EFFORTS DURING 1931–1932

A glance through the Congressional Record shows plainly how the demand for a stable dollar grew with the intensity of the depression:

[78] *Ibid.*, p. 393.

On December 8, 1931, *Mr. Burtness* of North Dakota re-introduced his [79] "Bill to stabilize the Buying Power of Money," and also his [80] "Bill to raise the commodity price level to the debt-incurring stage and to stabilize it thereafter."

On the same day *Mr. Ramseyer* of Iowa introduced his [81] "Bill to restore and maintain the level of wholesale prices" which intended to direct the Federal Reserve System to use all its powers for restoring the general price level of 1926, and then stabilize it at that basis.

On December 9, 1931, *Mr. Goldsborough* introduced his [82] "Bill to stabilize the purchasing power of money" and on January 15, 1932, his [83] "Bill to stabilize the purchasing power of money" and on January 19, 1932, his [84] "Bill for increasing and stabilizing the price level of commodities."

On January 22, 1932, *Mr. Keller* of Illinois presented his [85] "Bill to amend the Federal Reserve Act, to stabilize the average whole-sale prices of commodities at the average level of the year 1926, thereby to correct the price decline suffered since September 1928, to promote economic justice, to steady industry, agriculture, commerce and employment, and for other purposes." [86]

On April 14, 1932, *Mr. Burtness* addressed the House of Representatives on the stabilization problem. On April 21, 1932, an address of Mr. Clarence Poe, editor of the "Progressive Farmer Ruralist" on "Honest Money" was reprinted in the Congressional Record through the efforts of *Senator Bailey* of North Carolina. On May 5, 1932, *Senator Howell* of Nebraska addressed the Senate on stabilization and inserted in the Record a number of charts

[79] H.R. 20.
[80] H.R. 21.
[81] H.R. 128.
[82] H.R. 5078.
[83] H.R. 7800.
[84] H.R. 8026.
[85] H.R. 8246.
[86] The complete text of the above bill was reprinted in the Congressional Record of February 18, 1932.

showing the fluctuations of the dollar from 1891 to 1931, together with statements of economists on stabilization.

From now on stabilization bills, provided not simply for the *maintenance* of the price level, but also for *reflation,*—the correction of the recent severe fall in that level.

CHAPTER VI

LEGISLATIVE STAGE (1932–1934)

SECTION 1. GOLDSBOROUGH BILL HEARINGS (1932)

The Bill

FROM March 16, 1932 until April 14, 1932 hearings were held before a subcommittee of the Committee on Banking and Currency of the House, on the Goldsborough bill of 1932. Mr. Goldsborough himself was Chairman of the Subcommittee. The bill charged the Federal Reserve System with the duty of reflating wholesale commodity prices "to the level existing before the existing deflation," and stabilizing at that level. To the stabilization powers already at the disposal of the Federal Reserve Board, the bill added the power to raise or lower the price of gold when necessary. The bill read as follows:[1]

"A Bill for increasing and stabilizing the price level of commodities and for other purposes.

"Be it enacted. . . . That the Federal reserve act is amended by adding at the end thereof a new section to read as follows:

"Sec. 31. The Federal Reserve Board and the Federal reserve banks are hereby authorized and directed to take all available steps to raise the present deflated wholesale commodity level of prices as speedily as possible to the level existing before the present deflation, and afterwards to use all available means to maintain such wholesale commodity level of prices.

"Sec. 2. If, in carrying out the purposes of the preceeding

---

[1] H.R. 10517 (72nd Congress, 1st Session).

section, the Federal Reserve Board and/or the Federal reserve banks, in selling securities, should exhaust the supply, the Federal Reserve Board is authorized and directed to issue new debentures. "Sec. 3. If, in carrying out the purposes of section 1, the gold reserve is deemed by the Federal Reserve Board to be too near to the prescribed minimum the board is authorized to raise the official price of gold if the other methods already authorized appear inadequate; if, on the other hand, the gold reserve ratio is deemed to be too high the Federal Reserve Board is authorized to lower the official price of gold if the other methods already authorized appear inadequate."

Farmers' Support

The farmers' organizations were almost completely represented at these hearings, and in reading their testimony, one gets an idea of what these severe fluctuations in the price level have meant to the farming population, and what suffering has been caused by the recent severe decline of the general price level.

Mr. Edward A. O'Neal, President of the American Farm Bureau Federation, was the first witness. He cited resolutions adopted by his organization jointly with the two other major Farm organizations, the National Grange, and the Farmers' Union, endorsing reflation and stabilization. He expressed himself in favor of the purposes of the bill. He was, however, somewhat disturbed lest the bill should not go far enough.

Mr. Henry A. Wallace, the next witness, repeated much of what he had said at previous hearings. He thought that a proposal made by *Professor L. D. Edie* might well also be considered for stabilizing the dollar. This proposal, incorporated in a separate bill, was read by *Mr. Charles R. White,* President of the New York State Farm Bureau and Member of the Board of Directors of the American Farm Bureau Federation. Mr. Edie's proposal differed from the Goldsborough bill, in that it would measure out bank credit in proportion to the estimated volume of business. The volume of production and trade, rather than the price level, was to be the test.

". . . the Federal Reserve Board and the Federal Reserve banks shall establish as one of their prime objectives of policy the maintenance of a rate of growth of bank credit approximately equivalent to the average long-term rate of growth of production and trade in the United States." [2]

Mr. White referred particularly to the recent investigations of Professors Warren and Pearson, and introduced a paper which they had prepared about the development of the price level and the effects of price fluctuations.

Mr. C. A. Ewing, of Decatur, Ill., gave his sentiments about the gold standard as follows:

"I feel about this gold standard, Mr. Chairman, a good deal like the man who got a wire announcing that his mother-in-law had passed on to her reward, and which inquired, 'Shall we embalm, cremate or bury?' and he replied, 'Embalm, cremate and bury her; take no chances.' " [3]

Mr. Charles E. Hearst, President of the Iowa Farm Bureau Federation and *Mr. L. J. Taber,* Master of the National Grange expressed their doubts whether the bill would go far enough, and urged the inclusion of every possible provision that would increase its effectiveness.

Mr. John A. Simpson, the late National President of the Farmers' Union, was also of the opinion that the bill might not go far enough; he believed that the remonetization of silver was essential for the reflation of the price level. Mr. Simpson backed his testimony by a dramatic recital of his own experience; how in January, 1920, when he was in Washington on behalf of his organization, he went to see John Skelton Williams, the Comptroller of the Currency and asked him when deflation would begin. Mr.

Williams told him "in May"; so he went back home and warned the members of his organization and wrote an article about it in his paper. A week later, he sold all of his possessions, cattle, live-stock, and everything else he owned. Six months later he could not have gotten one-fourth of the prices he had realized. And since then, he said, he had kept his cash, and still had it, because he had no confidence in any of the measures Congress had passed since that time.

Other Supporting Testimony

Ex-Senator Robert L. Owen capped Mr. Simpson's experience with his own story of how the 1920 deflation was started. He told of his first efforts to have stabilization made part of the Federal Reserve Act, back in 1913,[4] and expressed himself in favor of the present bill, which he regarded as one of the most important legislative efforts to end the depression.

The last of the farmers' representatives was *Mr. C. C. Talbot,* President of the Farmers' Union of North Dakota, who also testified in favor of the measure.

Professor Willford I. King was the first economist to be heard. He gave a very detailed description of the present situation, particularly with respect to the increase in the debt burden, and believed that it was high time to replace this "chance standard of one commodity" by a more scientific system. He thought that the provisions of the bill would be adequate to stabilize the dollar, but he would like to see in it more specific regulations regarding the variations in the price of gold, in order to insure the success of the bill over a long period of time.

His opinion of the officials of the Federal Reserve System was that they were bankers who looked at the problem from a banking standpoint. While they wanted credit conditions sound he said,

[4] See Chapter 5, Section 2.

they would not admit that stabilization was one of their functions. He said:

". . . my feeling is that bankers are very expert in their line, and they think, because they deal in money, that it has to do with the monetary needs of the country. I really think there is no more connection necessary between being a good banker and being a good money economist, and being a good shoe maker and being a good monetary economist. I think these things are not related.

"These men [meaning the Federal Reserve officials] are experts in banking, but they are not interested in monetary economics; but the monetary system of the country has turned over to them something that they are not interested in, and it ought to be put in the hands of monetary economists, or else they ought to be instructed to do something in the way of learning something about it. They have plenty of good men, and they can learn about it." [5]

Mr. Alvin T. Simonds,[6] President of the Simonds Saw and Steel Co., also testified. He called attention to the vague test by which the bill proposed to determine the price level, "before the depression," and suggested that the 1926 level be specifically mentioned if that was what was meant. He also thought that the regulation of the price of gold should be more clearly provided for.

Mr. Ethelbert Stewart of the Bureau of Labor Statistics gave the reasons which had caused his Bureau to adopt the 1926 price level as = 100. He said that the economic life of the country had become so well adjusted to that price level that unless this level were restored, a large part of the population would remain economically ruined.[7]

Mr. Malcolm C. Rorty, the next witness, agreed with the purposes of the bill but contended that a mere mandate to the Federal Reserve Board to reflate would not enable them to carry out such

[5] Hearings on H.R. 10517, op. cit., p. 202.
[6] See also Chapter 4, Section 1.
[7] Hearings on H.R. 10517, op. cit., pp. 262 ff.

reflation. In order to facilitate reflation, he suggested that a subsidy be offered to contractors amounting to from 10% to 15% of the work to be done. In that manner he would expend five billion dollars, which should produce fifty billion dollars' worth of new work. Thus the subsidy would work out as the cheapest possible form of relief.[8]

Mr. W. C. Hushing, the legislative representative of the American Federation of Labor, said that his organization was in favor of the stabilization of the price level.[9]

The present writer [10] also made an extended statement in favor of the bill. He maintained that the reason why the Federal Reserve had failed in preserving to date the stable price level which had prevailed in 1922–1929 was that they had no mandate from Congress to do it.

He submitted a detailed and elaborate outline for a complete stabilization bill dividing the proposed legislation into three sections, namely a) legislation of immediate urgency; b) provisions for enabling the Federal Reserve System to stabilize, independently, if need be, of member or other banks; c) provisions for bringing about fuller cooperation among banks and for a unified banking system. He also mentioned bank deposit insurance as another possible improvement on the banking system.

He would not agree to the substitution of a production index as proposed by Professor Edie for the price index. Instead he suggested that the authorities be permitted to use whatever statistics they deemed best in order to arrive at a stable level of wholesale commodity prices. Among these would be the same figures for the volume of trade and production.

He also expressed the thought that if the Federal Reserve System did not want to take over this new responsibility, another body would have to be established to carry out the provisions of the bill.

[8] *Ibid.,* pp. 307 ff.
[9] *Ibid.,* p. 323.
[10] *Ibid.,* pp. 333 ff.

A number of Congressmen, some of whom had introduced stabilization bills of their own, also testified in favor of the Goldsborough bill. *Mr. Burtness* of North Dakota expressed the belief that the responsibility for carrying out stabilization should not rest with the Federal Reserve Board but with an independent Government Bureau, established for that purpose, and responsible directly to Congress and the country.[11]

Mr. Ramseyer of Iowa reported that recently a meeting had been held in the Caucus room of the House Office Building, called by the Congressmen who had introduced stabilization bills. About 100 members of the House had attended this meeting. To his mind, the proposed measure was not just another temporary relief measure, but fundamental legislation which was inevitable if the present economic order was to be maintained.

". . . this problem," he said, "is in a class by itself; and the other issues that are before the country and before Congress do not compare at all in importance with this issue here. The other relief measures, unless we have stability in the commodity price level . . . will prove to be partial and temporary. This is something of a permanent nature, and it has simply got to come, if we are to survive as a people." [12]

Mr. Selvig of Minnesota expressed himself in similar terms:

"The bills now under consideration by the members of your committee are the first before the present Congress that strike at the heart of the economic problems before us. The other bills that we have passed, were mere palliatives and nothing else." [13]

Mr. George H. Shibley was the last witness to testify in favor of the bill, and he condemned the Hoover administration for not having made any determined effort to stop deflation.

[11] *Ibid.*, pp. 296 ff.
[12] *Ibid.*, p. 424.
[13] *Ibid.*, p. 427.

Federal Reserve Opposition

In opposition to the bill, *Governor Harrison* of the Federal Reserve Bank of New York was the first witness. Mr. Goldsborough had said, that if the Federal Reserve system was going to buy Government securities (as announced) at the rate of twenty-five million a day, the price level would rise, partly by reason of the psychological effect in restoring confidence, and particularly, because credit would become so much easier. Mr. Harrison disagreed. He believed that any number of events could defeat the purpose of such action: Foreign investors might lose confidence and withdraw their deposits; there might be a revival of fear, leading to hoarding and runs upon banks; there might be a rush for goods by speculators who would sell again as soon as the price level was half-way up, thus helping to depress it again.

Yet, as Mr. Harrison explained, the Federal Reserve System was already making efforts to expand credit, only business was disinclined to borrow as there were few buyers.

The members of the Subcommittee charged the Federal Reserve with lack of confidence in its own powers. So long as they kept repeating, "we do not know what we are going to do," the country would naturally have no confidence. But a definite announcement of the Board's intention to reflate could restore confidence. To this Mr. Harrison retorted that it was a matter of record that, as soon as there was even a mention of America's intention to raise its price level, there was an international raid on the dollar, that is, an effort to get gold in order to speculate for a rise in its price.

Although he was very sympathetic with the attempt to raise the American price level, Mr. Harrison was not sure whether the Reserve System could accomplish reflation, and consequently did not want to have the responsibility for reflation imposed upon the System, nor the impression to go abroad that the System was able to do what the bill demanded.

"I just wonder whether it is wise to let the country think that, through the use of the Federal Reserve machinery, it is possible to do a thing that is influenced by so many other factors than credit alone. I do not mean, however, that we should not, in these circumstances, use our powers, so far as we have got them, to influence the volume of credit, hoping that it, in turn, will influence the price levels. I believe it will have some effect. Now, how far that may be offset by other factors, no man is wise enough to tell." [14]

When his attention was called to the fact that the bill also provided for a variable price of gold, Mr. Harrison indicated that he was opposed to such action:

"I am afraid" he said, ". . . that while I will go a long way with you in your efforts to influence prices through appropriate action of the Reserve System relating to the price and volume of credit, I think I would not agree at all in the wisdom of a law which provided for a varying gold content in the dollar. I think the dangers of that are immeasurable, and any law which provides for a change in that content may work untold injuries, not only upon us domestically, but in our foreign trade as well." [15]

Mr. Harrison was also of opinion that the Federal Reserve System was already doing all it could, and that the passage of the bill would not change any of its proceedings. "Let us reduce it to a practical case. I do not see what we could or should be doing differently from what we are doing to-day, even if you should pass this bill. I am looking for light and help." [16]

Mr. Eugene Meyer, the Governor of the Federal Reserve Board, who was the next witness, expressed himself very strongly in favor of a "unified banking system" which he thought would be of the first importance in bringing about a more efficient control of credit. With regard to the bill under consideration, he believed its purposes were impossible of accomplishment, mainly be-

[14] *Ibid.,* p. 483.
[15] *Ibid.,* p. 496.
[16] *Ibid.,* p. 498.

cause the procedures required by it were matters of judgment.
". . . You cannot accomplish it by law because it is a matter of
judgment. You cannot supply judgment by law." [17] He also said:

"If it were possible to take your resolution and put it into effect
and accomplish the result you have in mind—I would like to say
absolutely this is the thing for you to do and I will do my best to
help to carry out every purpose, or if I cannot somebody else
should be put in my place who can. But this bill contemplates, it
seems to me, that a small group of men will understand things in
the future that men nowhere understood within the last 10 years."

Mr. Meyer expressed ideas about business fluctuations which
disregarded any relationship to monetary fluctuations:

"An economically youthful country, with a rapidly growing
population, is likely to have periods of extreme activity and
of speculation at the end of it, and reactions and depressions after
that.

"I think that now we are more matured and our population is
more settled and will increase less rapidly, with the restrictions on
immigration, and the reduced birthrate, I think that is one of the
important fundamental factors in the situation." [18]

Asked by a member of the Subcommittee whether the restrictions on immigration and the reduced birthrate would lead to a
stabilization of commodity values, Mr. Meyer answered:

"No, it will not; but I will say this, that those violent movements which are the characteristics of rapid growth, and the inter-
ruption in that growth, on account of overdoing the rate of
growth, economically, in proportion to the fundamental stability
of the country, ought to be now more susceptible of control in the
direction of relative stability."

He was asked whether the index number of commodities would
not be better than gold as a yardstick for measuring the value of

[17] *Ibid.*, p. 530.
[18] *Ibid.*, p. 546.

money and as a basis for the issuance of currency. From his reply
we may gather that he did not consider the question of the monetary standard a fundamental one. He thought that ultimately
monetary fluctuations were caused by the changing moods of the
people.

"Well, I say this to you," he replied, ". . . I am not prepared
to answer that, because I do not feel as though I have any definite
views as to whether or not the commodity base for money is workable and practicable, and I have not been able to figure it out to
its ultimate conclusion. I can see the weakness of one system. I
can see the weakness of the maladjustments in our economic
structure, many of which are attributable to other things than the
gold standard; and I can also say that I can not see where some
weakness would develop under a new system, and I do not believe
you or anybody else can, but a whole lot of these maladjustments
come from neither one standard nor another, but from the
conduct and behavior of people; and sometimes a large number of people, en masse, get optimistic together, and overdo
things; then they get pessimistic and overdo things on the other
side. . . ." [19]

Passage of the Bill in the House

The Goldsborough bill was revised in the Banking and Currency Committee and passed the House of Representatives on
May 2, 1932, by the overwhelming vote of *289 to 60*. In its final
form, which was a simplification of the first draft, it read as
follows:

"An act for restoring and maintaining the purchasing power of
· ·   *the dollar.*

". . . That the Federal Reserve Act is amended by adding at
the end thereof a new section to read as follows:
"Sec. 31. It is hereby declared the policy of the United States

[19] *Ibid.*, p. 550.

that the average purchasing power of the dollar as ascertained by
the Department of Labor in the wholesale commodity markets
for the period covering the years 1921 to 1929 inclusive, shall be
restored and maintained by the control of the volume of credit
and currency.

"Sec. 2. The Federal Reserve Board, the Federal reserve banks
and the Secretary of the Treasury are hereby charged with the
duty of making effective this policy.

"Sec. 3. Acts and parts of acts inconsistent with the terms of
this act are hereby repealed."

This was the first time that any bill embodying the principle of
stabilizing the purchasing power of a monetary unit had passed
any legislative body in the world, although, as we shall see, stabilization, having the force of law had been officially adopted in
Sweden in 1931.

<h3>SECTION 2. FLETCHER BILL HEARINGS (1932)</h3>

Financial Interests Oppose

Senator Fletcher now introduced in the Senate his bill, practically identical with the Goldsborough bill. Hearings were held
on it May 12, 13, and 18, 1932. Before reviewing these hearings, let
us see what reception the passage of the Goldsborough bill had received in financial circles. Stabilization, until then, had been looked
upon to a large extent as a more or less academic proposal. It had
been easily blocked by its opponents. But now such a bill had actually passed the House and by an overwhelming majority. Public
sentiment in favor of stabilization was growing.

As a consequence of the passage of the bill in the House there
was consternation abroad and among the conservative business
men at home who had no understanding of what it was all about.
These facts had produced a slight effect upon the foreign exchange
rates, which was intensified by the Federal Reserve System's new
policy of buying securities in the open market at the rate of one

hundred million dollars a week—a policy which was perhaps a result of the discussions of the Goldsborough bill.

Nevertheless, it could hardly be expected that financial interests and financial writers should be much better acquainted with the stabilization problem than certain officials of the Federal Reserve System who have been quoted; and the stabilization provision of the bill was generally regarded as impossible of fulfillment. Thus an editorial in the "Commercial and Financial Chronicle" of May 7, 1932 even charged the Federal Reserve officials with a part of the blame in supporting the movement for stabilization by the large scale open-market purchases mentioned above:

"It seems useless to argue against follies such as those embodied in the Goldsborough Bill" said the editor, "when our legislators have lost all sense and reason, and the only hope is that the movement can be held under definite control before it is carried too far. We grieve to have to say that the Federal Reserve authorities are chargeable with a portion at least of the blame in inculcating the unsound doctrines which are finding such wide acceptance to-day through the Reserve policy of the large-scale purchases of United States Government securities."

In an editorial of May 21, 1932, the same paper cited a report authorized by the Executive Committee of the New York Merchants' Association. It had been drafted by the Association's Committee on Banking and Currency and amounted to nothing but a sneer, betraying complete misunderstanding of the practical possibility of stabilization:

"Theoretical schemes for stabilization of the price level" said the report, "have been discussed more or less for several years, but have hitherto made no progress in a practical way. To transmute such a theoretical concept into a rigid statutory requirement and to bind our banking system to an arbitrary and quite inflexible price level is so unsound as to be absurd, if it were not potentially so dangerous."

The following words from the same report show how little care the Association's Committee had taken to study the bill and the hearings on it.

"The Goldsborough Bill is essentially in a class with measures to stabilize prices by governmental purchases of uncontrollable surpluses and to help debtors by the destruction of creditors through the issuance of fiat money. Your Committee, therefore, recommends that the Association oppose any and all attempts to impose the statutory duty of maintaining price stability upon our banking system."

Here the ground was prepared for a dramatic battle: Congress, the farmers and a good share of public sentiment were for the measure; some New York bankers and most of the Federal Reserve authorities were against it. Yet, as we shall see, it did not come to a clash.

Supporting Testimony

The Fletcher Bill [20] was identical with the Goldsborough bill except for a small change in Sec. 3.

The members of the House Subcommittee who were present at the Senate hearings agreed to this change. Mr. Goldsborough explained that ever since 1922 the various stabilization measures had had extensive hearings, and that it could therefore not be looked upon as a "mushroom growth of the depression." Congressman Strong and Mr. Busby concurred in Mr. Goldborough's statement.

We need not record the supporting statements made by the various witnesses, most of whom had already appeared before the House Subcommittee. It will be more interesting to consider what finally prevented the bill from passing the Senate.

[20] S. 4429.

Opposition of the Treasury

As a first attack, the Senate Committee received a letter from the Secretary of the Treasury, *Mr. Ogden A. Mills,* which gave the Treasury's opinion of the Fletcher bill and discouraged in the strongest terms its passage by the Senate. The gist of this letter read:

". . . In my opinion it would not be possible for the Government of the United States to carry out such a mandate. Price levels are dependent upon a large number of factors that are beyond the control of the Federal reserve system, the Treasury Department, or any other agency of the Government, and I do not believe that it would be wise to impose upon them a duty and a responsibility which they could not discharge. Such an attempt would tend to undermine the confidence of the people in the various agencies of the Government and the result would be unfortunate.

"In this connection a subcommittee of the Committee on Banking and Currency of the House of Representatives held extensive hearings on the subject matter of a bill having a similar purpose, which has passed the House of Representatives and has been referred to your Committee. During the course of these hearings, Governor Meyer of the Federal Reserve Board and Doctor Goldenweiser, chief of its division of research and statistics, appeared before that committee and testified very fully as to the factors which are beyond the control of legislation of this character, and which would render it ineffective. For your convenience I enclose a copy of the part of these hearings which contains this testimony.

"I may add that the passage by the House of the bill referred to was a disturbing factor both at home and abroad and that the members of the Federal Reserve Board unanimously oppose the enactment of legislation of this character and approve the position taken by Governor Meyer in his testimony on this subject." [21]

[21] *Hearings* before the Committee on Banking and Currency, U.S. Senate, 72nd Congress, 1st session, on H.R. 11499 and S. 4429, p. 101.

Federal Reserve Opposition

When *Governor Meyer* of the Federal Reserve Board appeared to testify, he explained that the Board had passed a resolution, approving and endorsing the position he had taken with regard to the Goldsborough bill. He added that the Board did not possess the stabilization powers which the bill presupposed:

"The proposed bill assumes that the Federal Reserve Board has the power to carry out the policy enunciated in the bill. . . . The attitude which I expressed in the hearing was that the Board did not have this power and that the assumption therefore is not justified. . . ." [22]

Answering Senator Fletcher's remark that "You have the powers, do you not, now, that are conferred by this Goldsborough Bill," Mr. Meyer said:

"We think we have not; I think we have no power to determine a price level or to restore a given price level. . . ."

"I am opposing this as a measure because, although the proponents of it say 'Well, in any event it can not do any harm and it may do some good,' I feel quite the opposite; I think it can not do any good and may do harm. In fact, the passage of the bill through the House was very disturbing. I did not want to say at the hearing that I felt it would be. . . . It disturbed people all over the world, there were many excited articles in the newspapers and individual inquiries were numerous. I don't say the disturbance was justified, but it did have a disturbing influence. It disturbed the foreign exchanges." [23]

"And I think it is a matter of very fine judgment and experience, and I do not think a resolution of Congress can contemplate all the circumstances under which that judgment must be exercised, and therefore any definite policy laid down by a congressional

[22] *Ibid.*, p. 202.
[23] *Ibid.*, pp. 214–5.

enactment, in my opinion, is inappropriate and unwise." [24]

Dr. Miller, of the Federal Reserve Board, did not hesitate to state his opposition to the bill in the plainest of terms; he even indicated that a stabilization provision would produce worse conditions than existed already, and would end in a breakdown.

"I have been in full sympathy" he said, "with the position the Board has taken on previous occasions against the advisability of any instruction to the Federal Reserve banks or to the Federal Reserve Board, or to the Federal Reserve System as a unity which is based on the assumption that any such guide to credit control is going to result in a better situation than we can have without it. It has been my belief that such instructions will result in a very much worse situation and will eventually produce a disaster, a breakdown." [25]

Asked by Senator Couzens, whether he did not believe that the condition of business could have become even worse than it was, Dr. Miller replied that the depression would have been worse, had the Federal Reserve System acted under a stabilization provision during the years from 1926 to 1928.

". . . it is my opinion" he said, "that if the Federal Reserve System had had such an instruction to experiment with credit as is proposed in this bill, back in 1926, 1927 and 1928, the situation might have been and probably would have been materially worse to-day than it is." [26]

Dr. Miller gave no evidence for these assertions. With equal dogmatism he made a pronouncement against index numbers, as follows:

"The average of commodity prices does not mean anything. It is merely a metaphysical concept, something that has been invented by economists. It has no counterpart in actuality—it can not be traded in, bought, or sold. It is purely a figment of the mind."

[24] *Ibid.,* p. 217.
[25] *Ibid.,* p. 223.
[26] *Ibid.,* p. 223.

Here *Senator Brookhart*, the Chairman of the Committee, who perhaps had not believed his ears, asked: "Do you think it is imaginary altogether and not real?"

"Mr. Miller: The price level concept is wholly metaphysical. It is a statistical summation of the movements of an infinite variety of commodities in a vast number of markets scattered over the face of the world." [27]

Dr. Miller took a somewhat fatalistic view as to currency and credit administration:

"Whether the 1926 price level will be restored or not, or how far it will be restored, I do not know. Nature will have more to say about that than the Congress of the United States or the Federal Reserve Board. In the long run the play of economic forces acting in this country and over the face of the world determines these things." [28]

The Fate of the Goldsborough and Fletcher Bills

What became of the Fletcher Bill? Let us quote from the Congressional Record of June 8, 1932, when Congressman *Goldsborough* addressed the House on the fate his bill had met in the Senate Committee:

"A few days ago the Senate Committee on Banking and Currency adopted an amendment . . . being known as the Glass amendment, it having been introduced by the distinguished Senator from Virginia, Senator Glass. Up until this time no report has been filed covering the Glass amendment. Therefore it is impossible for me to discuss from the standpoint of the report just what the theory is upon which the Senate Committee proceeded when it adopted that amendment.

"However, I can say, quoting from the New York Times, the

---

[27] *Ibid.*, p. 227.
[28] *Ibid.*, p. 232.

Herald Tribune, the Baltimore Sun, The United States Daily, the Philadelphia Ledger and the Philadelphia Record, that after the meeting of the Committee on Banking and Currency, at which this amendment was adopted, Senator Glass—(I am reading from the New York Times of June 2, 1932)—said—

" 'Mr. Glass said that he did not believe that his or any other legislative device was necessary for such an end at this time—'

"That is inflation—'but he had offered the plan in order to stop the Goldsborough Bill, which he opposes.'

"Quoting again from Senator Glass:

" 'I dissent from the view that there is any need of artificial inflation of the credit or currency of the country, but nevertheless, if there is to be any more inflation it should be brought about by a simple method which everybody may understand and not by the roundabout process which is being vainly tried by the Federal Reserve authorities.' [29]

"And again he said:

" 'I distinctly disavow the belief that any of these legislative devices is necessary at this time. I simply offered the bill in question as a substitute for the Goldsborough Bill which I regard with utmost aversion.'

"The distinguished Senator from Virginia who offered this amendment and who evidently feels he has no confidence in his own legislative proposal, did not attend any of the hearings which took place before the Senate Committee on Banking and Currency. Neither did he appear at the hearings before the House Committee on Banking and Currency. . . ."

Mr. Goldsborough continued with a severe criticism of the Federal Reserve Board:

"There has been absolutely no courage shown in the policy of the Federal Reserve Board. There has been no imagination de-

---

[29] The reader will remember that the Federal Reserve Board at this time, despite its hostile attitude towards a mandate to raise the price level, was nevertheless trying to raise it by means of open-market operations.

veloped. There has been no recognition of the fact that, unless this condition of depression is stopped by bold steps, that the country has got to go through a condition of bankruptcy. None of this has been visualized by the Federal Reserve System, and so when we come to the stabilization bill passed in the House of Representatives on May 2 . . . the administration came out in advance and said that if the Senate passed that bill and it was put up to the Executive he would veto it.[30]

". . . If this stabilization bill had the support of the administration it would pass the Senate without five dissenting votes, and I know exactly whereof I speak. . . .

"Some 10 days ago the distinguished Senator from Virginia stated on the floor of the Senate that he would not be willing to give the power provided in this bill to any seven men that God ever made. Does not the Senator from Virginia know that the Federal Reserve System is now exercising these vast powers in an absolutely uncontrolled manner, and does he not know that this legislation would be a limitation upon their powers and their discretion? . . ."

This was the end of the Goldsborough and Fletcher bills. It is clear that this legislation would have been enacted had it not been for the opposition of Secretary Mills, Governor Meyer and Senator Glass. Had it been enacted, however, it is possible that it would have been vetoed by President Hoover.

The defeat of the Goldsborough bill did not stop the legislative attempts to confer on some authority a legal mandate to reflate and stabilize the price level.[31]

[30] This referred to the statement, widely quoted, that President Hoover would veto the Goldsborough bill if it passed both houses.
[31] A list of bills introduced towards the end of the 72nd and at the beginning of the 73rd Congress which began with the Roosevelt administration, in 1933, is given in Appendix V.

SECTION 3. MONETARY AUTHORITY BILL HEARINGS (1934)

The Bill

On January 20, 1934, Mr. Goldsborough, backed by Mr. Frank A. Vanderlip [32] and also by the Committee for the Nation, introduced his bill for the establishment of a "Federal Monetary Authority." [33]

The bill provides for the establishment of a Government agency to be called the "Federal Monetary Authority," and to consist of seven directors appointed by the President. The directors would represent industry, agriculture and banking and to be subject to removal by the President or by Congress. This Authority would have the sole right of issuing legal tender currency. The present privilege by national banks to issue bank notes would cease three years after enactment of the bill.

The Authority would also have jurisdiction over the nation's monetary gold. It was to purchase gold bullion or coin at home or abroad at a price to be fixed, from time to time, by the Authority. It would further sell gold bullion in lots of $5,000 value each at the market price, but only for the settlement of international trade balances. The Authority was also to buy and sell silver coin and bullion at the prevailing market prices (but, not to exceed $1. an ounce), and would sell this silver to the Secretary of the Treasury for subsidiary coinage at his discretion. The Federal Monetary Authority would be required to rediscount commercial paper for the Federal Reserve Banks at rates to be fixed by it; to purchase and sell short-term Government securities; commercial paper and foreign exchange.

These powers of the Monetary Authority were however to be exercised only to the extent necessary for carrying out the following policy:

[32] See also Frank A. Vanderlip, *Tomorrow's Money*, New York, Reynal & Hitchcock, 1934.
[33] H.R. 7157 and H.R. 8780 (73rd Congress, 2nd Session).

". . . To restore as promptly as possible and maintain the normal purchasing power of the dollar, which shall, for the purposes of this Act, be the average purchasing power of the dollar for all commodities during the year 1926." The Index for the Purchasing Power of the Dollar in Terms of the Wholesale Prices for all Commodities of the Bureau of Labor Statistics was designated as representing the purchasing power of the dollar, and the establishment of a "Price Index Commission" was provided for to revise, from time to time, the basis of compilation, so that the price index may represent more adequately the average purchasing power of the dollar.

General Review of Testimony

The hearings on the bill (H.R. 7157 and H.R. 8780) were held before a Subcommittee of the Banking and Currency Committee of the House of Representatives under the chairmanship of Mr. Goldsborough. They began January 30, 1934, and ended March 8, 1934.

Although the bill is definitely a reflation-stabilization proposal most of the testimony related to its silver and gold provisions, and its proposal for the establishment of a central currency issuing body. There was unanimous opinion in favor of having five, instead of seven members on the Monetary Authority, these men to represent not any particular interests, but the interests of the country at large. As amended by the subcommittee and re-introduced as H.R. 8780, the bill provided that the five Directors of the Federal Monetary Authority were to be appointed because of their fitness and not as the representatives of banks, industry and agriculture, and that they should, in order to lessen political influence, serve during good behavior, and be subject to removal only by impeachment. The purpose was to give the Monetary Authority an independent status, analogous to that of the Supreme Court of the United States.

Some of the members of the subcommittee, in particulai Mr. Goldsborough, repeatedly raised the question whether it would not be possible to construct a system of currency entirely divorced from the nation's debt structure. At present, when a debt is paid to a bank, the volume of deposit currency is decreased by that amount; and if, as during the depression, there is a wholesale net liquidation of debts, the volume of circulating medium is drastically contracted, involving deflation. On the other hand, there is inflation of deposit currency when many people go into debt to the banks.

In order to prevent the loan policies of banks—a private industry—from thus determining the circulating medium of the United States, many people have thought that there should be a divorce between the loan function and the monetary function, that it ought to be possible to loan and liquidate loans *without affecting the volume of the circulating medium*. Of this problem no witness offered a solution.

Several witnesses suggested that the Monetary Authority not only be made responsible for maintaining a stable purchasing power of the dollar but that, if there should be fluctuations of more than 5%, 10% or 20% above or below the fixed "normal," the inefficiency of the Authority would be deemed to have been established, and its members automatically removed. The proposal was also made that the permissible variations should be reduced every year, as the Authority gained experience in the technique of stabilization.

The Secretary of the Treasury, *Henry Morgenthau, Jr.,* expressed the desire of the administration that it be not disturbed in its monetary program, and that Congress wait for a period of nine months, or even a year, before making any changes. He said that the result obtained from the currency devaluation and gold buying policy had been favorable, but thought that more experience and more time were needed to work out the permanent monetary policy of the country.

"What the future policy of this country will be," he said, "I do not think anybody is wise enough to tell at this time, because we have not had sufficient experience." [34]

Mr. Rand's Testimony

In an extended statement, Mr. James H. Rand, Jr.,[35] the Chairman of the Committee for the Nation (a "Founder" of the Stable Money Association) enumerated the advantages to business men of having an independent Federal Monetary Authority instead of the present miscellaneous division of power over the American monetary system—powers distributed among the privately-owned Federal Reserve System and the politically appointed Secretary of the Treasury. Mr. Rand also believed that rules and regulations could be adopted as to the method and technique of effecting control over the price level. In their order of importance, he named these methods as follows:

". . . the mildest step, in my opinion, should be taken first, such as a change in the rediscount rate upward or downward; second, open-market operations in the purchase or sale of Government securities; third, a change in the margin requirements on security accounts of investment bankers; fourth, regulation of the reserve requirements behind deposits . . . in member banks. Then fifth, a change in the price of either gold or silver, or both. . . ." [36]

One of Mr. Rand's chief criticisms of the present system was that no effective control was possible over the expansion of the volume of the circulating medium, as 90% of that medium con-

---

[34] *Hearings* before the Subcommittee of the Committee on Banking and Currency, House of Representatives (73rd Congress, 2nd Session), on H.R. 7157 as amended and reintroduced as H.R. 8780, p. 379.

[35] President, Remington Rand, Inc., New York.

[36] *Hearings* on H.R. 8780, *op. cit.*, p. 40.

sisted of bank deposits which do not come under Federal control. He suggested that the quantity of cash money of the country should never fall below an amount equal to 25% of the volume of bank deposits; he cited France and England where the ratio of cash money to deposits is much higher than ours, and where bank failures are very rare.

"The Monetary Authority" he said, "would have ample power to apply the brakes and to control the building up of the monetary structure in this country in such a way that it would contain a higher percentage of actual tangible money and a lower percentage of credit, either in the form of bank deposits or in the form of pieces of paper which are convertible into bank deposits on demand—namely, of listed securities." [37]

Mr. Rand also submitted a written statement in which he emphasized the importance of assigning to the Government the power of determining and stabilizing the purchasing power of money.

"Sovereignty over money and the control of its purchasing power are so vitally important to our nation that, if they are left with the Federal Reserve System, the Government will inevitably be compelled to assume direct control of that system.

"Control of banking by the Government would tend to restrict the profit motive and capitalism in favor of socialized public control. Decisions as to the flow of private credit are beyond the powers of any government to administer efficiently.

"We must not permit a situation to develop that will impose an impossible burden upon governmental machinery.

"It is far better for the Federal Reserve to surrender the functions of currency issue and control of government credit that rightfully belong to the sovereign power, and keep for itself and its member banks the field of legitimate commercial banking, with decisions as to granting of loans uninfluenced by politics, in which only private initiative can function satisfactorily. Thus the Federal Reserve System can stand as a bulwark for the institutions and functions of private property."

[37] *Ibid.*, p. 47.

Opposing Statements

In opposition to the bill, *Mr. Rufus Tucker* took the ground that the comparative stability of the price level during 1922–1929 was responsible for the depression, as well as for the crash in 1929. He said:

"If wholesale commodity prices had been allowed to fall, during that period, in accordance with the reduction in costs of production, that crash would have been avoided. . . ." [38]

"I think this depression has been so bad, because of so much attempt to maintain prices in those years, and that was the cause of building up of a debt structure.

". . . What was going on between 1922 and 1929 was stabilization of prices to prevent them from going down, which meant borrowing a large amount of money to hold goods off the market, and that was the technical cause of the collapse.

"If commodity prices had come down during that time there would not have been so much trouble. You take the case of rubber, tin, wheat, they were all held off the market on borrowed money in order to prevent prices from going down, and you see what the consequence was." [39]

This seems to imply that, for a period of seven years, a preponderant number of commodities out of the 784 that make up the Wholesale Price Index of the Department of Labor Statistics had been held off the market, to prevent a decline in prices!

Dr. Benjamin M. Anderson, Jr., Economist of the Chase National Bank of New York, has, for many years, been actively opposed to the stabilization of the dollar. His testimony is of interest as representing the views of a great bank.

"*Mr. Busby:* 'I am just wondering by what unit you would measure the value of our dollar today.'

[38] *Ibid.,* p. 207.
[39] *Ibid.,* p. 212.

"Mr. Anderson: 'I measure it first by gold.'

"Mr. Busby: 'By weight only?'"

"Mr. Anderson: 'Yes.'

"Mr. Hancock: 'Which is not a constant buying force?'

"Mr. Anderson: 'There are no constant units of value for anything, for neither goods nor gold; they are not constant in value.'

"Mr. Hancock: 'We have a standard of weight, rather than a standard of gold, do we not?'

"Mr. Anderson: 'No, because the value is the important thing, the value of a particular weight of gold.'

"Mr. Hancock: 'The only thing that is constant about it is its weight, and not its buying power or value.'

"Mr. Anderson: 'I agree, and I say there are no constant units of value whatever.' [40]

"Mr. Busby: 'Do you regard it as the duty of the Federal Government to furnish a medium of exchange to business and the people of the country?'

"Mr. Anderson: 'Yes, I think it is, as far as the Government establishes the standard of value, controls the coinage and things of that kind, but in the provision of paper money and other media of exchange of a credit character, I think it is done best through a banking machinery working rather automatically and adapting the volume of these credit media to the needs of trade and commercial transactions.'

"Mr. Busby: 'Legal tender is the currency issue of the Government of the United States.'

"Mr. Anderson: 'I don't think there ought to be any legal tender except full-weight gold coin.' " [41]

This means that the Government should have to furnish the country simply with gold coins of a given weight and fineness, and that the bankers would take care of the remaining 90% and more of the circulating medium.

Another witness was *Governor Black* of the Federal Reserve Board. As compared with the testimonies of Dr. Miller and Gov-

[40] *Ibid.,* p. 252.
[41] *Ibid.,* p. 247.

ernor Meyer in behalf of the Federal Reserve Board, opposing previous stabilization bills, Governor Black's testimony showed considerably more sympathy for the stabilization idea as represented in the Monetary Authority bill. Governor Black was not in favor of it, nor did he think its purposes possible of accomplishment, but he said:

"Let's just put it this way. I doubt very much if you could establish, as a permanent dollar in America, a dollar based on 784 commodities with their different variations. I think you would need a Monetary Authority to do that. If you can do it, and if it will work toward making a stable currency in America, then I am not opposed to it." [42] When he was asked what he thought of the idea of having a dollar with constant purchasing power, a dollar that might buy at any time the same amount of composite goods, Governor Black answered:

"Well, I think it is a theory that won't work." [43]

The conclusion from this blunt and honest statement is that the nation cannot expect a stable dollar, as proposed by President Roosevelt, so long as the monetary and credit system is controlled by the Federal Reserve with its present personnel.

Supporting Statements

Father Coughlin, well known as a radio talker and a most ardent fighter against "bankers' monopoly," made an extended statement in support of the bill in which he said:

"I am in favor of this bill, wholeheartedly, because it undertakes to reclaim for the United States Government the power to issue its own currency, not predicated necessarily, upon gold; predicated also upon silver.

[42] *Ibid.,* p. 405.
[43] *Ibid.,* p. 406.

"I would go even further than that, although it is not within the compass of this bill, but I would predicate currency upon the real wealth of the Nation, on its farms, and homes, and mines, and fields, and factories, and facilities. . . ." [44]

Professor F. A. Pearson, the co-worker of Professor Warren on the stabilization problem, was the last witness in favor of the bill. In an extended statement, he explained that the price level actually depended upon the price of gold, and that a country could, by determining its price for gold, obtain any price level it desired. With the help of statistical data he described the effects of America's recent adjustment of the gold price and insisted that,

". . . the fundamental problem is not the distribution of gold, nor the amount of paper money, nor the amount of credit. The total amount of gold relative to the total amount of goods to be exchanged for gold, controls prices . . . regardless of where the gold may be located. The fundamental question is the amount and not its location." [45]

Professor Pearson closed with the following, hopeful statement:

"We should not be too disturbed because so little progress has been made in the past toward obtaining a stable measure of value. Inertia is such a dominant force in our thoughts and actions, that great changes rarely occur until an unusual event forces them upon us. The unparalleled peace-time rise in the value of gold forced the issue and very rapid progress is now being made. As a result of the unparalleled chaos of the last three years and the present wide-spread knowledge concerning the problem, it is possible that we may get a stable measure of value so that our children and our children's children will not suffer from the violent fluctuations in the value of gold which this generation has experi-

[44] *Ibid.,* p. 424.
[45] *Ibid.,* p. 507.

enced. If we get it, the price we are paying, although high, is cheap in terms of human progress." [46]

The Monetary Authority Bill was unanimously favorably reported by the Subcommittee which held these hearings. But at this writing no further action has been taken on it.

[46] *Ibid.*, p. 514.

CHAPTER VII

THE FEDERAL RESERVE SYSTEM (FROM 1920)

To understand the history of the stable money movement it is important to know to what extent the policy of the Federal Reserve System influenced developments of the American price level, and particularly whether the comparative stability of the dollar's purchasing power during 1922–1929 was due to the voluntary effort of the Federal Reserve officials, or whether this stability just happened as a result of conditions over which the Federal Reserve had no control.

The controversy over this question came to light at the stabilization hearings. On the one side were the officials of the Federal Reserve System, resenting the stabilization provision on the ground that they were already doing all they thought proper and that they could not, if they would, stabilize the price level definitely. On the other side were the advocates of stable money, who argued that the Reserve System had the powers needed for stabilization and had used them at times, but had failed at other times because the law did not compel them to exercise their powers for the specific purpose of stabilization.

Section i. The 1920 Deflation

Domination of the Secretary of the Treasury over Federal Reserve Policy

As a consequence of war activities wholesale commodity prices had risen from 100 in 1913 to 196 in March 1919. This price increase was accompanied by all the symptoms of a real inflation:

high cost of living; the price level rising faster than wages; profiteering; speculation, etc., so that those in charge of the monetary system became more and more alarmed about the situation. Governor Harding of the Federal Reserve Board related [1] that as early as August 1919 he was anxious to have the discount rate raised. Under special war legislation, however, the policy of the Federal Reserve System was largely determined by the Secretary of the Treasury, who naturally wanted a low interest rate so as to reduce the cost of Government financing. When in September 1919 the Federal Advisory Council met to reconsider whether all rediscount rates should be advanced, Mr. Leffingwell, the Assistant Secretary of the Treasury, appeared before it and objected to such an advance because it would increase his difficulties in trying to place a contemplated Liberty Loan. That is, increased discount rates would have a depressing influence upon the bond market. He said that after January 1920, the Treasury would not object to an advance. For this reason the Council was induced to postpone its contemplated recommendation.[2]

Reasons for Contracting Credit

However, the obvious inflation was not the only thing that alarmed the Federal Reserve authorities. In fact, in their opinion, it seems, the rise of prices was due more to a scarcity of goods because of the War, than to an oversupply of credit and currency. The real reason, then, for alarm was the danger to the Federal Reserve System that its gold reserves approached the legal minima of 40% and 35%. The desire to avoid reaching that limit and to maintain the gold standard was perhaps the most powerful factor in making up their minds to contract the credit and currency of the country.

[1] W. P. H. Harding, *The Formative Period of the Federal Reserve System*, Houghton Mifflin Company, The Riverside Press, Cambridge, 1925, p. 157.
[2] *Ibid.*, p. 158.

Accordingly, on January 23, 1920, the discount rate for commercial paper was raised from 4¾% to 6% in five of the twelve reserve districts, and within two weeks the same procedure was adopted in the other seven districts. At the same time the Federal Reserve Board "urged the importance of discouraging non-essential loans, and putting the banks back into a position where they could expand or contract their loans according to the industrial and commercial requirements of the country." [3] Such were the words used by Governor Harding on January 6, 1920 at a meeting of bankers representing 25 clearing-house associations.

Although this action affected the prices of a few agricultural products, the wholesale commodity price level continued to rise until in May 1920 it reached its peak of 247. [4] The Federal Reserve Board, however, was determined to use more drastic measures to prevent a further increase in credit. For that purpose the Board, on May 18, 1920, in Washington at a conference attended not only by the Board but by the Federal Advisory Council, and by the Class A Directors of the Federal Reserve banks, outlined a policy.

Governor Harding, in his opening address on that occasion, explained the need of checking expansion because of the reduced gold reserves which were approaching the legal minimum, and explained the need for "sacrifices" on the part of the public, "for the general economic good."

"Our problem," he said, ". . . is to check further expansion and to bring about a normal and healthy liquidation without curtailing essential production and without shock to industry, and, as far as possible, without disturbance of legitimate commerce and business. . . .

"The average [gold] reserves of the Federal Reserve banks are now about 42%, as against 45% at the beginning of the year, and about 51% twelve months ago. The solution of the problems con-

[3] *Ibid.,* p. 169.
[4] Index of the U.S. Bureau of Labor Statistics (revised).

fronting us will require the cooperation of all the banks and the public. Whatever personal sacrifices may be necessary for the general economic good, should be made. The war-time spirit to do things that are worthwhile must be revived, and there should be the fullest cooperation in an effort to produce more, save more, and consume less. . . ." [5]

Governor Harding put it up to the member banks themselves, to bring about the stringency of credit which was to result in reduced prices:

". . . there is nothing in the Federal Reserve Act" he explained, "which requires a Federal Reserve bank to make any investment or to rediscount any particular paper or class of paper. . . . It is the view of the Board . . . that discrimination might much better be made at the source by the member banks themselves. . . ." [6]

Governor Harding's words were quite typical of this meeting. All other members of the Board joined him in the demand for credit contraction. Even *Mr. Williams,* the Comptroller of the Currency who was not at all in sympathy with deflation, said,

". . . it is tremendously important that every individual bank, besides being a missionary for thrift, should each admonish and warn and hold the strings of their money-bags with a very discriminating hand, and should bring about a proper and reasonable degree of contraction. . . ." [7]

The Senate Resolution

Three days previous to this meeting, Senator Medill McCormick of Illinois had introduced and passed a resolution on the floor of the U.S. Senate, asking for information as to what the Federal Reserve Board were going to do about the undue inflation of credit and currency. This resolution, presented to the Board at

[5] Harding, *op. cit.,* pp. 171-2.
[6] *Ibid.,* p. 174.
[7] *Ibid.,* p. 177.

the time of this important conference, at any rate reinforced the efforts of the Board. Doubtless, a slight "reflation" downward was needed. But what happened was not slight.

The Federal Reserve Board was later severely criticized as being the instigator of the deflation which followed from 1920–1921. Hundreds of thousands of farmers lost their farms, millions of workers were thrown out of work. Twelve years later Ex-Senator Owen, in a statement before a Congressional committee, went so far as to say that the McCormick resolution "was instigated by those great financial forces behind the Federal Advisory Council and the Federal Reserve Board. At a secret meeting this principle was approved. ...." [8]

Governor Harding, on the other hand, in his book wrote that Senator McCormick's move did not bring about the action of the Federal Reserve which had been determined before the resolution was introduced:

". . . in justice to the memory of the late Senator McCormick it is only fair to state that his resolution had no bearing upon the policies of the Board, which had already been developed, and its adoption by the Senate on the day before the conference . . . was merely a coincidence." [9]

Nevertheless, Dr. Miller, in defending the Federal Reserve Board at a Stabilization Hearing before a Congressional Committee, on May 2, 1928, put the blame for the 1920 deflation altogether upon Congress, when he said:

"I think one of the chief troubles with the Federal Reserve System in 1920 was hysteria—hysteria in part due to the interference of Congress through a Senate resolution, with the maintenance of a well-balanced frame of mind in the Federal Reserve System." [10]

However, Dr. Miller hastened on the same occasion, to modify

---

[8] *Hearings* before the Subcommittee of the Committee on Banking and Currency on H.R. 10517 (Goldsborough Stabilization Bill), March 16, 1932, p. 124.
[9] Harding, *op. cit.*, p. 180.
[10] *Stabilization Hearings* on H.R. 11806 (1928), *op. cit.*, p. 163.

this statement somewhat, by dividing the blame equally between Congress and the bankers, who had acted according to the exhortation of the Federal Reserve Board:

"The mistake that the Federal Reserve made then, was in not saying there was no use doing those things, and of putting itself in the position of accepting responsibility for what happened more or less under the impulse of fear of the investment and banking community; and more or less the impulse of fear of the Senate of the United States." [11]

Credit Contraction in Practice

For the purpose of determining the question whether the Reserve System has the power to stabilize the price level, this conference of May 18, 1920 is of particular interest. For the first time in the history of the Federal Reserve Board, its power of "moral suasion" had been brought into play. It proved that any policy, initiated centrally at Washington and followed out by 10,000 of the most important banks in the country, could not fail to have an effect upon the currency situation of the entire country. The effectiveness of such suasion was vividly described by Congressman Swing of California, on May 23, 1922 before the House of Representatives: He related his personal experience with California bankers who were being ordered by the Federal Reserve to stop discounting paper.

"I was present at a meeting of the bankers of Southern California, held at El Centro, in my district, in the middle of November, 1920, when W. A. Day, then Deputy Governor of the Federal Reserve bank of San Francisco, spoke for the Federal Reserve bank, and delivered a message which he said he was sent there to deliver. He told the bankers there assembled that they were not to loan to any farmer any money for the purpose of en-

[11] *Ibid.,* p. 185.

abling the farmer to hold any of his crops beyond harvest time.
If they did, he said, the Federal Reserve bank would refuse to rediscount a single piece of paper on such transaction. He declared
that all the farmers should sell all their crops at harvest time unless they had money of their own to finance them, as the Federal
Reserve bank would do nothing toward helping the farmers hold
back any part of their crop, no matter what the condition of the
market. . . .

"No one could be in doubt for one minute as to what the natural,
logical, and necessary consequences of such policy would be. If
the entire crop of the country is thrown on the market at the time
of harvest, of course, the market would be depressed. You can
'bear' the market, or you can 'bull' the market. The Federal Reserve bank deliberately set out to 'bear' the market. They succeeded
so well that they broke the market—not only broke the market,
but broke the farmer as well. . . ."

Professor Commons cited this speech by Congressman Swing
when testifying before a Congressional Committee on Stabilization in 1927. He said:

"Now, if they could do that at that time, have they not done
that with other commodities, and can not that same system be
used to stabilize money and stabilize wholesale prices?" [12]

Had the Federal Reserve Board acted merely to stop inflation
and produce a very mild reflation downward so as to attain a
sounder price level, this would have been an effort towards stabilization. The high interest rate of 7%, and other credit restrictions
were, however, still maintained, *long after the price level had
fallen well below a desirable level,* and deflation was permitted.
The Board seemed to have thought of nothing but protecting the
gold standard, regardless of the effect of such action upon agriculture, commerce and industry.

The decline of the price level began in June 1920, and by De-

[12] *Stabilization Hearings* on H.R. 7895, *op. cit.,* p. 1111.

cember 1920 it had fallen from its peak of 247 in May, to 179; yet the 7% discount rate was maintained until May 5, 1921, when in New York, it was reduced to 6½%. The index number had meanwhile declined to 145. The discount rates were further reduced to 6% on June 16, 1921, to 5½% on July 21, 1921, and, on June 22, 1922, they were down to 4%.

Whether or not the Reserve Board intended more than a reasonable reflation downward can never be ascertained. But the fact cannot be disputed that as a result of their action, there was a disastrous deflation. The important point here is that this demonstrates the tremendous power over the price level possessed by the Federal Reserve System.

Non-Monetary Explanation of the Deflation

Apparently, the Federal Reserve Board did not foresee to what extent its deflationary measures would be effective. Like the general public, it believed that the high price level of the post-war period was due primarily to a scarcity of goods. When, as a consequence of falling prices, the markets were suddenly flooded with unsalable goods, the Federal Reserve Board in its annual Report for 1920 explained this phenomenon as being due mainly to nonmonetary causes. They said that the year had been one of "reaction," that the steps taken "did not produce deflation but . . . checked the expansion which had been proceeding at a dangerous rate. . . ." The Report continued:

"A gradual expansion then developed which culminated in much higher production early in the year 1920, and during this time the inability of the railroads to provide adequate transportation facilities brought about an unusual and serious congestion at initial points. This circumstance was due partly to an unusually severe winter, and partly to the renewed increase of production and larger volume of goods to be shipped. All the factors of the situation taken together brought about an accumulation of commodities until the late spring and early summer, when, as the result of more favorable weather and better transportation facilities, delayed consignments began to reach the markets in volume, but too late for sales on terms as advantageous as probably would have been obtainable had they reached distributors earlier and in a normal way." [13]

But the address of Governor Harding, to a group of bankers on January 6, 1920, shows a somewhat revised view. He said:

"While we have turned our backs upon the period of war financing, and have directed our steps toward a more normal banking policy, we can not expect, this year or next, nor in the immediate future, to regain a banking position which would be regarded as normal when judged by pre-war standards.

"We can only reach such a position when, as the result of increased production and reduced expenditure on the part of the people and the Government, outstanding obligations of the Government have been greatly reduced and the remainder has been absorbed by the investing public. The process is one which will require time and patience. *But we can formulate our policies now. We must have a definite policy.*" [14]

Thus, as a first step of a new policy, the Board effected a rigorous deflation which put the dollar upon a "sound" gold basis, and ruined millions of American citizens. At the same time it proved beyond any reasonable doubt the power of the Federal Reserve System to affect, for weel or woe, the value of the dollar, even the gold dollar.

The Agricultural Inquiry

The story of the 1920 deflation is told in the three volumes of hearings which were held before the Joint Commission of Agricultural Inquiry.[15] This Commission was appointed for the pur-

[13] *Annual Report* of the Federal Reserve Board for 1920, p. 6.
[14] *Federal Reserve Bulletin,* February 1920, p. 117; italics mine.
[15] *Hearings* before the Joint Commission of Agricultural Inquiry, 67th Congress, first Session, Senate Concurrent Resolution 4, 3 vol., 1922.

pose of finding out the causes of the deplorable condition of agriculture and the testimony consists mainly of statements of farmers' representatives who were complaining of the high cost of distributing their products, and the disastrous effect of the sudden fall of prices. Officials of the Federal Reserve System, notably Governors Harding and Strong, also testified and delivered extensive statements on the operations of the Federal Reserve System.

The most interesting part of these hearings is the testimony of *John Skelton Williams,* formerly the Comptroller of the Currency, and as such ex officio member of the Federal Reserve Board, who put the blame for the deflation entirely upon the Federal Reserve Board. He stated that he had repeatedly asked the Board to reverse its deflationary policy, once the rise of prices had been halted. Prompt action, he claimed, could have prevented the severe fall in prices. He said:

"I have stated clearly and repeatedly, that the curbing efforts of the Board and the Reserve banks were, for part of the time in the past two years, distinctly helpful and beneficial in restraining inflation and stabilizing values. But when the upward movement was halted and the downward rush of prices set in, the Federal Reserve Board, whether from inertia or from inability to comprehend the meaning of events and the radically changed conditions, distinctly failed in the supreme trial. The lack of sympathy displayed by the Board, and its apparent impotence to meet courageously and resourcefully a situation demanding instant and sagacious action was in my opinion unpardonable.

"I am convinced that if the Federal Reserve Board had heeded the urgent suggestions, recommendations and warnings contained in my clear-cut letters and memoranda of August 9, 1920, August 26, 1920, October 18, 1920, October 21, 1920, and December 28, 1920, and had revised its policies and methods to meet and respond to the great changes which had already taken place and were going on in the world of business and finance, that it could, as I said in my Washington address of April 15, 1921, 'have saved us from a fall so precipitate and smashing, and from much of the distress and ruin through which we have been dragged.' It could have made the shrinkage of values more gradual and uniform instead of violent and sporadic, could have helped strongly to keep the circulating currents of commerce at more even flow, so that the losses of each producer might be offset by a reasonable reduction in the cost of what he must consume. . . ." [16]

This quotation indicates how strongly this ex officio member of the Federal Reserve Board believed that the Board and the System had influenced the dollar (injuriously) and could influence it (beneficially).

The Reserve officials, on the other hand, maintained that the System was concerned merely with the maintenance of "sound credit conditions," and that the regulation of the price level was not one of its functions.

Although the problems under discussion at these hearings were created largely by the instability of the dollar, the Stable Money Movement had not yet advanced sufficiently to prompt the demand for stabilization legislation to prevent the recurrence of such violent fluctuations.

Section 2. Federal Reserve Opinion on Stabilization

By Governors of Federal Reserve Banks

The maintenance of comparative price level stability by the Federal Reserve System during 1922 to 1929 is usually credited to the wise leadership of *Governor Strong* of the New York Federal Reserve Bank. From his statements before Stabilization Committees it can be seen that he was by no means an outspoken advocate of a stable price level, although he considered such stability highly desirable, and used the powers of the system con-

[16] *Ibid.*, Vol. II, p. 124.

sciously to that end. In 1923 he was still of the opinion that

". . . the power and responsibility of fixing prices . . . never has, and I hope never will be granted to boards and to banks in this country." [17]

But whether he meant the fixing of individual prices, or the stabilization of the price level it is difficult to determine. It is likely that he meant price *fixing*.

The following quotations, however, show that he was greatly in favor of general stability and believed that the banking system, through regulation of the credit supply was in the position of making an important contribution to the attainment of this stability.

"What this country and the world needs is stability,—social, political and economic; stable thoughts, habits, and methods. The contribution to be made by our banking system just now can be but a part, though a helpful one, toward stability. Its best policy is to supply enough credit and not too much—enough for legitimate enterprise, but not enough to satisfy those who want simply cheap and limitless supplies of credit regardless of the consequences they are too blind to perceive." [18]

But Governor Strong did not think that the price level alone was an adequate guide for the determination of credit policy. He thought that other indexes had to be consulted by the central bank when deciding upon its course of action. He said:

"Just as credit is *one* of the influences upon the price level, so the price level should be *one* of the influences in guiding a credit policy. There are other influences which affect prices, and so there must be other influences which affect a credit policy. Here are a few briefly suggested:

"Is labor fully employed? Are stocks of goods increasing or

[17] *Interpretations of Federal Reserve Policy* in the Speeches and Writings of Benjamin Strong. Edited by W. Randolph Burgess, New York, Harper Brothers, 1930, p. 229 (Unpublished article, "Prices and Price Control").

[18] *Ibid.,* p. 234.

decreasing? Is production to the country's capacity? Are transportation facilities fully taxed? Is speculation creeping into the productive and distributive processes? Are orders and repeat orders being booked much ahead? Are bills being promptly paid? Are people spending wastefully? Is credit expanding? Are market rates above or below Reserve bank rates?" [19]

Governor Strong's great contribution to the stabilization movement, however, was his discovery of the open-market powers of the Federal Reserve System. When he had realized by actual experience to what extent the Federal Reserve could influence the money market through the purchase and sale of securities in the open market—a procedure which the advocates of stabilization had proposed in their theories long before—he organized the Governors of the most important Reserve Banks as an Open-Market Committee, in order that these powers might be used to the best advantage.[20]

In 1928 (as mentioned above), Governor Strong helped draft a bill directing the Federal Reserve System to use its powers for the maintenance of a stable purchasing power of the dollar. This was evidence that he had, to some extent, changed his views on the subject, and that he now thought it necessary to restrain the discretionary powers of the System.

Advocates of stabilization have often said that the depression would never have got so far—perhaps never occurred—had Governor Strong lived; that, just as he had acted in 1923 to prevent inflation and used the open-market powers of the system to maintain stability, so in 1929–1930 he would have made vigorous and prompt efforts to maintain stability. Governor Strong has perhaps given the best sketch of himself in a little statement that was found in his desk drawer after his death:

"To the Governor of this bank: Never forget that it was

[19] *Ibid.*, p. 233.
[20] See also Chapter 8, Section 1.

created to serve the employer and the working man, the producer and the consumer, the importer and the exporter, the debtor and the creditor, all in the interest of the country as a whole." [21]

As to *Governor Norris* of the Federal Reserve Bank of Philadelphia we have already seen that he was opposed to all efforts to interfere with a "movement of prices." [22] On the same occasion, however, he claimed that, although the Federal Reserve System was not obliged to do so, it had already acted to the best of its ability in preventing extreme fluctuations in the price level. In other words, while he believed that the demand for stabilization was unreasonable, the System had already stabilized. He said:

"While there is no responsibility of that sort imposed upon us at the present time, and while, on the contrary, the striking out of that provision in the original Federal Reserve act relieved us of the responsibility, we have, as a matter of fact—and I suppose there are a great number of people in the country who can not believe it—but we have acted conscientiously and done the best we knew how in our respective districts. We have realized the bad effect of extreme price fluctuations, and as far as it has been within our power to do it, without doing it for a definite purpose or acknowledging it as our prime purpose or object, we have worked in that direction." [23]

Governor Harrison of the New York Federal Reserve Bank, successor to Governor Strong, seems to have preserved the tradition which Governor Strong had established. The following statement of his is an almost perfect expression of how a central bank should function for the maintenance of stability by counteracting the disturbing actions of the private banks.

"It is almost inevitable that the Federal Reserve System or any central bank will always have to be going contrary to what the

[21] *Stabilization Hearings* on H.R. 10517, *op. cit.*, cited by Mr. Harrison, p. 502.
[22] See Chapter 5, Section 4.
[23] *Stabilization Hearings*, 1926, on H.R. 7895, *op. cit.*, p. 396.

banks are doing. When they are inflating, we have to put pressure on them, and when they are deflating, we have to boost them up. I think that is what we should do." [24]

"I would much prefer to operate the system with a view to maintaining the stability of prices and business, as far as it is in our power to do it, without either any promise on our part that we would accomplish a certain result, or without any direction from Congress that we must accomplish a certain result; because I do not believe that credit alone is an inexorable control of the price level." [25]

Governor Harding of the Federal Reserve Bank of Boston (formerly Governor of the Federal Reserve Board) opposed the Strong bill on the ground that so great a responsibility should not be imposed on any organization: "Even were it possible to place the control of the money market in the hands of a small official body, it would not be wise to do so. Such a responsibility is too great to place in the hands of any organization." [26]

From this he deduced that: "The Federal Reserve System should not undertake to control the money market, but rather to guide it in the right direction."

Federal Reserve Board and Federal Advisory Council

The Board's position on stabilization was best stated in its Tenth Annual Report, covering activities of the year 1923.

The Board stated that, even if stabilization were administratively and politically possible, better results might be obtained by other means.

"Entirely apart from the difficult administrative problems" the report reads, "that would arise in connection with the adoption of

---

[24] *Stabilization Hearings* on H.R. 10517 (1932), *op. cit.*, p. 503.
[25] *Ibid.*, p. 487.
[26] In "Trust Companies," Vol. XLII, No. 1, July, 1926, p. 12.

the price index as a guide, and entirely apart from the serious political difficulties which would attend a system of credit administration based on prices, there is no reason for believing that the results attained would be as satisfactory as can be reached by other
means economically valid and administratively practicable. In saying this the board is not unmindful of the abundant evidence recent years have given of the economic and business disturbances
occasioned by violent fluctuations of prices. But it must not be overlooked that price fluctuations proceed from a great variety of
causes, most of which lie outside the range of influence of the
credit system. No credit system could undertake to perform the
function of regulating credit by reference to prices without failing
in the endeavor. . . .

"No statistical mechanism alone, however carefully contrived,
can furnish an adequate guide to credit administration. Credit
is an intensely human institution, and as such reflects the
moods and impulses of the community—its hopes, its fears, its
expectations. The business and credit situation at any time is
charged with these invisible factors. They are elusive and cannot
be fitted into any mechanical formula, but the fact that they are
refractory to the methods of the statistical laboratory makes them
neither non-existent nor non-important." [27]

The Federal Advisory Council, in 1926, opposed stable money
legislation because in its opinion, the Reserve System's powers
were inadequate, adding that the attempts to stabilize would
produce pressure for changes in credit policy, if individual prices
or groups of prices fluctuated:

"In the opinion of the Council, stabilization of the price level
can not be accomplished by means of rediscount rates and open-
market operations. In the main, fundamental conditions of the
business situation are not subject to control by the Federal Reserve
banks. Moreover, the council believes it would be extremely dangerous were the Federal Reserve System charged with the responsibility for promoting a stable price level for commodities by
means of the powers vested in the Federal Reserve System. The

[27] *Annual Report* of the Federal Reserve Board for 1923, pp. 31–32.

index of prices represents merely an average, and it has often been true in the past and it will be so in the future that the prices of some commodities are high while those of others are low. Whenever such a situation should arise, the interests of various lines of business would be in conflict, and the system would become subject to most undesirable pressure exerted now in favor of one commodity and then of another." [28]

The various statements of *Dr. Miller* of the Federal Reserve Board are of particular interest, as they show the vacillation and uncertainty of his attitude. In 1921, Dr. Miller apparently thought that stabilization was a quite reasonable demand, and that the technical details of a stabilization plan could be worked out.

"As an abstract proposition," he wrote, "the proposal to substitute a price indicator for the reserve ratio as a guide to discount policy has much economic merit. The rigors of the recent price adjustment process through which the United States, in common with the rest of the commercial world, has been passing, have emphasized the value of price stability. Price disturbances not originating from inevitable natural causes are bad and costly alike to producer and consumer. It is not surprising, therefore, in view of the trying experiences of recent years, that effort should be made, in reviewing the working of present-day credit and banking machinery, to find some guide to credit policy that will give to the community greater protection against unsettling changes in the price level. . . .

"As a theoretical proposition, therefore, it is entirely conceivable that the discount policy of the Federal Reserve System might be governed by indications of impending price changes, with a view of mitigating their cyclical fluctuations. While such an undertaking would raise some new and difficult problems of credit administration, no doubt in time the technique of a plan of credit regulation based on price indices could be worked out

[28] *13th Annual Report* of the Federal Reserve Board for the year 1926, p. 485.

and be made administratively practicable if public sentiment demanded." [29]

And again, when speaking on "Federal Reserve Credit Policy," Dr. Miller could almost have been taken for a representative of the Stable Money Association. He made the following statement in favor of a credit policy that would neither inflate nor deflate the price level.

". . . We should seek just as earnestly to avoid deflation as we should to avoid inflation. By inflation I mean an expansion of credit that eventuates in a rise of general prices. By deflation I mean a restraint of credit that eventuates in a fall of prices. Good economic and credit policy will endeavor to steer a middle course between these two dangerous shoals. . . ." [30]

But when it came to putting the stabilization principle into the law, Dr. Miller developed an entirely different attitude. In May, 1928, at one of the Congressional hearings, he apparently thought that such wise credit policy as he described above would be an attempt to interfere with the laws of nature.

". . . to my mind, undertaking to regulate the flow of Federal Reserve credit by the price index, is a good deal like trying to regulate the weather by the barometer. . . . Your price index indicates slowly, very slowly—what is in process. It does not indicate much until after the change has gone so far that there is an actual disturbance." [31]

Other, similar statements by Dr. Miller have already been cited.

Governor Meyer, of the Federal Reserve Board, whose statements before the Subcommittee of the Committee on Banking and Currency of the House were approved by all members of

[29] A. C. Miller, *Federal Reserve Policy* in the American Economic Review, June, 1921, p. 192.
[30] At the Joint Conference of the Chairmen and Governors of the Federal Reserve Banks, October 25–28, 1921, Doc. #24, pp. 1–4.
[31] *Stabilization Hearings* on H.R. 11806, *op. cit.,* p. 348.

the Board,[32] declared himself in full sympathy with the purpose of stabilization, when he said:

". . . I regard the efficiency of the banking structure as an important element in achieving stability in the price level, and in using for that purpose, to the extent it can be used, the regulation of the volume of currency and credit." [33]

Yet, what Governor Meyer meant by such stability it is difficult to guess. A member of the Subcommittee asked him:

"I wish you would give us any light that you might have regarding the subject of securing stabilization. . . ."

Following is his answer:

"I am not, Mr. Congressman, a believer in the idea that you really want to achieve a static position in all respects, economically speaking. No matter how much a steady condition appeals to anyone as an ideal, I think when you get down to it, any business man will try to go ahead, and want to go ahead in the world. . . .

"That does not alter the fact that relative stability is desirable, and limits to the area of fluctuation are desirable. Therefore, I do not think that you and I differ, and I only make the distinction because I do not believe the human race wants a static position. . . ." [34]

SECTION 3. FEDERAL RESERVE POLICY

No Definite Policy

These expressions of the most prominent officials of the Federal Reserve System clearly show that the System did not avowedly use the price index as a guide in determining its credit policy. As a definite policy was never publicly announced, it is difficult to say what most influenced the Board in making its

---

[32] See Chapter 6, Section 2.
[33] *Stabilization Hearings* on H.R. 10517 (1932), p. 522.
[34] *Ibid.*, p. 542.

decisions. There is no doubt but that many officials of the System resented the idea of being tied down to a policy; but apparently they were trying to build up a tradition, like that of the Bank of England which, in spite of wide discretionary powers, proceeds according to time-honored principles. As Mr. W. W. Stewart expressed it at one of the hearings, the Federal Reserve Board had a policy, although it never definitely stated what this policy was.

". . . I have felt that the frequently repeated statement that the Federal Reserve Board has no policy was based upon the fact that it has made no declaration of intention. I do not regard a policy as a declaration of intention. Consistency and continuity of action does not require a declaration of purpose, though it does require the exercise of judgment and the realization that action in one set of circumstances may bring a different result than upon another." [35]

Governor Harrison on another occasion said: "The system is announcing a policy through action. . . ." [36]

Dr. Miller, as far back as 1921, said that, ". . . Our principal pre-occupation, I repeat, should be to deal with conditions and circumstances rather than with principles." [37]

That is the System wanted the utmost liberty in doing at any moment what it felt was the most appropriate. Yet, in retrospect, certain definite guiding principles can be traced which have influenced the determination of the System's credit policy.

Restoration of International Gold Standard

Foremost among such influences has been the desire to help the world get back to an effective gold or gold-exchange standard. The desire to maintain the gold standard was one of the

[35] *Stabilization Hearings* on H.R. 7895, *op. cit.*, p. 759.
[36] *Stabilization Hearings* on H.R. 10517 (1932), p. 479.
[37] At the Joint Conference of the Chairmen and Governors, *op. cit.*, pp. 1–4.

main reasons for the inauguration of the deflationary measures of 1920. All of the Federal Reserve officials who testified against stabilization were unanimously in favor of the re-establishment of an effective international gold standard, and except for a statement by Dr. Miller, apparently not one of them ever expressed any fear that this policy might lead to a gold shortage and a mal-distribution of gold and an instability of gold in terms of commodities. Warnings as to these possible results made by the advocates of stable money were entirely disregarded.

Governor Strong was a great believer in the benefits of the gold standard. It was due to his efforts, perhaps more than to those of any other official of the Federal Reserve System, that America lent a helping hand to nations desiring to return to gold. The following expressions show his belief that unless the world was brought back to the gold standard as it existed before the War, the Federal Reserve System would never be able to function satisfactorily in every respect:

"You cannot have a banking system conducted under conditions such as have existed since the War where there is not a free movement of gold between the nations, and expect to bring about that more or less automatic stability which comes by re-adjustment of domestic and world prices. Until we get back to the automatic flow of gold which affects bank reserves and brings into play the automatic reactions from loss of reserves, until that time comes I do not believe we are going to have all the satisfaction in the Federal Reserve System that we will have after that time comes." [38]

". . . the gold standard is a much more automatic check upon excesses in credit and currency than is a system where gold payment, if you please, is suspended and it is left to the human judgement of men to determine how much currency shall be issued which they do not need to redeem in gold—do you see

[38] *Stabilization Hearings* on H.R. 7895 (1926), *op. cit.*, p. 378.

the distinction? And when you speak of a gold standard, you are speaking of something where the limitation upon judgment is very exact and precise and the penalty for bad judgment is immediate." [39]

And yet, it was in fact a better judgment that led the Federal Reserve officials chiefly under the influence of Governor Strong to impound the surplus gold, and *not* to permit it to have its natural inflationary effect upon the domestic price level.

Governor Harding, discussing Congressman Strong's bill at a dinner of the Stable Money Association, also said that the restoration of the international gold standard was the first step to be taken:

". . . We cannot ignore the world level of prices, and it seems to me that as a first step toward stabilization, our efforts should be directed toward promoting the restoration of the gold standard in those countries which, because of the war, were forced to abandon it. . . ." [40]

Dr. Miller was also a very outspoken advocate of a general return of the world to the gold standard which, he believed, would produce better results than any obtainable by other means, even if the stability of the price level was used as the test.

"There has been a notable movement for the restoration of the gold standard, in the course of the last year and a half particularly, and it can only be a question of a rather short time when the three or four important remaining commercial countries that are still on a paper standard, will go back to gold, and gold will, therefore, again become in a very important sense a regulator and stabilizer. My own belief is that, when that point is again reached, . . . we shall get results that are comparable to those that were produced by the gold standard before the

---

[39] *Stabilization Hearings* on H.R. 11806 (1928), *op. cit.,* p. 20.
[40] Dinner of the Stable Money Association, May 3, 1926, quoted from *Stabilization Hearings* on H.R. 7895 (1926), *op. cit.,* p. 1041.

war, and probably better than anything that you could get, taking stability in the price level as the test, if you please—better, I repeat, than you could get under any artificial device or formula or any series of substitute expedients." [41]

Dr. Miller, however, realized that a general return to gold might cause a scramble for it; and he realized that the Federal Reserve System, possessing so much gold, had a responsibility to those countries that wanted to return to it. Unless this factor were taken into consideration, he said, there might be trouble.

The Annual Report of the Federal Reserve Board for 1928, says with some pride that the System had done its part in helping the world back to the gold standard:

"The credit policies of the Federal Reserve System, which during the period from 1924 to 1927, when the gold standard was being reestablished, were a factor favoring the redistribution of gold, have, therefore, contributed to the maintenance of the gold standard and indirectly to the improvement of world trade." [42]

But later on, Dr. Miller, having praised this Federal Reserve gold policy, which favored redistribution, became a severe critic of it. He said:

". . . I think there was also more or less the illusion (that became more pronounced in 1927) that the Federal Reserve System could do something to correct what was then described, and is still described, as the maldistribution of gold in the world. I am afraid that illusion still obtains in certain Federal Reserve circles, and in certain parts of the country. It is one of the most misleading illusions that any body of men charged with the responsibility of administering the fundamental credit mechanism of the country could allow to enter its mind." [43]

[41] *Stabilization Hearings* on H.R. 7895 (1926), *op. cit.,* p. 791.
[42] *Annual Report* of the Federal Reserve Board for 1928, p. 16.
[43] *Hearings* before a Subcommittee of the Senate Banking and Currency Committee, 71st Congress, 3rd Session on Senate Resolution 71 (1931). Survey of the National and Federal Reserve Banking Systems, p. 132.

Production—Consumption Indices

Federal Reserve officials seemed to see an inconsistency between the interests of the price level and the interests of the distribution of goods. The 10th Annual Report of 1923 emphasized the importance of the movement of goods from producer to consumer as criterion for the functioning of the credit system:

"A characteristic of the good functioning of the economic system is to be found in the smooth and unobstructed movement of goods from the producer through the channels of distribution to their several ultimate uses. The characteristic of the good functioning of the credit system is to be found in the promptness and the degree with which the flow of credit adapts itself to the orderly flow of goods in industry and trade. So long as this flow is not interrupted by speculative interference, there is little likelihood of the abuse of credit supplied by the Federal Reserve banks and consequently little danger of the undue creation of new credit." [44]

Mr. W. W. Stewart preferred the production-consumption index to the price index as criterion of Federal Reserve credit policy. He said:

". . . rather than use the price index as a test or as an indicator of Federal Reserve credit policy, I would prefer to know what the inventories were and whether or not production was moving promptly into distribution." [45]

Dr. Miller also pointed to this factor many times when testifying before Congressional Committees. In May, 1928, he explained that price quotations may be ignored and had been ignored, when credit policy was being determined. He said:

". . . when goods move into consumption about as rapidly as they are turned out of production, you have what is here de-

---

[44] *10th Annual Report* of the Federal Reserve Board for 1923, p. 34.
[45] *Stabilization Hearings* on H.R. 7895 (1926), *op. cit.*, p. 764.

scribed as an equilibrium between the volume of consumption and the volume of production and trade."

Asked why prices were thus ignored, he answered:

". . . Because this [production-consumption index] is a more competent guide and detector of changes in the volume of credit needs than prices or any other single factor possibly can be; . . . you have got to have an indication of the direction in which the economic situation is tending quicker than you can get it from a price index." [46]

The Federal Reserve officials testified that this production-consumption index was definitely consulted in 1923. Perhaps it was consulted on other occasions, but there is no evidence which is generally known that it ever had the effect of preventing disequilibrium between production and consumption.

Declining Price Level

Another factor, although perhaps not comparable in importance with the gold policy and the production-consumption indices, may nevertheless, at times, have had a definite influence in shaping Federal Reserve credit policy. This is the idea that, as a consequence of increased efficiency and keener competition, the price level ought to decline in periods of prosperity. Dr. Goldenweiser had mentioned this theory [47] which was, however, vigorously opposed by Professor Commons. The latter's argument was that by discouraging production, a declining price level was definitely a cause of unemployment.[48]

It is quite possible that a slow fall in the price level may take place without reducing profits, trade and employment, if there is a wide-spread improvement in costs and efficiency. But the

[46] *Stabilization Hearings* on H.R. 11806 (1928), *op. cit.,* p. 346.
[47] See Chapter 5, Section 5.
[48] *Stabilization Hearings* on H.R. 11806 (1928), *op. cit.,* p. 432.

Federal Reserve officials seemed to assume that a fall in the price level is itself a convincing evidence and expression of such technological improvements.

SECTION 4. POWERS TO STABILIZE

The Powers and their Limitations

The advocates of stable money insisted that the officials of the System had all the powers needed for stabilizing the dollar. The officers of the System said they had not. What then, in the opinion of these officials were their powers and what were the limitations on them, legal or practical, that interfered with stabilization?

Governor Strong, in 1926, said that because the System held the country's gold and could control the reserves of many banks, it could influence the volume of credit; that is, by means of rediscount rates and open-market operations.

"I think," he said, "the fundamental thing about the Federal Reserve System is that, holding the reserves of so many banks, the gold reserve of the country, and being the source of supply of additional credit when it is required by business, and the means, if you please, of retiring that credit when it is no longer needed by business, the Federal Reserve System, through changes in the rate of discount and preliminary purchases or sales of securities in the market, has the power to influence to some extent, at times, the total volume of credit in the country and its cost." [49]

On the other hand, he believed that there were a number of practical limitations to the powers of the system—that is, factors beyond its control which might lead to inflation in spite of all Federal Reserve efforts.

[49] *Stabilization Hearings* on H.R. 7895 (1926), *op. cit.,* p. 296.

1) The management of the system might deteriorate. Governor Strong said that their best men were often hired away by commercial concerns that paid higher salaries.

2) The administration of the Treasury might interfere with the operations of the system, by inflating the currency.

3) Congress might change the reserve requirements of the member banks, and the additional credit facilities thus placed at their disposal might bring about inflation which the system could not control.

4) Uncontrollable and unavoidable importations of gold, might occur at times when the system could not "sterilize" it for want of sufficient earning assets wherewith to buy it. This would lead to credit expansion which the Reserve authorities could not control.[50]

So long as the system had sufficient earning assets, Governor Strong believed it might bring pressure to prevent inflation, unless Congress or the Treasury interfered. But,

"When you come to arresting a deflation of credit, you are coming into the most difficult problem that the Federal Reserve System can possibly have to face." [51]

In his opinion, if agricultural products declined due to the state of the world market, this would start a decline of the price level. If then the System attempted to make money cheap, their efforts, instead of correcting the price level, might lead to speculation in securities. Nor could business men be forced to use credit if they did not want to.

A very comprehensive statement of the stabilization powers of the Federal Reserve System was presented by *Mr. W. Randolph Burgess,* then the Assistant Federal Reserve Agent stationed at the New York Federal Reserve Bank. Although it is but an elaboration of the points mentioned by Governor Strong, the

[50] *Ibid.,* pp. 554 ff.
[51] *Ibid.,* p. 577.

essential points of the statement are quoted below in part for their clearness:

"The powers the Federal Reserve System possesses for stabilization are of two principal types: First, those which arise from the very existence of the system; and second, those which involve some policy decision. The first group is perhaps the most important, the influence for stability which arises, not from any specific decision, but from the facilities which the Reserve System is continuously offering member banks and to the public. These facilities include the following:

"(1) Facilities for the elasticity of credit

"(2) Facilities for fluidity of credit

"(3) Influence upon credit practice

"(4) The publication of information on credit and business

"(5) Providing an agency to handle Government finance.

"The second group of powers which the Reserve banks may use to encourage stability of credit and business consists of those which involve definite policy decisions. The principal such powers are the following:

"(1) Changes in the rediscount rate

"(2) Purchases and sales of Government securities

"(3) Informal influence upon member banks

"(4) Regulatory action." [52]

Denial of All Powers

In spite of these comprehensive statements the opponents of stable money persisted in their denials. Thus Mr. W. W. Stewart said in 1926:

". . . My own interpretation is that they have not exercised their powers to stabilize prices, nor have they the power to stabilize prices." [53]

[52] *Ibid.*, p. 1018.
[53] *Ibid.*, p. 768.

And in 1928 Congressman Strong had the following little discussion with Dr. Miller:

"Mr. Strong: 'My conception is when we give to a board of men the right to control the volume of money in circulation among the people, and largely to control the price of money, and the right to control the expansion or contraction of credit, that is the greatest power that has ever been given to any men by any government, except the power of life and death and liberty.'

"Dr. Miller: 'I would say that is all right for oratorical purposes.'

"Mr. Strong: 'Is it not true?'

"Dr. Miller: 'No; it is not true. . . . I deny that it even has these powers that you say it has; that it can contract or expand as you say. When has the Federal Reserve Board contracted credit? Has it in this last year?' " [54]

The following review will show how the Federal Reserve used the open-market and discount policies for the maintenance of a stable dollar from 1922 to 1929, and also what brought such stability to an end.

[54] *Stabilization Hearings* on H.R. 11806 (1928), *op. cit.,* p. 184.

CHAPTER VIII

THE FEDERAL RESERVE SYSTEM (CONTINUED)

SECTION 1. THE OPERATION OF THE FEDERAL RESERVE, 1921–1929

Preventing Gold Inflation

LET us first see how the excessive gold imports can be prevented from creating inflation.[1]

The first method is to prevent a "secondary expansion." Member banks, by depositing their imports of gold with their Federal Reserve Bank create reserves which enable them, under the law, to extend credit to their customers amounting to several times the value of the deposits. The Federal Reserve banks, in turn, may also use the gold thus received to increase their own investments and loans to member banks. These credits are called secondary expansion, and this the Federal Reserve banks resisted.

The second method is to prevent gold from backing either Federal Reserve notes or credit, by compelling it to back gold certificates. Such certificates require a 100% backing in gold, whereas Federal Reserve notes require only a 40% gold reserve and credit much less. By January, 1928, for instance, the Federal Reserve System had put one billion dollars of gold certificates into circulation, and had accordingly stored a like amount of gold, which might otherwise have backed Federal Reserve notes two-and-a-half times that sum, or credit many times that sum.

The third method of preventing gold from backing an ex-

[1] For a full description see W. Randolph Burgess, *The Reserve Banks and the Money Market*, New York, Harper & Brothers, 1927.

cessive credit expansion is to raise the rediscount rate. This the Federal Reserve System did from 1922-1929, at the same time trying not to raise it so far as to attract gold imports.

Discovery of Open-Market Powers

The bottom of the 1920-1921 deflation was reached in the Summer of 1921. Due to the existing deflation the member banks offered less paper to the 12 Reserve banks for rediscount, thus decreasing the earnings of these 12 banks from that source. At the same time the Federal Reserve banks, merely in order to increase their earning assets, began purchasing Government securities in the open market. To the surprise of the Reserve officials, the purchase of Government securities by the 12 Reserve banks seemed to have the effect of further reducing their profits. This was because member banks, having thus increased their reserves (*i.e.* deposits) in the Reserve banks, curtailed their other methods of obtaining such reserves, *i.e.* curtailed their rediscounting of paper at the Federal Reserve banks and the latter lost more earnings through loss of rediscount opportunities than they gained by increasing their "earning assets."

At first they did not know why the purchases of earning assets was thus followed by a diminution of rediscount opportunities [2] but they soon found out and noticed the correlation: that by selling and buying bonds, etc., they would raise and lower the member bank reserves and thus raise and lower the volume of credit issued by the member banks to the public. It was because of this discovery that Governor Strong used the Open-Market Committee to control credit by this newly found principle, the principle of "open-market operations," although the Open-Market Committee may originally have been established informally by

[2] See also John R. Commons, *Price Stabilization and the Federal Reserve System* in "The New York Times Annalist," April 1, 1927.

Governor Strong for the purpose of preventing the several Federal Reserve banks from interfering and competing with each other when purchasing securities.

Through these purchases of securities, the Federal Reserve banks, in 1921, furnished the member banks with new credits. Member banks first used these funds to liquidate some of their indebtedness with their respective Federal Reserve banks, and then *to establish reserves* which enabled them more freely to extend loans to their own customers. The resulting easier credit conditions, supplemented by lower discount rates, had a very gratifying influence upon industry and trade. During 1922 the basic production index of the Federal Reserve Board rose 33%. The wholesale commodity price index of the Bureau of Labor Statistics rose from 138 in January 1922 to 156 in December 1922. In fact, recovery from the previous depression became so rapid that there was a general fear of another inflation.

Preventing Inflation in 1923

But the Federal Reserve System now reversed its "let-alone" policy as to inflation and deflation. The Open-Market Committee, which in the Spring of 1923 became officially recognized by the Federal Reserve Board, began to exert a definite and conscious influence upon the development of the money market. During June 1922–July 1923, this Committee *sold* Government securities to the amount of $525,000,000. As the purchasers were largely member banks, the chief effect was to reduce their own reserves and thus diminish their power to extend credit. In other words, money had been taken out of circulation and in order to accommodate the public, the member banks were forced to rediscount in increased volume with their Federal Reserve banks.

This compulsion to rediscount would ordinarily make the member banks less inclined to lend money. In addition rediscount rates were increased in the Spring of 1923, and the Federal Reserve Board, in its own and in other publications, warned the public of the danger of a new inflation through over-expansion of credit. In that manner the Federal Reserve System used all three of its powers, viz., open-market operations, the rediscount rate, and moral suasion, and as a result the advance of prices was stopped—inflation was prevented.

The Federal Reserve Board, however, later denied that these measures had been of deciding influence, and argued that the supply of goods had caught up with the demand for them, and thus interrupted the rise of prices.

Dr. Miller expressed this non-monetary influence as follows: "We began to sell some securities. We sold the market, which means we took money out of the market. . . . We absorbed some portion of the cash in the market and also resorted to the discount rate advance in February 1923; in other words, we began to test the real need of the existing volume of credit in order to enable industry to function smoothly; and the fact is that as we liquidated open-market investments a demand in the shape of rediscounts of practically equivalent volume made its appearance and rather satisfied us that the existing amount of credit was needed. A further testing of the situation by the movement of trade and prices, pay-rolls and employment, satisfied us, on the whole, that the situation was not an unsound one; and although it looked expanded by the test of price changes alone, inherently there was nothing wrong and there was no inflationary development in connection with it." [3]

Yet, Professor Commons seemed quite justified in asking what developments might have followed if the Federal Reserve had bought securities instead of selling them, and had lowered its discount rate instead of raising it.

He showed how the steadiness of the price level in 1923 was

[3] *Stabilization Hearings* on H.R. 7895 (1926), *op. cit.,* pp. 840-1.

the net result of the action of two factions in the Federal Reserve, one of which tried to restrain inflation and the other of which concluded that no restriction was then needed. He said: "There arose in 1922 and 1923 within the System itself, two conflicting theories, not as to the economic effect of the open-market operations and discount rates, but as to their timeliness and amount."

The one side—alarmed at the rapid rise of prices—demanded extreme, drastic measures immediately—and was able to carry through the extensive sale of securities just mentioned but not to carry out an increase in discount rates. The other side maintained—(based on new statistical evidence)—that easy credit had not yet produced speculation nor excessive inventories, nor exceeded the needs of increasing production, trade and employment.

"The two conflicting theories worked out happily in combination, for the year 1923 turned out to be a year of full employment without any further increase in the price index after April. . . ." [4]

Open Market Operations and Changes of Discount Rates,
1923 to 1928

But presently, the credit restraint proved excessive. From April, 1923 to May 1924, the price index fell from 159 to 147; business receded; there were serious bank failures in the West; the perilous condition of the cattle industry threatened a national disaster. [5]

Very well: the System now proceeded to counteract this down-

[4] *Stabilization Hearings* on H.R. 11806 (1928), *op. cit.,* pp. 427–8.
[5] See also O. M. W. Sprague and W. Randolph Burgess, *Money and Credit and their Effect on Business,* Chapter X, of *Recent Economic Changes in the United States.* Report of the Committee on Recent Economic Changes of the President's Conference on Unemployment. New York, McGraw-Hill Book Co., Inc., 1929, Vol. II, pp. 657–707.

ward trend. Beginning with December, 1923 and up to September, 1924 it bought $510 millions of Government securities [6] and reduced the discount rates from 4½% to 3%. As a consequence of these easier credit conditions, the price level rose 11% from June, 1924 to March, 1925; agricultural prices increased as much as 20%. Business reached a new high peak in the early part of 1925. This recovery was, however, accompanied by excessive speculative activities which induced the Federal Reserve to sell again—it sold some 200 million dollars of securities which it had previously bought. For the same reason it raised the rediscount rate. This was done in Boston in November, 1925, and in New York, in January, 1926.

From then on, until the early part of 1927, business conditions were satisfactory, and the price level maintained comparative stability, except, perhaps for a short period of hesitation during the summer of 1926, when the system bought a small amount of securities and the New York discount rate was lowered for a few months.

In the beginning of 1927, Professor Sprague expressed himself as favoring a reduction of the rediscount rate. Indeed, he said, in the interest of continued prosperity, increased open-market purchases and a lower discount rate should already have been employed late in 1926.[7] Beginning in the summer of 1926, the wholesale price index had gradually declined, and agricultural conditions became very unfavorable. Professor Sprague admitted that easier credit conditions might produce speculation, but thought that this should not prevent the Federal Reserve from acting so long as trade and industry were benefited. In May 1927, the System resumed the purchases of Govern-

[6] Benjamin Haggott Beckhart, *Federal Reserve Policy and the Money Market,* 1923–1931, Vol. IV, of *The New York Money Market,* New York, Columbia University Press, 1932, p. 6.

[7] O. M. W. Sprague, *Lower Discount Rates May Prove Advisable,* "New York Times Annalist," January 14, 1927.

ment securities, acquiring 230 million dollars' worth [8] until November 1927. In the late summer of that year, the rediscount rates were also reduced to $3\frac{1}{2}\%$.

A main reason for action at that time seems to have been the condition of the European exchanges. Unless America's interest rates were kept low, foreign gold would flow into the United States; and such a flow would have necessitated the raising of bank rates abroad which was considered inadvisable because of the depressed condition of world trade and world prices. The Governors of the most important European Central Banks had come to this country in the Spring of 1927, to discuss this matter with the Federal Reserve officials, and it is very likely that the System acted upon the representation and advice of these European bankers—that is, kept the rates low.

The beginning of 1928 brought a new outburst of speculative activity which the System attempted to curb by selling about 400 million of securities from December 1927 to June 1928. At the same time the rediscount rates were raised again from $3\frac{1}{2}\%$ to 4% and $4\frac{1}{2}\%$. Clearly, this action was not taken with regard to the business, agricultural, or industrial situation of the country, but with the intention of curbing speculation in the securities markets. Naturally, the price level and business conditions were also affected by this new restriction which came just at a period when business was recovering and prices were rising due to the previous reductions in rates and open market operations.

Beginning in 1928, there now followed a series of contradictory actions by the Federal Reserve System, precipitated largely by the stock market situation. In spite of these, the price level and business conditions held their own quite well until late in 1929, although the index had started on its downward movement earlier that year.

[8] Beckhart, *op. cit.,* p. 6.

Timeliness of Action

Almost without exception, the above adjustments of the Federal Reserve System were made too late, if judged by the criterion of the commodity price index. And when a corrective measure was taken it was permitted to exert its influence too long, so that the pendulum swung too far in the opposite direction. Apparently, the System made no use of its production-consumption indices which some of the officials said were more prompt in detecting disequilibrium than the price level. For correcting disequilibrium *timeliness of action* has frequently been called more important than the *method* of it. Even during the above period of comparative stability of the price level, the Federal Reserve's greatest failure was in the lack of *timely* action.

Later, in 1928 Dr. Sprague, at the stabilization hearings, agreed with the proponents of the Strong bill that the lack of a definite policy apparently left the System unable to make prompt decisions. The hesitating manner in which policies were carried out, was, in his judgment, the greatest defect in the operation of the Reserve System. He said:

"Well, if it [the Strong bill] would accomplish that result,—make the decision in matters of policy at times a little more immediate, and the decision itself a little more definite,—then there would be, I think, an advantage from the passage of the bill. I probably agree with you that the defects in the operation of the Federal Reserve System are not so much in positive errors of judgment that have been made, but rather in the hesitating manner in which, at times, policies have been decided upon and then executed." [9]

This consideration led Dr. Sprague to express himself definitely in favor of legislation that would limit the discretionary

[9] *Stabilization Hearings* on H.R. 11806 (1928), *op. cit.*, p. 156.

powers of the System with regard to the determination of its policy:

"For a number of years now, measures directing the Reserve Banks to use their powers to maintain price stabilization have been before Congress. At hearings, first in 1926, and later in the Spring of 1928, I expressed great doubts of the advisability of such amendments to the Federal Reserve Act. Assuming, however, definite recognition of the limitations to which price stabilization is subject, I have reached the conclusion that a stabilization amendment might prove serviceable. . . .

"A few general principles taken as desirable objectives should neither unduly hamper nor enforce action, and, in particular, a price stabilization provision in the Reserve Act might well prove helpful in its bearing upon future monetary legislation and in the development of co-operative policies and arrangements with foreign bank officials." [10]

Section 2. Stock Market Speculation

The comparative stability of the price level ended in the Fall of 1929, when the decline became more pronounced. What, then, were the reasons that prevented Federal Reserve policy from being effective in counteracting this decline—or did the System take any action at all to prevent deflation?

Speculation in securities was the main disturbing factor. As mentioned above, Governor Strong as early as 1926 had called attention to the danger of a speculative use of Federal Reserve credit when extended to ease the credit situation. This had happened during 1924–25, and the System then immediately took corrective measures by selling securities and raising the discount rate.

[10] *Price Stabilization,* in "American Economic Review, Supplement," Vol. XIX, No. 1, March 1929, pp. 67–68.

Opinions on Federal Reserve Responsibility

The question whether the Federal Reserve should interfere with such speculation, and whether the stock market was one of its concerns, was a warmly disputed one. *Carl Snyder,* during the stabilization hearings of 1926, being asked whether the System should interfere with stock prices, replied:

"I would prefer, Mr. Congressman, not to go into questions of that kind further than to say I do not think that is any concern of the Federal Reserve System in this country any more than to interfere with the price of cottage cheese." [11]

During 1927–1928, as a consequence of open-market operations and reductions of the discount rates, credit had become cheaper and more abundant, and consequently securities speculation had received another strong stimulus. At the time of the stabilization hearings of 1928 this speculative trend had become very annoying to the Federal Reserve officials, and they frequently expressed their displeasure. *Gustav Cassel,* being asked for his opinion, stated his fears that the attempt to curb speculation by increasing discount rates might produce a decline in commodity prices with reduced production and unemployment as results.

"It would be a great benefit to the country if some means could be devised by which it would be possible to limit speculation on the New York Stock Exchange without increasing the Federal Reserve's bank rates, because such increases may be very unwelcome. They may disturb the whole monetary policy, and it may have an effect on the general level of prices that will result in a depression in production in this country, followed by a decrease of employment, all only for the purpose of combating some speculators in New York." [12]

[11] *Stabilization Hearings* on H.R. 7895 (1926), *op. cit.,* p. 602.
[12] *Stabilization Hearings* on H.R. 11806 (1928), *op. cit.,* p. 381.

Professor Commons also discussed this problem on that occasion and advised that the Federal Reserve pay no attention to securities prices:

"I will classify stock-market prices along with rents and wages and retail prices as things we do not need to pay attention to when we are looking forward to keeping the business of the country continuing in prosperity, keeping employment as stable as possible, and thus having the productive energies of the country stabilized. You cannot stabilize everything; that is true. . . ." [13]

In his summary of the various statements made at these hearings, Professor Commons also warned that the attempt to regulate stock prices might have a detrimental effect upon the price level. He said: "To attempt to control so volatile a matter cripples the power to control the purchasing power of the dollar. . . ." [14]

The members of the Federal Reserve Board presented a different point of view. However, *Mr. Hamlin* revealed the painful sense of responsibility which the Board may have felt in arriving at its decisions. Apparently he foresaw the detrimental effect upon the entire country of the deflationary measures applied to curb stock exchange speculation, but could find no other way out:

"I feel that the Federal Reserve Board and the Federal Reserve System primarily has nothing to do with the operations in the stock market, and I have always hesitated to think of increasing a rate—for example, on agriculture and commerce— because some people are speculating in Wall Street. But, on the other hand, I think a condition can arise where that speculation so threatens business, threatens to curtail, perhaps, business credits that may be demanded, that the Board would

[13] *Ibid.,* p. 100.
[14] *Ibid.,* p. 437.

have a right to act. I should always be reluctant to act. The only direct power you give to us over any speculative transaction is to put up the rates on agriculture, commerce and industry. That is like telling a father that he must cut the ears off his child, because a drunken man is carousing in the street. . . . I hate it; but I do admit that a condition may arise where it is the only thing to do, and it has got to be done; and, in the long run, it will be better for agriculture, commerce and business, to do it." [15]

And *Dr. Miller* said that although the Federal Reserve System was not concerned about the stock market, it was responsible for the use to which its credit was being put; and as Federal Reserve credit was employed for stock market speculation, the System became responsible for such speculation:

"My view is that the Federal Reserve has nothing to do with the stock market as such; that the Stock Market is of no concern to the Federal Reserve.

"It is, however, a matter of great concern to the Federal Reserve what becomes of the credit that it creates. When as a result of policies adopted for other considerations, it develops that a part, and more particularly when it is a considerable part, of the credit released by it goes into the stock exchange loan account, the resulting situation becomes its responsibility." [16]

This statement by Dr. Miller seemed to express the position of the Federal Reserve System correctly. The System was created particularly to see to it that business, industry and agriculture, that is, the so called "legitimate" users of credit, would not be deprived of their credit requirements because of Wall Street speculation. Although it is still a controversial question whether, in recent years, such speculation actually did deprive business, industry and agriculture of their credit requirements, the Federal Reserve System seemed to have taken its position

[15] *Ibid.*, p. 396.
[16] *Ibid.*, p. 119.

from the mere fact that some of the credit it had created was used for speculation, ignoring the further fact that its own corrective measures might also curtail the supply of "legitimate" credit.

Proposals for Controlling Speculation

The proposals which were advanced for the control of speculation in securities came from two groups.

One comprised those who would deal with the situation in such a manner as not to interfere with the legitimate credit needs of the country, and not to hurt the price level.

The second group comprised those who would discourage speculation by such a general credit restriction as would (in the opinion of the other group) have a detrimental effect upon the general business situation, and thus indirectly have more than the intended effect on stock values.

Foremost in the first group was *Professor O. M. W. Sprague.* His suggestions may be summarized as follows:

The Federal Reserve banks should refuse to rediscount at any rate and for any appreciable period of time for banks that have a large line of call loans on their books.

In Dr. Sprague's opinion, speculation could easily be controlled by such direct means. "It is perfectly feasible to bring about a reduction of call loans by informing the 100 largest banks of the country that the Reserve banks will be indisposed to lend as much as they may ask when they have a large volume of call loans which they can liquidate. It is perfectly possible to reduce the volume of call loans without any further advance in discount rates by the Federal Reserve banks." [17]

Of the same mind was *Mr. Hamlin* of the Federal Reserve Board. He also believed that speculative loans might be stopped by restricting further loans to banks which used their funds for

[17] *Stabilization Hearings* on H.R. 11806 (1928), *op. cit.*, p. 148.

speculative purposes. The Board or Federal Reserve banks should be given the power, "to go to any bank and, if they found that the proportion of its loans for speculative purposes has reached such a percentage of its total deposits, that it is threatening business conditions, they should have the right to increase the reserve requirement of that individual bank. . . ." [18]

Professor Commons in his summary of the proceedings, noted the following methods which had been suggested: ". . . requirement that time deposits be invested in securities; or higher rates of discount be imposed on notes secured by Government collateral than on commercial paper, thus reversing the practice during the war and until 1921; or no discount less than seven days, following the practice of the Bank of England; or refusing to lend to a member bank which is extending its stock exchange loans at such period; or by the extension of branch banking." [19]

In contrast to the above suggestions, some of the most prominent officials of the Federal Reserve banks were quite definite in their advocacy of higher discount rates to curb speculation. At a hearing before the Senate Banking and Currency Committee, Governor Harrison, of the New York Bank, was asked the following question by *Senator Glass:* "Why do you apply the rediscount rate to a situation of that sort and penalize the legitimate commerce in order to control something you say you have no right to control?" [20]

To this *Mr. Harrison* answered: "I think we have a perfect right to control an expansion of credit, regardless of the cause of it, when credit is expanding as it was in 1928 and 1929 at a great rate all through the country. Because of the demand for money for speculative purposes we wanted to put up our redis-

[18] *Ibid.,* p. 404.
[19] *Ibid.,* p. 436.
[20] *Hearings* on Senate Res. 71 (1931), *op. cit.,* p. 56.

count rate believing that was a proper means of limiting a too rapid use of the country's assets for speculative or other purposes."

Governor Harding of the Federal Reserve Bank of Boston in the Spring of 1929, also defended the policy of high discount rates which, by curbing business activities, would also eventually bring down securities values. He said: ". . . Continued high rates of interest will eventually bring about a slowing down in business and industry. Such a slowing down would inevitably affect, adversely, security values. While the Federal Reserve System is not engaged in any kind of economic warfare, and has no desire to destroy values, it is my belief that under the terms of the Federal Reserve act its first duty is to the industrial, commercial and agricultural interests of the country. That there can be no dependence upon the effective discharge of this duty if the resources of the System are permitted to be diverted through indirect methods into channels expressly prohibited directly by the law, appears to me so clear as to be beyond dispute." [21]

What Was Done to Stop Speculation

It is not the purpose here to explain the crisis of 1929 nor the Stock Market crash. We are interested only in the operations of the Federal Reserve System as to stable money and as to the elimination of the destabilizing influence of security speculation.

The sale of about 400 million dollars of Government securities from January to June, 1928, the increase in the rediscount rates from 3½% to 4½% in May 1928, and their further increase to 5% by eight of the twelve Reserve banks in July, 1928, were the first corrective measures to be taken. During the same

---

[21] Speaking before the Economic Club of New York, March 18, 1929; quoted from "The Consensus," of June, 1929, publ. by the National Economic League, Boston, p. 17.

period the System's monetary gold stock declined by about 258 millions and the System made use of "moral suasion," discouraging the use of Federal Reserve credit for speculative purposes, and warning the public of the dangers of an over-expanded security market.

The United States Senate also took an active interest in the matter. Hearings were held before the Senate Banking and Currency Committee,[22] and on May 12, 1928 this Committee passed a resolution to the effect that the Federal Reserve Board should ask the Federal Reserve banks to prevent further expansion of speculative loans, and suggests legislative remedies if any were practical.[23]

As a result of the above mentioned measures, the growth of the speculative movement was brought to a stop in the summer of 1928, although the speculative loans were not reduced. But the credit stringency made itself felt in legitimate business.

Thereupon, with the desire to be helpful to seasonal financing, the Federal Reserve System purchased Government securities and bills to the amount of 358 million, during August and December, 1928.[24] Legitimate business, however, did not greatly benefit by this expedient, while speculation was again encouraged by it. Consequently, immediately after the turn of the year, the Federal Reserve reversed its open-market operations, reducing its holdings by 398 million.

The power of moral suasion was now again resorted to, in preference to an advance of discount rates. A letter addressed to the Federal Reserve Banks on February 2, 1929, stated:

"A member bank is not within its reasonable claims for rediscount facilities at its Federal Reserve bank when it borrows

[22] *Hearings* on Brokers' Loans before the Banking and Currency of the U.S. Senate, 10th Congress, 1st Session, S. Res., 113.
[23] *Report*, No. 1124, U.S. Senate, 70th Congress, 1st Session; quoted from Beckhart, *op. cit.*, p. 99.
[24] Beckhart, *op. cit.*, p. 112.

either for the purpose of making speculative loans or for the purpose of maintaining speculative loans." [25]

At its meeting on February 15, 1929, the Federal Advisory Council approved the Board's attempt to influence the speculative situation by "moral suasion":

"The Federal Advisory Council approves the action of the Federal Reserve Board in instructing the Federal Reserve banks to prevent, as far as possible, the diversion of Federal Reserve funds for the purpose of carrying loans based on securities. The Federal Advisory Council suggests that all the member banks in each district be asked directly by the Federal Reserve bank of the district to cooperate in order to attain the end desired. The council believes beneficial results can be attained in this manner." [26]

On April 19, 1929, however, the Council changed its attitude and asked the Board to permit the Federal Reserve banks to raise their discount rates in order to check speculation:

"The Council in reviewing present conditions finds that, in spite of the cooperation of the member banks, the measures so far adopted have not been effective in correcting the present situation of the money market. The council, therefore, recommends that the Federal Reserve Board permit the Federal Reserve banks to raise their rediscount rates immediately and maintain a rate consistent with the cost of commercial credit." [27]

The Federal Reserve Bank of New York, from February 14 until May 23, 1929 had applied to the Federal Reserve Board in all ten times for permission to raise its discount rates from 5% to 6%. But the Board still had faith in the effectiveness of its policy of "direct action," as the method of moral suasion was sometimes called.

On May 21, 1929, the Federal Advisory Council repeated its recommendation that the Federal Reserve banks be permitted to increase their rates:

[25] Quoted from Beckhart, *op. cit.*, p. 128.
[26] *16th Annual Report of the Federal Reserve Board for* 1929, p. 218.
[27] *Ibid.*, p. 218.

". . . the council recommends to the Federal Reserve Board that it now grant permission to raise the discount rates to 6 per cent to those Federal Reserve banks requesting it, thus bringing the rediscount rates into closer relation with generally prevailing commercial money rates. The council believes that improvement in financial conditions and a consequent reduction of the rate structure will thereby be brought about more quickly, thus best safeguarding commerce, industry and agriculture." [28]

Not until August 8, 1929 was the Federal Reserve Bank of New York authorized to raise its discount rates to 6%. Yet, at the same time, the acceptance buying rate of the New York Federal Reserve Bank was lowered from 5¼ to 5⅛%. The purpose of this contradictory measure was evidently to check speculation by higher discount rates, while facilitating the financing of legitimate business enterprise through open-market operations. Accordingly the Federal Reserve System proceeded to purchase bills in the open market and between August 10 and October 19, 1929, added 261 million of bills to its portfolio.

The net results were, however, quite contrary to expectation. Business and agriculture which were to have received the advantage of the easier credit conditions created by these open-market operations, had already covered their seasonal requirements of credit months before, and at the then prevailing high rates.

The credit tension was relieved by the System's open-market purchases and the fact that member banks were no longer subject to the application of "direct pressure." The funds thus made available, finding no other use, found their way into the speculative market. The net result was a sharp increase in speculative loans.[29]

[28] Ibid., p. 218.
[29] Beckhart, op. cit., pp. 142 ff.
For a very incisive study of Federal Reserve Policy, see also Lauchlin Currie, The Failure of Monetary Policy to Prevent the Depression of 1929–32 in "The

Section 3. After the Stock Market Crash

Fear of Inflation

The Federal Reserve System prevented the stock market crash which began in September, 1929, and culminated in the panics of October 21, 28, 29, 1929 from creating an immediate money panic, by the purchase of securities and bills in the open market, and progressively decreasing the rediscount rates. But while the System thus acted to prevent the demoralization of the money market, it paid little or no attention to the commodity price level. An attempt seems to have been made early in 1930, to avert deflation; but when, as a consequence, the stock market started to go up again, the attempt was given up.

During the summer of 1930, after the depression had set in, the Federal Reserve was urged to expand credit in order to stem the deflation. As an expression of the business world's demands for such action, the following expert advice in the Bulletin of the Royal Bank of Canada may serve. It advocated large scale open-market purchases by the Federal Reserve banks in order to put new credit into the member banks, restore confidence, and prevent further deflation:

". . . immediate and decisive action on the part of the Federal Reserve banks in putting new funds into the market in large volume is what is necessary to arrest the present serious and protracted price decline and to change the present psychology of business. . . .

"The only means by which the Reserve banks can affect the

Journal of Political Economy," Vol. XLII, April, 1934, No. 2, pp. 145–177, Chicago, The University of Chicago Press.

Mr. Currie thoroughly approves of the Federal Reserve policy of 1927, and also, though less enthusiastically, that of 1928; but he believes that the restrictive policies of 1929 were altogether wrong and largely responsible for the depression.

market would be through the purchase of Government securities. The latest balance sheet shows that they hold 597 million dollars of such securities.

"If the Reserve banks should increase these holdings to one billion dollars, the member banks would find their credit balances with the Federal Reserve System increased by substantially a like amount. . . ." [30]

This suggestion for credit expansion should, however, have been addressed to the Federal Reserve Board, which, through a reorganization of the original Open Market Committee in the Spring of 1930 had come into full control of the System's open-market operations. An Open-Market Policy Conference consisting of the Governors of the 12 Reserve Banks, had been substituted for the original Committee of five and the actions of the new body were subject to approval by the Board. As a consequence, the System had lost its power to act quickly. Moreover, any reflationary action would have had to be carried out so as to counteract, to some extent, the deflationary effect of a declining trend of the world price level.

According to Dr. Miller, the system was drifting previous to the crash.

"It was my opinion, expressed several times in discussions at Federal Reserve meetings, in the opening months of the year 1929, that the Federal Reserve System was drifting; that it was in the midst of a perilous situation without a policy." [31]

But even after the crash there was still no evidence that the system was following a policy, except, perhaps, that it was constantly afraid of inflation, and consequently resisted all efforts that might have led to credit expansion. This fear of inflation was frequently expressed by Dr. Miller. At one of the Congressional hearings he put it thus:

[30] *Bulletin of the Royal Bank of Canada*, July, 1930.
[31] *Hearings* on S. Res. 71 (1931), *op. cit.*, p. 143.

"I would say this, . . . if I may say it without carrying the implication that I have in mind my colleagues, that I think one of the main conditions affecting the operation of the Federal Reserve banking system is that most Americans are, by temperament, inflationarily inclined. Under such a law as this [meaning the Strong Stabilization Bill] were it enacted, there might be a disposition, perhaps, to seize the first indication or appearance that things were running off, that prices were down, to put into effect a pretty energetic open-market policy. . . ." [32]

The year of 1930 undoubtedly presented such a situation. "Things were running off" and a "pretty energetic open-market policy" might have spared the country much of the consequent deflation. But the Federal Reserve Board controlled the monetary policy, and nothing happened. There is no evidence that the Board made any effort to relieve the condition, either by buying securities, or by re-establishing confidence through moral suasion.

The evidence is to the contrary. Speaking for the Board in 1931, in the midst of the most devastating deflation, Dr. Miller again had nothing to suggest except advise against the danger of inflation:

". . . You must not leave it too easy for the Federal Reserve System to inflate. We have had too much inflation in the Federal Reserve System, and its favorite instrument is the open-market purchase of Government securities.

"We have had something of an obsession for easy money in the System, a feeling that it makes the atmosphere of business; that it can stop a recession of business, and turn a period of depression into one of recovery." [33]

As late as 1932, Dr. Miller opposed the Goldsborough stabilization bill on the ground "that the thing to be expected in this

[32] *Stabilization Hearings* on H.R. 11806 (1928), *op. cit.,* p. 363.
[33] *Hearings* on S. Res. 71 (1931), *op. cit.,* p. 147.

country if we operated under a stabilization philosophy, would be inflations." [34]

Deflation Prevails

Therefore, industry and agriculture soon learned that deflation ruled. In October, 1930, a representative business magazine,[35] portrayed in an editorial the fear and helplessness of the business community, and ridiculed the notion that deflation was a good thing, while inflation was the essence of all that is bad. It said:

"The Deflationists are in the Saddle.

". . . what was a comparatively mild business recession during the first half of 1930, has now become a case of world-wide reckless deflation. When a Governor of a Federal Reserve bank can stand up before a convention of investment bankers, condemn the American people for using automobiles, electric refrigerators, and radios, and proclaim that he does not agree with those who say that there must be no retrogression from the present living standards in this country, we need no further sign of the arrogant self-assurance of the night-riders of defeatism. . . .

"For some reason, to this type of mind, inflation enjoys a monopoly of evil and sums up all the economic sins; deflation is altogether a good thing, and there can never be too much of it. It seems to be wholly forgotten that, while a measure of deflation may be necessary after a period of speculative excess, it is a process just as dangerous and calling for as vigilant control as its opposite. . . ."

And Mr. R. G. Hawtrey, after explaining that "The only real remedy [for a Trade Depression] is the expansion of credit by the central banks," [36] came to the sad conclusion that

"The real obstacle to measures of credit expansion is not the

---

[34] *Stabilization Hearings* on H.R. 11499 and S. 4429 (1932), *op. cit.*, p. 250.
[35] Editorial in "The Business Week," October 22, 1930.
[36] R. G. Hawtrey, *Trade Depression and the Way Out*, London, Longmans, Green & Co., 1931, p. 74.

fear that they will not be effective, but the fear that they will." [37]

An exception to the deflationary policy of the Reserve System was the period from March to July 1932, when for seven weeks, the Federal Reserve bought securities amounting to 100 million a week. This action was taken after the passage of the Glass-Steagall bill which authorized credit expansion far beyond the limits previously set by the gold standard. But why the expansion stopped after seven weeks, or why it was decided to buy just 700 million of securities, it is difficult to say.

The actual addition to the reserves of the member banks was, however, small, due partly to a renewed outflow of gold, and partly to large scale hoarding by the public as a consequence of lack of confidence. Moreover, in many cases, the member banks, instead of expanding credit, often used their increased reserves to pay off or reduce their indebtedness to their respective Reserve banks.

SECTION 4. OTHER INTERFERENCES WITH STABILIZATION

Internal Friction

The stock market was not the only factor that interfered with an efficient operation of the Federal Reserve System. The fundamental set-up of the System produced much internal friction, division of counsel, desire for personal domination, and the like. It is impossible to put the blame on a single factor. There were other important factors.

Early in 1929, as already mentioned, there was a serious difference of opinion between the Federal Reserve Board and the New York Federal Reserve Bank. This bank applied several times for a drastic increase in the discount rates. The Board disregarded these applications, and when the increased rates were finally granted, they did not have the effect intended. Governor Harrison, testifying

[37] *Ibid.*, p. 84.

at the stabilization hearings in 1932, attempted to explain the importance of such an increase in the discount rates and of other possible measures at that time which might have prevented or mitigated troubles that followed:

". . . I think that had it been impossible for others than the banks to make loans to brokers during that period, and had the Reserve banks been in a position to raise rates as rapidly as some of us would have liked, you would have had a very different picture." [38]

With reference to this period, Dr. Miller had said that the system was "drifting," and in the "midst of a perilous situation" was "without a policy." He further said that:

". . . in default of any program on the part of the Federal Reserve banks for dealing with the situation, the Federal Reserve Board owed a responsibility to the country and to the future of the Federal Reserve System, for which it must find a solution. That solution was found in a rejection of discount policy as a suitable expedient in the circumstances, as they had then developed, and the adoption of 'direct pressure.' " [39]

In other words, according to Dr. Miller, the Board had to make this decision, because the banks did not know what to do—and this although the New York Bank, at least, had advanced a definite proposal which was rejected. Mr. Hamlin of the Federal Reserve Board explained this matter more in detail. The Board had previously agreed on the "direct pressure" method, as the more effective procedure to stop speculation. This policy was inaugurated on February 7th, 1929. On February 14th, the New York Bank, for the first time, applied for the rate increase, but the Board rejected it as it wanted to give its own method a fair trial. "Direct pressure" was abandoned on May 31, upon receipt of a letter from the Chairman of the New

[38] *Stabilization Hearings* on H.R. 10517 (1932), *op. cit.*, p. 464.
[39] *Hearings* on S. Res. 71 (1931), *op. cit.*, p. 143.

York Bank explaining that, under this method, member banks were really afraid to borrow at all.[40]

But later on, Mr. Hamlin explained that the New York application was rejected because of its form and this shows by what considerations important decisions of the Board have sometimes been influenced:

". . . This application, by the way, and I am not criticizing the Bank, was made over the telephone from New York. Governor Harrison, when advised of our decision, replied to Governor Young, that he had not given us the full vote of the New York Board, which contained a condition that our board should immediately decide it; and that his board of directors were waiting, and could not leave until we decided it. On that first application the Board was unanimous in rejecting it. I want to add in fairness to my associates that some who favored the application for increase, agreed that the condition imposed of an immediate decision could not be accepted by the Board, and therefore joined in an unanimous rejection of the application." [41]

For an understanding of this controversy it is necessary to refer to the time when, under the initiative of Governor Strong, the main power of the System rested unquestionably with the New York Bank and was exercised mainly by Governor Strong's Open-Market Committee. The Open-Market Committee, as mentioned above, was constituted informally in 1922, but confirmed officially in 1923.[42] But some of the members of the Board, particularly Dr. Miller, objected to the supreme power exercised by the New York Bank, whose judgment was sometimes opposite to that of the Board. The Federal Reserve Board therefore eventually reduced the Open-Market Committee almost to impotence.

Another apparent cause of jealousy among the members of

[40] *Ibid.*, p. 164.
[41] *Ibid.*, p. 172.
[42] *Tenth Annual Report* of the Federal Reserve Board, 1923, pp. 11–16.

the Federal Reserve Board was the intimate contact which the
New York Bank, due to its location, was able to maintain with
the central banks of foreign countries. When, in 1927, the heads
of the leading European central banks (English, French and
German) came to this country to discuss the need of a change
in credit policy,[43] they went to Governor Strong, and visited
Washington merely as a matter of courtesy. At a Congressional
hearing, Dr. Miller revealed his feelings about this matter as
follows:

". . . That was a rather sorry and shabby episode. On the
other hand, if the Federal Reserve Board had taken a position
at that time, as was its power and duty to do, on the matter
which was the occasion of that visit to which you have referred,
I think the contact, brief and informal though it was, would
have sufficed to leave the visiting central bankers in no doubt
where the ultimate responsibility and source of power in the
matters which brought them to the United States resides—in
the Federal Reserve System." [44]

Changing Dominating Influences

Dr. Miller also complained of the fact that the moving force
in the System was so hard to identify:

"I have in mind," he said, "vaguely, whatever happens to be
the dominant influence in the Federal Reserve System, and that
is expressing itself in the line of policy undertaken. It may today
be this individual or group; tomorrow it may be another. But
wherever any important line of action or policy is taken there
always will be found some one or some group whose judgment
and whose will is the effective thing in bringing about the result.
Their's is the ear which does the hearing for the System." [45]

[43] See also Chapter 8, Section 1.
[44] *Hearings* on S. Res. 71 (1931), *op. cit.,* p. 160.
[45] *Stabilization Hearings* on H.R. 11806 (1928), *op. cit.,* p. 165.

This amounts to saying that in the absence of a specific policy laid down by the law, the Federal Reserve System would vacillate, listening first to one, and then another proposal. However, the objection was made that the duty of stabilization would expose the Board to political pressure, which would make it impossible for it to fulfill its mandate successfully.

The advocates of stable money, on the other hand, have often claimed that the Board was already under political influence and that a definite mandate would be the only way for the Federal Reserve System to *escape* political influence, as manifested in the following instances:

Political Considerations

(1) In 1921, according to Professor Reed, Congress was investigating the activities of Federal Reserve Banks, and bills were proposed that the assent of Congress should be asked before the rediscount rates could be raised, to prevent the recurrence of a deflation as just experienced in 1920. If discount rates were lowered, there would be less insistence upon this point.[46] Therefore, according to Professor Reed, the Federal Reserve changed its policy in 1921 by lowering the discount rates. Of course, it is not argued that this action of Congress was the only cause for lowering the discount rates, but it might well have been one of the causes.

(2) Professor Commons, at the stabilization hearings in 1927, asked, "Why did they stop deflation in 1924?"[47] and answered that the System acted to prevent radical legislation.

"Governor Strong told you," he said, "the reason why they reversed their policy. . . . He said they found the reason they had to change was because of the depression in agriculture

[46] Quoted from Harold L. Reed, *Federal Reserve Policy*, 1921–1930, New York, McGraw-Hill Book Co., 1930, p. 15.
[47] *Stabilization Hearings* on H.R. 7895 (1926–27), *op. cit.*, pp. 1114–5.

in the West, the failure of agricultural banks and the menace of radical legislation. I would add also the Presidential campaign. We had to have prosperity in 1924 and they brought on prosperity. They began buying, began reducing the rates, increased the volume of money, sent prices up from 145 to 161 . . ."

Professor Reed, agreeing with Professor Commons, said: ". . . Political discontent in the Middle West, and the desire to avoid Congressional remodelling of the Reserve System, supplied strategical reasons for a further hearkening to the difficulties of the farm elements in our population." [48]

(3) Professor Reed asserted also that the credit policy of the Federal Reserve during 1928 was influenced by considerations of a political character, namely the 1928 elections which could not have been won by the party in power, unless economic conditions were favorable. He said:

"The elections of 1928 were to take place in the fall and the slackening tendencies of trade and employment in 1927 must have created considerable embarrassment to the leaders of the party in power with respect to their ability to employ the prosperity argument. On several occasions both the President and the Secretary of the Treasury had seized the opportunity to indicate their confidence in the soundness of the business and financial situation. Early in January 1928, for instance, the Treasury announced the issuance of new 3.5 per cent notes to replace the Second Liberty 4.25 per cent bonds. Since the bonds were not to mature until September 15, this announcement could scarcely be interpreted otherwise than as a declaration that the Treasury's influence would be exerted to maintaining easy money rates." [49]

Such considerations led to the discussion of the possibility of

[48] Reed, *op. cit.*, p. 72.
[49] *Ibid.*, p. 136.

eliminating the Secretary of the Treasury as a voting ex-officio member of the Federal Reserve Board. A constructive suggestion to that effect was made by Dr. Miller at the stabilization hearings in 1928, but was opposed by Mr. Hamlin.[50]

(4) In 1932, as another presidential election was coming, the open-market operations were under suspicion as possibly prompted by political considerations.

SECTION 5. EXPRESSIONS ON THE FEDERAL RESERVE SYSTEM

By Members of the Board

The preceding pages show some of the various forces which created and disturbed the stability of the purchasing power of the dollar under Federal Reserve administration. We have seen that the System always admitted that it had no policy. Governor Harding said so in 1920,[51] when the American monetary system was ". . . a good deal like a ship at sea without adequate equipment of rudder and compass to guide it." [52]

However, the system was active in developing its equipment, and as Dr. Miller said on the same occasion, in 1926: ". . . it is to the everlasting credit of the Federal Reserve System that it soon recognized the need for new instruments of regulation and began to set about their construction. . . ." [53]

But there was little, if any evidence that these new instruments, by which apparently the production-consumption index was meant, were employed to guide the ship safely. In 1928, Dr. Miller again declared that the System was in the same perplexed state of mind as in 1920–1921: ". . . It is my opinion that the Federal Reserve mind at the present time is more perplexed than it has been since the troublesome period of 1920–21; that

[50] Stabilization Hearings on H.R. 11806 (1928), op. cit., p. 407.
[51] Federal Reserve Bulletin, February, 1920, p. 117.
[52] Dr. Miller at the Stabilization Hearings on H.R. 7895 (1926), p. 696.
[53] Ibid., p. 696.

it is in a state of mental confusion largely because of surprise." [54]

Nevertheless, the Federal Reserve officials opposed Congressional action which would have defined their policy and limited their responsibility by the elimination of the discretionary powers which caused the confusion. Thus Dr. Miller suggested on the same occasion that the System be left alone:

"I do not want to be instructed where I know the instruction is going to be an embarrassment to me and a source of confusion to others who are, perhaps, less prepared by training to deal with matters of this kind." [55]

". . . I believe that you will get on the whole a more competent performance from the Federal System if you will let it go ahead and develop a procedure that grows out of its own experience. . . ."[55a]

So the Federal Reserve System was left to develop its "procedure." But in 1929, as Dr. Miller later said, the system was again "drifting." The Federal Reserve Board was powerful, it had supreme control of discount rates, open-market operations, and "direct pressure" methods. Yet, in 1931, Dr. Miller warned, "Without a strong Board I see trouble ahead for the Federal Reserve System." [56]

In 1928, Dr. Miller had stated [57] that the outflow of Federal Reserve funds into the speculative field was the most serious problem confronting the system; that, if a way could be found to stop this leakage he would be more sympathetic with the stabilization proposal. For this dilemma a number of practical solutions were proposed by experts, but not one of them was adopted.

[54] *Stabilization Hearings* on H.R. 11806 (1928), *op. cit.*, p. 162.
[55] *Ibid.*, p. 162.
[55a] *Ibid.*, p. 359.
[56] *Hearings* on S. Res. 71 (1931), *op. cit.*, p. 133.
[57] *Stabilization Hearings* on H.R. 11806 (1928), *op. cit.*, p. 363.

By a Congressman

Congressman Goldsborough, at the stabilization hearings in 1932, bitterly complained that the Federal Reserve System never even asked for help from Congress:

"Have you ever,—in spite of the fact that all we can get from the Federal Reserve System is that they have been compelled to devote their activities to trying to control prices on the New York Stock Exchange,—have you ever heard of anybody connected with the Federal Reserve System coming down here to help us get legislation through, to control the New York Stock Exchange?" [58]

By an Economist

After the painful experience of the stock market crash, and after measures had been applied to prevent a repetition of it, the Federal Reserve officials were even more opposed to stable money than before. Professor Willford I. King, at the stabilization hearings in 1932, attempted to explain this attitude by saying that the Federal Reserve officials looked at the problem from the bankers' viewpoint:

"They do not seem to have been particularly interested in stabilizing the price level during the last two or three years, and I do not suppose that they would change their views in that regard. My impression is, I do not think the Federal Reserve Board has any feeling that that was one of its functions. They are bankers, and they look at the thing from the banking standpoint, and they think of it just as the bankers think of banking in general. They want the credit conditions sound, but they do not think it is one of their functions. They feel that this is some-

[58] *Stabilization Hearings* on H.R. 10517 (1932), p. 507.

thing the people are trying to pull on them, and they do not want it. They have said so repeatedly. . . ." [59]

By a Banker

In June, 1932, Mr. Russel C. Leffingwell, himself a prominent banker and Assistant Secretary of the Treasury during the Wilson administration, and a partner of J. P. Morgan & Co., summarized the whole problem of Federal Reserve policy in a statement submitted to the Congressional Committee investigating "Stock Exchange Practices." On the basis of the above analysis, it is difficult to improve upon its conclusions:

". . . It is evident that the Federal Reserve System failed to control the inflation and has as yet failed to control the deflation. Ultimately the New York discount rate was raised to 6% in August 1929, but the country paid dearly for the months of delay and indecision in the superinflation of that year. Similarly, the System has been unable to evolve and operate and persist in an effective policy to counteract the deflation in the last three years. Its anti-deflationary policy has found only hesitant, tardy and intermittent expression in action. In matters of monetary management, in the control of inflation and deflation, a stitch in time saves nine. Twelve scattered banks, each with its Governor and its Chairman, and its Board of Directors, loosely ruled by a Board of eight in Washington, composed of men of diverse opinions, do not provide the country with an organization well adapted to act promptly and decisively. Some remedy must be found for this." [60]

---

[59] *Stabilization Hearings* on H.R. 10517 (1932), *op. cit.*, pp. 201–2.
[60] *Hearings* before the Committee on Banking and Currency, U.S. Senate, 73rd Congress, 1st Session on S. Res. 84 (72nd Congress) and S. Res. 56 (73rd Congress), Part II, p. 952.

CHAPTER IX

OFFICIAL RECOGNITION ABROAD (FROM 1919)

SECTION 1. CONFERENCES OF INTERNATIONAL IMPORTANCE

The Cunliffe Committee (1918–1919)

In January 1918, the famous but ill-advised Cunliffe Committee was appointed by the English Government,

". . . to consider the various problems which will arise in connection with currency and the foreign exchanges during the period of reconstruction and report upon the steps required to bring about the restoration of normal conditions in due course."

The following words were subsequently added to the Terms of Reference:

"and to consider the working of the Bank Act, of 1844, and the constitution and functions of the Bank of England with a view to recommending any alterations which may appear to them to be necessary or desirable." [1]

The Committee was headed by Lord Cunliffe who was the Governor of the Bank of England. All its thirteen members were bankers with the exception of Professor Pigou and Mr. Upcott, the latter representing the Treasury and Ministry of Reconstruction. In August, 1918, an Interim Report was issued; and on December 3, 1919, this was followed by a Final Report.

The recommendations of the Cunliffe Committee were very important if very unfortunate. They furnished the basis for the monetary policies which were subsequently followed, not

[1] Quoted from *Federal Reserve Bulletin,* December, 1918, pp. 1178–1192.

277

only in Great Britain, but in the entire world. The Report was largely an exposition of the mechanism of the pre-war gold standard—the "free gold-standard," as it was called. Under the free gold standard gold could move freely from one country to another, and central banks determined their credit policies according to their gold reserves. In the opinion of the members of the Committee, the return of the world to normal conditions was possible only by way of a restoration of this gold standard. Their conclusions were, therefore:

". . . In our opinion it is imperative that, after the war, the conditions necessary to the maintenance of an effective gold standard should be restored without delay. Unless the machinery which long experience has shown to be the only effective remedy for an adverse balance of trade and an undue growth of credit is once more brought into play, there will be grave danger of a progressive credit expansion which will result in a foreign drain of gold, menacing the convertibility of our note issue and so jeopardizing the international trade position of the country. . . ." [2]

One of the first critics of this Report was Mr. Arthur Kitson.[3] He pointed out that it was based on various dubious assumptions, *viz.*, that the pre-war prosperity was due to the gold standard; that the rise of the price level in England during the war was due to the suspension of the gold standard; that stability of the foreign exchanges was more important than the stability of the internal purchasing power of the currency; that the national welfare depended upon the volume of foreign trade. Many of the criticisms made by Mr. Kitson were later sustained by actual developments, and the abandonment of the gold standard by England in 1931 was the final collapse of the theories upon which the Cunliffe Report was based.

In a later brochure, Mr. Kitson explained the failure of the

[2] *Ibid.*, p. 1191.
[3] See *A Criticism of the First Interim Report of the Committee on Currency and Foreign Exchanges,* January 11, 1919.

Cunliffe policy by the fact that it embodied the views of the foremost English bankers. Their advice, he said, was favorable to banking interests, but not to British and world trade and industry. He said:

"In no other business or profession—save that of banking— would the Government of any civilized country so brazenly offend the public sense of justice as to appoint a committee composed exclusively, or even mainly, of members engaged in that particular business, to determine the legal privileges which such a business should enjoy.

"What would the public say if the Government of this country were to appoint a committee drawn exclusively from the Brewers or Whisky Distillers Association to determine the character of our licensing laws; or a committee composed exclusively of criminals to determine the criminal laws? . . ." [4]

Mr. Kitson was not the only critic of the Report. Even conservative banking opinion soon found the Cunliffe solution unsatisfactory. The following is quoted from the Bulletin of Barclays Bank, Ltd., December 1921. It criticizes the deflationary effect of attempts to restore the pre-war gold standard:

"It will be remembered that the [Cunliffe] Committee suggested that it was imperative that the conditions necessary to the maintenance of an effective gold standard should be restored without delay, and advocated as a means to this end the adoption of a policy which in its operation involved monetary deflation. . . . Clearly this is only practicable during a period of prosperity, yet the report contained nothing in the nature of a close analysis of the position which would arise with a slump in trade. This is the more curious, as effective monetary deflation must, in the long run, tend to depress industry, since a steady and persistent fall in prices necessarily diminishes and discourages trading activity. . . ."

---

[4] Arthur Kitson, *The Bankers' Conspiracy*, London, Elliot Stock, 1932, p. 38.

In spite of these and many other criticisms the Cunliffe recommendations were followed out to their ultimate consequences; but at the Brussels International Economic Conference, in 1920, they were for the first time put on an international basis.

The Brussels Conference (1920)

In September, 1920, in order to obtain a general outline of the conditions necessary for a program of international reconstruction, a conference was held in Brussels. Thirty-nine countries sent representatives, not as official spokesmen, but merely as technical experts. For the first time since the war, the former enemies and the neutrals sat together around a table to discuss their common economic problems.

Advocates of stable money were present and tried to persuade the conference to adopt a resolution which might induce the several countries to consider an internally stable money. Professor Gustav Cassel submitted his paper on "The World's Monetary Problems" [5] in which he advocated the immediate stabilization of each currency unit in terms of its domestic purchasing power over commodities.[6]

With regard to the gold question, Cassel suggested that the main task was to keep the value of gold stable relative to commodities and meanwhile to prevent its value from rising, after its recent depreciation.

Sir Henry Strakosch warned of the danger of fixing the price of gold, as this might effect a decline in the gold output, and bring about currency "starvation," or deflation. He suggested, on the contrary, that the price of gold be permitted to rise in accordance with market conditions.[7]

---

[5] See also Chapter 3, Section 4.
[6] *International Financial Conference*, 1920, Brussels. Printed for the League of Nations, Brussels, Th. Dewarichet, Vol. II, p. 61.
[7] *Ibid.*, p. 78.

Dr. G. Vissering, the Chairman of the Netherlands Bank made the following interesting recommendations:

First, decrease the fiduciary circulation of money. Second, stabilize the value of money, and, if possible, the rates of exchange—both (if possible) being based on some fixed standard of value. Third, consider the question whether gold could in the future be adopted as a standard of value.[8]

"A stable currency is needed," he said, "to permit of a return to normally operating monetary traffic. . . ." [9]

Dr. Vissering recommended a double currency, a stable "banco currency," or money of account; and a cash currency which, for the time being, might fluctuate as compared with the stable currency; saying that as times became more normal, the cash money would also become stable. Dr. Vissering thus upheld the tradition of the famous "banco money" of the Bank of Amsterdam,[10] proposing essentially the plan which was later taken up again by Dr. Eisler.[11]

The Conference, however, did not commit itself to any statement favorable to stable money. But the Commission on Currency and Exchange of the Conference referred the question to a special committee by means of Resolution XI which read:

"Resolution XI. We cannot recommend any attempt to stabilize the value of gold and we gravely doubt whether such attempt could succeed; but this question might well be submitted to the Committee . . . , if it should be adopted." [12]

This was the first instance of the problem of stabilization being considered by an international economic conference, and the above resolution furnished a basis upon which the Genoa Conference afterwards proceeded.

[8] *Ibid.*, p. 52.
[9] *Ibid.*, p. 54.
[10] See Chapter 1, Section 2.
[11] See Chapter 3, Section 4.
[12] *International Financial Conference*, 1920, *op. cit.*, Vol. I, p. 20.

The Genoa Conference (1922)

The Genoa Conference, in the Spring of 1922, gave the first real international stamp of approval to the proposal of stabilizing the purchasing power of money. This Conference had its origin in the sessions of the Supreme Council of the League of Nations at Cannes, in January 1922. It was assembled mainly on the initiative of Mr. Lloyd George, who was then the Premier of Great Britain, for the purpose of discussing the economic reconstruction of Europe.[13] Some thirty-three nations were represented, among them Soviet Russia. This was the first time that the Soviet Government had attended an official international gathering.

The resolutions adopted by the Financial Commission of the Conference [14] have for years served as the potent armory for the advocates of stable money all over the world. Although these recommendations adopted at Genoa were never followed out, they have stimulated further study of the stabilization problem, and valuable data have been gathered by the League of Nations to substantiate the demands made by them. The essence of these famous resolutions, in so far as they referred to stable money was the advocacy of the internal stability of each currency; the suggestion of an international convention to determine measures for preventing a scramble for gold which would result from a general return of the world to the gold standard and which would undoubtedly increase the value of gold; and the cooperation of central banks in regulating credit so as to maintain the purchasing power of gold.

The resolutions read as follows:

[13] See J. Saxon Mills, *The Genoa Conference,* New York, E. P. Dutton and Company, 1922, pp. 9 ff.

[14] This Commission included: Sir Basil Blackett; Professor Gustav Cassel; Dr. Havenstein; Dr. Vissering; Mr. M. Avenol; Sir Henry Strakosch; Mr. M. Dubois; Mr. Coom; Mr. Bianchini and Mr. R. H. Brand.

"*Resolution 1.* The essential requisite for the economic reconstruction of Europe is the achievement by each country of stability in the value of its currency.

"*Resolution 9.* . . . its [the gold standard's] successful maintenance would be materially promoted, not only by the proposed collaboration of central banks, but by an international Convention to be adopted at a suitable time. The purpose of the convention would be to centralize and coordinate the demand for gold, and so *to avoid those wide fluctuations in the purchasing power of gold,* which might otherwise result from the simultaneous and competitive efforts of a number of countries to secure metallic reserves. The convention should embody some means of economizing the use of gold by maintaining reserves in the form of foreign balances, such, for example, as the gold exchange standard, or an international clearing system.

"Resolution 11. It is desirable that the following proposals to form the basis of the international Convention contemplated in Res. 9, be submitted for the consideration of the meeting of central banks, suggested in Res. 3. . . .

". . . Credit will be regulated, not only with a view to maintaining the currencies at par with one another, but also with a *view to preventing undue fluctuations in the purchasing power of gold.* It is not contemplated, however, that the discretion of the central banks should be fettered by any definite rules framed for this purpose, but that their collaboration will have been assured in matters outside the province of the participating countries." [15]

Progressive and desirable as these resolutions were, Mr. Hawtrey finds them defective for lack of definite criteria as to time and condition for being complied with:

"In one respect" he said, "the Genoa resolutions are really unsatisfactory. It is impossible to point to any particular time at which effect can be given to them. Not only must they wait for the balancing of budgets before they can take effect in the weaker countries; even in the stronger they must wait for the

[15] *Papers Relating to International Economic Conference,* Genoa, 1922. His Majesty's Stationary Office, pp. 60–65. Italics mine.

establishment of a gold parity, whether the restoration of the old one or the adoption of a new. . . .

"Some countries whose currencies are less than half their pre-war gold parities, are nevertheless extremely unwilling to give up the prospect of restoring them. France, Belgium and Italy all took this attitude at Genoa. It seems to involve an almost indefinite postponement of stabilization so far as they are concerned." [16]

There was also a resolution to the effect that stabilization should be accomplished at approximately the post-war price levels of 1922—*i.e.* that some of the currencies should be devalued in terms of gold. But several nations seemed to see something humiliating in such a course. As to this question of pride Sir Charles Addis had an amusing comment:

"I remember at the Genoa Conference in 1922 when a resolution was passed stating that those countries would deserve well of the world who decided to adopt the gold exchange standard at about the level of prices then current.

"The resolution was adopted unanimously, but not before the French and the Italian delegates rose to their feet and declared that nothing but a return to the pre-war parity would satisfy the prestige of their respective countries. Well, the whirligig of time has brought about its revenges. But old prejudices are hard to eradicate. . . ." [17]

In the word "revenges," Sir Charles, of course, referred to the fact that both France and Italy were eventually forced to stabilize their currencies far below the pre-war parities. Britain refused to make any such concession, and thereby suffered more than France and Italy.

[16] R. G. Hawtrey, *The Genoa Resolutions on Currency*, "The Economic Journal," September, 1922, Vol. XXXII, Macmillan, & Co. London, p. 303.

[17] Sir Charles Addis in an Address before the British Institute of Bankers, April 3, 1930.

Section 2. International Organizations

League of Nations Committee on Economic Crises

In 1921, the General Labour Conference called for an inquiry into the national and international aspects of unemployment, and the means of combating it. The Conference invited the International Labour Office of the League of Nations to suggest a solution. For this purpose a special sub-committee was set up which was to be responsible to the Economic Committee of the League of Nations. Later, a *Joint Committee on Economic Crises* was formed, consisting of the above sub-committee with three members of the Financial Committee of the League of Nations and four experts appointed by the International Labour Office. This new Joint Committee conducted most of the investigations into the relationship between unemployment and monetary fluctuations. Probably the leading rôle in these studies was taken by Mr. Albert Thomas, M. Henri Fuss and Major Bellerby, in whose writings the subject of monetary stability constantly recurs.

In 1923 the Official Journal of the League of Nations printed a report by *Albert Thomas* which stated that the stabilization of a country's exchange rate has usually resulted in increased unemployment:

". . . In the course of the investigations undertaken in the last few months, the International Labour Office has been enabled to realize clearly the close relation between rates of exchange and the condition of the labour market in each country. . . . The stabilization of the rate of exchange and the improvement in the monetary situation have undoubtedly resulted in renewed or increased unemployment."

This surprising statement becomes clearer when he explains

that such stabilization in terms of gold was achieved by deflationary measures:

"A return to the gold standard will result in a fall of prices; a fall in prices almost invariably appears to cause unemployment. . . ." [18]

International Congress on Social Policy

The International Congress on Social Policy, held at Prague, October 1924, being a Joint Conference of the International Association for Labor Legislation and the International Association on Unemployment, adopted the following resolution, proposing the stabilization of the price level, as mentioned in the Genoa resolutions, for the purpose of preventing unemployment:

"The International Congress on Social Policy invites the partisans of social progress in all countries to promote the newer policy of preventing unemployment by calling on Governments to adopt the necessary economic measures in particular, those directed towards the stabilization of the general level of prices in conformity with the resolutions adopted by the International Conference at Genoa for the economic reconstruction of Europe." [19]

The *Joint Committee of the League of Nations,* mentioned above, held three meetings at Geneva on June 2nd and 3rd, 1925 at which it confirmed several resolutions adopted at a previous meeting. In its proceedings (in which it mentioned the Genoa resolutions) attention was again called to the relationship between credit policy, price tendencies, trade fluctuations, and unemployment:

"The Mixed Committee is . . . of opinion that the evils caused to regularity of employment by excessive trade fluctuations might

[18] Official Journal, 1923, p. 963.
[19] Quoted from *Stabilization Hearings* on H.R. 7895 (1927), *op. cit.,* p. 959.

to some extent be mitigated if, in arriving at decisions governing credit policy . . . due regard were paid to all data as to relevant economic conditions, including the tendencies of employment and prices. . . .

"2) The Mixed Committee, by an unanimous decision also recalls and adopts the resolutions mentioned in the report of the Financial Committee of the Genoa Conference held in 1922, being convinced that the principles laid down in these resolutions are entirely applicable in the present circumstances." [20]

In an article on "Unemployment in 1925," *M. Henri Fuss* of the International Labour Office gave an interesting account of the effect of price changes upon the employment situation, and arrived at the conclusion that because of the influence of changes in the price level upon employment, it was necessary to stabilize not merely the exchange rates, but the internal purchasing power of each currency as advocated in the Genoa resolutions. He said:

". . . changes in the general price level have a very important influence on fluctuations in unemployment and employment. . . . Considerable progress has been made in recent years towards stable exchange rates and international parity of prices. But even when such stability and parity have been universally achieved by the restoration in all countries of the gold standard or the gold exchange standard, it will still be necessary, as was recommended by the International Economic Conference at Genoa, to stabilise the purchasing power of gold itself. . . ." [21]

International Association for Social Progress

At its meeting in Vienna, September 14–18, 1928, the International Association for Social Progress dealt with the problem of credit control in a comprehensive report on the subject. This was prepared by a Committee of experts headed by *M. Max*

[20] Quoted from League of Nations, *Official Journal,* July, 1925, pp. 961–2.
[21] Henry Fuss, *Unemployment in* 1925, in "International Labour Review," 1926, pp. 228 and 230.

Lazard of Lazard Frères, Paris. The committee reached the conclusion that the stability of the general price level was desirable and that central banks as well as private banks might, by the timely control of credit, do much to maintain such stability. The relevant part of the report reads as follows:

"8. The Committee wishes to make it clear that credit restrictions at the beginning of a period of rising prices, though it may seem a hardship for enterprises which are flourishing or expanding, constitutes the most effective and economic means of limiting an artificial expansion of business and at the same time avoiding the depression which would inevitably follow any such expansion. If it is applied in time, such a restriction need be only slight. If its application is deferred the need for it is not avoided but only increased: the restriction must then be applied more harshly and more generally."

International Labour Office

The International Labour Office continued its investigations as to monetary stability, and in an article in 1928, *Henri Fuss* dealt with "Rationalisation and Unemployment." [22] On the basis of exhaustive statistical data M. Fuss came to the conclusion that while rationalization (*i.e.* "scientific management") measures ". . . may lead to unemployment, they do so only to a modified extent." If workers were dismissed because of rationalization, then the time they were unemployed depended entirely upon the general business situation, which naturally was under the direct influence of monetary fluctuations.

In a report on "Unemployment and Monetary Fluctuations" [23] the International Labour Office made a statistical investigation.

[22] See also *The Effects of Rationalisation on Unemployment*, in "Unemployment Problems in 1931," International Labour Office Studies and Reports, Series C, No. 16, Geneva, 1931.

[23] *Report* presented to the Twelfth Session of the International Labour Conference, May–June, 1929. *Unemployment, Some International Aspects, 1920–28.* International Labour Office Studies and Reports, Series C. N. 13. Geneva, 1929, p. 36.

They came to the conclusion that variations in the price level are an important cause of unemployment crises, and efforts should therefore be made to mitigate these variations:

". . . it seems to be possible to declare emphatically that abrupt, or even slow but prolonged, variations in the general price level, or in other words, disturbances in the equilibrium between production and the means of payment, play no small part in determining the alternating acceleration and retardation of economic activity, and are hence an important cause of the recurrent unemployment crises which mark one phase of the cycle.

"If, then, the magnitude of variations in the general price level could be reduced, an important cause of unemployment would be rendered less potent. . . ."

Section 3. League of Nations Gold Delegation

Origin

The establishment of the famous League of Nations Gold Delegation was the logical sequel of the Brussels and Genoa Conferences. Professor Gustav Cassel, was perhaps more than any one else, responsible for its formation. The International Economic Conference in Geneva, 1927, induced the Economic Consultative Committee of the League of Nations to include the following paragraph in its final report, mentioning the advantages of stability and warning of the evil economic consequences of fluctuations in the purchasing power of gold:

". . . Without desiring to express an opinion as to the technical methods, the Committee wishes to emphasize the great advantages to economic development of a monetary policy which should, as far as possible, reduce fluctuations in the purchasing power of gold, and has adopted the following resolution:

"The Consultative Committee, while recognizing the great benefit to international commerce that has already resulted from stabilization in terms of gold of the currencies of most countries of the world, recalls the fears entertained by the Genoa Conference of the dangers that might arise from undue fluctuations in the purchasing power of gold. In view of the detrimental effects upon industry, agriculture and the conditions of employment that would result from such fluctuations, the Committee appreciates the great interest which the central banks take in this problem and recommends it to the attention of the Financial and Economic Organisation of the League." [24]

The Financial Committee of the League of Nations declared itself ready, if the Council of the League so desired, to study the question raised by the Economic Consultative Committee. The Council considered the matter on June 8th, 1928, and requested the Financial Committee "to consider to what extent and in what way the League of Nations could most usefully assist in the study and solution of the problem of undue fluctuations in the purchasing power of gold." [25]

Inspired particularly by a memorandum on "Monetary Stability and the Gold Standard" by Sir Henry Strakosch, who was one of its members, the Financial Committee dealt with the matter again during its sessions of September and December 1928, and submitted a report to the Council. Among other things, the report contained the following recommendation: "The Financial Committee suggests that a special Committee of some eight or nine persons should be constituted, 'to examine into and report upon the causes of the fluctuations in the purchasing power of gold and their effect on the economic life of the nations' . . ." [26]

First Report

Thus the Council eventually appointed the Gold Delegation [27]

[24] *League of Nations Official Journal*, July, 1928, p. 1033.
[25] *Unemployment and Monetary Fluctuations, op. cit.*, p. 42.
[26] *Ibid.*, p. 39.
[27] The Delegation was composed of the following members:

Prof. M. Albert Janssen (Chairman)   Sir Reginald Mant (England)
  (Belgium)   Dr. Feliks Mlynarski (Poland)
Prof. M. J. Bonn (Germany)   Dr. Vilem Pospisil (Chzechoslovakia)
Prof. Gustav Cassel (Sweden)   Prof. O. M. W. Sprague (U.S.A.)
Comte de Chalendar (France)   Sir Henry Strakosch (England)
                                       Dr. L. J. A. Trip (Netherlands)

whose first Interim Report was issued on June 17, 1930. On the basis of a large mass of statistical data the conclusion reached in this report was that the available new supply of monetary gold was inadequate, and that in the not distant future, the shortage might depress the world price level unless remedial measures were applied to prevent this development:

"In view of all the circumstances" the report says, ". . . the probable trend of prices in the future must obviously give rise to some anxiety. We wish, therefore, at once to record our opinion that, if the need is recognized, remedial measures can be found which can be expected, for at any rate the next decade, to correct the consequences we fear. . . ." [28]

The report also expressed the hope that the policy of keeping gold in the central banks and out of circulation, should be more generally adopted. This would enable the available stock of gold to go farther and would thereby make the currency more elastic. Other recommendations of the report were: reduce the minimum gold reserve requirement of central banks; and as additional measures for economizing gold, prefer the use of checks and other bank transactions to the use of gold. The report stated specifically that only the long-term trend of prices had been considered, as only this type of fluctuations were caused by the fluctuations in the supply of gold.

Second Report

The Second Interim Report of the Gold Delegation appeared in January, 1931. The first report had called attention to the inadequacy of the gold supply, but the second report dealt mainly with the dangers of the maldistribution of monetary gold. In its introduction the report mentioned that because the distribution

[28] League of Nations, *Interim Report of the Gold Delegation of the Financial Committee*, Geneva, June 17, 1930, p. 18.

of the monetary gold stock influences the purchasing power of money, this factor must be considered by the Gold Delegation:

". . . the adequacy or inadequacy of gold to serve as the basis of the credit structure and of prices in gold standard countries must depend, not only on the total amount of gold available for monetary purposes, but also upon the manner in which the monetary stocks held at any moment are divided between various centres. The distribution of gold is, therefore, one of the factors influencing the purchasing power of money which falls under our mandate for consideration by us. . . ." [29]

Particular stress was placed upon the obligations of those countries which had adopted the gold, or the gold-exchange standard. Unless they should all strictly observe certain rules, difficulties would arise which might lead to the breakdown of the system.

Although an economy in the use of gold had been secured, the report said [30] the functioning of the gold standard had been rendered more complicated. The task of central banks had therefore become more difficult to perform, while at the same time their monetary policy had acquired new importance.

Final Report

The Final Report of the Gold Delegation did not appear until June, 1932, when almost all of the former gold standard countries had for the second time since the beginning of the World War, suspended gold payments. However, this final report was not unanimously agreed to by the members of the Delegation, and a special note of dissent was attached to it. In the main, the final conclusions were that the gold standard was the ideal currency system, and that its breakdown was simply proof that the game had not been played according to rules:

[29] League of Nations, *Second Interim Report of the Gold Delegation of the Financial Committee,* Geneva, 1931, p. 7.
[30] *Ibid.,* p. 14.

"78.) The Delegation, however, records its belief that at the present stage of world economic development, the gold standard remains the best available monetary mechanism. . . .[31]

"80.) Although it is obvious that the time and level—as well as the particular form of restoration of the gold standard that should be decided upon—can be determined only by the proper authorities in the countries concerned, the Delegation considers the return within the shortest possible time, to the international gold standard system of such vital importance for financial and economic development that it feels its obligation to consider the policy that should, in its view, be followed in order to facilitate the achievement of that aim. . . ."

In other words, although by terms of its appointment the matter was none of the Delegation's concern, the majority of it felt called upon to advocate the immediate restoration of a monetary system that had been found wanting. By way of explaining this unauthorized act the Delegation refers to the cyclical fluctuations of business which are considered unavoidable, except in a static society. The past attempts at controlling changes in the price level were even held to have been the cause of the aggravation of the present crisis. That is, attempted regulation had merely deferred the crisis which eventually and thereby became the more severe. The Delegation said:

"134.) We view the business cycle as a more or less rhythmical oscillation of a very complex price-structure and business activity around a hypothetical norm of stable relationships. The normal position of the equilibrium is never reached and never can be realized except upon the assumption of a static society. . . . The forces producing instability are inevitably complex, so that the resultant price-changes have defied any attempt at simple analysis or explanation. . . .

". . . attempts to control fluctuations in the general or average level of prices may accumulate strains within the price-structure and therefore cause deferred and possibly more violent paroxysms

[31] League of Nations, *Report of the Gold Delegation of the Financial Committee*, Geneva, June, 1932.

of readjustment eventually. We are, indeed, convinced that the violence of the present crisis, for example, is due in large degree to the fact that readjustments in industry, trade and prices in the post-war period have been thwarted by various forms of control and manipulation. . . ."

With certain limitations, however, the Delegation was in favor of stable money:

"184.) . . . We consider it highly desirable that monetary policy should be directed to an avoidance of violent fluctuations in purchasing power. . . ."

But they held that monetary policy alone was insufficient for the attainment of desirable stability and that, in a dynamic society, "complete" stabilization was impossible.

"185.) . . . (1) . . . we do not consider it possible to avoid all oscillations in the general level of prices, and (2) . . . we are fully aware that even that measure of stability, which we all wish to achieve, cannot be secured by monetary policy alone. . . . Complete stabilization and identity of group movements are, indeed, impossible in a dynamic society, and society must either develop or decay."

As part of the necessary procedure for stabilization, the Report prescribed the following rather contradictory method: as a test of stability, use a wholesale price index, but at the same time determine your currency by the size of your gold reserve:

"187.) . . . The relative stability of these index-numbers of wholesale prices over a term of years will, however, provide a test of the success of the policies that have been pursued. . . .

"195.) In considering monetary policy from the national point of view, the primary index should, in our opinion, be the historic index of the gold reserve. . . ."

Note of Dissent

A Note of Dissent, was signed by Mr. M. Albert Janssen, Sir Reginald Mant, Sir Henry Strakosch, and was later agreed to by Prof. Gustav Cassel. In the opinion of these four men, the mal-distribution of gold was *the main cause* for the international fall of prices, a factor to which the majority report had attached no importance. A second point of divergence had to do with the objective of all monetary policy: the majority aimed apparently, at mere mitigation of short term fluctuations, while the dissenters aimed at permanent stabilization. They said:

"The second important issue on which we differ from our colleagues is the objective of monetary policy. They define this objective (paragraph 186) as 'a relative, but not an absolute, stability of wholesale commodity prices as measured by their movement over a long series of years,' and they add that the measure of stability which they envisage is not inconsistent with slow movements of the long-term trend either upward or downward.

"We are not clear what is intended by the reference to relativity, but we understand that our colleagues would aim merely at restricting the range of short-term fluctuations of prices, and would not attempt to influence the long-term movement by monetary policy, though this seems hardly consistent with other parts of the report, which stress the desirability of economizing the use of gold, the most potent factor in determining the course of long-term movements.

"But whatever may be the meaning of our colleagues' recommendation, we think it desirable to make it perfectly clear that, in our view, the prime objective of monetary policy should be stability in the general level of wholesale commodity prices." [31a]

The Note of Dissent particularly denied the point (134) that attempts to control price movements had accumulated strains in the price structure, and caused the recent fall of world prices.

"We believe, on the contrary," the dissenters said, "that a readjustment of industry, trade and of relative prices is likely to proceed with far less strain, if fluctuations in the general level of prices are avoided, for such fluctuations necessarily superimpose upon the price structure the additional strain which arises from

[31a] *Ibid.,* pp. 67 ff.

the consequent redistribution of incomes and from all the reactions which such redistribution has on production, trade and finance."

The dissenters suggested that it might be a practical plan for all the countries which were off gold to agree, for the time being, on a common objective in the management of their paper currencies, namely the stabilization of their internal wholesale commodity price levels. This might be the best preparation for a general return to the international gold standard. They did not fail, however, to add their point of view as to the gold standard in general, which implied that they believed in a gold standard only if it was properly managed:

". . . we think it desirable to add, that we do not endorse without qualification the statement in paragraph 45 of the report that 'at the present stage of world economic development the gold standard remains the best available monetary mechanism.' We would only go so far as to say that the gold standard is the best mechanism *if properly managed.*"

Section 4. The Macmillan Committee

Appointment of Macmillan Committee

The famous British "Committee on Finance and Industry" was appointed on November 5, 1929, by the Chancellor of the Exchequer, Philip Snowden, "To inquire into banking, finance and credit, paying regard to the factors both internal and international which govern their operation, and to make recommendations calculated to enable these agencies to promote the development of trade and commerce and the employment of labour."

The Committee was headed by the Right Hon. H. P. (now Lord) Macmillan, and included among its members such outstanding advocates of stable money as the Right Hon. Reginald MacKenna, and Mr. John Maynard Keynes. During 1930–1931 the Committee held 49 meetings and examined 57 witnesses, including bankers, industrialists, business men, labour representatives and economists. In its "Minutes of Evidence" are also included the written statements received from 15 organizations and 31 individuals.

The Macmillan Report, is divided into two distinct parts: Part I, "Historical and Descriptive," in which the experiences and facts concerning money, banking and prices, are reviewed; and Part II, "Conclusions and Recommendations" in which remedies for the national as well as the international situations are proposed.

From the following quotations it can be seen that the Report was one of the most progressive documents that has ever resulted from an official investigation of currency and banking. Its conclusions read like the crowning proof of the assertions which advocates of stable money had been making for many years.

Functions of a Central Bank

It is recognized that profit is the motive for action of a private institution, while a central bank should only be guided by considerations of the public welfare. The report says:

". . . the functions of a Central Bank and the obligations resting upon it are of a very special character, calling for skill, experience and judgment of a kind different from those which must be possessed by commercial bankers. No banker can neglect the rules of prudence and safety, but the object of a commercial banker is to make a profit. The situation of a Central Bank is such that it must often undertake operations which are not only not profitable, but result in losses. Its aims must be the safety of the financial system and the economic welfare of the country." [32]

[32] *Report of the Committee on Finance and Industry* (Chairman Macmillan), London, H. M. Stationary Office, June, 1931, p. 16 (No. 31).

In its view of the international gold standard the Macmillan Committee mentions the stability of the world price level as the desirable object of policy, which should not be interfered with by the actions of individual central banks:

"(47) . . . (I) The international gold standard system involves a common agreement as to the ends for which it exists.

"(II) It should be an object of policy to secure that the international gold standard should bring with it stability of prices as well as that it should guarantee stability of exchange.

"(III) Action by individual Central Banks which, by repercussions on the policy of the others, imperils the stability of the price level should, as far as possible, be avoided." [33]

Objectives of Domestic Monetary Policy

The following quotation defines the desirable objectives of monetary policy as reflation and stabilization, that is, the policy afterwards adopted by the Roosevelt administration. The report mentions especially that the general adoption of a price index as criterion would represent a "great and notable change" in central bank policy.

"(275) Thus our objective should be, so far as it lies within the power of this country to influence the international price level, first of all to raise prices a long way above the present level and then maintain them at the level thus reached with as much stability as can be managed.

"(276) We recommend that this objective be accepted as the guiding aim of the monetary policy of this country. The acceptance of such an objective will represent in itself a great and notable change. For before the War scarcely anyone considered that the price level could or ought to be the care and preoccupation, far less a main objective of policy, on the part of the Bank of England or any other Central Bank." [34]

[33] *Ibid.*, p. 23.
[34] *Ibid.*, p. 117.

The Committee had perceived the myth of the "automatic gold standard" and demanded recognition of the fact that the monetary standard must be managed:

"(280.) The monetary system of this country must be a Managed System. It is not advisable, or indeed practicable, to regard our monetary system as an automatic system, grinding out the right results by the operation of natural forces aided by a few maxims of general application and some well-worn rules of thumb. . . ." [35]

Let us here pause for a moment, and compare this passage with the statement made in 1932 by Dr. Miller of the Federal Reserve Board, a year after the publication of the Macmillan Report. Dr. Miller said, "Nature will have more to say" than the Congress and the Federal Reserve System about the reflation of the American price level.

In the following Conclusions the Macmillan Committee summarized once more its recommendations, particularly that of a stable price level as the aim of central bank policy. It mentioned that this stabilization was to be achieved by the central bank's regulation of the supply and cost of credit, while for the purpose of attaining international stability, it recommended frequent conferences of the world's central banks:

"(I) The aim of the Central Banks should be to maintain the stability of international prices both over long periods and over short periods; *i.e.* they should both keep the average steady over a period of years and avoid fluctuations round this average from year to year.

"(II) The method of achieving this object should be so to regulate the volume and terms of bank credit as to maintain as much stability as possible in the rate of new investment and new enterprise generally, both at home and abroad. By these means alternate excesses of enthusiasm and depression might be avoided and the demand for new output of the instruments of production and other forms of capital in the world at large kept in better

[35] *Ibid.*, p. 118.

equilibrium with the proportion of income which is currently available for such purposes—neither in excess nor in defect.

"(III) With this end in view the Central Banks should confer together at frequent intervals to decide whether the general tendency of their individual policies should be towards a relaxation or a tightening of the conditions of credit; and their bank rates and other instruments of credit control should then be adjusted accordingly, without prejudice to their policies relative to one another remaining at the free discretion of each separate institution. Nor should they be afraid of small and frequent changes. For otherwise action may be unduly deferred. Such small and frequent changes would also have the advantage of accustoming the public not to attach undue importance to every necessary adjustment. The Central Banks must be prepared to keep in touch with conditions, to make small changes in response to small indications, and to reverse the tendency with any noticeable change in the underlying facts.

"(IV) This form of joint policy should be consistent with a full measure of autonomy for each national institution." [36]

The Macmillan Committee suggested that the Bank of England carry out the monetary and credit policies just mentioned, and listed the following well known chief means at the disposal of the Bank:

"(I) The official Bank Rate.

"(II) 'Open-market' operations which . . . have the effect of changing the aggregate amount of the Bank's Private Deposits.

"(III) 'Open-market' operations which consist in changing the form of the Bank's assets without changing their quantity. . . .

"(IV) There are certain technical devices for directly influencing the foreign exchanges, namely sales or purchases of foreign balances, dealings in forward exchange, and small variations in the Bank's buying price for gold.

"(V) The use of the Bank's personal influence over, or advice to, prominent elements in the money market." [37]

[36] Ibid., pp. 131 ff.
[37] Ibid., p. 152.

SECTION 5. THE OTTAWA CONFERENCE

The *Imperial Economic Conference 1932* which met in Ottawa (Canada) from July 2, 1932 to August 20, 1932, comprised representatives of the entire British Empire [38] who had assembled primarily to improve trade conditions among themselves. As a consequence of the world-wide decline in the prices of primary products, conditions of serious disequilibrium had arisen in every one of these British nations. At Ottawa this disequilibrium had created the demand of all the assembled nations for a rise of the wholesale price level which was to be achieved by the united action of the several members of the British Empire.

The question of money, in relation to the level of wholesale prices thus became the object of serious discussion at this Conference.

Agenda

The Provisional Agenda of the Conference contained the following reference to the problem of raising and stabilizing the price level:

"Consideration of existing inter-relationships of the various currencies and monetary standards of the Empire, and of the desirability and feasibility of taking steps to restore and stabilize the general price level and to stabilize exchange." [39]

Mr. S. M. Bruce, the leader of the Australian Delegation, among other things, said in his opening statement:

". . . We must not only arrest the fall in prices but must find the means to raise them to a reasonable level and then introduce elements of stability to prevent the disastrous effects of violent

---

[38] The representatives of the following nations were assembled: Australia; Canada; India; Irish Free State; Newfoundland; New Zealand; Southern Rhodesia: United Kingdom; Union of South Africa.

[39] *Imperial Economic Conference* 1932. Report to the Conference, Ottawa, F. A. Acland. Printed to the King's Most Excellent Majesty, 1932, p. 35.

fluctuations. This great and urgent problem is certainly one which the Imperial Economic Conference must consider, and it is one in the consideration of which the Australian Delegation is prepared to play its part." [40]

Sir Atul C. Chatterjee, the leader of the Indian Delegation, in his opening address also referred to the problem of stable money in the following words:

". . . There is one item in the agenda, the importance of which cannot be stressed too strongly. I mean the inter-relationship of monetary standards of the Empire and the desirability and feasibility of restoring and stabilizing the general level of prices and achieving exchange stability. For here we come to factors which affect the very foundations on which any structure of fiscal preferences has to rest. The benefits to production and trade of a preferential system may easily be swept away unless it is supported by a monetary and credit policy which assures a reasonable measure of stability of general wholesale prices." [41]

On July 22, 1932, a Committee on "Monetary and Financial Questions" was constituted, which again appointed a subcommittee to report on two questions: one, relating to the possibility or desirability of securing a rise in the general levels of wholesale prices, and the other, relating to the stabilization of currencies within the Empire. [42]

Canadian Viewpoint

Mr. R. B. Bennett, Prime Minister of Canada, and Chairman of the Ottawa Conference, delivered the first statement before the Committee on "Monetary and Financial Questions." He cited in particular the evil effects of falling prices in Canada, as well as the evils of fluctuating exchanges. "Personally I cannot see,"

[40] Ibid., p. 93.
[41] Ibid., p. 91.
[42] Ibid., p. 36.

he said, "how we can carry on business with the world at large, unless there is some commodity or yardstick of universal acceptance. I confess that gold seems to me to be the commodity which can perform this function most effectively, but others may disagree with me. In that connection I would call your attention to the fact that the British empire produces about 80 per cent of the world's gold supply." [43]

He mentioned further the possibility of stabilizing exchange within the British Empire by means of an "Empire Exchange Pool" with a credit of half a billion dollars.

The following part of his statement is of interest for its reference to stable money. He said:

"As a permanent program for the more distant future, we also believe that it should be a responsibility of our monetary authorities to do their utmost to *eliminate* the long-run secular fluctuations, and to *moderate* the short-run cyclical fluctuations, in the world level of prices. So pernicious are the social and economic effects of such price changes that the elimination of monetary instability would constitute one of the most important contributions which statesmanship could make to the buttressing of our present economic and social system." [44]

Australian Viewpoint

Mr. S. M. Bruce of Australia emphasized again that his country believed in solving its difficulties by an increase of commodity prices. After relating Australia's experience during the depression [45] he indicated that if a definite lead towards raising the wholesale price level were given by Great Britain, it would be followed not only by the other countries of the sterling area, but also by the countries still on gold. "I believe" he said, "that a

[43] *Ibid.*, p. 118.
[44] *Ibid.*, p. 118.
[45] See Chapter 10, Section 3.

definite declaration of their policy by the British Government
and the maturing of plans already put in hand would have a
tremendous effect and would quite probably turn indecision into
confidence and give strength to deep-rooted forces already at work."

During the period of rising price levels, that is, during reflation, Mr. Bruce thought it important to maintain parity of exchange within the British Empire. This exchange stability to be
"managed" through the close co-operation of the central banks.
He suggested that the Dominions which have no central banks
set up autonomous boards which were to be charged with the
management of the exchange.

Regarding the re-establishment of a workable international
monetary standard, which he held to be desirable, Mr. Bruce
believed that central bank co-operation could bring about such a
standard. He also said:

"In this connection the Hon. the Leader of the South African
Delegation may be right when he claims that stable exchanges
are a necessity to commerce. On his part he will no doubt admit
that a reasonable stable measure of value is a necessity for the
production, without which there can be no commerce. We know
all too well the poverty in the midst of plenty that has mocked
our increased capacity to produce during the fall in prices. It
is this that has deranged commerce and thrown the exchanges
into confusion." [46]

Mr. J. G. Coates, Minister of Public Works Transport and
Employment of New Zealand, and leader of his country's delegation, largely concurred in the statement of Mr. Bruce. He demanded most urgently that Great Britain take action to raise
her general price level. "We can" he said, "make some local
adjustments, but it is simply impossible to restore even a reasonable measure of sound conditions in the Dominion unless
and until the general price level in Great Britain is increased,

[46] *Imperial Economic Conference*, 1932, *op. cit.*, pp. 123-124.

and increased substantially. That is something which cannot be left to take care of itself." [47]

South African Viewpoint

Mr. N. C. Havenga, Minister of Finance of the Union of South Africa, represented his delegation's point of view. He agreed that the fall of prices had caused disastrous effects all over the world. But in analyzing the currency problem, he distinguished between two questions which he mentioned as follows:

"There is first, the breakdown of a large part of the world's machinery of exchange of commodities and services, reflecting itself strongly, as is to be expected, in currency, the instrument with which we account for our commercial transactions.

"There is secondly, the evil caused by the fact that while the world has reached a marvellous degree of perfection in its industrial processes, it has not yet, in the sphere of the measurement of material values, emerged beyond the somewhat primitive stage of employing a measuring rod which expands and contracts under the influence of the commodities which it measures.

"The first problem" he continued, "is one of restoration of economic health in a world which has, in the last quarter century, engaged in practices which have materially undermined its physique. The second is the more difficult problem of the invention of machinery which will be as great an advance on the present measures of value as the steam engine was an advance on the animal-drawn transport which preceded it."

The latter statement is interesting as it comes from the representative of the richest gold mining country in the world. It is a recognition of the shortcomings of the gold standard. Mr. Havenga said further:

"If the world cannot invent a more perfect standard of value,

[47] Ibid., p. 126.

we shall be forced to put up with the best we have. But if the world is to go on enjoying a high degree of material civilization, it will be necessary to concentrate our attention on the subject of the restoration of economic health, the convalescence to which is proving to be such a long and painful process. We consider therefore that the first approach to the solution of our present monetary problem should be by way of a restoration of world confidence. . . ." [48]

"We hold the view, therefore, that to blame the monetary part of the economic machine for not having stood the strain when the whole machine broke down is to make a false, and therefore misleading approach to the subject."

Mr. Havenga seems here not to blame the monetary machinery, but the "world's machinery of exchange of commodities and services." He goes on to say:

". . . we are of opinion that a re-establishment of at least that degree of certainty which is associated with the use of one commodity as a measure of value, will help materially to revive trade.

"We realize the difficulties with which many states will be faced for some time to come in restoring the gold standard. We realize too that the old parities are no longer sacrosanct. We consider, however, that if the states here represented can affirm their determination to restore as soon as practicable at least the relative stability of the gold standard, such action will have a settling effect on many people, who in ignorance of the intricacies of a very involved subject, are now so doubtful of the future of world currencies that this factor has a very unsettling effect on enterprise and on confidence in general."

Mr. Havenga thought that the question of a more stable standard of value should be dealt with by a conference representing the nations of the entire world, and not merely those of the British Empire. He concluded:

[48] *Ibid.*, p. 127.

"As a preliminary indication of our views we are, however, prepared to say first that we consider some commodity basis will be essential to an improved standard. As long experience has proved gold to be the most satisfactory, we consider that any scheme for the inauguration of a better standard of value must necessarily be based on gold . . ."

"What is wanted" he further concluded, "is an upward trend of the international price-level, and not an upward trend in the local price-level, while world prices fall." [48a]

The leaders of the Irish Free State and of the Newfoundland Delegations also affirmed the necessity for their countries of higher price levels, as did Sir George Schuster, Member of the Council of Governor-General of India.

Indian Viewpoint

Sir Henry Strakosch, Member of the Council of India, amplified Sir George Schuster's statement. According to Sir Henry Strakosh, the differences of opinion as to the fundamental factors that had brought about the fall of price levels were "mainly of emphasis and not of substance." After surveying the general effects of falling price levels, he concluded that:

". . . pending the re-establishment of a stable international monetary standard the Empire countries should as far as possible adopt a common standard of value and . . . the wholesale level of prices in terms of that common standard should be raised to a point at which an equilibrium is re-established between costs and that level of prices.

"Further, . . . on the attainment of that level, monetary policy should be directed towards maintaining it stable, both in terms of commodities and in terms of other Empire currencies.

"The United Kingdom, being the greatest center for Empire

48a *Ibid.*, p. 128.

trade and finance, and being in a very strong creditor position *vis à vis* the rest of the Empire, the trend of prices in terms of the common standard must depend in the main upon the monetary policy she decides to pursue." [49]

Sir Henry believed that for a restoration of the prosperity which existed before the depression, the restoration of prosperity all over the world was essential; and for the restoration of world prosperity the re-establishment of an international monetary standard seemed to him inevitable. An international monetary system, however, which "can be relied upon to assure all reasonable conditions of stability, both in regard to the purchasing power of money in terms of commodities, and in regard to the exchanges. The measures for Empire co-operation in the monetary field must therefore be regarded as no more than a preliminary stage to alleviate the position and pave the way to the restoration of an international monetary standard."

English Viewpoint

Mr. Neville Chamberlain, Chancellor of the Exchequer, spoke for the Delegation of the United Kingdom. He answered as follows the Dominions' demand that England take the lead in raising her price level:

". . . there was a general, though not perhaps universal, feeling that the United Kingdom could contribute more to a solution of how to raise prices than any other of those who are met here.

"However flattering to our vanity may be this attribution to the United Kingdom of such far-reaching powers, I fear I must submit to you some considerations which will show our limitations." [50]

[49] *Ibid.*, p. 141.
[50] *Ibid.*, p. 142.

He made it clear that England was as anxious as the Dominions to raise her wholesale price level:

". . . I want to make it perfectly clear at once that upon the desirability of raising wholesale commodity prices the United Kingdom Delegation is in full sympathy and agreement with the Dominions and India."

Regarding the re-establishment of an international monetary standard, Mr. Chamberlain made the following remarks which indicated that for the time being, England did not intend to return to the gold standard:

". . . there is the question of the measure of value which should be ultimately adopted. I venture to express my agreement with Mr. Bennett's observation when he said that he failed to see how we could carry on business with the world unless there were some universal yardstick, and I am not disposed to differ from him when he said that he was unable to see a yardstick other than one based on gold which would be universally acceptable. The Leader of the South African Delegation also made some extremely weighty observations on the same subject. At the same time we must make it clear that we have no intention of returning to the gold standard unless we can be thoroughly assured that a remedy has been found for the maladjustments which led to the breakdown of that standard last year. It would be useless for the countries now on a sterling basis to revert to gold if the fundamental conditions—economic and political, as well as monetary—had not been so changed as to obviate the risk of a fresh fall in gold prices. Before we change our present basis we must be sure that the change can be maintained and that we shall not have to do our work all over again in a few years' time." [51]

Mr. Chamberlain also mentioned that "it is in wholesale much more than in retail prices that we desire to see a rise, . . ." and

[51] *Ibid.*, p. 143.

summarized the opinion of the English Delegation as follows: "I am now in a position to summarize the views I have put before you. In the opinion of the United Kingdom Delegation it is not desirable to embark upon any rash experiments in currency policy for the central position of the United Kingdom in world commerce and finance and the wide-spread use of the sterling bill as a medium of international trade will always require us to proceed with great circumspection. We do not see any prospect of a speedy return to the Gold Standard, nor are we prepared to say at the present time at what parity such a return should be effected if and when it takes place. We are doing and shall continue to do our utmost to prevent wide fluctuations in the value of sterling caused by speculative movements and we believe that we have now established effective machinery for this purpose." [52]

Ottawa Report

The report submitted by the subcommittee and adopted unanimously by the Committee on Monetary and Financial Questions, and later by the entire Conference, provided, in part:

I

"(a) A rise throughout the world in the general level of wholesale prices is in the highest degree desirable. The evil of falling prices must be attacked by Government and individual action in all its causes whether political, economic, financial, or monetary.

"(b) For dealing with the problem in its widest aspects the Governments represented at this Conference record their conviction that international action is urgently necessary and announce their desire to co-operate with other nations in any practicable measures for raising wholesale prices.

"(c) The Conference has considered what action can be taken by the nations of the Commonwealth to help towards raising prices.

[52] *Ibid.*, p. 146.

"As regards monetary factors, the Conference recognizes that the central position of the United Kingdom, not only among the countries of the Commonwealth but in world trade and finance, makes the United Kingdom a main factor in anything that can be done. The Conference therefore welcomes the following statement made on behalf of the United Kingdom by the Chancellor of the Exchequer:

" 'His Majesty's Government desire to see wholesale sterling prices rise. The best condition for this would be a rise in gold prices and the absence of a rise in gold prices inevitably imposes limitations on what can be done for sterling. A rise in prices cannot be effected by monetary action alone, since various other factors which have combined to bring about the present depression must also be modified or removed before a remedy is assured. His Majesty's Government nevertheless recognize that an ample supply of short-term money at low rates may have a valuable influence, and they are confident that the efforts which have successfully brought about the present favorable monetary conditions can and will, unless unforeseen difficulties arise, be continued.' "

(d) Under this subdivision it was stated that the monetary policy of the British Commonwealth of Nations should be on sound lines toward raising price levels by low interest rates and a plentiful supply of short-term money. This should not take the form of financing public expenditure, but should be directed toward stimulating private industry and reviving confidence in business.

(e) Under this subdivision it was stated that efforts should be made to stabilize exchange among the various empire countries; no machinery was proposed for this purpose but it was suggested that all units of the empire co-operate for the purpose of obtaining stable exchange rates.

II

"The Conference recognizes that the ultimate aim of monetary policy should be the restoration of a satisfactory international monetary standard. Such a standard should so function as not merely to obtain stable exchange rates, but also to insure the smooth and efficient working of the machinery of international trade and finance.

"This postulates international agreement among the great trading nations of the world, and while certain of the States here represented hold very definite views on the question of the most desirable standard, the Conference refrains from making any recommendations on the subject in view of the fact that the subject is shortly to be discussed at an international conference.

"There are, however, several conditions precedent to the re-establishment of an international monetary standard. The most important among them are: a rise in the general level of commodity prices in the various countries to a height more in keeping with the level of costs, including the burden of debt and other fixed and semi-fixed charges; and an adjustment of the factors, political, economic, financial, and monetary, which have caused the breakdown of the gold standard in many countries, and which, if not adjusted, would inevitably lead to another breakdown of whatever international standard may be adopted.

"It is also, in the view of the Conference, of the utmost importance to the future working of any international standard that international co-operation should be secured and maintained with a view to avoiding, so far as may be found practicable, wide fluctuations in the purchasing power of the standard of value." [53]

Conclusions

From the foregoing discussion it will be seen that while there was no general agreement concerning the gold standard and other questions of specific detail, there was apparently agreement on two great objectives, namely reflation and stabilization, the same two objectives as President Roosevelt's today.

But the chief importance of this Conference consisted not so much in the sentiments expressed, as in the fact that these senti-

[53] *Ibid.,* pp. 22–24.

ments were expressed by responsible political leaders. In no previous Conference, national or international, had this ever been true in any marked degree. Even at the Genoa Conference, the resolutions adopted were the work of technical experts and their adoption was more or less perfunctory, and without much discussion, by the official delegates.

The Ottawa resolutions became of particular importance when, a year later, they were endorsed in the "Imperial Declaration," signed at the close of the London World Economic Conference by representatives of the British Empire.[54]

[54] See Chapter 11, Section 2.

CHAPTER X

MONETARY PRACTICE ABROAD

Section 1. England off the Gold Standard

(September 21, 1931)

Causes

In September, 1931, the difficulties which had led to the appointment of the Macmillan Committee came to a head, only a few months after the publication of its Report. From the beginning of 1929 to the middle of 1931, France had increased her monetary gold stock by about 964 million dollars, and the United States, during that time, had added about 847 million of gold to her hoard.[1] In order to defend their gold reserves, the other central banks were forced to raise discount rates, that is adopt deflationary measures. These caused a stringency of credit all over the gold standard world. Countries began calling their loans, and England which had made a practice of lending at long-term and borrowing at short-term, was subject to heavy withdrawals of foreign credits. During 1931, the English situation became more acute; therefore France and the United States extended huge credits to the Bank of England. Nevertheless, the withdrawals did not stop; and on September 21, 1931 England was forced to suspend the payment of gold.

The measure authorizing this suspension read as follows:

"1.) Unless and until his Majesty by proclamation otherwise directs, Subsection 2 of Section 1 of the gold standard act of 1925

[1] See *Final Report of the Gold Delegation, op. cit.,* p. 37.

shall cease to have effect, notwithstanding that Subsection 1 of the said section remains in force.

"2.) The Bank of England is hereby discharged from all liabilities or risk for anything done by the Bank in contravention of the provision of said Subsection 2 at any time after September 18, 1931, and no proceedings whatsoever shall be instituted against the Bank or any other person for anything so done as aforesaid.

"3.) It shall be lawful for the Treasury to make and from time to time vary orders authorizing the taking of such measures in relation to exchanges and otherwise as they may consider expedient for meeting difficulties arising in connection with the gold standard. This subsection shall continue in force for a period of six months from the passing of this act. This act may be cited as the gold standard (amendment) act of 1931."

One by one the other gold standard countries followed England's example, with the exception of the United States, France and a few smaller countries. This produced a general fear of inflation, because now these countries would be no longer restricted in their currency issues by the limitation of gold reserves. But nothing of the sort happened. For the time being, deflation was stopped in those countries, but the very fear of inflation seems to have prevented them from having the full benefits of a rising price level, up to a normal pre-depression level. Most of these nations had linked their currencies more or less definitely to the pound sterling, and England's monetary policy, therefore, determined the price level in almost all countries off gold, known collectively as "Sterlingaria."

Advantages Lost

When England left the gold standard, her budget was balanced. There was no fear that the Government might resort to the printing press to pay its expenditures. Concurrently with the abandonment of gold, the Bank of England raised the bank rate to 6%. This is extraordinarily high for England; but some such action seemed necessary to prevent the pound from depreciating too much in comparison with gold currencies. The high bank rate was maintained, however, unnecessarily long, so that British industry and trade could take but little advantage of the otherwise favorable situation which had resulted from going off gold. *Mr. Hawtrey* explained this lost opportunity as follows:

"The 6 per cent rate lasted five months. The purchases of foreign exchange by the Bank of England during that period did but little to counteract its deterrent effect. The value of the pound was never clearly brought down to the equilibrium level, and at no stage was that prospect of expanding demand and rising prices, which had given so hopeful a tone to business immediately after September 21, revived.

"By the 18th of February, 1932, when the Bank rate was reduced, the vicious circle of deflation had been once again joined, and it was as impossible as it had been a year before to induce traders to extend their borrowings by cheap money alone. The opportunity had been lost, deflation and falling prices prevailed in spite of the abandonment of gold, and the pound sterling had become a currency only one degree less intolerable than gold itself.

"The transition to cheap money, when it came, was prompt. In four weeks the rate came down from 6 per cent to 3½ per cent (17th March 1932). Then by slower stages it was reduced to 2 (June 30th). But it was too late." [2]

Up to June 1932, the Bank of England was accumulating foreign exchange to pay off its credits in Paris and New York, and through these purchases was able, to some extent, to influence the foreign valuation of the pound sterling. After this operation was completed, the Bank on June 16, 1932, was provided with an Exchange Equalisation Account in order to be in a position to continue this influence over the foreign exchange rates.

[2] R. G. Hawtrey, *The Gold Standard in Theory and Practice,* London, Longmans, Green & Co., 1933, p. 185.

Advantages Gained

Reginald MacKenna, in the Midland Review for June–July, 1932 gave expression to the hopes of advocates of stable money at that time. They believed that the time had come for England to lead the way by reflation and ultimate stabilization:

". . . Extracting the essence of various statements, direct and indirect, of spokesmen of the Government, we may summarize Britain's policy in monetary affairs under three clauses: first, to maintain, by the provision of cheap and plentiful money, the technical conditions for a substantial rise in the general level of wholesale commodity prices in terms of sterling; secondly, to eliminate, as far as possible, wide and rapid fluctuations in the gold exchange value of sterling, particularly those due to speculation and 'capital flights' this way or that, while allowing exchange rates in the longer run to adjust themselves to altered price-level relationships; and thirdly (in the indefinite future, when the mists have rolled away), to effect final stabilization of the pound."

More than *two years after the abandonment of gold,* in the October-November 1933 issue of the Midland Bank Review Mr. McKenna summarized the benefits which the several countries had obtained from the abandonment of the gold standard. In particular he mentioned the fact that further deflation had been halted, although it was permitted to go on in the countries which were still on gold:

"The main point which emerges from this survey is that, since our departure from gold, recovery has been steady and has been shared in, one after another, by those countries which, having themselves at different times taken the same step, have participated in the benefits of a monetary policy unhampered by more or less fortuitous bonds. The general average of commodity prices in the sterling group as a whole is now roughly the same as in September 1931. This, taken by itself, is a disappointing result, since the average at that time was far too low and is still below the level which can be designated as healthy, having regard to debt obligations, internal and international, and budget requirements. Yet, how much more satisfactory is even this record than that of the gold countries, where prices have fallen by ten to twenty per cent, intensifying their difficulties in many directions. There can be no doubt that our departure from gold has paid us already a handsome dividend. . . ."

Future Policy

It is apparent then, that England has, in effect, turned definitely to a policy of credit expansion and may be heading towards ultimate stabilization of the purchasing power of the pound sterling, without, however, being avowedly committed to such a course. The British credit situation appears similar to that of America under Governor Strong's manipulation. Strong always avoided being committed to a stabilization policy, although he was actually pursuing one, and like the United States during the "prosperity" of 1922–1929, England is today progressing steadily, under her currency management. But the American experience indicated that, without a definite stabilization policy, crystallized in legislation, we cannot be safeguarded against fluctuations in the purchasing power of the currency. It remains to be seen whether, in England, where tradition and usage, as instanced by the Bank of England, often function in place of written statutes, stabilization may be accomplished by a different route from that taken by Sweden or expected in the United States.

However, Mr. McKenna believed, that the signature of the "Empire Declaration" [2a] by England, in July 1933, together with most members of the British Empire, placed upon the Bank of

2a See also Chapter 11, Section 2.

England a new monetary policy. In this declaration the view was reaffirmed that the final objective of monetary policy should be "the re-establishment of an international gold standard reformed in such a manner that stability of exchange rates could be reconciled with a reasonable measure of stability in world prices." [3]

Mr. McKenna is emphatic in pointing out the importance of this step. "This declaration," he says, "may well prove the most important profession of faith the world has yet had on the subject of monetary policy." It seems that in fact, the vast British Empire is actively proceeding on the principles laid down in the Imperial Declaration and is thus quietly, but successfully paving the way for the ultimate attainment of a world wide stable money.

SECTION 2. THE SWEDISH STABILIZATION EXPERIMENT

(FROM SEPTEMBER 28, 1931)

Formulation of a New Policy (1931)

On September 28, 1931, one week after Great Britain went off the gold standard, Sweden followed suit. During the war, Sweden had suspended gold payments, but she was the first country to return to gold in 1924. In the war period the Swedish paper krona was worth more than the gold krona; at one time its value was 20% above the old gold par. But in 1931 it seemed to have been a foregone conclusion that as a consequence of the abandonment of gold, prices would rise, that is, the purchasing power of the krona would depreciate. This idea seemed to have been current as a consequence of the fact that during the two years previous to 1931 the krona had appreciated 20% in purchasing power. There was now considerable disagreement as to how far prices should be permitted to rise, and there was also a general fear of inflation.

[3] *Midland Bank Monthly Review*, January–February, 1934.

Mainly perhaps to reassure the public of its intention to prevent inflation, the Riksbank, upon abandoning gold announced (with the agreement of the Swedish Government) that it intended at least to maintain the purchasing power of the krona in the hands of the consumers. Thus, for the first time in history, a country announced that its policy would be that of stabilizing its currency, not with regard to gold or with regard to foreign exchange, but with regard to the internal purchasing power of its money.

Knut Wicksell, whose work has been reviewed above,[4] is sometimes called the father of the Swedish experiment; at all events, including Wicksell, Sweden has had an unusual number of authorities who advocate stable money. Among those who made suggestions that influenced the official formulation of the Riksbank's stabilization policy have notably been Professors Heckscher, Ohlin, Myrdal and others. The efforts of these outstanding Swedish economists have no doubt been instrumental in educating the Swedish public. And, as Professor Lindahl expressed it, "The economists in Sweden have always had a comparatively strong influence on political decisions having an economic bearing." [5]

Nevertheless, what has been done would certainly never have been done, had not the Governors of the Riksbank sympathized with the proposal. The cooperation of the Banking Committee of the Riksdag and of the Minister of Finance were also essential and were forthcoming. Most central banks are owned privately or semi-privately. But the Swedish Riksbank is a state institution and, although the Crown appoints the Chairman of the Board of Governors, the bank is directly responsible to the Swedish Parliament.

[4] See Chapter 3, Section 4.
[5] Erik Lindahl, *Sweden's Monetary Program,* in "Economic Forum," June–July, 1934.

Modification of Policy (1932)

Immediately after the Riksbank in September 1931 set out on its new policy which had been temporarily established, the Minister of Finance gave his approval of its object, namely, *"preserving the internal purchasing power of the krona in the hands of the consumers."* In January 1932 the Minister modified his statement by adding that the policy did not "preclude certain modifications of prices, especially wholesale prices." He also said that "stabilization of the international value of the krona should be attempted as soon as conditions permit."

The explanation of this modification of policy seems to be that the Riksbank, during these first months after abandoning the gold standard, was surprisingly successful in preventing inflation, and there also occurred an amazing stability of the retail price level. Confidence in the possibility of managing the consumption price level was thus established, and it was then hoped that the Riksbank would overcome, by reflation, some of the evil effects of previous deflation.

The Governors of the Riksbank, in a statement of February 1932 said that "The Riksbank's intention is to endeavor to maintain more or less unaltered the average level of prices of home-market goods and of the most important services that form an integral part of consumption. A monetary policy along these lines is compatible with a certain rise in the Riksbank's index. . . ." [6] In other words, under this modified policy, even the Riksbank's retail index was to be permitted to rise slightly, under the influence of the increased prices for imported goods.

When, in May of 1932, the Banking Committee of the Riksdag met, it was decided that for the time being, the stabilization of the international value of the krona, that is, the pegging of its

[6] Quoted from Bertil Ohlin, *Sweden's Monetary Policy*, in "Index" of Svenska Handelsbanken, Vol. VII, No. 81, September, 1932.

external exchange value to gold or to sterling, was out of the question, but that, on the contrary, the internal wholesale price level ought to be raised, in so far as this could be done without also seriously affecting the cost of living. Swedish retail prices and wages had not fallen as drastically as had the wholesale price level, so that the gap between wholesale and retail prices had become abnormally wide. By raising wholesale prices, while maintaining the retail price level, it was hoped to correct this disequilibrium. At the same time this procedure was to make production profitable again.

Establishment of Consumption Index

Dr. Dog Hammarskjöld was employed by the Governors of the Riksbank to devise for the Statistical Department of the bank a special weekly retail price index, the Consumption Index of the Riksbank, comprising the average retail prices of goods and services which represent the "cost of living" of a representative cross section of the Swedish people. In order that this index might represent the average purchasing power of the krona in the hands of the consumer as accurately as possible, the prices are collected in fifteen different localities; the basis of the index is subject to constant readjustments, corresponding to changes in consumption. The "weighting" of the individual items is also adjusted from time to time.[7] Nor does the Riksbank look only at this special index when making its decisions; on the contrary, other available indexes are consulted. Dr. Hammarskjöld even constructed a special wholesale price index for this purpose, but other available indexes, such as production, trade and employment indexes are also consulted.

[7] Erik T. H. Kjellstrom, *Managed Money The Experience of Sweden*, New York, Columbia University Press, 1934, pp. 48–52.

The Riksbank's Powers and their Limitations

By what methods may the Riksbank influence the price level, and what are the limitations on these methods? The Swedish money market, which is under the Riksbank's influence, is concerned largely with the financing of national projects and has few of the complications of an international money market. This is an advantage which adds to the stability of the situation; but, on the other hand, it excludes the facilities of a short-term market which the central bank would be able to regulate through "open-market" operations. Thus, the Riksbank is limited in its control over the volume of outstanding currency mainly to the manipulation of the interest rate, the purchase and sale of gold, and of foreign exchange and of Government securities.

Even in these operations the Riksbank is limited. For instance, the Riksbank might decide to lower its bank rate and the commercial banks might cooperate by lowering their discount rates on commercial paper, and yet other interest rates, particularly for long-term financing might remain high, through the slow action of the savings banks (which in this field compete with the commercial banks).[8] Even the commercial banks might be slow in supporting an easy money policy on the part of the Riksbank, preferring liquidity. These clashes of bank policies may prevent the Riksbank's attempts to expand credit from having an immediate and complete effect upon the national money market, particularly as it has only a limited possibility of making direct loans to credit seekers. In general, however, Sweden has an homogeneous and unified banking system, and the commercial banks raise or lower their discount rates to correspond to the raising or lowering of the Riksbank's rates.

When we consider the additional, even though temporary,

[8] The slow action of the savings banks can be explained by the fact that they are depending in their interest policy on the yield of Government bonds and other gilt edge securities.

difficulties occasioned by the collapse of the Kreuger concern, the import restrictions of Sweden's chief customer, Great Britain, also the foreign exchange restrictions and price reduction policies of Germany and, above all, the continued decline of prices in gold standard countries, and serious labor troubles occasioned by the expiration of wage agreements, the accomplished fact of a krona stable in the hands of the consumers, ever since September 1931, appears the more remarkable.

Stability of the Riksbank's Consumption Index

The official cost of living index (which alone the Riksbank undertook to stabilize) kept remarkably stable. Starting with 100 in September, 1931, it never rose higher than 101.7, and never fell below 98.4, for thirty-five months, that is, up to the present writing, August, 1934. In other words, it ranged from 1.7% above, to 1.6% below, the chosen par; and usually the deviation from par was less than 1%. The change in any one week was usually less than ½ of 1%.[9]

The Riksbank's Operations (1931–1933)

Such stability did not simply "happen." The Riksbank had to make use of much active management. First, in March–April 1932, when the Kreuger concern collapsed, skilful management was required to prevent a serious depreciation of the external value of the krona, without creating deflation at home. Later, management was required to prevent the Swedish price level from following the downward trend of the world price level.

[9] Professor Bertil Ohlin has made a revision of the official figures of the Riksbank, taking account of seasonal variations and increased taxation and has thus computed a retail index number which during the two years gradually sagged until it is for 1933 about 2% below the official index of the Riksbank. There are undoubtedly a number of methods of adjusting the index, but the only exact measure of the success or failure of the Riksbank must, of course, be the index which the Riksbank itself used for its criterion.

The Swedish wholesale price index moved only from 109 in March 1932 to 108 in July 1932, while the English wholesale price level declined from 105 to 98 in the same period. The Riksbank effected this stability mainly through the purchase of foreign exchange and of Swedish Government securities. In September, 1931, the Riksbank's holdings of foreign exchange amounted to a mere 33 million kronor which by December, 1932 had been increased to 214 million. Largely, therefore, the stability of Sweden's wholesale price level at that time was maintained through a depreciation of the gold-exchange value of the krona, in proportion as prices in other countries declined. But these expedients were supplemented by regulations of the discount rate.

For instance, on September 21, 1931 when England abandoned the gold standard, the Riksbank raised its discount rate from 4% to 5%. Four days later it raised the rate to 6% and afterwards (when Sweden abandoned gold) to 8%. At the same time, it asked the commercial banks to restrict credits for import as well as for speculative purposes. Obviously, this action was taken from fear of inflation. On October 19, the rate was reduced to 6%, equal to the English bank rate, and both rates (England's and Sweden's) stayed at 6% until the middle of February, 1932. From then on the Swedish rate was reduced gradually:—to 3½% towards the end of 1932; to 2½% beginning June, 1933; and to 2% in December, 1933. While the initial rise of the discount rate may have been effective in preventing inflation, the subsequent reductions seem to have been helpful merely in not interfering with an expected credit expansion, without, however, bringing about such expansion.

The Swedish wholesale price level, which was 107 in September, 1931 was kept comparatively stable during the first year, and even rose a few points, in September, 1932 to 110.

Report of the Commission of Experts (1933)

From September, 1932 until April, 1933 the Swedish whole-sale price level, however, declined from 110 to 105. The Government, therefore, in April, 1933, appointed a Committee of Ex-

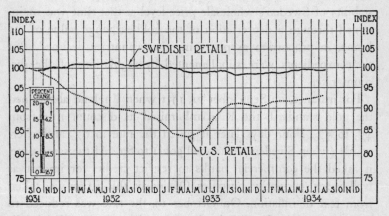

Chart 1. Retail Indexes (American, National Industrial Conference Board; Swedish, Official Riksbank)

perts, whose unanimous report of May 22nd was subsequently adopted by the Government and the Swedish Parliament.[10] This report was made a part of a "Memorandum by the Swedish Delegation on the Monetary Policy of Sweden," which was submitted to the London Economic Conference, on June 21, 1933. In this memorandum the whole problem of Sweden's management of

[10] See Gustav Cassel, *Sweden's Monetary Policy,* in "Skandinaviska Kreditaktiebolaget, Quarterly Report," July, 1933.

the krona is explained in all its details. In part this statement read as follows: [11]

"In examining the problem of setting out the lines on which to pursue our monetary policy in the present situation, the first point to be considered is whether the directions to be indicated

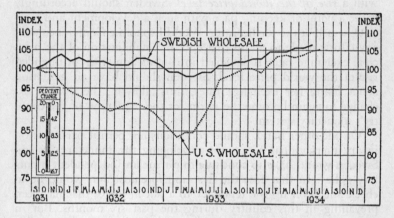

Chart 2. Wholesale Indexes (American, U. S. Bur. Labor Statistics; Swedish, Kommerskollegium)

should deal specifically with the internal purchasing power of the krona, or with its foreign exchange value. Being fully in agreement with the official statements made on the occasion of Sweden's adoption of a free standard in September, 1931, and during the last session of Parliament, the experts are of the opinion that Sweden's monetary policy should continue to aim at a regulation of the internal purchasing power of the krona along lines favourable to the economic life of the country, and a cor-

[11] League of Nations, *Monetary and Economic Conference, Monetary and Financial Commission*, Conf./M.L./C.M.F./11.

responding adjustment of the foreign exchange value of the currency. The experts are of the decided opinion that Sweden should, however, not embark upon a policy of depreciating the foreign exchange value of the Swedish krona with a view to gaining advantages in the field of commercial policy.

"A regulation of the internal purchasing power of the krona on lines favourable to Sweden's economic life would probably be most easily and most advantageously accomplished in connection with a *rise of the world price level*. Sweden should accordingly make a point of keeping pace with such a development and associate herself at the forthcoming World Economic Conference with any efforts made to attain that end. If a stabilization of the principal exchange rates is achieved in conjunction with an intended rise of the world price level, Sweden should have no hesitation about fixing her exchange rates, thus allowing the foreign exchange to again become the norm for the regulation of the country's monetary system.

"On the other hand, should conditions not permit participation in an international action for developing the monetary system, Sweden would have to continue to pursue an independent monetary policy. In that case the first and foremost aim would be to check and level up the tendency to a fall in prices that has been prevailing in this country during the past six months. But in addition to this, the objectives of an independent monetary policy —as has also been the declared aim in official pronouncements in other countries, including the British Empire—should be to bring about a moderate *rise of the internal wholesale price level*. Seeing that the cost of living consists largely of factors of cost that are independent of the rise in wholesale prices, and as retail prices react but slowly to changes in wholesale prices, it is to be expected that no appreciable rise will occur in the cost of living standard as a whole.

"Among the *means* at the disposal of the Riksbank for achieving the aims indicated above, *discount policy and credit policy* in general deserve special emphasis. Further, there are the possibilities that the Riksbank has of *active* intervention towards the same end. Should, contrary to expectation, an isolated Swedish rise in prices occur on a scale greater than is intended, the means just mentioned should be employed to counteract any such tendency with a view of controlling the value of the Swedish krona."

It was with this program of international reflation that the Swedish Delegation, headed by Richard Sandler, Sweden's Foreign Minister, and Ernst Wigforss, Minister of Finance, went to the London Economic Conference. Although England at first appeared favorable to this course, and the United States, through President Roosevelt's message, was later committed to it, Sweden could not obtain any international agreement at that time, and proceeded independently with her domestic monetary policy.

Operations of the Riksbank in 1933

Accordingly, in the course of the year, the Riksbank increased its gold and foreign exchange holdings, thus maintaining the foreign exchange rate of the krona at a low level; incidentally such purchases served to minimize the effects of foreign exchange fluctuations, and provided investment for the bank. From March, 1933 until December, 1933, 164 million kronor of gold and 186 million of foreign exchange were thus added to the bank's portfolio.[12]

As early as May, 1933, aided, no doubt, by a world-wide tendency of prices to rise, Sweden's wholesale price index began to recover, and, by July 1933 it rose to 108 and had thus practically regained the position it held when the gold standard was abandoned. The latest available figure of this index, for June, 1934, is 114, which shows that the recovery continued.[13]

[12] Skandinaviska Kreditaktiebolaget, *Quarterly Reports*.
[13] In considering the stability or instability of the Swedish wholesale price level since September, 1931, comparison should be made relatively to 107, which was the position of the wholesale index in September, 1931 (relatively to 100 in 1913).

Conclusions

The success of the Swedish stabilization experiment appears so much more remarkable in consideration of the difficulties which the Riksbank had to encounter, due to world deflation; the smallness of the country; its dependence upon foreign trade; the Kreuger disaster; as well as labor troubles and other difficulties. The Riksbank had to contend with the same difficulties we had in the United States, namely, during a depression business men are reluctant to borrow.[14]

At this writing it is still a matter of controversy in Sweden, to what extent the Riksbank's policy was instrumental in accomplishing the stability of the consumption index.

Some maintain that the Riksbank deserves the main credit for accomplishing stabilization. They believe that this was done chiefly by its wise adjustments of foreign exchange operations to the domestic requirements of the country; that is, purchasing foreign exchange to maintain a low foreign valuation of the krona; abandoning the exchange stability of the krona with the English pound when such exchange stability tended to pull down the Swedish price level; but maintaining a stable sterling exchange when the beneficial influence of a rise of British wholesale prices could thus be made to effect a corresponding rise of the Swedish wholesale price level.

These people also say that there is no reason to believe that the Riksbank would have pursued its policy with equal efficiency and determination, had it not been pledged to the maintenance of the consumption price index.

Others believe that, while these operations of the Riksbank were helpful, the stability of the consumption price index was due chiefly to the inherent stability of Swedish industrial, agri-

[14] See also Bertil Ohlin, *The Inadequacy of Price Stabilization*, in "Index," Vol. VIII, No. 96, December, 1933, Svenska Handelsbanken, Stockholm.

cultural, and social relations. These people would have us think that it was not so much the purposeful management of the Riksbank but simply sheer good luck that, for some hundred and fifty weeks in succession the chosen index number has simply happened to remain invariable—within 1 or 1¾ per cent —something which had never happened before.

In any case, the two simple facts: (1) that the Riksbank announced its intention to maintain the internal purchasing power of the krona in the hands of the consumer, and (2) the subsequent stability of that purchasing power, stand out as among the most remarkable facts of the depression.

Efforts have been made in the United States to disprove the benefits to Sweden of her stabilization. Such efforts seem to have been inspired by those who oppose stable money for the United States. These efforts are discussed in Appendix II.

Section 3. Australia's Experience

Australia attacked her depression in two ways; the monetary way (correcting the *value* of money); and the tabular-standard way (changing the *amount* of money payable, to thus offsetting the uncorrected change in its value), that is, she adjusted her internal cost and debt structure to the lowered income created by a fall in prices—especially export prices. Australia's great achievement, however, during the depression of 1929-1933, was in the monetary way. She gave the world a successful demonstration of *reflation*. This she accomplished mainly by the following methods: Depreciation of the currency, *i.e.* lowering the gold value of her money (raising the price of gold); and expansion of central bank credit. This unconventional attack upon Australia's depression was launched in the summer of 1931, chiefly according to the directions and proposals given by a group of Australian economists.

Professor Copland

In order to better understand the significance of these developments in Australia as they bear upon the world struggle for a stable currency, let us note several statements made by Professor Douglas Copland of the University of Melbourne. He is one of the most outstanding Australian economists, and his advice has frequently been sought by the Australian Government.

Professor Copland had for a number of years been an advocate of Stable Money. As early as in 1921, he listed the following advantages of a stable standard of value:

"It would," he said,

"a) Lead to a more equitable distribution of wealth
"b) Discourage speculation
"c) Reduce uncertainty in industry
"d) Render Public Finance more stable; and
"e) Promote more settled industrial relations." [15]

Professor Copland then suggested regulating the issuance of Australian currency so as to maintain a stable price index. That is, when there was a tendency towards rising prices, he would contract the currency, and when there was a tendency towards falling prices, expand it.

As the machinery by which this stabilization could be accomplished he mentioned:

"(I) An index of *responsive* wholesale prices.

"(II) The automatic variation of the note issue according to movements in the index number.

"(III) The use of notes as legal tender bank reserves and for clearing house operations.

"The evils of a fluctuating standard," he concluded, "are

[15] D. B. Copland, *Currency and Prices in Australia,* The Joseph Fisher Lecture in Commerce, delivered June 15, 1921, at the University of Adelaide, p. 24.

now so obvious to the mass of men that a new standard must
be adopted eventually. . . . Monetary theory has gone beyond
the gold standard, as we knew it before the war, and the simple
return to it will be no real advance. On the other hand, the
successful adoption of a multiple standard is the next step
forward." [15a]

In 1924, on the occasion of a Presidential address given before
the Social and Statistical Section of the Australasian Association
for the Advancement of Science, Professor Copland referred to
the need for currency management in the following words:

"Whatever standard of value is ultimately adopted, it will be
subject to some form of control. The direction in which this
control should be exercised is the central problem of monetary
policy." [16]

He concluded that a stable price level should be the objective
of monetary policy:

". . . for the short period it is obvious that stability is the goal
to be aimed at—that is, stability within the secular trend. This,
I believe, would be theoretically most beneficial if the trend was
slightly downwards, but such a proposal is in practice out of the
question. It is therefore necessary to aim generally at stabilization, and this is the goal upon which there is general agreement." [17]

In a recent book on "Australia in the World Crisis" [18] Professor Copland has given a comprehensive picture of Australian
monetary and financial developments during the depression, and
explained the action by which the depression was eventually
overcome.[19]

[15a] *Ibid.*, p. 43.
[16] D. B. Copland, *Monetary Policy and Its Application to Australia*, Melbourne
University Press, 1926, p. 509.
[17] *Ibid.*, p. 511.
[18] Cambridge, *England at the University Press and New York*, Macmillan Co.,
1934, 212 pp.
[19] See also:
E. O. G. Shann and D. B. Copland (Compilers), *The Crisis in Australian*

The Course of Australia's Depression

The Australian depression began in the middle of 1928, and was greatly aggravated during 1929, when the world prices of Australia's most important export products—mainly wool and agricultural products—fell heavily. The total value of Australia's wool exports fell from £61,615,245 in 1928–1929 to £36,600,510 in 1929–1930.[20] The fall of export prices which in 1932 had declined to roughly one half of their pre-depression level, resulted in an immediate and serious decline in the national income. From 1928 to 1932 the loss in the national income was more than one-third.

A serious disequilibrium was created by declining prices and lower income on the one side, and a rigid debt and cost structure on the other. The balance of trade became increasingly adverse; unemployment rose; state budgets showed alarming deficits, and profits in agriculture and industry almost disappeared. In November, 1929, these difficulties had forced the country virtually to abandon the gold standard, without, however, immediately depreciating the foreign exchange value of the currency. The gold standard was given up in order to permit Australia the full use of her gold reserves to meet her external obligations.

Inflationists; Deflationists

In this serious situation, two schools of economic thought advanced their proposals for overcoming the crisis, and their arguments soon became a matter of serious political controversy.

Finance, 1929 to 1931. Angus & Robertson, Ltd., Sydney, 1931. XIX, 201 pp.
The Battle of the Plans dto., 1931, XVIII, 169 pp.
The Australian Price Structure, 1932 dto., 1933, XIX, 253 pp.
Douglas Copland, Economic Adjustment in Australia, in Lloyds Bank Limited, "Monthly Review," November, 1933.
[20] Official Yearbook of the Commonwealth of Australia, Commonwealth Bureau of Census and Statistics, Canberra, No. 25, 1932, p. 619.

The *Inflationists,* on the one side, proposed the issuance of fiduciary currency in order to balance the budget and in order to provide for emergency unemployment relief, and also in order to provide for a subsidy to the wheat growers. They further urged the depreciation of the exchange rate, and the continuation of these measures until the price level of 1925–1929 should be restored. In addition they demanded drastic reorganization of banking with the object of greater control by the government over credit and the interest rate.

The *Deflationists,* on the other hand, proposed parity of the Australian pound with the English pound, and a deliberate deflation policy with regard to all income, which, they hoped, would also bring about a deflation of future costs and future debts.

The Middle Course; Copland Committee

A third group of economists advocated a "middle course," later also called the program of *Stabilization.* This was to be a blend of inflationary and deflationary measures, which were to restore income by higher export prices; reduce costs and the interest on debts, while at the same time inauguarating an expansionist monetary policy. Professor Copland lists the points of this program as follows:

"1) Depreciation of the currency sufficient to restore real income in export industries to [within] 10% of its former level.

"2) A reduction of real wages of 10%.

"3) A general reduction in real government salaries and wages and expenditures of 10%.

"4) A super-tax of 10% on income from property.

"5) An expansionist monetary policy based upon the purchase of Government securities by the Commonwealth Bank with a view to maintaining the general level of prices as measured by the *complete* retail index number." [21]

---

[21] *Australia in the World Crisis, op. cit.,* pp. 66–67.

On the basis of this program of "stabilization" a memorandum was submitted in September, 1930, to the Treasurer of the Commonwealth by Professors Copland, Giblin, and Mr. Dyason. In January, 1931 the Social and Statistical Section of the Australasian Association for the Advancement of Science also concurred in these demands in a statement which called for:

"1) Reduction of costs, including labor costs.

"2) Balancing of budgets.

"3) The improvement of external and internal prices." [22]

The first step in the direction of this policy was taken on January 22, 1931, when the Arbitration Court ordered a reduction of 10% in the real basic wage. The Arbitration Court is a permanent Australian institution in the field of a tabular standard which makes quarterly adjustments of the wage rate according to a cost of living index. In April, 1931, the Government appointed the "Copland Committee," consisting of four economists and five Under-Treasurers, with Professor Copland as chairman. The function of the Committee was to recommend a way out of the depression.

The Premiers' Plan

The report of the Copland Committee (May, 1931) was adopted almost in its entirety by the Premiers of the several Australian States at a Premiers' Conference in May–June, 1931. The following are the main points of the "Premiers' Plan," adopted on June 10, 1931:

"(a) A reduction of 20 per cent in all adjustable Government expenditure, as compared with the year ending June 30, 1930, including all emoluments, wages, salaries and pensions paid by the Governments, whether fixed by statute or otherwise, such reduction to be equitably effected;

[22] *The Crisis in Australian Finance, op. cit.*, p. 73.

"(b) Conversion of the internal debts of the Governments on the basis of a 22½ per cent reduction of interest;

"(c) The securing of additional revenue by taxation, both Commonwealth and State;

"(d) A reduction of Bank and Savings Bank rates of interest on deposits and advances;

"(e) Relief in respect to private mortgages." [23]

The basis of the Premiers' Plan was, of course, the attempt to make production (and export) again profitable, and to distribute equitably over the entire population the loss of income which was an inevitable effect of world-wide deflation. It was by means of the slogan, "Equality of Sacrifice," that the plan was subsequently popularized.

While the Premiers' Plan, which reduced the income of a large part of the population, thus had the appearance of a deflationary measure, it was, in reality, what Professor Copland calls, a measure of "constructive deflation."

"There is," he says, "no precedent for this in the action taken by Australia in 1931 to adjust fixed charges to the fall in national income and the rise in the value of money. . . . It is only necessary to draw attention to the proposals of economists for a tabular standard or a more stable price level. Until the problem of reasonable stability has been solved, the use of some form of tabular standard would overcome the injustices suffered by both debtors and creditors by the payment of fixed charges in a unit of currency that fluctuates in value.

"Justice cannot be done by forcing payment in a currency that is so appreciated as to destroy or greatly reduce capacity to pay. Australia was acting prudently in revising contracts on the principle that the real meaning of the contract itself had been altered by the rapid economic changes forced upon her in the depression. Interference with contract, in these circum-

[23] *The Battle of the Plans, op. cit.,* p. 127.

stances, was an integral element of a constructive policy. Deflation was applied to all incomes with the object of correcting a distortion in the cost and price structure by spreading quickly and equitably the loss of real income. We may legitimately designate this as *constructive deflation* in contrast to the type of deflation that attacks certain incomes only, and thus adds to the disparity in real incomes among different classes. The deflationary policy pursued by Australia had the additional merit that it was accompanied by certain inflationary action." [24]

In other words, Australia attacked the problem of "stabilization," not only by changing the gold value of her currency, but by adjusting partly her cost and debt structure to the drastically changed purchasing power of her currency. She "stabilized" by an application of the principle of the tabular standard.

Domestic Effects of the Plan

The country's dependence upon export trade, which was under the direct influence of declining world prices, had, besides loss of income caused a wide gap between the rigidly high costs of production in Australia, and the prices which were obtainable for Australian goods on the world market. Consequently production had become unprofitable; and Australia now reduced the gap by altering both, the prices and the costs. The prices of her exports were raised by depreciating her currency in terms of gold. In August, 1933 this depreciation had proceeded to a point where 185 Australian paper pounds were equivalent to 100 gold pounds, that is, the price of gold was raised 85%.

On April 12, 1932, the "Wallace Bruce Committee," consisting of four economists and two business men [25] submitted to the

---

[24] *Australia in the World Crisis, op. cit.,* pp. 138–9.
[25] Wallace Bruce (Chairman).   L. G. Melville
    G. S. Colman   R. C. Mills
    L. F. Giblin   Edward Shann

Australian Government its report on the economic situation, advocating the continued application of the following three basic recovery measures:

1) A further reduction of wages
2) Further depreciation of the foreign exchange
3) Extension of bank credits; loans for public works, and other measures to increase enterprise.[26]

Point (2), the further depreciation of the exchange rate was considered the easiest and quickest method for bringing costs and prices into equilibrium. This expedient would particularly have increased the prices, in Australian currency, obtained by exports on the foreign markets, and thus have raised the purchasing power of an important part of the population, engaged in production for export. But the Board of the Commonwealth Bank, which had been entrusted with the control of the foreign exchange rate refused, at that time, further depreciation.[27]

The report of the Wallace Bruce Committee also mentioned some of the results which had been obtained through the application of the Premiers' Plan. It also complained that in some instances full cooperation of all states and individuals with the Premiers was still lacking.

According to this Committee's report, the costs of Australian production were reduced (pursuant to appropriate legislation, where necessary) by reducing industrial wages and salaries (20% to over 30% between 1928 and 1932); lowering interest rates on all debts, mortgages, etc. (22½% was made permissible on private debts, but reductions ranged from 15% to 33%); and other costs, not necessarily involved in the export trade were reduced, including rents, railroad charges (the latter especially on export products); the balancing of the state budgets through the reduction of expenditures by 20% to 30% (both administra-

26 *The Australian Price Structure, op. cit.,* pp. 38–78.
27 *Ibid.,* pp. 99–100.

tive and other expenses). The Government reduced some of its interest burdens by conversion of bond issues, thus saving about 22½% (and over, in some instances) in interest payments.

During 1933, Australia succeeded in converting in London £109,849,000 of maturing obligations, the original interest rate of which had varied from 4% to 6½%. The conversions were effected at rates ranging from 3½% to 4%, thus saving annually £2,280,000 to Australia.[28]

Imports, which before depression had amounted to over £140 millions were in 1931-32 reduced to £44 millions, leaving a favorable trade balance of £34 millions, which was more than sufficient to meet the debt charge of about £26 millions. During 1932-33 again the trade balance was sufficient to meet charges on foreign debts, although imports had increased from £44 millions to £56.6 millions. This favorable development naturally obviated the necessity for incurring new borrowings in London.

The domestic situation was also improved by the extension of central bank credit (amounting to a net expansion of 40% in the crisis) for the financing of public works, and for the payment of Government deficits; by low money rates (the rates for three months' deposits was 2% in June 1933, as compared to 4½% in January 1931; by the cooperation of the private banks in extending credit in industry.

These drastic measures brought speedy relief to the manufacturing and export industries. While the gold value of exports continued to decline, the decline of the value of exports in terms of the Australian paper currency was mitigated. That is, while gold prices of export products had fallen 70%, the fall in terms of Australian currency was only about 45%. The volume of exports, however, was maintained, and even increased through

[28] See The Record of the Lyons Government, January, 1933 to December, 1933, pp. 23-25.

favorable seasons. But in spite of the depreciation of the currency in terms of gold, the Government's credit was restored which made possible the conversions of loans, mentioned above.

One of the most convincing evidences of the increasing confidence in Australia's condition was given by the increasing prices of stock in industrial and other business companies. The index of Ordinary Shares rose from a low of 52.1 in January 1931, to 86.5 in July, 1933 (basis May 1926=100) Preferred Shares rose from 80.8 to 106.9 in the same period. Five and one-half per cent Government Securities which in June 1931 sold at 80%, after having been converted in Securities bringing only 4%, sold at 94% in June 1932. That is, they were higher in price, despite a reduction of the return to a purchaser from 8½% in 1931, to 3¾% in 1932.

In due time, unemployment began to decline gradually, and this improvement was helped by public works. In general, Australia began to recover from the depression earlier, and recovered faster, than most other countries.

International Effects of the Plan

In thus maintaining, and even increasing, her export trade in a period of declining consumption, it was inevitable that Australia should sometimes take trade from those countries which continued to adhere to the gold standard and to a deflationary policy. At the Ottawa Conference, in July–August, 1932, this fact was apparently discussed in connection with the demand for the stabilization of the foreign exchange rates. On this occasion, the Rt. Hon. S. M. Bruce, the leader of the Australian Delegation, delivered a speech in which he gave the following explanation regarding Australia's monetary policy:

"Some may accuse Australia of too rough an energy in her

struggle to pay her debts. Be it so. I should prefer conviction on such a charge to responsibility for the appreciation in the purchasing power of money and the slow paralysis of trade. We have at least avoided that infection. We have produced more heavily than ever before and marketed our products as we went. They have gone into current consumption, feeding and clothing both East and West.

"With this growing trade, no one will welcome stable exchanges more than we will if they come with higher prices. But any attempt to restore stable exchanges without a tolerable level of prices would be a mockery. A true international standard must give us stability of prices both in place and in time. By that I mean that we need currencies stable in their relations all around the world. We need, even more sorely, money that will enable a debt contracted in one year to be repaid by a comparable service when it falls due in another. If out of the present universal distress we can learn something of the art of reconciling these two stabilities we may yet extract from adversity a lesson of unrivalled value. Perhaps that reconciliation is not so difficult. Even now, the way to it may be clearing." [29]

Australia's Present and Future Policy

Professor Copland's view of Australia's present and future monetary policy is contained in the following sentences:

"In refusing to tie the currency to sterling or any other standard at present, the [Commonwealth] Bank [of Australia] is adding to, rather than detracting from, the security of Australian currency; for it is endeavoring to preserve a currency unit less variable in internal purchasing power than other and more important currencies. This is a constructive exchange policy. By promoting export production and thus adding to sterling assets,

[29] *The Australian Price Structure,* 1932, *op. cit.,* p. 142.

it improves the security of the currency. In changing world conditions, internal stability is preferable to exchange stability whatever be the inconveniences of variations in the rate of exchange.

"Until it is safe to link the currency again with the international standard, control can be exercised by the Commonwealth Bank to maintain any rate that promotes recovery and ultimate price stability in Australia, whatever be the temporary accumulation of London funds. Australian currency is in fact at present more stable than most other currencies, and therefore more secure." [30]

"The currency policy pursued during the depression has also a place in the monetary policy of the immediate future. . . . Its objectives are to sustain enterprise, to render elastic the internal financial structure, and to avoid the serious disturbances of unnecessary monetary changes. . . . The policy should, of course, be left to the Commonwealth Bank to administer with a general direction that currency policy is to aim at promoting a balanced price structure, with as far as practicable general stability, after a certain position (say, the 1928 level) has been attained. Early stabilization of the exchange should be avoided not less than an heroic attempt at restoring parity with sterling." [31]

Lessons from Australia's Experience

Professor E. O. G. Shann in a book "Quotas or Stable Money" [32] also argues for the maintenance of domestic stability of the currency and charging the central banks with the responsibility of accomplishing the necessary control. He severely criticizes as futile and restrictive the proposed methods of giving "Quotas"

[30] Australia in the World Crisis, op. cit., pp. 169–170.
[31] Ibid., p. 189.
[32] Three Essays on the Ottawa and London Conferences, 1932–33, Sydney, Australia, Angus & Robertson, Limited, 1933.

to the several countries of the British Empire according to which they should be permitted to export their products.

Nor does Professor Copland fail to point out that Australia had, for many years, applied and found wanting, the restrictive methods of economic control—control of output—which have recently been favored in the United States. He offers to the world, and to the United States in particular, the benefits of Australia's experience on this point and his warnings ought to be carefully considered.

"To one who has lived through the later years of Australia's policy of economic control there is something tragic in the universal enthusiasm now shown by the Northern Hemisphere for measures of economic control, frequently of a restrictive nature. In the heyday of our socialistic experiments in Australia we were fit subjects for academic study. But men of affairs in the old world with our example before their eyes, and that of our sister Dominion [New Zealand] across the Tasman Sea, now warmly embrace economic doctrines which Australia, after thirty years' experience, has found in some respects unsatisfactory. Apart from excess in tariff policy, which we now struggle to correct, the economic policy we pursued in the crisis was designed to encourage private enterprise.

"New measures of control were confined largely to management of the currency to give private industry a monetary unit reasonably stable in purchasing power. It is no exaggeration to say that this remains, even in Australia, and much more so in the world at large, the most important immediate economic problem. . . ."

"In the past we went too far along the wrong road in economic control. By a direct attack upon development, wages and working conditions we sought to maintain a high standard of living for a population that was growing much more than is commonly supposed. We did nothing to control the flow of investment at a reasonable rate of interest or to insure reasonable stability in the price level. Consumers' income was maintained at the expense of increasing costs—real wages, the real rate of interest, the real burden of taxation. Perhaps the United States is treading the same path at present. Time alone will tell. We do know that the experiment has failed in Australia to reach its objective, partly because it was forced too much along wrong lines, and partly it neglected some vital elements of economic control.

"The evils of a varying price level are now widely understood and public policy that aims at promoting stability of prices, after economic equilibrium has again been reached, will be widely supported." [33]

[33] *Ibid.,* pp. 176 and 178.

CHAPTER XI

BEGINNING WITH F. D. ROOSEVELT (FROM 1933)

Section i. America Off the Gold Standard

Meeting an Emergency

PRESIDENT ROOSEVELT is the first statesman of any great modern nation who has given the problem of stabilization of the purchasing power of money an important place in his administrative program. On the occasion of his first public pronouncement as President of the United States, in his Inaugural Address on March 4, 1933, he said that "there must be provision for an adequate but sound currency." Not only has he stated repeatedly that he wants to establish a currency which shall not vary in its purchasing and debt-paying power over a period of a generation, but up to this writing, he has acted consistently with this aim.

The first step in the President's currency-reform program was the separation of the dollar from gold. This was partly effected on March 6, 1933 by the proclamation declaring a national bank holiday and prohibiting, until March 9th, withdrawals of gold for hoarding and also prohibiting with certain flexible exceptions, all exports and earmarkings of gold and foreign exchange. On March 9th, this prohibition was extended for an indefinite period, and made applicable to all gold exports, whether coin or bullion, and to the export of gold certificates. An exception was made of such transactions as should be especially licensed by the Secretary of the Treasury. Also purchases of foreign exchange in limited quantity for purposes of travel and business transactions were permitted. Thus foreign money changers could, for the time being, turn American paper into gold at the old rate of equivalence.

On April 20, 1933, by Executive Order,[1] the President ended such equivalence by clamping a more rigid embargo on all exports of gold and foreign exchange, except such as might be licensed. This action definitely put the United States off the gold standard and freed the administration's hands for the purposes of (1) raising domestic prices; (2) facilitating domestic credit expansion; (3) dealing with foreign countries at the forthcoming Washington parleys and the forthcoming London Economic Conference; (4) preventing any congressional action that might take the initiative as to reflation out of the President's hands.

The New American Policy

On May 7th, 1933, Mr. Roosevelt, explained for the first time, the aims of his monetary policy—reflation and stabilization—in an address over the radio, as follows:

"The administration has the definite objective of raising commodity prices to such an extent that those who have borrowed money will, on the average, be able to repay that money in the same kind of dollar which they borrowed.

"We do not seek to let them get such a cheap dollar that they will be able to pay back a great deal less than they borrowed. In other words, we seek to correct a wrong and not to create another wrong in the opposite direction. That is why powers are being given to the administration to provide, if necessary, for an enlargement of credit, in order to correct the existing wrong. These powers will be used when, as, and if it may be necessary to accomplish the purpose. . . ."

[1] No. 6111.

The President's Powers

The President had thus placed his intentions before the country, and Congress acted promptly to give him the powers necessary for carrying out those intentions. The *Thomas Amendment to the Farm Relief Act,* provided the President with supreme inflationary powers, and virtually made him the master over the value of the dollar. This amendment enacted May 12, 1933, authorized the President to arrange with the Federal Reserve banks and Board for the open market purchases of up to 3 billion dollars' worth of Government obligations, including stock in those corporations of which the United States is the majority stockholder.

It further provided that if the President were unable to effect this purpose, or if it proved inadequate, he could:

Direct the issuance of United States notes up to 3 billion dollars, wherewith to retire Government obligations at the rate of 4% annually;

Reduce the gold content of the dollar by not to exceed 50%;

Provide for the unlimited coinage of silver at a fixed ratio with the gold dollar.

In addition, the bill authorized the President to accept silver up to 200 million dollars in the payment of war debts during the next six months, valuing the silver up to 50 cents an ounce; the silver thus obtained to be used as the basis for the issuance of silver certificates;

As a curb against too much inflation, the Federal Reserve Board was authorized to declare the existence of an emergency and increase or decrease reserve balances required of member banks to be held against deposits.

On May 29, 1933, a Joint Resolution was passed [2] outlawing the gold clause in all public and private contracts—the con-

[2] H.J. Res. 192. The vote in the House was 283 to 57.

ventional clause calling for payment in gold. This resolution,

1) declared that the clause in question is contrary to public policy;

2) provided that obligations, public or private, expressed to be payable in gold or in a specific coin or currency, may be discharged dollar for dollar in legal tender;

3) provided that no future obligations, public or private, should be expressed as payable in any specific coin or currency;

4) made certain technical amendments to the Thomas amendment which were necessary to carry out the intention of that legislation regarding what shall be legal tender in the United States.[3]

On June 5th, President Roosevelt affixed his signature to this resolution.

On June 16th, he signed the "Banking Act of 1933," heralded at that time as the most important banking legislation since the Federal Reserve Act. This legislation provides among other things, for bank deposit insurance, and the divorce from the banks of their speculative affiliates dealing in securities. Unquestionably, it was intended to effect greater stability of the banking system and to prevent runs upon banks and speculative excesses. In these ways it is part of the program for stabilizing the dollar. The "New Deal" contains numerous other measures which directly or indirectly are intended to bring about greater economic stability. But we are interested here only in the *Monetary* measures of the New Deal.

Section 2. London Economic Conference

Origin and Preparations

On June 12, 1933, the World Economic Conference opened in London, with sixty-six nations participating, representing practi-

---

[3] See *Journal of Commerce,* New York, May 30, 1933.

cally the entire civilized world. Almost every one of them, had suffered intensely from the evils of prolonged deflation; and they were bent on finding a common ground of action for remedying the situation.

The London Conference had its origin at the Lausanne Conference in July, 1932, where the nations which were principally concerned with reparations decided to ask the League of Nations "to convoke at a convenient date and at a place to be fixed, a Conference on Monetary and Economic Questions." [4]

Towards the end of October, 1932, a committee of experts, appointed by the League, met to discuss the subject of the proposed Conference and to prepare the agenda. The Committee included representatives from Belgium, France, Germany, Italy, Japan, the United States, the United Kingdom, the Bank for International Settlements and the League of Nations.

In January 1933, the Committee issued its *"Draft Annotated Agenda"* in which certain recommendations were set forth. It recommended in particular the restoration of an effective international gold standard, provided the factors which had led to its breakdown could be eliminated. Reference was also made to the possibility of cooperation by central banks in order to obtain greater stability of future price levels:

"In the field of monetary and credit policy," the Agenda reads, "the objective must be the restoration of an effective international monetary standard to which the countries which have abandoned the gold standard can wisely adhere. Each Government must, of course, remain free to decide when and under what conditions it would adopt such a standard, and we do not suggest that this can or should be done without the most careful preparation. The notes appended clearly show that there are a great number of economic as well as financial conditions which must be fulfilled before the restoration of an international gold standard can be a

[4] Quoted from *Midland Bank Monthly Review,* May–June, 1933; *The Coming World Conference.*

practical possibility. Moreover, it will be necessary to provide effective safeguards against such a restoration of the gold standard leading to a fresh break-down. The question has to be considered whether measures can be taken with the co-operation of Central Banks on the lines of the recommendations suggested in the report of the Gold Delegation of the League of Nations, to ensure a greater stability of price-levels in the future." [15]

The Commission found that, as the first essential step the equilibrium between prices and costs should be restored and that this should be followed by "such a reasonable degree of stability of prices as the world measure of value should properly possess." [6]

While thus recommending the return to the international gold standard, the Commission also emphasized that "any declarations in favour of the restoration of an international gold standard should, at the same time, indicate certain essential principles for its proper functioning under modern conditions." [7] The Final Report made by the Gold Delegation of June, 1932 [8] was held to be of great importance and was endorsed as a starting point for re-organizing the gold standard system.

In summary, therefore, the Commission recommended a program of international reflation, which was to be followed by the restoration of a reformed gold standard under which a reasonable stability of the world price level could be attained.

The Clash of Policies

In order to understand President Roosevelt's famous message which practically disrupted the London Conference, let us review the development of two essentially different viewpoints about

---

[5] League of Nations Monetary and Economic Conference. *Draft Annotated Agenda*, Geneva, January 20, 1933, p. 1.
[6] *Ibid.*, p. 11.
[7] *Ibid.*, p. 13.
[8] See Chapter 9, Section 3.

the idea of reflation and stabilization. The difference was that France, and England, and the other countries of the two classes —gold and sterling—favored a temporary stabilization of their exchange rates, to be followed by measures for raising their respective price levels. The United States (and also Sweden) on the other hand, insisted on settling the problem of reflating domestic price levels, *before* entering into any agreements to stabilize exchange. To *raise* the price level *first* was the President's plan.

The Chancellor of the British Exchequer, Neville Chamberlain, on the other hand stated that, in his opinion, stable exchange rates were first in importance and should come first. In an address, delivered to the Conference, on June 14, he said:

"The immediate objective should be to secure approximate stabilization between the currencies of the principal countries of the world in order that trade may not be hampered by violent, unpredictable fluctuations of basic currencies. This end will be achieved in so far as the principal countries use their resources in order to counteract fluctuations in the value of their currencies caused by temporary movements of capital rather than fundamental economic factors. This first step should be dealt with immediately." [9]

Mr. Chamberlain then mentioned, as second in importance, the general return to the gold standard, provided the three following objects could be accomplished: The raising of the wholesale price level; the conquest of the factors that had caused the break-down of the gold standard; the administering of the gold standard in the future in such a way as to prevent wide fluctuations in the purchasing power of gold.

The main subject under discussion at the beginning of the Conference was therefore that of the stabilization of the American, English and French exchange rates. In practice this

[9] New York *Times*, June 14, 1933.

meant the pegging of the dollar and pound to the franc, or, in other words, to gold, no matter how much the commodity purchasing power of gold itself might fluctuate. Among the proposals for carrying out this currency truce, the establishment of a joint tri-partite equalization fund was discussed, and a plan for the stabilization of the three exchanges during the life of the Conference was cabled to Washington.[10]

On June 21, President Roosevelt rejected this plan, to the dismay of those who conceived recovery only in terms of an immediate restoration of the international gold standard.

On June 22, the American Delegation issued the following statement indicating that America believed in first raising the domestic price level and then stabilizing it; that is, the policy of reflation-stabilization was again clearly set forth:

"Undue emphasis has been placed upon consideration of a plan proposed for temporary de facto stabilization of currencies.

"The fact is this never has been an affair of the delegation. It was considered by representatives of the Treasuries and Central Banks of the United States, Great Britain and France, Oliver M. W. Sprague having been specially sent to represent the United States Treasury for this purpose. The American Government at Washington finds that measures for temporary stabilization now would be untimely.

"The reason why it is considered untimely is because the American Government feels that its efforts to raise prices are the most important contribution it can make and that everything that would interfere with these efforts and possibly cause a violent price recession would harm the Conference more than the lack of an immediate agreement for temporary stabilization.

"As to the ultimate objective, the American Delegation has already introduced a resolution designed for ultimate world-wide stabilization of unstable currencies, and is devoting itself to the support of measures for the establishment of a co-ordinated monetary and fiscal policy to be pursued by the various nations in co-

[10] See also Leo Pasvolsky, *Current Monetary Issues,* Washington, D. C., The Brookings Institution, 1934.

operation with the others for the purpose of stimulating economic activity and improving prices."

On June 27th, according to the press,[11] France brought pressure upon England to tie the pound sterling to the franc, *i.e.* to gold, regardless of America's action. On the next day, France, Holland, Italy, Belgium and Switzerland (known collectively as "the gold bloc") discussed measures for defending the gold standard against America's reflationary plans.

On June 30, the situation had become tense. The dollar-pound rate was fluctuating sharply. A plan for preventing the speculative movement of exchange during a certain period was drawn up by several leading nations and transmitted to President Roosevelt, in the hope that America would support it. It read as follows:

"DECLARATION, in which nations on the gold standard and those not on that standard join:

"It is agreed that stability in the international field should be obtained as quickly as practicable, and the common interest of all concerned is recognized;

"That re-establishment of gold as a measure of international exchange value should be accomplished with recognition that the time at which each of the countries off gold could undertake stabilization and the time at which parity is established must be determined by the respective governments;

"It is reasserted by Governments, the currencies of which are on the gold standard, that it is their intent to maintain the free working of that standard at current gold parities and in conformity to their respective monetary laws, believing that maintenance of existing gold parities is in the interest of world recovery.

"Governments subscribing to this declaration whose currencies are not on the gold standard take note of the above declaration and recognize its importance without in any way prejudizing their own future ratios to gold and reiterate that the ultimate

[11] New York *Times,* June 27, 1933.

objective of their currency policy is to bring back an international standard based on gold under proper conditions.

"Each Government whose currency is not on the gold standard agrees to adopt such measures as deemed most effective to limit exchange speculations, and other signatory governments undertake cooperation to the same end.

"Each of the governments signatory hereto agrees to ask its central bank to work together with the central banks of other governments which sign this declaration in limiting speculation and, at the proper time, reinaugurating an international gold standard." [12]

President Roosevelt's Message

President Roosevelt declined this proposal, and a few days later, on July 3rd, sent his famous message to the London Conference which made it clear that he adhered to his plan of American reflation to be followed by American price level stabilization, and that he would not be diverted from this plan by those for whom the old-fashioned idea of exchange-stability seemed the most important objective of monetary policy. It was a declaration that the United States intended to be the master of its own currency.

The President put it up to the other nations to adopt a similar course. The effect of the message upon the Conference was compared by the President's opponents to that of a bomb shell, by his friends to that of a fresh clear wind, that drive away uncertainty. It effected healthy, honest clarification of the issues. It read as follows:

"I would regard it as a catastrophe amounting to a world tragedy if the great conference of nations called to bring about a more real and permanent financial stability and a greater prosperity to the masses of all nations should, in advance of any serious effort to consider these broader problems, allow itself to

[12] New York *Times,* July 2, 1933.

be diverted by the proposal of a purely artificial and temporary experiment affecting the monetary exchange of a few nations only.

"Such action and such diversion show a singular lack of proportion and failure to remember the larger purposes for which the economic conference originally was called together.

"I do not relish the thought that insistence on such action should be made the excuse for continuance of the basic economic errors that underlie so much of the present world-wide depression.

"The world will not long be lulled by a specious fallacy of achieving a temporary and probably artificial stability in foreign exchange on the part of a few large countries only.

"The sound internal economic system of a nation is a greater factor in its well-being than the price of its currency in changing terms of the currencies of other nations.

"It is for this reason that a reduced cost of government, adequate government income, and ability to service its government debts are all so important to ultimate stability.

"So, too, old fetishes of so-called international bankers are being replaced by efforts to plan national currencies with the objective of giving to those currencies *a continuing purchasing power which does not greatly vary in terms of commodities* and the need of modern civilization.

"Let me be frank in saying that *the United States seeks the kind of dollar which a generation hence will have the same purchasing and debt-paying power as the dollar value we hope to attain in the near future.* That objective means more to the good of other nations than a fixed ratio for a month or two in terms of the pound or franc.

"Our broad purpose is permanent stabilization of every nation's currency. Gold or gold and silver can well continue to be a metallic reserve behind currencies, but this is not the time to dissipate gold reserves. When the world works out concerted policies in the majority of nations to produce balanced budgets and living within their means, then we can properly discuss a better distribution of the world's gold and silver supply to act as a reserve base for the national currencies.

"Restoration of world trade is an important factor both in the means and the result. Here, also, temporary exchange fixing is not the true answer. We must rather mitigate existing embargoes to make easier the exchange of products which one nation has and another nation has not.

"The conference was called to better—and perhaps to cure—fundamental economic ills. It must not be diverted from that effort.

FRANKLIN D. ROOSEVELT." [13]

Many of the assembled diplomatists were dismayed by the un-conventional and straight-forward tone óf the President's mes-sage, stressing price level stabilization as distinguished from parity of exchange.

"It is not difficult to see how the tone of this document shocked the representatives of the nations assembled in London perhaps even more than its content." [14] Thus did Mr. Warburg, New York banker, of the American Delegation describe his personal feel-ings upon the receipt in London of the President's message. And Will Rogers, our national jester discussed the incident in the following words:

"Now Europe is saying that they didn't get so sore at what Mr. Roosevelt said as they did the way he said it. You see, diplomats have a thing they call diplomatic language. It's just lots of words, and when they are all added up, they don't mean anything. Well, on account of the President having something to say, and wanting to say it, there is no diplomatic language for that. A diplomat has a hundred ways of saying nothing, but no way of saying something because he has never had anything to say. That's why they call 'em diplomats. . . ." [15]

While the gold standard countries acted immediately to protect their currencies, deciding to cling to gold, the advocates of real stabilization rejoiced. The following quotation from an article

[13] Franklin D. Roosevelt, *On Our Way*, New York, The John Day Company, 1934, pp. 124–126. Italics mine.
[14] James P. Warburg, *The Money Muddle*, New York, Alfred A. Knopf, 1934, p. 119.
[15] New York *Times*, July 6, 1933.

by Mr. J. M. Keynes gives good expression to that sentiment:
". . . the President's message has an importance which transcends its origins. It is, in substance, a challenge to us to decide whether we propose to tread the old unfortunate ways or to explore new paths; paths, new to statesmen and to bankers, but not new to thought. For they lead to the managed currency of the future, the examination of which has been a prime topic of post-war economics.

". . . on the broad political issue—on the things which it should be the business of Presidents and Prime Ministers to understand—he is magnificently right in forcing a decision between two widely divergent policies." [16]

On July 5, 1933, the American Delegation issued another official statement relative to the President's message in which it said: "The first task is to restore prices to a level at which industry and above all agriculture, can function profitably and efficiently. The second task is to preserve the stability of this adjustment once achieved."

Failure of the American Delegation

But apparently the American representatives were, in part at least, ill chosen to interpret the President's intentions. Mr. Warburg says that, after the receipt of the message, "the cables were kept humming between the White House and the Claridge's Hotel [Home of the American Delegation] in a vain effort to understand what the President meant by a dollar of constant purchasing power." [17] Because it was Mr. Warburg's job to explain to the other representatives the significance of the new American monetary policy, and he found himself "completely unable to do so," he resigned his position on July 6th in a letter to the Chairman of the American Delegation, Secretary Hull.

[16] New York *Herald Tribune*, July 4, 1933.
[17] James P. Warburg, *The Money Muddle, op. cit.,* p. 121.

Mr. Warburg gives a clear picture in his book of the consternation of the American, as well as the English and French delegates, and their complete failure to understand what sort of "stabilization" the President referred to in his message. It seems that the ultimate collapse of the Conference was due mainly to the unpreparedness of the American delegation; for had the Americans taken a firm lead they could, with the cooperation of the Scandinavian countries and of Australia, New Zealand, and perhaps Canada,[18] have forced a decision from England, and thus brought about international agreement on a reflation-stabilization policy. There is no question but that the President and Congress were ready and anxious to join such international action.

Monetary Clarification

The world now became divided into three camps: The United States, proceeding on her way towards reflation and eventual stabilization; the gold bloc, or gold standard countries, continuing on gold, apparently without any aspirations at all toward monetary reform; the United Kingdom and the "Sterlingaria" countries, that is, those countries which kept their moneys at exchange parity with the English pound. The majority of this third group signed a so-called "Imperial Declaration" which said that a continued rise in commodity prices was most desirable in order "to restore the activity of industry and employment, insure an economic return to the producer of primary commodities, and harmonize the burden of debts and fixed charges with economic capacity." This position was not very different from Mr. Roosevelt's. We have already seen what Mr. McKenna thought of its importance.[19] Somewhat removed from these three camps were

[18] On April 29, 1933, a joint statement issued by President Roosevelt and Prime Minister Bennett of Canada stated (among other things): "We are agreed that our primary need is to insure an increase in the general level of commodity prices."

[19] See Chapter 10, Section 1.

Sweden and Australia, whose monetary policies have been reviewed above.

Thus, the World Economic Conference, which adjourned on July 27, 1933, yielded one valuable result: "Monetary Clarification," as Reginald McKenna termed it. In his review of the Conference, Mr. McKenna said further:

". . . In a sense this clarification is the fruit of wide-spread disappointment, for to many people the negotiations concerning immediate monetary measures, which are often described as having 'wrecked' the Conference, provided the one hope of solid accomplishment. With that hope extinguished, all hope perished in their breasts."

He added:

". . . first, . . . the proposed declarations [of the gold bloc] would have tied the world to the wrong end of the stick; and secondly, . . . they drew from President Roosevelt a clear indication that he at least was for seizing the right end. . . ." [20]

SECTION 3. BEGINNINGS OF A NEW MONETARY SYSTEM

Opposition Begins

The President had meanwhile secured the assistance of Professors George F. Warren of Cornell and James Harvey Rogers of Yale who were to advise him as to monetary policy. His unconventional utterances, combined with the great and discretionary powers for reflation which Congress had granted him, caused misgivings in the minds of some bankers and some conservative economists, and soon aroused a vigorous opposition.

Among the earliest criticisms were those of *Dr. H. Parker Willis* of Columbia University, formerly Secretary to the Federal Reserve Board and *Mr. Edmund Platt,* Vice President of a large Bank and formerly Vice Governor of the Federal Reserve Board.

[20] In *Midland Bank Monthly Review,* August, Sept., 1933.

The occasion was a meeting of the Institute of Public Affairs held at the University of Virginia.[21] Both of these speakers denounced America's temporary abandonment of the gold standard as unnecessary. Dr. Willis went so far as to say that it was "the result of hysteria." Both spoke of an "unsound experiment" with a "depreciated dollar." The "inflationary projects" of the administration were called "unsound and unnecessary." Some three years before, the business world was conscious of the fact that the "deflationists" were "in the saddle."[22] Mr. Platt now declared that the "monetary theorists" were "in the saddle," and that they were "determined to use the Federal Reserve System to prove their theories." He foresaw that this group intended to "get its hands on" the gold of the Federal Reserve System; or as Mr. Platt put it: "steal it, I might say—for payment of government debts or for public works, or for purchase of unnumbered billions of government securities. . . ."

These statements were but the first of a great number of similar attacks. The cry of "inflation" was again sounded, and taken up by all who thought they had reason for opposing the President's efforts towards reflation as a preliminary to stabilization. In his message to the London Conference, the President had declared that the objects of his monetary policy were *reflation* and then stabilization of the purchasing power of the dollar. The opposition in denouncing his monetary policy as "inflation" was in effect telling him that he did not know where he was headed. In the same way, in 1932, after the Goldsborough stabilization bill had passed the House, public sentiment was aroused against a supposed "uncontrolled inflation."

The President had not yet made use of any of his reflationary powers; business was improving mainly on the basis of restored confidence, and on the expectations raised by the President. This

[21] New York *Times,* of July 4, 1933.
[22] See: Chapter 8, Section 3.

is much the same as saying that it was on the basis of an increased velocity of circulation and less hoarding. But now the
introduction of codes under the NRA, as well as of the processing
taxes under the AAA seemed to have a deterrent effect upon the
activities of industry. Nor were the persistent attacks upon the
administration's monetary program conducive to confidence.

A series of 16 syndicated articles on "Money and Inflation" was
printed in many of the most important newspapers. These articles were sponsored by a group of prominent men and went on
record as follows: ". . . there has not been the slightest relation
between the volume of money available and the prices of commodities in the depression . . . there has been no breakdown in
the gold standard." [23]

The Gold Buying Policy

It was in this period of uncertainty and business hesitation that
the President again spoke over the radio to explain his new
monetary plans. The following is quoted from his radio talk of
October 22, 1933, when he reiterated his reflation-stabilization
policy:

". . . Finally, I repeat what I have said on many occasions, that
ever since last March, the definite policy of the Government has
been to restore commodity price levels. The object has been the
attainment of such a level as will enable agriculture and industry
once more to give work to the unemployed. It has been to make
possible the payment of public and private debts more nearly at
the price level at which they were incurred. It has been gradually
to restore a balance in the price structure so that farmers may
exchange their products for the products of industry on a fairer
exchange basis. It has been and is also the purpose to prevent
prices from rising beyond the point necessary to attain these ends.
The permanent welfare and security of every class of our people
ultimately depends on our attainment of these purposes. . . ."

[23] New York *Times*, October 10, 1933.

To his critics, to those who were continuously demanding the immediate stabilization of the foreign exchanges, which meant stabilization of the value of the dollar in terms of gold, and not in terms of general purchasing power the President said:

"Some people are putting the cart before the horse. They want a permanent revaluation of the dollar first. It is the Government's policy to restore the price level first. I would not know, and no one else could tell, just what the permanent valuation of the dollar will be. To guess at a permanent gold valuation now would certainly require later changes caused by later facts.

"When we have restored the price level we shall seek to establish and maintain a dollar which will not change its purchasing and debt paying power during the succeeding generation.[24] I said that in my message to the American Delegation in London last July. I say it now once more."

In order to arrive at a better regulation of the value of the dollar, the President now announced a new policy of Governmental control over the price of gold:

"Because of conditions in this country, and because of events beyond our control in other parts of the world, it becomes increasingly important to develop and apply the further measures which may be necessary from time to time to control the gold value of our own dollar at home.

"Our dollar is now altogether too greatly influenced by the accidents of international trade, by the internal policies of other nations and by political disturbance in other continents. Therefore, the United States must take firmly in its own hands the control of the gold value of our dollar. This is necessary to prevent dollar disturbances from swinging us away from our ultimate goal, namely, the continued recovery of our commodity prices.

"As a further effective means to this end, I am going to establish a Government market for gold in the United States. Therefore, under the clearly defined authority of existing law, I am authorizing the Reconstruction Finance Corporation to buy gold newly mined in the United States at prices to be determined from

[24] Italics mine.

time to time after consultation with the Secretary of the Treasury and the President. Whenever necessary to the end in view, we shall also buy or sell gold in the world market.

"My aim in taking this step is to establish and maintain continuous control.

"This is a policy and not an expedient.

"It is not to be used merely to offset a temporary fall in prices. We are thus continuing to move toward a managed currency.

"You will recall the dire predictions made last Spring by those who did not agree with our common policies of raising prices by direct means. What actually happened stood out in sharp contrast with those predictions. Government credit is high, prices have risen in part.

"Doubtless, prophets of evil still exist in our midst. But Government credit will be maintained, and a sound currency will accompany a rise in the American commodity price level."

While thus declaring that the country was moving towards a "managed currency," the President also indicated that he was going to do the first managing himself. As the first act of such management he determined that the United States would pay $31.36 for an ounce of newly mined gold; on October 25, 1933, this price was established. It was 27¢ above the free world price for gold; and gradually the figure was raised until, on December 18, 1933 it reached $34.06. On November 1, the gold buying policy was modified somewhat in that the New York Federal Reserve Bank, acting as the agent for the Reconstruction Finance Corporation, was to buy gold offered in the world market.

The Gold Controversy of 1933

President Roosevelt's assurance that he intended not more than a limited rise in the price level, and that ultimately he would stabilize the purchasing power of the dollar, meant little to those who opposed him.

Caught unaware, or, perhaps, unprepared by previous study of the stabilization problem, many economists (though fewer monetary economists), all over the country fell in line protesting against the new monetary policy. In fact, even some who had for years been enthusiastic friends of stable money in the sense of stabilizing the purchasing power of the dollar, now opposed the President on his "reflation" policy while, apparently, still in favor of stabilization of the price index. They evidently did not realize that after the violent fall during the depression, a corresponding price rise was essentially part of complete stabilization.

The complaints ranged from intimations of incompetence on the part of the President's advisers, to the outright charge that an attempt was being made to defraud the American people of its savings. Such an attitude bore the marks of unfamiliarity with the practical possibilities of monetary management, as well as of a disregard of the monetary cause of deflation and the fall of prices. A great number of the country's newspapers, however, supported the President's monetary policy, notably The Philadelphia *Record* which, under *David Stern* had been one of the first advocates of reflation and stabilization.

The farmers and the business leaders associated with the "Committee for the Nation" also stood by the President in favor of reflation to be followed by stabilization. What the opposition demanded was immediate stabilization—and only in terms of gold.

The attitude of the Chamber of Commerce of the State of New York was typical of such opposition. In a hurriedly called meeting, it passed a resolution which said: "Gold has been the basis of our currency for more than half a century. It must still be the basis of any sound monetary unit." [25]

The Chamber of Commerce of the United States, in a resolution adopted November 18, 1933, demanded: ". . . early return to a gold basis, with complete avoidance of monetary experimentation, greenbackism and fiat money, and with complete re-

[25] *Christian Science Monitor,* November 16, 1933.

cession from theoretical or arbitrary ideas of 'price index' fixation of the value of gold." [25a]

An "Economists' National Committee on Monetary Policy" was formed with Professor E. W. Kemmerer as Honorary Chairman, and Professor Ray B. Westerfield of Yale as President, to organize academic opposition against reflation. The membership of this Committee proved again that evidently there had been a division among economists who advocated stabilization in terms of purchasing power, namely, into those who considered reflation a part of stabilization, and those who merely wanted stabilization without reflation. The former group, of course, supported the President's monetary policies; the latter opposed the reflationary part.

Professors from Columbia, Cornell, Yale and other universities issued manifestos which, however, not only opposed reflation, but usually demanded the immediate return to the gold standard.

Typical of such resolutions passed by university professors, is the following excerpt from a letter of 44 economists to the President: "The degree of public confidence essential for economic recovery will be attained most quickly by a return to the gold standard." [26]

On November 21, 1933, Professor Sprague published a letter addressed to President Roosevelt, tendering his resignation as adviser to the United States Treasury, because of his opposition to the administration's monetary policy. He had become convinced, he wrote, that, ". . . there is no defense from a drift into unrestrained inflation other than an aroused and organized public opinion," and that he had left his post in order to contribute to such an arousing and organizing.

Sprague's resignation and his series of articles opposing the President's monetary program, naturally stimulated the opposi-

[25a] N. Y. *Times,* November 19, 1933.
[26] New York *Herald Tribune,* November 9, 1933.

tion. The Advisory Council of the Federal Reserve Board endorsed Dr. Sprague's attitude, and issued a resolution in favor of early gold stabilization. Mr. James P. Warburg, Professor Kemmerer and others advanced the proposals for "stabilizing the dollar" in foreign exchanges at a purchasing power somewhat reduced, but not as much as Mr. Roosevelt intended it. Mr. Warburg advocated a "reformed gold standard," while Professor Kemmerer was satisfied with the original gold standard, revaluating the dollar at two-thirds of its former gold content.[27] On the other hand, following the President's lead, Mr. Vanderlip, proposed a gold bullion standard, under which the price of gold may be varied. Another feature of Mr. Vanderlip's proposal was a continuation of the exchange restrictions, in order to prevent the speculative import and export of foreign currency which are a main factor in foreign exchange fluctuations.[28]

Not since the "silver controversy" of 1896, had such a general interest in monetary questions been expressed in this country. This time the controversy came to its culminating point in two large meetings held in New York, on November 27, 1933, the one sponsored by the so-called "sound," or "hard" money advocates under the auspices of the "Crusaders" who had been organized to oppose prohibition. The other meeting was sponsored by the advocates of reflation, notably Father Coughlin of Detroit. The contrast between the drab meeting for "sound money," and the jubilant mass of people who gathered to hear Father Coughlin—many thousands of whom could not get into the large hall—startled many in New York, who had not previously followed the movement for monetary reform. For the time being it practically put an end to the open opposition to the President's monetary policy. At any rate, as the decision rested with the President, both sides aimed entirely at influencing his decision.

[27] New York *Herald Tribune*, November 28, 1933.
[28] New York *Times*, November 24, 1933.

President Roosevelt Proceeds

On December 21, 1933, by proclamation, the President called for the coinage of silver in conformity with a resolution introduced at the London Conference by the Delegates of the United States, which was then adopted by the assembled 66 nations. In this proclamation Mr. Roosevelt said that the action was taken, ". . . to cooperate with other Governments and [was] necessary to assist in increasing and stabilizing domestic prices. . . ."

Accordingly, the U.S. Mint would receive for coinage into standard silver coins, any silver mined in the United States at *half* the old mint price. This act for "re-monetizing" silver was another step in the direction of reflation and stabilization, mainly in reviving hope for international action on these two basic principles.

On December 28, 1933, the President, by proclamation, recalled all hoarded gold into the U.S. Treasury, providing for heavy penalties against any one holding gold unless specially licensed.

On January 3, 1934, on the occasion of the assembling of Congress, the President addressed that body, reiterating his intention to stabilize the purchasing power of the dollar:

"With the two-fold purpose of strengthening the whole financial structure and of arriving, eventually, at a medium of exchange which will have, over the years, less variable purchasing and debt-paying power for our people than that of the past, I have used the authority granted me to purchase all American-produced gold and silver and to buy additional gold in the world markets. Careful investigation and constant study prove that in the matter of foreign exchange rates, certain of our sister nations find themselves so handicapped by internal and other conditions that they feel unable at this time to enter into stabilization discussions based on permanent and world-wide objectives. . . ."

The Gold Reserve Act of 1934

On January 15, 1934, President Roosevelt sent a special message to Congress, which was again a confirmation of his intention of ". . . restoring the price level, and, . . . arriving eventually at a less variable purchasing power for the dollar. . . ." He asked Congress for special legislation in order to enable the government to appropriate the gold held by the Federal Reserve, and paying for it with bullion certificates. Already authorized by the Thomas amendment [29] to fix the content of the gold dollar as low as 50% of its former content, the President now asked for legislation that would establish an upper limit of 60% for such final revaluation and authorize him, for a period of three years, to vary the content from time to time between these two limits. At the same time he declared that because of the uncertainties of the world situation, it was undesirable at the moment to fix upon a definite weight of the dollar in gold. From the profits of devaluation, he proposed to create a fund of 2 billion dollars for the purchase and sale of gold and foreign exchange, or of government securities to be used, ". . . as the regulation of the currency, the maintenance of the credit of the Government and the general welfare of the United States may require."

The closing paragraph of this message was perhaps intended to remove the doubts of those who still thought it possible that the President was not in earnest about reflation but had hitherto acted merely to forestall inflation by Congress.

"Permit me once more to stress two principles. Our national currency must be maintained as a sound currency which, in so far as possible, will have a fairly constant standard of purchasing power and be adequate for the purpose of daily use and the establishment of credit.

"The other principle is the inherent right of Government to

[29] Compare Section 1 of this Chapter.

issue currency and to be the sole custodian and owner of the base or reserve of precious metals underlying that currency. With this goes the prerogative of government to determine from time to time the extent and nature of the metallic reserve. . . ."

Concurrently with this message, the administration's tentative draft of a bill was introduced in both Houses of Congress. On the same day, an Executive order extended the prohibition of all transactions in foreign exchange, except under special license. The official price of gold was also raised from $34.06 to $34.45 an ounce.

A statement by Governor Black of the Federal Reserve Board of January 16, 1934 revealed that it was upon the special request of the Federal Reserve authorities that President Roosevelt had asked for legislative action to effect the transfer of all Federal Reserve gold to the U.S. Treasury. The Federal Reserve Board had agreed that the "profit" from devaluation belonged to the Government, but suggested that the matter ought to be decided by Congress in order to remove responsibility from the President as well as from the Reserve authorities.

On January 17, 1934, the Attorney General of the United States, Mr. Homer Cummings, informed the Secretary of the Treasury that the payment of the Federal Reserve gold with special Gold Certificates, as contemplated, was constitutional.[30]

On January 20, 1934, the House of Representatives passed the Administration Gold Bill, and on January 27, the Senate passed it. On his birthday, January 31, 1934, the President signed it. To supplement the measure he issued a proclamation on the same day, revaluating the gold dollar, by fixing for the time being its content at 13.71 grains fine, which corresponded to a price of $35—per ounce of fine gold. The "Gold Reserve Act of 1934"

[30] New York *Times*, January 18, 1934.

gives, for the time being, supreme power to the President and to the Secretary of the Treasury to manage the currency.

Besides furnishing means of regulating exchange, it further puts "Open-Market" powers in the hands of the Secretary of the Treasury, in addition to those already existing in the Federal Reserve System. With the enactment of the Gold Reserve Act, it had therefore become impossible for a hostile Federal Reserve System to altogether block the reflationary efforts of the administration. Of course, the presence of open-market powers, both with the Secretary of the Treasury and the Federal Reserve System, makes it possible, theoretically, that the two authorities might work at cross-purposes.

Mr. Norris, of the Philadelphia Reserve Bank, demanded that the Federal Reserve should be allowed to retain at least the 40 per cent of gold as backing for its outstanding notes. Asked by Senator Perkins, whether the Federal Reserve banks would not rather keep the gold in their vaults than turn it over to the government and accept its promise, Governor Norris frankly answered "Yes." "You have more faith, then, in gold than in the government?" was Senator Perkins' next question, to which, however, he got no answer.[31] This may have been the thought of the Federal Reserve, namely to retain the power that comes from the possession of gold. Governor Norris also stated that he believed private interests were more capable of conducting banks than the Government. And Dr. Benjamin M. Anderson, Jr., on the same occasion suggested that the Government leave the gold in the Federal Reserve, and establish a stabilization fund through "regular sources," namely by means of borrowings (from the banks) and taxation.

J. P. Morgan, at the Pujo investigation in 1911 had stated that

[31] See New York *Times* report on the *Hearings before the Senate Banking and Currency Committee on the Gold Reserve Act,* January 19, 1934 (in the New York *Times,* January 20, 1934).

"Money is gold, and nothing else." The very fact that the Government had taken all the gold there is in this country, undoubtedly had its effect upon gold-psychology.

The Silver Purchase Act of 1934

On May 22, 1934 the President (in a message to Congress, recommending Silver Legislation) referred to the "Gold Reserve Act of 1934" as a step towards the organization of a currency system "that will be both sound and adequate." In submitting the draft of the "Silver Purchase Act of 1934," the President now declared that this was but another step on the road towards stable money.

"We should move forward," he said, "as rapidly as conditions permit in broadening the metallic base of our monetary system and in stabilizing the purchasing and debt-paying power of our money on a more equitable level."

The closing paragraph of the President's message referred to his desire to bring about international action for reflation and stabilization, and that apparently he was attempting to achieve it.

"I have begun," he said, "to confer with some of our neighbors in regard to the use of both silver and gold, preferably on a co-ordinated basis, as a standard of monetary value. Such an agreement would constitute an important step forward toward a monetary unit of value more equitable and stable in its purchasing and debt paying power."

In a radio address on June 28, 1934, the President, referring to the achievements of his administration, said:

"Finally, and I believe most important, it reorganized, simplified and made more fair and just our monetary system, setting up standards and policies adequate to meet the necessities of modern economic life, doing justice to both gold and silver as the metal bases behind the currency of the United States."

.   .   .   .

This book ends with the recording of what happened last. In a history there is no place for either a final conclusion or a prophecy. The author, as historian, can not go beyond this point; but he will use the Appendix to record his own opinions.

APPENDIX I

Section I. Autobiographical

My own interest in the problem of stabilizing the purchasing power of money began almost as soon as my economic studies began—about 1892. That was at the end of a quarter of a century of deflation which was about to culminate in the "sound money" campaign of 1896.

But my attitude at that time was very different from what it subsequently became; for I had not then come to realize how serious were the evils of unstable money, nor how impossible it was for business men to provide against them through foresight alone. I even thought I had discovered that these evils were largely overcome in business by compensatory adjustments in the rate of interest—the rate being low during periods of falling prices and high during periods of rising prices. One of my earliest economic monographs—Appreciation and Interest—was devoted to this idea.

My conclusion was naturally welcomed by the opponents of Bryan; and one of them, Byron W. Holt, who had charge of the Sound Money campaign of the New York Reform League, wrote me on January 15, 1898: "I consider your discussion of 'Appreciation and Interest,' if not the greatest, at least one of the greatest contributions ever made to monetary science."

Subsequent statistical studies have shown, however, that I then greatly exaggerated the extent to which the rate of interest compensates for changes in the purchasing power of money, though

374

these studies have confirmed the original conclusion that *some* degree of compensation is effected in this way.[1]

Having the substantial faith which the young and inexperienced often do have in things as they find them, I felt scandalized, when attending the meeting of the American Economic Association at Indianapolis in 1895, at what seemed to me to be the too light-hearted way in which Professor E. A. Ross and others were willing to "tamper with the currency."

I took part in the "Sound Money" campaign against Bryan in 1896. Had that campaign occurred at the present time, I would not have been so strenuous an opponent of Mr. Bryan; for I now know that the evil of which he complained was more real than I then thought. His proposed remedy—"national bimetallism," at 16 to 1,—was, I still think, far from good; nor would "international bimetallism," as proposed in a plank in the Republican platform of the same year, have been much better. That plank was practically ignored during the campaign and has been forgotten ever since.

As the years went by, I became increasingly aware of the imperative need of a stable yardstick of value. I had come into economics from mathematical physics, in which fixed units of measure constitute the essential starting point; but, at that time, the science of index numbers had received little attention, and we economists tried to get along without any clear quantitative idea of a dollar's *average* purchasing power—over goods in general.

Beginning about 1905, the subject of a better standard of value was considered in my class room for many years. The first solution offered by me was in 1911.[2] I then avoided any attempt to

---

[1] My present appraisal of this interest factor will be found in *The Theory of Interest,* Macmillan Co., New York, 1930, 566 pp.

[2] In *The Purchasing Power of Money* (Assisted by Harry G. Brown), Macmillan Co., New York, 1911, 492 pp.

This book was written, however, to establish the basic principles by which the purchasing power of money is determined (according to what I called "the

APPENDIX I

state my proposal in popular language because it is easy to laugh out of court anything as new about money as stabilization seemed to be at that time. The thought, therefore, was to try out the idea first in academic circles and, after a few years, to consider the possibility of popularizing it.

This program would doubtless have been followed out literally had it not been for an invitation, from Professor Taussig of Harvard, to present a paper on the proposal before the International Congress of Chambers of Commerce, meeting in Boston in 1912. This seemed too good an opportunity to lose for publicly launching the plan.

Within five minutes after the reading of my paper, which was entitled "An International Conference Regarding the Cost of Living," [3] a business leader of Chicago asked for the floor and made a fervent speech against the plan. He had taken alarm at the idea of even hinting that anything could be wrong with our dollar, and still more at the idea of allowing "labor" to think that the "high cost of living" could be cited as a proper cause for complaint or as a reason for adjusting money wages. On the contrary "we must not" he said, "disturb confidence in our money." The gentleman's alarm amused Professor Taussig, who replied that there was no thought at that meeting of endorsing the proposal but merely a desire to give it a hearing.

Meantime, Hamilton Holt, then editor of the "Independent," had offered to print the substance of my address in his magazine and to supply a "broadside" reprint of it for wide distribution among newspapers and individuals.

"The fat was now in the fire." The Boston address had "started something." Up to that time plans for stabilization had been disconnected or sporadic suggestions and were always thought of

equation of exchange") and only incidentally to suggest how such purchasing power could be made stable.

[3] Publications of the Fifth Congress, Boston, 1912.

as "academic playthings" rather than practical proposals to be taken seriously. It was not long before the *Commercial and Financial Chronicle* (in 1912) had a series of editorials ridiculing the idea and asseverating that our gold dollar is "the Rock of Gibraltar"—the one thing that never varies!

One result of this and other controversies was to stimulate me, from that time forth, to write and speak in defense of stabilization and in answer to criticism. My secretary counts up, since then, 99 addresses, besides 37 letters to the press, and 161 special articles, as well as 9 testimonies at hearings held by Government bodies and 12 privately printed circulars, together with 13 books bearing on the subject. These 331 items constitute my written and spoken statements on the stabilization problem. Of these, some of the most representative are those noted in the footnotes of this Appendix and the additional references listed at the end.

These writings are of two sorts—popular and technical; each of which fall under four heads: (1) fundamental principles; [4] (2) the measurement of purchasing power; [5] (3) studies of this purchasing power, in relation to current events, especially in relation to the "high cost of living" [6] and "depression of trade;" [7] (4) writings on methods of stabilization.[8]

---

[4] As typified in *The Purchasing Power of Money,* already cited; "Our Unstable Dollar and the So-Called Business Cycle," *Journal of the American Statistical Association,* Vol. XX, New Series, No. 150, June, 1925; and *Booms and Depressions,* The Adelphi Company, New York, 1932, 258 pp., where evidence is given to show that the greater depressions are usually due, in large part, to a combination of "the debt disease" and "the dollar disease"—a volume of unpayable debt and a swollen dollar.

[5] As typified in *The Making of Index Numbers,* Publication No. 1 of the Pollak Foundation for Economic Research, Cambridge, Houghton Mifflin Co., 1922, 526 pp.

[6] As typified in *Why Is the Dollar Shrinking?* Macmillan Co., New York, 1915, 245 pp.

[7] As typified in *The Stock Market Crash and After,* Macmillan Co., New York, 1930, 286 pp.

[8] As typified in *Stabilizing the Dollar,* Macmillan Co., New York, 1920, 305 pp. and *The Money Illusion,* The Adelphi Company, 1928, 245 pp.

The phrases "compensated dollar" and "stabilizing the dollar," suggested by me, have come into general use. I had also tried several other phrases, such as "standardizing the dollar" and "an unshrinkable dollar." Latterly, all these have been largely replaced by the phrase "commodity dollar," as more nearly self-explanatory. But the various phrases are not quite synonymous. Thus "compensated dollar" refers only to one particular method of stabilizing, namely the method of compensating for any rise or fall in the purchasing power of gold by putting less or more gold content into the gold dollar, *i.e.* by raising or lowering the price of gold.

At one time I had supposed that I was the first to think of this compensated dollar plan; but, on looking up the literature, I found anticipations in almost every particular, leaving unanticipated only a few details like the provision ("brassage fee") to guard against speculation in gold injurious to the Government Treasury. All the known anticipators, nine in all, are mentioned in the preface to *Stabilizing the Dollar.*

Besides writing and speaking, my work has included: organizing the movement; enlisting the interest and help of key men —economists, business men, bankers, statesmen; raising and contributing money.

A few words here regarding the first of these three—organizing the movement—will supplement what is said in the text. While preparing *The Purchasing Power of Money,* I had conceived the idea of an international commission to study the money problem, with special reference to the "High Cost of Living," and had secured the adherence of a hundred or more influential people.[9]

[9] Including: President Taft; his Secretary of War, Henry L. Stimson; his Secretary of the Treasury, Franklin MacVeagh; Woodrow Wilson, then Governor of New Jersey; Gifford Pinchot; seven Senators; about a hundred other American leaders—economists, bankers, and industrialists; about twenty-five similar leaders in England, including Lords Brassey and Courtney; Professors Marshall, Edgeworth, Keynes, and thirteen other leading economists; about a score in France,

President Taft sent a special message to Congress on February 2, 1912, favoring an appropriation for such an International Conference. The wording of this message was prepared by me in cooperation with his Assistant Secretary of State, Huntington Wilson, afterwards author of an excellent book on stable money. The bill for such a commission was introduced by Senator Crawford and passed the Senate under suspension of the rules. In the House it was introduced by Congressman Sulzer, but was never reached on the calendar, despite efforts to bring it up before midnight of March 3, 1913, when the Taft administration expired.

Soon after Mr. Wilson's nomination for the Presidency, in 1912, I had visited him in Trenton. He said: "I think we might curb rising prices by increasing the weight of the gold dollar." He was much surprised to find that I had advocated something similar—the "Compensated Dollar Plan"—and took with him on his vacation trip to Bermuda, before inauguration, a typed copy of my first draft of what eventually became *Stabilizing the Dollar*. It is interesting to note that President Roosevelt has now actually applied the same principle as President Wilson's but in reverse, *reducing* the dollar's weight to compensate for a fall of prices.

But, after Wilson's inauguration, consideration of the money problem was elbowed aside in the rush of more pressing questions. Nevertheless these efforts were not wholly wasted; for they got numerous friends for what was now a growing movement.

On October 2, 1919, I addressed the American Bankers Association at its annual convention at St. Louis on "A Monetary Remedy for the High Cost of Living." This address was heard attentively and with apparent approval. In fact, many afterward

including President Poincaré; about a dozen each in Germany and Austria; and a few others scattered among seven other countries.

went out of their way to express their approval. But the sequel was not so satisfactory. Hoping to induce the younger and more progressive bankers to make a special study of the subject, I asked to have a committee appointed for that purpose. The President of the Association happened to have a special aversion to appointing new committees. He therefore insisted that the matter be referred to a standing committee, which, as it happened, consisted of old and very conservative men, most of whom had been appointed many years before to stop Bryan. At the head of this Committee was A. Barton Hepburn, then Chairman of the Board of the Chase National Bank. Mr. Hepburn was a personal friend of mine, but our ideas on monetary questions were diametrically opposed.

Of this standing committee, only two actually signed the report: Mr. Hepburn, Chairman, and James B. Forgan, Vice Chairman. Mr. Forgan (who was Chairman of the Board of the First National Bank of Chicago) was careful to add a qualifying statement in which he admitted that "it is possible that Dr. Fisher's plan might work out if established under normal conditions and if a guaranty could be had that normal conditions would permanently prevail."

Although scores of business bodies had appointed committees on the subject, this was the first committee to return an adverse report. The report was not so much an analysis of the proposal as it was a pronouncement. The key sentence seems to be: "We believe it is unwise to agitate changes in the gold standard at the present time." But, if my view is correct, the only gold standard which could have survived during the last few years would have been the very compensated gold dollar against which the bankers' report was written. Then was the time for them to recognize that fact and save the gold standard! Since that time, by the irony of fate, thousands of bankers have been ruined because (if my analysis is correct) they were adamant against any "change in the gold standard."

After the adverse report on the compensated dollar plan, many bankers who had previously favored the plan were, for a long time, unwilling to say so publicly. A dozen bank presidents had previously written me favoring the idea. Some now asked not to be quoted further.

This adverse report was published in the *Journal of the American Bankers Association* in November, 1920. To it I replied in the same *Journal,* June, 1921.

On March 8, 1920 Mr. Frank A. Vanderlip gave me a dinner to which he invited the leading presidents of banks of New York City in order that I should have the opportunity to address them on the subject of my book *Stabilizing the Dollar,* copies of which he had sent them in advance. The criticisms were mostly adverse, although President Hadley of Yale, who had from the first approved my proposal, spoke in its favor. Afterward he commented caustically to the effect that the bankers present "seemed merely to be thinking in terms of three to six months ahead."

In view of the growing prevalence of banker opposition, to what had then come to be called the "Fisher plan"—though never with my consent—it became evident that, in order to win support from bankers and make the movement succeed, the lead must now be taken by others and that other plans than mine (or what had come to be thought of as mine) for stabilizing money should be given prominence.

For some time it seemed clear that there should be an organization devoted to stabilization, and, on publishing *Stabilizing the Dollar* in January, 1920, I had asked the publishers to insert a post card in each copy, with a request that the reader mail it to me in case he was interested in the formation of such a society. On December 31, 1920, at the New Willard Hotel in

Washington, a dinner was held for discussing the advisability of forming a "Stable Money League." There were 25 present,[10] and I was able to announce that I had names of about 1,000 other persons interested in the project. The meeting ended with a midnight visit by many of us to the Washington Monument where we ushered in the New Year by dedicating ourselves to the new movement. The official organization meeting of the proposed Stable Money League was called for May 28, 1921, at Washington.

Up to that time I had been almost the only active proponent. Now, in the belief that the real hope of the movement lay in a great deal of team work, the lead was passed on to others. Although urged frequently by several loyal friends to accept the presidency of the League and to try to commit it to the "compensated dollar plan," I declined both suggestions. I had never believed that the compensated dollar plan was the only possible plan, nor even ideally the best. In *Stabilizing the Dollar* I had been careful to call it "a" solution, not "the" solution. I had offered it as requiring the least radical change from the existing gold standard, and therefore perhaps politically the most feasible.

If the gold standard is to be retained, the compensated dollar plan is almost necessary, as has been so well shown by Professors Warren and Pearson. I am therefore still in favor of it for America, as part of a general plan, although, for simplicity, the method recently adopted by Sweden (a managed currency independent of gold) seems better. But when *Stabilizing the Dollar* was written, any proposal to "go off gold" completely, as Sweden has done, would have been lampooned and hooted down; and even more preposterous at that time would it have

[10] Including Secretary of War, Newton D. Baker; Robert D. Kent, President of the Merchants National Bank of Passaic, N. J., from the first an unflinching friend of stable money; Professor James Harvey Rogers, then at Cornell University; various other economists and business men; and Dr. Harvey W. Wiley, of pure food fame, who made an excellent speech in favor of stabilization.

seemed to advocate a purely discretionary "managed money."
Previous to the formation of the Stable Money League, the practicability of any plan was generally denied.

Norman Lombard, a California business man, was one of the
earliest to share my enthusiasm for stable money. I first met him
in person in 1919, when I was giving the Hitchcock Lectures on
Stable Money at the University of California. He struck me as
a most promising leader and I told him that, if certain business
ventures of mine succeeded as I hoped, I would expect to support financially—until others could be found to take up the load
—a stabilization movement, provided he would come East and
devote himself to it. We both kept this in mind for several years
and eventually, in 1926, when the conditions specified had been
fulfilled, he gave up his business in California and came East
with his family. Preliminary to taking office as executive director of the Stable Money Association, he spent a year with
me, studying and collecting historical material, showing that the
Stable Money Movement, far from being a one man affair had
always had supporters and now had a number of them. This
research work was the beginning of the present book. In his
work with the Stable Money Association, Mr. Lombard accomplished all that could be expected, and more.

After turning over to others the work of organizing and conducting the Stable Money Movement, I continued my special
studies in the subject.

One of the greatest obstacles then standing in the way of
stabilization was a prevalent idea that index numbers were un-
reliable. Until this difficulty could be met, stabilization could
scarcely be expected to become a reality

In order to do my bit toward solving this problem, I wrote
The Making of Index Numbers, a work requiring several years
of costly calculations, partly financed by the Pollak Foundation
for Economic Research. It was published in 1922. One of its con-

clusions was that, while what I called the "ideal" formula was the best, all formulæ for index numbers agreed with each other, for all practical purposes, provided they were so constructed as to work both ways—that is, to give consistent results when comparing two years, whether the first or the second year was taken as the base. It was shown that the simple arithmetical average of price relatives, then a common form of index number, was inaccurate because, in particular, it would not work both ways. This form of index has, since that time, been very largely abandoned and replaced by the geometric average or by what I called the "aggregative." While this test was purely concerned with the question of formula, and did not solve all the problems of index numbers, it did remove the chief complaints; and the faith in index numbers, at least partly as a result of this book, was definitely strengthened.

This is not the place to discuss the question as to the best index number for stabilization purposes further than to state the following opinions: First, that almost any reasonable index, wholesale, retail, or general (Snyder's) would be better than none at all, and that, under any sort of stabilization, all indexes would differ from each other less than is commonly imagined, as well as far less than they differ now when none of them is stabilized; secondly, the Swedish choice—namely a retail index of the cost of living—is, on the whole, the best of those practically available, one reason being that it means almost the same thing to everybody, since all people consume similar goods (while they produce dissimilar goods).

In January, 1923, I began the publication in the newspapers of a weekly Index Number of Wholesale Prices, starting with the *New York Times*. This was the first *weekly* index ever published, being made possible by certain short-cuts in calculation. This index series, with revisions, has been continued to the present time, and now appears in several countries and in various official publications of the United States and other Governments.

The chief purpose, however, of this newspaper publication was to invert the ordinary index number representing the price level, thereby obtaining an index representing the purchasing power of the dollar, the idea being to accustom the public to the thought that the dollar is not a constant but a variable. For I had come to realize that people could not get interested in stabilizing the dollar until they saw that it was unstable; and this could scarcely happen until they could read a statistical record of its instability.

The index of the dollar's purchasing power gave to several million people every Monday morning the opportunity to read of the weekly change in the dollar. It was apparently as a result of this that the phrases "the purchasing power of the dollar," "the pre-war dollar," "the dollar of 1913," "the dollar of 1926," and other expressions, implying a consciousness that the dollar changes, came into general use; whereas previously all indexes were thought of as representing price movements of commodities —money being forgotten. Other issuers of index numbers followed suit and gave figures to measure "the farmer's dollar," the "business man's dollar," and so forth.

It had taken a long time for me to realize the need for this sort of public education and to perceive that, in the popular psychology of money, there was what I came to describe as "The Money Illusion." In 1922, I visited Germany expressly to find out whether the instability of the mark could possibly escape attention of its victims. As noted in the Introduction, I found it had most decidedly escaped attention. That is, to Germans, the dollar had risen, and commodities had risen; but the mark had not fallen!

With such object lessons before me, I lectured in the School of International Studies at Geneva in 1927 and, on the basis of these lectures, I wrote the *Money Illusion*.

Besides helping the public to understand that their monetary yardstick is not a fixed and dependable one, the publication of its changes can serve a very practical purpose for business men by showing them how their business is likely to be affected by "general conditions." In "Our Unstable Dollar and the So-called Business Cycle" it was shown that every enlargement of the dollar tends to hurt business shortly afterward and that every shrinkage of the dollar tends temporarily to boost business. Either effect begins at once but is spread over a number of months, tapering off gradually, according to what I called a "distributed lag." Thus the dollar's changes forecast, so far as any one factor can do so, the volume of trade and unemployment. The moral of this is that, as long as the dollar is allowed to fluctuate, business men should watch its fluctuations and learn how to take them into account.

And not only can the dollar's recorded fluctuations be used as one of the bases for forecasting, but those fluctuations can, to some extent, be themselves forecast from, for instance, the volume of money and credit, in the light of "the equation of exchange."

Both sorts of forecasting—the forecasting of business from the dollar and the forecasting of the dollar from credit—often go wrong, like the forecasts of the weather bureau, because of numerous disturbing influences not known to the observer. The chief of these, since 1913, have been unannounced changes in Federal Reserve Policies. As has been seen, the system's easy money policy immediately after the war caused a rising price level, or falling dollar; its restrictive policy decided on in May 1920 caused a collapse in the price level; its policy, through Governor Strong's open market committee, kept the dollar fairly stable until that policy lapsed with his death; the fluctuating policy since that time has made the dollar fluctuate correspondingly.

With advance information on these policies, supplemented by

other known data and interpreted in the light of the equation of exchange and distributed lag, any one could have foretold, almost without error, every important change in business and employment. At any rate, the record shows that the forecasts which were made on the above principles were substantially correct when the Federal Reserve policy was known in advance, and incorrect when those policies were unknown or the forecaster was misinformed about them.

Among those for whom correct forecasts of the dollar's changes are important are investors. Apparently the first book on this subject was a symposium to which I wrote the introduction.[11] After this came various articles by me, and several books by others, including Robert W. Pomeroy's *Stock Investments;* Edgar Lawrence Smith's *Common Stocks as Long Term Investments;* and Kenneth Van Strum's *Investing in Purchasing Power.* In reviewing these books I added some statistical studies.[12]

Forecasting is one of three ways of escaping or mitigating the baleful consequence of the unstable dollar, the other two being: (1) to stabilize the dollar, and (2) to frame contracts in terms of index numbers—that is, to use the tabular standard.

Regarding the last, I was apparently the first in this country to introduce the index wage for the purpose of offsetting the rising cost of living in the World War. This method was used in my personal office, in the office of the American Association for Labor Legislation, of which I was then President, and in a commercial business of mine—the Index Visible. When this business united with that of the Kardex Company of James H. Rand, Jr., of Buffalo, we two, with an able attorney—Charles P.

[11] *How to Invest When Prices Are Rising,* by Edwin W. Kemmerer, Harry G. Brown, Walter E. Clark, J. Pease Norton, Montgomery Rollins, G. Lynn Sumner. G. Lynn Sumner and Co., Scranton, Pennsylvania, 1912.
[12] Including "When Are Gilt Edge Bonds Safe?" *The Magazine of Wall Street,* New York, Vol. XXXV, No. 13, April 25, 1925 and "Stocks vs. Bonds," *Review of Reviews,* Vol. LXXII, No. 1, July, 1935.

Franchot,—prepared the "stabilized bond" issued by that company which is described in the text (Ch. 4, Sec. 1). This bond was an object of study, as a legal curiosity, by the dean and professors of the Yale Law School and other law schools.

When the Kardex Company again merged with others (ultimately becoming the Remington Rand Co.) the stabilized bond was retired in favor of gold clause bonds because the latter type, being familiar, had a wider market. Later, Mr. Rand and I, and Mr. Vanderlip tried to get the United States Treasury to issue stabilized bonds but without success. A few analogous types have been used by other commercial companies. After the war, at the request of "the Mitten Management" (a traction organization) and with the assistance of Benjamin P. Whitaker, I worked out "the market basket wage." This was adopted by the Mitten Management. It was dependent on a special index number of the cost of living in Philadelphia.

As indicated in the text, during the war millions of laborers worked under such wage agreements. But they never constituted a major portion of contracts even in the field of wages and were almost invariably dropped when prices fell, because the wage earner objected to a cut in money wages. As long as the high cost of living was getting higher, the "Index Visible" employees welcomed the swelling contents of their "High Cost of Living" pay envelopes. They thought their wages were increasing, though it was carefully explained to them that their real wages were merely standing still. But as soon as the cost of living fell they resented the "reduction" in wages, and refused to believe that their real wages were not reduced thereby.

Such experiences afford fresh proof of the practical omnipresence of the "money illusion" and of the impracticability of index wages and index bonds as a general solution of the great problem of unstable money. The only general solution must come, not from mending or patching the dollar from the outside, but from truing it up inside.

SECTION 2. MY SELECTED BIBLIOGRAPHY

(In addition to footnote references in the text and in Appendix I, Section 1)

Will the Present Upward Trend of World Prices Continue? *American Economic Review,* Boston, Mass., Vol. II, No. 3, pp. 531–558, September, 1912.

A More Stable Gold Standard. *Economic Journal* (London), December, 1912, pp. 570–576.

Preissteigerung und Reallohnpolitik. (In collaboration with Prof. Dr. Stephan Bauer, of the University of Basle.) *Annalen für Soziale Politik und Gesetzgebung,* Berlin, Herausgegeben von Dr. Heinrich Braun, Sonderabdruck aus 1. Band, 4. und 5. Heft. pp. 393–430, 1912.

Observations de M. Irving Fisher. Communication à la Société de Statistique de Paris, *Journal de la Société de Statistique de Paris,* Paris, France, 1913.

A Compensated Dollar. *The Quarterly Journal of Economics,* Cambridge, Mass., Vol. XXVII, No. 2, pp. 213–235, Three Appendices, pp. 385–397, February, 1913.

La Hausse Actuelle de la Monnaie, du Crédit et des Prix, Comment y Remédier. *Revue d'Economie Politique,* Paris, 1913, pp. 419–434.

Objections to a Compensated Dollar Answered. *American Economic Review,* Boston, Mass., Vol. IV, No. 4, pp. 818–839, December, 1914.

Some Contributions of the War to Our Knowledge of Money and Prices. *American Economic Review Supplement,* Vol. VIII, No. 1, March, 1918.

Business Depression and Instability of Money. (Two lectures before London School of Economics and Political Science, University of London, December 9 and 16, 1921.) *Bankers' Magazine,* London, No. 934, January, 1922.

How an Unstabilized Dollar Interferes with Efficient Management. (Address before meeting of the Taylor Society in Springfield, Mass., February 24, 1921.) *Bulletin of the Taylor Society,* New York, Vol. VI, No. 4, August, 1921.

Address and Examination before Select Standing Committee on Banking and Commerce of the House of Commons, Ottawa, Canada, on Bill No. 83, An Act Respecting Banks and Banking on the Resolution of Mr. Irvine, M.P., re Basis, Function and Control of Financial Credit, etc. Reprinted May, 1923.

Ethics in the Monetary System (in three parts). *Christian Work,* Vol. 118, No. 2, January 10, 1925, pp. 52-4; Vol. 118, No. 3, January 17, 1925, pp. 82-84; Vol. 118, No. 4, January 24, 1925, pp. 117-8.

A Statistical Relation Between Unemployment and Price Changes. *International Labour Review,* Vol. XIII, No. 6, June, 1926.

Dollar Stabilisation. *The Encyclopaedia Britannica,* 13th Edition, Vol. I, Aal-Eye, 1926.

Compensated Dollar. *The Encyclopaedia of the Social Sciences,* Macmillan Co., New York, Vol. IV, pp. 134-135, 1931.

Business Cycles as Facts or Tendencies. *Economische Opstellen* aangeboden aan Prof. Dr. C. A. Verrijn Stuart, Haarlem, De Erven F. Bohn N.V., 1931, pp. 140-157.

Statistics in the Service of Economics, *Journal of the American Statistical Association,* Vol. XXVIII, No. 181, March, 1933, pp. 1-13.

The Relation of Employment to the Price Level. *Stabilization of Employment,* edited by Charles F. Roos, Principia Press, Inc., Bloomington, Ind., 1933, pp. 152-159.

Inflation. The Adelphi Company, New York, 1933, 104 pp.

The Debt-Deflation Theory of Great Depressions. *Econometrica,* Vol. 1, No. 4, October, 1933, pp. 337-357.

Testimony at Hearings before the Subcommittee of the Committee on Banking and Currency of the House of Representatives on H.R. 7157 as amended and reintroduced as H.R. 8780 (to establish the Federal Monetary Authority and to Control the Currency of the United States), February 1, 1934. Government Printing Office, Washington, 1934, pp. 73-95.

After Reflation, What? Adelphi Co., New York, 1933, 137 pp.
Are Booms and Depressions Transmitted Internationally
    Through Monetary Standards? Paper for XXII Session of
    the International Statistical Institute in London, April, 1934.
    Separate reprint. Second printing slightly revised, 460
    Prospect St., New Haven, Conn.

SECTION 3. MY PERSONAL VIEWS

As the reader will have noted, there have been, and still are,
many conflicting views on the question of stable money. Some
readers may ask how it is possible to explain such conflicts of
opinion. I can, of course, only answer that question from my own
point of view. I shall now endeavor to do this very briefly, referring those who care for anything more elaborate to the writings listed above.

In the first place, every new idea has to fight its way. Andrew
D. White wrote a fascinating book [13] devoted almost entirely to
this thesis. We all know how evolution and the germ theory had
to fight their way.

In the second place, as has already been emphasized, especially
in the Introduction, the idea of stable money has an exceptional
handicap in the "money illusion." It may be recalled that the
somewhat analogous illusion that the earth is flat and immovable held back the spread of the Copernican theory for centuries.
This being so, the astonishing thing is not that so large a majority of people still imagine the dollar to be immovable but that
so large a minority have already learned that it is not. When
asked in 1912, at the meeting of the American Economic Association, how long it would take before stable money would come,
I replied, laughingly, "nine hundred years"; and at that time, I
had no realizing sense of the retarding influence of the money

[13] *A History of the Warfare of Science with Theology in Christendom,* D. Ap-
pleton and Company, New York, 1896, Vols. I and II.

illusion. But nineteen years later stabilization actually came (in Sweden); although most Swedes, like most Americans, do not yet comprehend it—and this despite the fact that forty years ago their great economist, Knut Wicksell, did his epoch making work.

Besides these two broad reasons—namely that it takes time for a new idea to spread, and more time when the idea is hidden by a specific illusion—there is what may be called the price confusion, that is, the failure to distinguish the concepts of a particular price and a general price level.

The observing reader must have noticed many instances of such confusion in the course of this history. Congressman Strong tells me that a case in point was evident at a meeting with the Federal Reserve Board when, after he had tried to explain the project of stable money by identifying it with that of a stable price level, one of his auditors said: "Congressman Strong, do you mean you want the Government to fix the price of wheat?" Thereupon Congressman Strong looked despairingly at Governor Strong, who responded by a significant wink.

Fixing the price of wheat or any other price is far more difficult than fixing the general level of prices, just as it is far more difficult (impossible in fact) to fix a little wave on the surface of a mill pond, than to regulate the level of the whole pond.

This price confusion traces back to the money illusion. That is, when most people talk of the price of wheat being determined by the supply and demand of wheat, they forget that these— the price and the supply and demand—are partly in terms of money and so depend partly on the supply and demand of dollars. The dollar's value (price level inverted) is a factor in every individual price. No one can get far in understanding the stable money problem until he rids his mind of the notion that the supply and demand of commodities fix the price *level*.

Moreover, fixing the price level does not imply any control over production, nor the buying of surplus products to boost their prices. Much less, in restoring the price level, should we try to raise it by destroying cotton, wheat, or other wealth. That amounts to "getting rid of poverty in the midst of plenty by destroying the plenty"; whereas true reflation is making the money plentiful to match the plentiful goods to be bought.

Nor is it true reflation arbitrarily to mark up prices or even to mark up wages beyond the point which accords with supply and demand. Such arbitrary mark-ups result in lessened buying, and lessened employment, while, on the other hand, increased money and credit, during a depression, revive buying, trade, production, and employment.

Another common perversion of the stable money idea is the vague notion that there is something in it which is unnatural and so improper or impossible. It is true that every unit is arbitrary. There is no "natural" yard, no "natural" kilowatt. So there is no "natural" dollar. But surely there is nothing unnatural or improper in preventing the yard, the kilowatt, or the dollar from varying. We can ordinarily make the dollar what we will, just as we can make the yard what we will.

But some confused minds, half-way convinced, take a half-way position. They admit that *some* influence can be exerted on the price level by monetary or credit control but, since this influence is only one among many, fear that other and greater forces may upset control. How is it possible, they argue, that so little an influence as a slight change in the rate of interest or in the volume of Federal Reserve open market operations can steer the monetary ship? One might as well ask: How is it possible that so little an influence as a slight turn of the rudder can steer a ship, despite the mightier forces of winds and tides?

Finally, we find people who are so determined not to favor stabilizing money that they deny that its instability has any meaning. One writer gravely professes that he does not even know what inflation and deflation mean. "How measure them?"

This is like professing not to know the difference between a big ship and a little one without first settling on exactly how the size is to be measured—by length of the ship? by gross tonnage? by net tonnage? by cubic contents?

Another writer professes to find that no measurement at all is possible, since all index numbers are meaningless, being, so he fancies, made up by adding together unlike items, such as horses and apples. This is like saying that, while there is such a thing as the price of bread and such a thing as the price of cheese, there is no such thing as the price of a cheese sandwich, or of a club sandwich containing many ingredients, or of a "hash" of many commodities, or of a whole cargo of miscellaneous goods—including horses and apples.

An index number is simply the ratio of the price of such a representative cargo at one time to its price at another time. The dollar is stable, or fixed, if it will always buy a fixed fraction of that cargo. I shall never forget what a fellow economist told me after playing golf with one of the leading bank presidents of the country. The latter suddenly asked, "What *is* an index number?" This, of course, is practically asking, "What is a dollar?" In view of what has been said, there seems little reason to wonder why so many educated and intelligent people are not yet convinced about stable money. They simply are not yet really "educated" on this particular subject.

We have now seen six reasons to explain the disagreements over stable money—namely (1) its apparent novelty; (2) the money illusion; (3) the price confusion; (4) the apparent unnaturalness of stabilizing the dollar; (5) its supposed dependence on so many uncontrollable forces; (6) its meaninglessness.

Besides these reasons others could be suggested—especially if I were to venture on a psychoanalysis of particular individuals.

As, one by one, the students of the subject learn its fundamentals they usually change their attitude completely and permanently. As Major Bellerby says, "once a stabilizer, always a stabilizer." The President of one of the largest life insurance companies, at a meeting of the Stable Money Association, explained for an hour, with humble frankness, how his eyes had been opened only a few weeks before by a young Canadian banker.

It seems to me as inevitable as anything human can be that some day the money illusion will be conquered, at least as fully as the illusion of sunrise and sunset has been conquered; that, therefore, almost every educated man and woman will know that gold is no more stable than copper; that stabilizing or standardizing money will be as much a matter of course as standardizing the yard or the ounce; that recent recorded pronouncements of certain bankers will be regarded with the same amusement as the pronouncements of the Governor and Vice-Governor of the Bank of England at the "Bullion Report" hearing in 1810; that the world will wonder why so simple a project as stable money should ever have met any opposition.

It also seems to me that there are certain definite conclusions on stable money as undebatable as the rotundity of the earth—such conclusions as that, at the bottom of this depression, a corrective upward reflation of the price level was needed; that the dollar's instability can be corrected; that it should be corrected; that all the corrections should be made by monetary or credit means, not by making goods scarce (the two have been confused; the first is merely reducing to normal the unit for measuring incomes; the second is reducing the incomes themselves); that limiting profits will tend to retard re-employment.

But, of course, there will always remain some honest differences of opinion; for there is always a debatable fringe on the outskirts of every area of undebatable truth. This is true even in astronomy and the other "exact sciences."

Among the debatable questions are these: Exactly what is the

best criterion for measuring stability and instability? Exactly
how far should reflation go? What are the best monetary or
credit means to use?

On several questions I have changed my own opinion, from
time to time, and especially as to whether stabilization should
wait on international agreement. Under present circumstances,
it seems to me that the quickest way to attain stable money
throughout the world is for each country to choose its own price
level, its own method of measuring that price level, and its own
method of attaining and controlling it. After, say, Sweden,
America, and the British Empire shall have achieved their respective stabilizations, the rest of the world will doubtless follow fast.

Incidentally, when stable money shall thus have displaced our
gold standard and our silver standard (though not necessarily
the monetary use of these metals), the minor problem of stable
international exchanges will have almost solved itself.

As to the problem of stable money in the United States, while
a rough stabilization could be obtained by sole reliance on adjusting the price of gold according to the compensated dollar plan,
I do not think a really accurate stabilization is feasible without
also a direct control of the total volume of checking deposits or
what may be called checkbook money.

I would (after reflation is over) make the adjustments of the
price of gold, which means adjustments of the gold content of
the dollar, as few and slight as possible, in order to keep foreign
exchange rates as steady as is compatible with the stabilization
of our domestic price level. I would, however, remove the present restrictive limits on the gold content of the dollar—50 per
cent and 60 per cent of the old legal gold content—so as to
avoid some day finding no further adjustments permissible under
the law. Also I would keep redemption in gold discretionary on
the part of the Government and not return to compulsory re-

demption, lest we also return to gold raids, runs, and hoarding. I do not think there would be any objection to the re-establishment of a free gold market as proposed by Mr. Vanderlip. I would confine the use of silver to the minimum politically feasible.

I would depend for a stable dollar mainly on open market operations and occasional adjustments of rediscount rates under the supervision of a special Monetary Authority or Commission, as proposed in the new Goldsborough bill sponsored by Mr. Vanderlip.

As soon as politically feasible, I would go even further, along the lines of Senator Cutting's bill. I would have the Government practically take away from the banks the entire function of creating or destroying circulating medium but leaving to the banks the strictly banking functions such as lending money.

This project, now favored by many economists, particularly Simons and others at the University of Chicago and by some bankers, such as George LeBlanc, is the subject of a book I am writing called "The 100% System of Money and Banking." Under this system all checking accounts would have behind them a reserve in lawful money of 100%. An incidental but, at the present time, very great advantage of this system would be that it would reduce the Government debt, now reaching alarming proportions. It would do this by substituting non-interest-bearing obligations for interest-bearing obligations, up to the point needed to restore and maintain a stable price level.

I will close this personal statement of opinion by repeating the last paragraph of *Stabilizing the Dollar,* written in 1919:

"The more the evidence in the case is studied, the deeper will grow the public conviction that our shifting dollar is responsible for colossal social wrongs and is all the more at fault because these wrongs are usually attributed to other causes. When the intelligent public who can apply the remedy realizes that our dollar is the great pickpocket, robbing first one set of people and then another—robbing them of billions of dollars a year, confounding business calculations, convulsing trade, stirring up discontent, fanning the flames of class hatred, perverting politics and, withal, keeping its sinister operations out of sight and unsuspected—when, I say, the public and legislators realize this, action will one day follow; and we shall have secured a boon for all future generations, a stable yardstick of contracts, a stabilized dollar."

APPENDIX II

THE CONTROVERSY OVER SWEDISH STABILIZATION

As THE importance of what Sweden has done comes to be fully recognized, it would seem that similar principles of monetary policy must in time be adopted everywhere. Of course, there are those who *fear* this—fear that Sweden may thus serve as an example for the future monetary policy of the United States. A number of articles have consequently been written by men who cling to the present system, and who are naturally alarmed by the good reports of the Swedish experiment, and would like to minimize its importance. The purport of such articles is that the significance of the Swedish experiment has been greatly exaggerated and that it has not been of much, if any, use to Sweden.

It is not necessary to impugn the motives of these writers. Doubtless many of them are quite sincere. But, like most people, some of them do not know the profound difference between a price level and a price, and so believe that the "supply and demand" of individual commodities not only determine individual prices relatively to the price level, but determine them absolutely and so determine the price level itself. One such man, an expert in foreign exchange, told the present writer with emphasis, "Sweden has not stabilized. The apparent stability was an accident due to the fact that one group of commodities happened to go up just enough to offset another group which happened to go down. Any other explanation is absurd, for no stabilization of all prices is possible. I don't see how it could be done. What we need is to stabilize foreign exchange."

399

Some commentators insist that Sweden has, in fact, stabilized merely in the sense of pegging the krona to sterling, and for that reason Sweden is often included in the list of "Sterlingaria" countries. Mr. James P. Warburg says,

"Sweden has 'managed' by the simple method of pegging its krona to the pound, which in turn was raising and lowering itself by means of the gold standard." [1]

It is true that, so far as was consistent with the internal stabilization of the krona, Sweden did try to keep foreign exchange from fluctuating widely. But this exchange control was not only secondary to, but was actually employed as a means toward, internal stabilization. The pound, at first, depreciated more rapidly than the krona, and in October, 1931, was quoted 7% below krona-parity. This was consistent with Sweden's determination to prevent inflation. In December 1931, the old krona-pound parity was almost restored, and beginning April, 1932, in accordance with Sweden's desire to reflate wholesale prices, the pound was quoted about 7½% above par, except for the period from November 1932 to March 1933, when the old parity with the pound was temporarily re-established.

This proves that the foreign exchange value of the krona was determined *independently of the pound,* that is, Sweden did *not* properly belong to the "Sterlingaria" group. Never did the Riksbank or the Riksdag Committee employ the English exchange rate as the real criterion for the Riksbank's monetary policy.

Professor H. Parker Willis's Foreword to Mr. Kjellstrom's exhaustive study on the Swedish experiment, "Managed Money, The Experience of Sweden" [2] gives a wrong impression of the book itself. In this introduction we find a reference to an alleged "superstition regarding Swedish 'management' of money

[1] James P. Warburg, *The Money Muddle,* New York, Alfred Knopf, 1934, p. 177.
[2] *Op. cit.*

and banking which has been widely advertised and exploited by
academic and other adherents of the view that it was possible
to move price levels about practically at will." [3]

Professor Willis recommends Mr. Kjellstrom's book as
"a valuable sedative for the excited minds which are now
evolving new and strange monetary theories which they (on
hearsay) ascribe to Sweden as the originating source of experimentation." [4]

The statement by Professor Willis seems to imply, though he
does not definitely say so, that he does not think stability of the
price level is possible and that he does not believe that Sweden
has accomplished such stability. If so, Dr. Willis is mistaken, as
the facts clearly indicate, and, so far as could be ascertained, no
other writer on the subject has denied the *fact* that Sweden has
accomplished it. It is not denied but is affirmed in the book to
which Dr. Willis writes the introduction.

The controversy over Sweden has been not as to this fact but
as to whether this regulation which Sweden has accomplished has
benefited her. These two questions—as to (1) the fact of Swedish stabilization and (2) the effects of that stabilization should
be carefully separated.

But when we read Mr. Kjellstrom's book itself we find it
clearly shown that the Swedish stabilization of the consumption
index had been not only successful, but remarkably so. Despite
his predilection for the gold standard, Mr. Kjellstrom admits
almost everything which the most enthusiastic friends of stabilization could desire.

"The following results have" Mr. Kjellstrom says, "been obtained, (1) the process of deflation has been halted; (2) the

[3] Kjellstrom, *Managed Money, op. cit.*, p. IX. The present writer is one of
those who believe that it is "possible to move price levels about practically at will"
—in other words that it is possible to select any desired value for our monetary
unit just as it is possible to select any length for a yardstick.
[4] *Ibid.*, p. IX.

danger of currency and credit inflation was averted; (3) the internal purchasing power of the krona has been maintained reasonably well; (4) a gradual rise of the wholesale price level has not taken place." [5]

Only the last point (4) sounds unfavorable; but on the next page, we find this explained as follows:

"In view of the *results* of the program it should be realized that, although it has been impossible to achieve a slow rise of the domestic price level, the Swedish wholesale prices *have not fallen as low as have corresponding prices in some other countries not having a definite monetary program.*[6]

The first three results are, as we have seen, precisely what Sweden set out to accomplish, namely, halting deflation, preventing inflation, and stabilizing the krona at home at the level of September, 1931. The last of these three—stabilization—is the part of the Riksbank's policy in which we are especially interested here. We have seen that the chosen index number was maintained over a period of over 2½ years—up to the present writing—with a degree of precision never believed possible by either the friends or the foes of stabilization. The measure of this remarkable precision was the deviations from par of 1.7% above the chosen par and 1.6% below it—a total spread of 3.3% in 2½ years—half above and half below.

As to the fourth point (raising the wholesale price level) it is true that the Riksbank did not at first, nor until after two years later, succeed in the attempt to restore a fair degree of balance within the price structure. Immediately after the abandonment of the gold standard, wholesale prices recovered. However, in 1932, in spite of the revision of Swedish monetary policy, not only did wholesale prices fail to rise further, but after September, 1932, until March, 1933, they declined somewhat. For some

[5] *Ibid.*, p. 92.
[6] *Ibid.*, p. 93. Italics mine.

time Sweden was therefore disappointed. For a good part of this development, the collapse of the Kreuger concern was probably responsible, as it impaired the liquidity of some of the Swedish banks, and made the remaining banks extremely cautious in their credit policies and desirous of remaining liquid.[7]

The adverse situation created by the Kreuger collapse, which amounted to a catastrophe for Sweden, and the continued decline of world prices, apparently found the Riksbank insufficiently prepared. What expansive measures were taken seem to have been sufficient merely to offset these unfavorable developments and so prevent them from depressing the Swedish wholesale price level, as has been noted. The resulting, perhaps unwanted, wholesale-price stability during 1932 may explain the assertion which is sometimes made that the Riksbank maintained the wholesale price level in spite of its intentions. Professor Bertil Ohlin criticized the Riksbank's lack of more determined action as follows:

"There would nevertheless have been, in my opinion, a chance of bringing about a rise in the price level through the taking of energetic measures by the Riksbank (*i.e.* large bond purchases) supplemented by an increased demand for capital for public works. No such policy was, however, inaugurated." [8]

Another Swedish economist [9] tried to explain the failure of wholesale prices to rise by the reluctance of the Riksbank to expand credit because it desired to return to the international gold standard as soon as possible. Writing in the beginning of 1932 he charged the Riksbank with maintaining high discount rates and restrictions on credit which prevented the increase of production, increasing unemployment and even causing numerous

---

[7] See Karin Kock, *Paper Currency and Monetary Policy in Sweden* in *Economic Essays in Honor of Gustav Cassel,* London, Allen Unwin Co., Ltd., 1933, pp. 343–356.

[8] Bertil Ohlin, *Sweden's Monetary Policy, op. cit.*

[9] Emil Sommarin, *Knut Wicksell's Auffassung der Entwicklung des Preisniveaus, op. cit*

farm foreclosures. "Everything points to the fact," he said, "that the directors of the Riksbank consider the return to a more or less revised gold standard the final aim of the present monetary policy."

The fact that the Riksbank failed at first in this point of her program, and this perhaps mainly for lack of enthusiasm, has been used by the enemies of stabilization to prove that the Swedish experiment was a "failure." Yet Mr. Kjellstrom shows that, through those two years, wholesale prices fell much less than in the gold standard countries, and fluctuated less than in England.

It may be here added that, since Mr. Kjellstrom's book was written, the recovery of Swedish wholesale prices has continued. The maximum fall of wholesale prices since the stabilization began, until December, 1933, was only 1.9% in Sweden, compared with about the same fall in England, but compared with 16% for the United States and 19% for France. The maximum swing of the wholesale price levels, that is the swing from the highest to the lowest point as compared with the chosen par, in that period was 5.6% for Sweden, 9% for England, and 19% and 16% for France and the United States respectively.

This relative stability of the Swedish wholesale price level is emphasized because of the unjustified criticisms of her policy. These have centered around this question of wholesale prices, and an impression has gone abroad that Sweden had suffered from deflation more than other countries, and this because of her stabilization policy. One writer says, ". . . there is strong reason to believe that Sweden is one of the three or four countries that have suffered most acutely in the past eighteen months, and equally strong reason to believe that the attempt to manage the currency has intensified her sufferings." [10] The exact opposite is

[10] From *Sweden's Managed Currency*, by Rufus S. Tucker, in "Barron's," June 19, 1933.

the truth. By April, 1934, wholesale prices were at 113.5, or 6.5 points higher than in September, 1931, when Sweden abandoned gold. The Swedish Board of Trade, in its review of the year 1933, said:

"Viewed against the background of the general trend in the rest of the world, the recovery in Sweden seems to have been more considerable than in most other countries." [11]

According to the League of Nations, in 1933, the Swedish production index showed more improvement than that of any other European nation. Of the 15 nations mentioned by the League's report, recovery of Sweden's production in 1933 was second only of that of Canada.[12]

Thus, reflation of wholesale prices eventually seems to have been attained, and therefore all four points of the program, and not merely three, carried out with reasonable success.

The increase of Swedish unemployment since the abandonment of gold has also been cited as conclusive proof that the stabilization did not benefit Sweden. Mr. Tucker says: "But the conclusive proof that Sweden has not benefited herself by abandonment of the gold standard is furnished by the statistics of unemployment . . ." But of course, we could not expect a Swedish stabilization started in September, 1931, to solve immediately the unemployment problem. There is always a lag of several months between movements in the price level and their effects on employment. Furthermore, in normal times, Sweden exports about 25% of her total production, and for this reason, Swedish employment of labor depends, to a considerable extent, upon conditions *in foreign countries*. During 1932, her exports to Great Britain were about 40% less than during 1930 and her exports to Germany declined about 60% in that period. Her total exports in 1932 were about 40% smaller than in 1930.

[11] *Kommerskollegium Economic Review,* No. 1, March, 1934.
[12] League of Nations, "Monthly Bulletin of Statistics," Vol. XV, No. 4, Apr., 1934.

Unemployment (of the members of trades unions) increased from 11.8% (average) in 1930, to 22.2% (average) in 1932 [13] or, an addition of about 10% of the total trades union membership. A simple calculation shows that the greatest part of this additional unemployment evidently was due to the decline in exports. Unfortunately, the unemployment was greatly increased by strikes in the building and wood-pulp industries. To compare unemployment in Sweden and elsewhere is difficult, but it seems evident that Sweden's unemployment would have been worse had she continued on the gold standard; in fact, so far as available figures indicate, Swedish unemployment has shown no worse a trend but rather a better trend than unemployment in gold standard countries.

Professor Bertil Ohlin summarizes the general effect of the Swedish stabilization policy as follows:

"As to the effect of the Swedish policy on economic conditions in general, it is important to remember that Sweden suffered considerably last year from the Kreuger crisis and, this year, has had to bear with a serious conflict in the building trade.

"Despite these unfavorable circumstances, the economic situation has not undergone a considerable change for the worst, and it is generally believed that this is due to the wholesome effect of a stable price level." [14]

Whether her index number was the best one that could have been chosen; whether she ought to have reflated before stabilizing, or devaluated her currency and adjusted her debt structure as Australia has done;—these are questions which need not be further discussed here. They are important questions and should be studied on their merits; but they are not the most important ones for this study. The main point here is that Sweden did con-

---

[13] Source: *Kommerskollegium Economic Review*.
[14] Quoted from New York *Times*, October 31, 1933.

trol her consumption price level as she set out to do, a feat formerly declared impossible.

Professor Erik Lindahl who was in constant touch with the monetary experiment in Sweden gave the following opinion as to the efficiency of the Riksbank's management and the lessons which can be derived from it:

"Most of us are of the opinion" he said, "that the management could have been better in several respects; that we could have achieved more with this national paper money experiment. Nevertheless, the policy carried on in Sweden has, upon the whole, proved beneficial; and consequently the Swedish experiment may be of some interest to other countries." [15]

Professor Lindahl emphasizes a number of practical advantages which have resulted from Sweden's stabilization and which should be of interest to other countries—advantages arose from the mere announcement of a definite monetary policy by a central bank. First the public is relieved of uncertainty about what the central bank will do. Secondly, the central bank is able to refer to its announced policy and thus enforce whatever measures may be needed to carry it out, without political interference. In the opinion of Professor Lindahl, the Riksbank would never have carried out so strong a policy with regard to the exchange rate, had it not thus been pledged to a definite policy. In fact, the Riksbank even acted despite the risk of loss of its income and capital; and this, Professor Lindahl feels, "is the most significant proof that we have had an effective monetary policy in Sweden during these years."

Advantages also arose from the establishment of a consumption index as criterion of the Riksbank's monetary policy and the weekly publication of this index. Such publication enables

[15] Erik Lindahl, *Sweden's Monetary Program,* in "Economic Forum," June–July, 1934, pp. 169–181.

the public as well as the directors of the bank to draw their conclusions as to the future development of the price level. "It seems
very suitable," Professor Lindahl says, "to link a monetary program to an index of this type, because more definite conclusions
can be drawn regarding the future development of prices. But"
he continues, "this does not imply that the index should be kept
unaltered." The monetary policy of Sweden has been laid down
merely in a provisional way, he explains, and perhaps a later
formulation may provide for a price level of consumption goods
which shall vary "in some sort of inverse order to the general
state of productivity."

Finally (according to Professor Lindahl), Sweden has shown
that the regulation of the foreign exchange rates prevents foreign price movements from having their full effect upon the
internal price level. But it has also been demonstrated that in
practice a complete stabilization of the level of import and export
prices cannot be attained in this manner. It seems best, he concludes, to maintain a stable exchange rate with the principal
foreign countries and occasionally to alter this rate in order to
regulate the domestic price level.

Professor Lindahl concludes that the Swedish experiment had
a favorable effect, although its effectiveness was hampered by
two facts: First, the Riksbank was unable to influence labor disputes, and similar interferences; and second, the country had
been suffering from the effects of two years of previous depression. He says:

"The fact that, in spite of this, the policy has had a comparatively favorable effect, offers ample evidence that the possibilities for a rational management of the money system are greater
today than man ever hoped for. This is perhaps the main lesson
of the Swedish experiment."

Whatever the future holds in store, this achievement of Sweden
will always be the most important landmark up to its time in

the history of stabilization; and the various efforts which have been made to discredit the importance of Sweden's example can never erase the simple fact that Sweden *did* stabilize the internal purchasing power of her krona according to the official measure set up for that purpose.

Since none, except possibly one, of the opponents of stabilization disputed the fact that Sweden has stabilized her consumption index as she intended to, some of them have sought to argue that, while little Sweden could do so, big America could not. But so far as size is concerned, the argument is obviously the other way. Sweden is so small as to be largely at the mercy of conditions in other countries. The United States is a world in itself. Sweden's slowness in restoring wholesale prices was largely due to the difficulty of stemming the downsweeping tide of wholesale prices in other countries. Swedish foreign trade and the dependence of her exporters on foreign prices are far more serious than in the case of America. If little Sweden can become an oasis in the world-wide desert of depression surrounding her, and despite the Kreuger disaster at home, can maintain her chosen index number almost unchanged, the same result is *economically* feasible almost anywhere.

On the other hand, as mentioned before, Sweden was particularly favored in her stabilization experiment because of her inherent economic stability, the comparative homogeneous and unified nature of her banking system, and her ability to use the foreign exchange for influencing her domestic situation.

SELECTED BIBLIOGRAPHY OF ARTICLES ON SWEDISH STABILIZATION

(In addition to the footnote references in the text and in Appendix II)

Benjamin Haggott Beckhart, *Sweden Seeks Return to Gold* (New York *Herald Tribune,* November 26, 1933).

Gustav Cassel, *Managed Money* (Skandinaviska Kreditaktie-bolaget Quarterly Report, January, 1934).

M. W. Childs, *Sweden: Where Capitalism is Controlled* (Harper's Magazine No. 1002, November, 1933, pp. 749–58).

Charles T. Hallinan, *Sweden's Managed Currency* (The Forum and Century, Vol. 90, No. 3, September, 1933, pp. 159–63).

Eli Heckscher, *La politique économique et les forces économiques en Suède* (Société Belge d'Etudes et d'Expansion Bulletin Periodique No. 92, Mars, 1934, pp. 88–95).

Baron Johan Liljencrants, *The Operation and Principles of a Managed Currency System* (Trust Companies Magazine, Vol. LVII, No. 4; October, 1933, pp. 369–72).

Erik Lindahl, *The Consumption Price Index of the Bank of Sweden,* Mimeographed Memorandum, April, 1933.

Henri de Man, *L'éxperience Suèdoise* (Banque Nationale de Belgique Bulletin d'Information et de Documentation VIIIe année, Vol. II, No. 1, 10 Juillet, 1933).

Midland Bank Monthly Review, *A Notable Experiment; Monetary Management in Sweden,* Issue of October–November, 1932.

APPENDIX III

PARTIAL LIST OF HONORARY VICE-PRESIDENTS OF THE STABLE MONEY ASSOCIATION

(In addition to those already mentioned in the text in connection with the Stable Money League and the National Monetary Association): Charles Rist (France); Sir Henry Strakosch (England); Sir Charles Addis (Great Britain); Sir Arthur Balfour (Great Britain); Eduard Benes (Czechoslovakia); Roland W. Boyden (U.S.A.); Nicholas Murray Butler (U.S.A.); John W. Davis (U.S.A.); Charles G. Dawes (U.S.A.); Robert W. De Forest (U.S.A.); William Green (U.S.A.); Sir Herbert Holt (Canada); Charles Evans Hughes (U.S.A.); Otto H. Kahn (U.S.A.); Baron Frederic De Koranyi (Hungary); Baron Maurice Kornfeld (Hungary); Max Lazard (France); Louis Loucheur (France); Frank O. Lowden (U.S.A.); Samuel Mather (U.S.A.); Lord Melchett (Great Britain); Carl Melchior (Germany); Emile Moreau (France); Alberto Pirelli (Italy); James H. Rand, Jr. (U.S.A.); Richard Reisch (Austria); George M. Reynolds (U.S.A.); Elihu Root (U.S.A.); Louis Rothschild (Austria); Sir Josiah Stamp (Great Britain); C. E. Ter Meulen (Netherlands); Albert Thomas (France); Norman Thomas (U.S.A.); Emile Vandervelde (Belgium); Eleutherios K. Venizelos (Greece); Gerard Vissering (Netherlands); Count J. H. Von Bernstorff (Germany); K. A. Wallenberg (Sweden); Paul M. Warburg (U.S.A.); Owen D. Young (U.S.A.).

Among the members of the Administrative Committee were: Francis H. Sisson; Fred I. Kent; Lawrence Chamberlain.

The following were Honorary Vice-Presidents, Ex-Officio: the Presidents of the following organizations, American Association for Labor Legislation; American Bar Association; American Farm Bureau Federation; American Farm Economic Association; American Statistical Association; Brotherhood of Railroad

Trainmen; Farmers' Educational and Co-operative Union of America; International City Managers' Association; International Photo Engravers' Union; National Association of Credit Men; National Association of Owners of Railroad and Public Utility Securities; National Association of Purchasing Agents; National Consumers' League; National Education Association of the United States; National Institute of Social Sciences; National Retail Dry Goods Association; United Mine Workers of America; United States Building and Loan League. The Chairmen of American Cotton Growers Exchange; and American Council on Education. The National Master of the National Grange.

The Presidents of the following Bankers' Associations: Alabama; Arkansas; California; Colorado; Connecticut; Delaware; District of Columbia; Florida; Georgia; Idaho; Illinois; Indiana; Iowa; Kansas; Louisiana; Maine; Maryland; Massachusetts; Michigan; Minnesota; Mississippi; Missouri; Montana; New Jersey; New Hampshire; New Mexico; New York State; North Carolina; North Dakota; Ohio; Oklahoma; Oregon; Pennsylvania; South Carolina; South Dakota; Tennessee; Texas; Utah; Vermont; Virginia; Washington; West Virginia; Wisconsin; Wyoming.

The Presidents of the following organizations: Chicago Association of Commerce; The Merchants' Association of New York; The Savings Bank Association of the State of New York.

APPENDIX IV

PUBLICATIONS OF THE COMMITTEE FOR THE NATION
SINCE ITS ORGANIZATION IN JANUARY, 1933.[1]

1. "Five Next Steps"—(The Committee's program for recovery).
2. "Interim Report"—(A survey of conditions in February, 1933).
3. "H.R. 5073"—(Bill to create Monetary Board) with the Committee's comment.
4. "Stabilization of the Measure of Value," by Professor G. F. Warren.
5. "The Business Situation"—by Professor G. F. Warren.
6. "The London Free Gold Market"—by Professor T. E. Gregory.
7. "An Analysis of the Proposal for an American Free Gold Market"—by National Industrial Conference Board, Inc.
8. "The Dollar of the Future—What Happened at London"—radio address by Earl Harding.
9. "The All-American Dollar"—radio address by James H. Rand, Jr., President of Remington Rand, Inc.
10. "Frozen Bank Deposits—A Drag on Recovery"—report by Committee for the Nation.
11. "Prices and Gold"—radio address by Frederic H. Frazier, Chairman, General Baking Company.
12. "Frozen Bank Deposits"—radio address by Lessing J. Rosenwald, Chairman, Sears, Roebuck and Co.
13. "Monetary Policy and Agriculture"—radio address by Fred H. Sexauer, President Dairymen's League Cooperative Assn. Inc.
14. "Why Deflation must be Stopped," a survey of the Effects

[1] Copies of some of these publications may be secured by writing to the Committee for the Nation, 205 East 42nd Street, New York City.

of the Drop in Price Level in a Typical American Community.

15. "President Roosevelt's Monetary Policy"—radio address by Frank A. Vanderlip.

16. "U.S. Gold Program—What Does It Mean?"—radio address by Earl Harding.

17. "The Price of Gold,"—by Professor Frank A. Pearson.

18. "Memorandum on the Stabilization of the Dollar," by Frank A. Vanderlip.

19. "Some Statistics on the Gold Situation,"—by Professor G. F. Warren and F. A. Pearson.

20. "Why A Federal Monetary Authority,"—by James H. Rand Jr., and Frank A. Vanderlip, with text of bill.

21. "Australia's Recovery Contrasted with AAA Regimentation."

22. "Wall Chart of Gold Price and Recovery Indices."

23. "The Money Muddle"—Domestic price level more important than exchange stabilization.

24. "Unemployment Chart."

25. "Gold Policy Has Worked"—How price of gold controls price of basic commodities.

26. "Who Says It Doesn't Work . . !" by Frank E. Gannett, American Agriculturist.

27. "The President's Gold Policy Has Worked," by Congressman Samuel B. Pettengill.

28. "Strikes"—Social Upheaval Feeds on Deflation.

29. "Can Industry Still Save Itself?"—Committee's current program.

30. "Money and Profits," address by U. S. Senator Elmer Thomas.

31. "The Rise and Fall of the Gold Standard," by Sir Charles Morgan-Webb.

APPENDIX V

List of Stabilization Bills

Introduced in the 72nd Congress—2nd Session, And in the 73rd Congress—first and 2nd Sessions

(In addition to foot note references in the Text)

On December 5, 1932, *Mr. John E. Rankin* of Mississippi, introduced his

"H.R. 13012, A Bill, to regulate the value of money, to stabilize its purchasing power by the controlled expansion and contraction of the currency, and for other purposes."

On December 23, 1932, *Senator Elmer Thomas* of Oklahoma, introduced the same bill as S. 5292. This bill was re-introduced by Mr. Rankin as H.R. 1703 in the 73rd Congress—1st Session.

On February 22, 1933, *Senator John H. Bankhead* of Alabama, and *Congressman Samuel B. Pettengill* of Indiana, introduced identical bills, H.R. 14757 and S. 5674 (72nd Congress—2nd Session), calling for the issuance of "stamp money." These bills were re-introduced in the 73rd Congress—1st Session, by Senator Bankhead on March 11, 1933 (S. 242) and by Mr. Pettengill on March 9, 1933 (H.R. 148).

On March 9, 1933, *Mr. Harold McGugin* of Kansas introduced the following bills in the 73rd Congress—1st Session:

"H.R. 20, A Bill to stabilize the buying power of money."

"H.R. 21, A Bill to raise the commodity price level to the debt-incurring stage and stabilize it thereafter."

On March 10, 1933, *Mr. Kent E. Keller* of Illinois re-introduced his bill (mentioned in the text) in the 73rd Congress—1st Session:

"H.R. 1619, A Bill to amend the act approved December 13, 1913, known as the 'Federal Reserve Act,' to stabilize the average

415

wholesale price of commodities at the average level of the year 1926, thereby to correct the price decline suffered since September 1928, to promote economic justice, to steady industry, agriculture, commerce and employment, and for other purposes."

He also introduced (at the same Session):

"H.R. 1624, A Bill to regulate the value of money and for other purposes."

On April 18, 1933, *Mr. O. H. Cross* of Texas introduced (73rd Congress—1st Session):

"H.R. 5066, A Bill, establishing a stabilized currency and adopting the wholesale commodity index of 1926 as a standard of value."

On April 20, 1933, *Mr. T. Alan Goldsborough* of Maryland introduced his "H.R. 5073" and on April 21, 1933, his "H.R. 5160" (73rd Congress—1st Session), both bills containing the following:

"A Bill, to regulate the value of money in accordance with article I, section 8, of the Constitution of the United States, to re-establish the gold standard, to provide for its maintenance and stabilization, and for other purposes."

On April 21, 1933, *Mr. John E. Rankin* of Mississippi introduced (73rd Congress—1st Session):

"H.R. 5158, A Bill, providing for the exercise of power conferred by section 8 of article I, of the Constitution: To coin money and regulate the value thereof."

On April 22, 1933, *Mr. Jeff Busby* of Mississippi introduced (73rd Congress—1st Session):

"H.R. 5172, A Bill, to declare a monetary policy and regulate the value of money in accordance with paragraph 5, Section 8, article I, of the Constitution of the United States, to provide for the maintenance and stabilization of the gold standard, and for other purposes."

On January 20, 1934, *Mr. Edward C. Moran, Jr.* of Maine introduced his "H.R. 7156" (73rd Congress—2nd Session) and on January 22, 1934, *Mr. Henry B. Steagall* of Alabama introduced his "H.R. 7216" (73rd Congress—2nd Session), both bills calling for the "Federal Monetary Authority," as described in Mr. Goldsborough's bill which is mentioned in the text.

On June 6, 1934 *Senator Bronson Cutting* of New Mexico introduced (73rd Congress—2nd Session):

"S. 3744 A Bill, to regulate the value of money in pursuance of article I, section 8, paragraph 5, of the Constitution of the United States; to create a Federal Monetary Authority; to provide an adequate and stable monetary system; to prevent bank failures; to prevent uncontrolled inflation; to prevent depressions; to provide a system to control the price of commodities and the purchasing power of money; to restore normal prosperity and to assure its continuance; and for other purposes."

On the same day, *Mr. Wright Patman* of Texas introduced the same bill in the House of Representatives as H.R. 9855.

On June 14, 1934, *Mr. George G. Sadowski* of Michigan introduced (73rd Congress—2nd Session):

"H.R. 9931, A Bill, to stabilize and standardize money and labor prices by the establishment of a labor-hour monetary system, to guarantee work at all times, to give normal prosperity, prevent depressions, and for other purposes."

On June 15, 1934, *Senator Elmer Thomas* of Oklahoma introduced (73rd Congress—2nd Session):

"S. 3798, A Bill, to provide for the taking over by the Government of the outstanding capital stock of all Federal Reserve banks, to substitute United States Treasury notes for outstanding gold certificates, silver certificates, Treasury notes of 1890, Federal Reserve notes, Federal Reserve bank notes, national currency and national bank notes; and to regulate the value of money in pursuance of article I, section 8, paragraph 5, of the Constitution of the United States; and for other purposes."

On June 18, 1934, *Mr. Andrew L. Somers* of New York introduced (73rd Congress—2nd Session):

"H.R. 9968, A Bill, to create a National Bank of the United States and to provide an adequate and stable monetary system in order to regulate the price level and the purchasing power of money within the United States, and to regulate the activities of all banks."

APPENDIX VI

Selected Bibliography

(In addition to the 285 titles mentioned in the text; 23 titles of publications of the Committee for the Nation; 39 titles mentioned in Appendix I; 10 titles mentioned in Appendix II.)

Academy of Political Science, New York, "The Future of Prices at Home and Abroad," *Proceedings of the Academy of Political Science,* William L. Ranson and Parker Thomas Moon, Editors. January 1925. New York, The Academy of Political Science, Columbia University. 205 p.

——————, "Money and Credit in the Recovery Program," *A series of addresses and papers presented at the semi-annual meeting of the Academy of Political Science.* March 21, 1934. Parker Thomas Moon, Editor. New York, The Academy of Political Science, Columbia University. 1934. IV, 124 p.

Anderson, B. M. Jr., "The Gold Standard Versus 'A Managed Currency,'" *Chase Economic Bulletin,* Vol. V, No. 1, March 23, 1935. 39 p. The Chase National Bank of New York.

——————, "The Practical Impossibility of a Commodity Dollar," *Chase Economic Bulletin,* Vol. XIII, No. 4, December 1933. 28 p. The Chase National Bank of New York.

Angas, L. L. B., *Inflate or Perish,* St. Clemens Press Ltd., London, 1932. 101 p.

——————, *The Coming Collapse in Gold,* St. Clemens Press Ltd., London, 1933. 91 p.

Angell, James W., *The Theory of International Prices,* Harvard University Press, Cambridge, 1926. XIV, 571 p.

Ayres, Leonard P., *The Economics of Recovery,* Macmillan Company, New York, 1933. VI, 189 p.

Barbour, Sir David, *The Standard of Value,* Macmillan & Company Ltd., London, 1912. XVI, 242 p.

418

——————, *The Influence of the Gold Supply on Prices and Profits,* Macmillan and Co., Ltd., London, 1913. XII, 104 p.

Barnes, Harry Elmer, *Money Changers vs. The New Deal,* Ray Long and Richard R. Smith, Inc., New York, 1934. 150 p.

Bauer, John and Gold, Nathaniel, *Permanent Prosperity and How to Get It,* Harper & Brothers, New York and London, 1934. VII, 251 p.

Baxendale, A. S., *Currency, An Indictment,* Cecil Palmer, London, 1925. 192 p.

Boissevain, G. M., "Een Ideale Waarde-Standaard," *De Economist,* The Hague, 1913. pp. 441–473.

Campbell, Homer Orpheus, *Socialized Money,* published by the author, 1525 Forty-Fifth Avenue S.W., Seattle, U.S.A., 1933. 160 p.

Cannan, Edwin, *Modern Currency and the Regulation of Its Value,* P. S. King & Son, Ltd., London, 1931. VIII, 112 p.

——————, *Money, Its Connection with Rising and Falling Prices,* (First edition 1918—seventh edition 1932). P. S. King & Son, Ltd., Westminster, 1932. XII, 127 p.

Christen, Theophil, "Die Kaufkraft des Geldes und ihre Bedeutung fuer die Volkswirtschaft," *Annalen des Deutschen Reiches,* 48. Jahrgang Muenchen, 1915. pp. 493–506.

Clark, J. M., "Possible Complications of the Compensated Dollar," *American Economic Review,* September 1913. p. 576–588.

Cole, G. D. H. (editor), *What Everybody Wants to Know About Money,* A Planned Outline of Monetary Problems by Nine Economists from Oxford. Victor Gollancz, Ltd., London, 1933. 544 p.

Coughlin, Rev. Chas. E., *The New Deal In Money,* The Radio League of the Little Flower, Royal Oak, Mich., 1933. 128 p.

Davidson, David, "Irving Fisher's Förslag att reglera penningens köpkraft," *Economisk Tidskrift,* Stockholm, Haft 3, 1913. pp. 88–107.

Dick, Ernst, *The Interest Standard of Currency,* G. Allen & Unwin, Ltd., London, 1925. 286 p.

——————, *The Problem of Interest in Its Relation to Cur-*

rency and Debt, Williams & Norgate, Ltd., London, 1929. XV, 381 p.

Döring, Herbert, *Die Geld Theorien seit Knapp*—ein dogmen-historischer Versuch. Greifswalden staatswissenschaftliche Abhandlungen Nr. 7. Greifswald, L. Bamberg, 1921. VIII, 239 p.

Economic Club, New York, "The Federal Reserve System and the Control of Credit," Discussion before the Economic Club of New York, March 18, 1929. *The Concensus,* June 1929. The National Economic League, Boston.

Edgeworth, F. Y., "Thoughts on Monetary Reform," *The Economic Journal,* Vol. V, pp. 434–451. Macmillan & Company, London, 1895.

Edie, Lionel D., *Money, Bank Credit and Prices,* Harper & Brothers, New York and London, 1928, XIV, 500 p.

——————, *The Banks and Prosperity,* Harper & Brothers, New York and London, 1931. XI, 179 p.

——————, *Dollars,* Yale University Press, New Haven, 1934. 293 p.

Fortune (editors of), "Federal Reserve," *Fortune Magazine,* New York, May 1934. pp. 65–68; 114–125.

Foster, William Trufant, and Catchings, Wadill, *Money,* Houghton, Mifflin Co., Boston and New York, 1923. 409 p.

Glückstadt, Hans, *The Mechanism of the Credit Standard,* Practical Proposals for a New Monetary Standard. P. S. King & Son, Ltd., London, 1933. XIII, 111 p.

Graziani, Augusto, "Di una nuova proposta per rendere più stabile il valore della moneta," *Reale Instituto d'Incoraggiamento di Napoli,* Nota letta nella tornata del 6 marzo, 1913.

Haberler, Gottfried, "Die Kaufkraft des Gelds und die Stabilisierung der Wirtschaft," *Schmoller's Jahrbuch,* 55. Jahrgang, 1931. pp. 993–1023. Dunker und Humblot, München und Leipzig.

Hahn, L. Albert, *Geld und Kredit,* J. C. B. Mohr (Paul Siebeck), Tübingen, 1929. VI, 278 p.

Hansen, Alvin Harvey, *Economic Stabilization in an Unbalanced World,* Harcourt Brace and Company, New York, 1932. IX, 384 p.

Harding, W. P. G., "Factors Which Govern Price Levels and Stability," *Trust Companies,* Vol. XLIII, No. 1, July 1926. pp. 11–13; 91.

Hardy, Charles O., *Credit Policies of the Federal Reserve System,* The Brookings Institution, Washington D.C., 1932. XV, 372 p.

Harris, S. E., *Twenty Years of Federal Reserve Policy,* Harvard Economic Studies, Vol. XLI, Harvard University Press, Cambridge, Mass., 1933. 2 vols.

Hayek, Friedrich A., *Prices and Production,* George Rutledge & Sons, Ltd., London, 1931. 112 p.

Hobson, J. A., *Gold, Prices and Wages,* Methuen & Co., Ltd., London (H. Doran Company, New York), 1913. XIII, 181 p.

——————, *Economics of Unemployment,* G. Allen Unwin, Ltd., London, 1922. 157 p.

Hodgson, James Goodwin (Compiler), *Stabilization of Money,* The Reference Shelf, Vol. VIII, No. 7, H. W. Wilson Company, New York, 1933. 238 p.

Huntington–Wilson, F. M., *Money and the Price Level,* The Century Company, New York and London, 1932. X, 222 p.

James, F. Cyril, *The Road to Revival,* Harper & Brothers, New York and London, 1932. XV, 235 p.

Kemmerer, Edwin Walter, *High Prices and Deflation,* Princeton University Press, Princeton, N.J., 1920. XII, 86 p.

——————, "The Gold Standard in the Light of Post-War Developments," *Journal of the Canadian Bankers' Association,* April, 1929.

Kerschagl, Richard, *Theorie des Geldes unter der Geldwirtschaft,* Gustav Fischer, Jena, 1923. IV, 144 p.

King, Willford, I., "The Movement for Sound Money," *Burroughs Clearing House,* October, 1927. pp. 5–7; 44–51. Burroughs Adding Machine Co., Detroit, Mich., 1927.

Kinley, David, "Objections to a Monetary Standard Based on Index Numbers," *The American Economic Review,* Vol. III, No. 1, March, 1913. pp. 1–19.

Knapp, Georg Friedrich, *Staatliche Theorie des Geldes,* Dunker & Humblot, München, 1923. XVI, 461 p.

Knibbs, G. H., "Consideration of the Proposal to Stabilize the

Unit of Money," *American Economic Review,* June 1919. pp. 244–255. Rejoinder by Irving Fisher, pp. 256–262.

Knies, Karl, *Das Geld,* (1885) Neudruck Hans Buske, Leipzig, 1931. X, 450 p.

König, Heinrich, *Die Befestigung der Kaufkraft des Geldes,* Bonner Staatswissenschaftliche Untersuchungen. Kurt Schröder, Bonn und Leipzig, 1922. 91 p.

Lawrence, Joseph Stagg, *Stabilization of Prices,* Macmillan Company, New York, 1928. XIX, 484 p.

Lloyd, E. M. H., *Stabilization,* An Economic Policy for Producers and Consumers. Alfred Knopf, New York, 1923. 140 p.

Lombard, Norman, "Interest of Comptrollers and Accounting Officers in Stable Money," *The Comptroller,* November 1927.

————, "The Future of Money Value," *The Bankers Magazine,* New York, September, 1929.

Low, Alvin H., *Stabilize the Value of the Dollar,* Pico Stationers, Los Angeles, Cal., 1929. 85 p.

McCracken, Harlan Linneus, *Value Theory and Business Cycles,* Falcon Press, New York, 1933. XIII, 270 p.

McCullough, Ernest, *Everybody's Money,* G. P. Putnam's Sons, New York and London, 1923. VI, 175 p.

March, Lucien, "Un Projet de Stabilisation des Prix," *Communication à la Société de Statistique de Paris,* le 15 janvier, 1913. *Journal.* pp. 10–24.

Menger, Carl, "Geld," *Handwörterbuch der Staatswissenschaften,* 3. Auflage 4. Band. pp. 555–610. Gustav Fischer, Jena, 1909.

Meulen, Henry, *Industrial Justice Through Banking Reform,* Richard J. James, London, 1917. XI, 324 p.

Mises, Ludwig, *Theorie des Geldes und der Umlaufsmittel,* Dunker & Humblot, München und Leipzig, 1924. XIII, 420 p.

————, *Geldwertstabilisierung und Konjunkturpolitik,* Gustav Fischer, Jena, 1928. 84 p.

Mlynarski, Feliks, *The Functioning of the Gold Standard,* League of Nations Publications Ser. 2A, No. 25, Geneva, 1931. 115 p.

Monroe, Arthur Eli, *Monetary Theory Before Adam Smith,* Harvard Economic Studies, Vol. XXV, Harvard University Press, Cambridge, 1923. XI, 312 p.

Morgan-Webb, Sir Charles, *The Rise and Fall of the Gold*

Standard, George Allen & Unwin, Ltd., London, 1934. 187 p.

Newlin, Gurney E., "How Monetary Instability Burdens the Law," *The Lawyer and Banker,* August, 1929.

Nicholson, J. Shield, *A Treatise on Money,* London, 1888. XIV, 375 p.

—— *Inflation,* P. S. King & Son, Ltd., London, 1919. IV, 143 p.

Nogaro, Bertrand, *Modern Monetary Systems,* P. S. King & Son, Ltd., London, 1927. XII, 236 p.

Ostrer, Isidore, *The Conquest of Gold,* Jonathan Cape, London, 1932. 142 p.

Palyi, Melchior, "Ungelöste Fragen der Geldtheorie," *Die Wirtschaftswissenschaft nach dem Kriege,* Bd. II, pp. 455–517. Dunker & Humblot, München und Leipzig, 1925.

Patterson, E. M., "Objections to a Compensated Dollar," *American Economic Review,* September 1913. pp. 863–875.

Pell, Charles Edward, *The Riddle of Unemployment and Its Solution,* Cecil Palmer, London, 1922. 217 p.

Persons, Warren M., *Forecasting Business Cycles,* John Wiley and Sons, Inc., New York, 1931. XIV, 295 p.

Puxley, H. L., *A Critique of the Gold Standard,* George Allen Unwin Ltd., London, 1933. 272 p.

Reed, Harold L., *The Commodity Dollar,* Farrar & Rinehart, New York, 1934. 56 p.

Richards, William, *The Standard of Value,* Washington, D. C., 1893. 62 p.

Roberts, George E., "The Gold Movement and Its Effect on Business," *Forbes Magazine,* February 1, 1928. pp. 18–20; 40.

Robertson, D. H., *Money,* Harcourt, Brace and Company, New York, 1922. XII, 182 p.

——————, *Banking Policy and the Price Level,* P. S. King & Son, Ltd., London, 1926. 103 p.

Röpke, Wilhelm, *Krise und Konjunktur,* Quelle & Meyer, Leipzig, 1932, 141 p.

Royal Institute of International Affairs, *The International Gold Problem,* Oxford University Press, London, 1931. 240 p.

——————, *Monetary Policy and the Depression,* Oxford University Press, London, 1933. VI, 128 p.

Sir Arthur Salter, Sir Josiah Stamp, J. Maynard Keynes, Sir Basil Blackett, Sir Henry Clay, Sir E. H. Beveridge, *The*

World's Economic Crisis and the Way of Escape, The Century Company, New York and London, 1932. 185 p.

Schumpeter, Joseph, "Das Sozialprodukt und die Rechenpfennige," *Archiv fuer Sozialwissenschaft und Sozialpolitik,* 44. Band, 1917–1918. pp. 627–715. J. C. B. Mohr, Tuebingen.

——————, *Theorie der Wirtschaftlichen Entwicklung,* Dunker & Humblot, München und Leipzig, 1926. XIV, 369 p.

Sewall, Hannah Robie, *The Theory of Value before Adam Smith,* Publication of the American Economics Association. Series III, Vol. II, No. 3, Macmillan Company, New York, 1901. 128 p.

Shaw, W. A., *Currency, Credit and the Exchanges During the Great War (1914–1926),* G. G. Harrap & Co., Ltd., London, 1927. 202 p.

Spahr, Walter Earl, *The Federal Reserve System and the Control of Credit,* Macmillan Company, New York, 1931. XVIII, 138 p.

——————, *The Monetary Theories of Warren and Pearson,* Farrar & Rinehart, New York, 1934. 26 p.

Stable Money Association, *The Movement for a Sounder Money,* by Owen D. Young; Norman Lombard; Frederick A. Delano; Sir Josiah Stamp; Henri Fuss; Carl Snyder. The Stable Money Association, New York, 1929. 54 p.

Taussig, F. W., "The Plan for a Compensated Dollar," *Quarterly Journal of Economics,* May 1913. pp. 401–416.

Tucker, Robert H., "Our Unstable Standard of Value," *The United States Banker,* January, 1929.

Valette, Marc de, *Stabilisation de la Valeur de la Monnaie,* A. Pedone, Paris, 1924. 46 p.

Walker, Karl, *Das Problem unserer Zeit und seine Meisterung,* Rudolf Zitzmann Verlag, Lauf a. Pegnitz, 1931. 226 p.

Wicksell, Knut, "Der Bankzins als Regulator der Warenpreise," *Jahrbücher für Nationalökonomie und Statistik,* III. Folge, Bd. 13. Jena, 1897. pp. 228–243.

Wieser, Friedrich von, *Social Economics,* Adelphi Publication, Greenberg Publishers, New York, 1927. XXII, 470 p.

Wiggelsworth, F., "Gold and Stability, the Problem of our Currency," *The Contemporary Review,* London, April 1928.

Wiggelsworth, Frederick and Alfred, *The Gold Tangle and the*

Way Out, John Lane, The Bodley Head Limited, London, 1931. X, 245 p.

Winn, Henry, "The Invariable Dollar," *The Traveler,* October 17, 1891.

Withers, Hartley, *Money,* Jonathan Cape & Harrison Smith, New York, 1920. 121 p.

——————, *Bankers and Credit,* Eveleigh Nash and Grayson, Ltd., London, 1924. X, 294 p.

Woodward, Donald B. and Rose, Marc A., *Inflation,* Whittlesey House, McGraw-Hill Book Company, New York, 1933. XII, 165 p.

Young, Allyn A., "Downward Price Trend Probable, Due to Hoarding of Gold by Central Banks," *The Annalist,* New York. January 18, 1929.

Owen D. Young, Walter W. Head, Carter Glass, Ogden L. Mills, "Recent Federal Reserve Policy" (A Symposium) *The American Review of Reviews,* September, 1929.

Zeuthen, F., "Irving Fisher's Forslag til Prisniveauets Stabilisering," *Nationalökonomisk Tidskrift,* Copenhagen. Hefte 4. July–August 1913. pp. 350–364.

INDEX

Barclays Bank Ltd., 279
Barker, Joseph W., 70
Bavaria, *stabilization attempt in revolutionary,* 142-143
Beauchamp, Earl, *quoted,* 137
Beckhart, Benjamin Haggott, 250, 262
Bellerby, Major J. R., *quoted,* 85, 86; *cited,* 161, 285, 395
Bendix, Vincent, 118
Bennett, R. B., *quoted,* 302-303; *cited,* 359
Berkeley, Bishop, *quoted,* 14
Bernoulli, Professor, 144
Bevan, Aneurin, M. P., 134
Bianchini, Mr., 282
Bibliography, selected, 418-425
Bimetallism, 3, 54, 375
Birtwell, Charles W., 106
Black, Governor, *quoted,* 212-213; *cited,* 370
Blackett, Sir Basil, *quoted,* 139-141; *cited,* 139, 282
Boeckh, Augustus, 6
Bonn, M. J., 290
Bourne, Mr., 39
Bracteates, 9, 10, 11
Brand, H. H., 282
Brassage, 378; *need for adequate,* Rogers, 153; King, 154
Brassey, Lord, 378
British Committee on Finance and Industry, *see* Macmillan Committee
British Conservative Platform, 135
British Empire, *common standard of value for,* Strakosch, 307; *monetary policy of, decided by England,* Strakosch, 208
British Employers' Group, 131
British Industrialists, *expression on stable money,* 130
British Labour Platform, 135
British Trades Union Congress General Council, 130, 133
Brokers Loans, Harrison, 268
Brookhart, Senator, 203
Brown, Harry G., 375, 387
Bruce, S. M., *quoted,* 301, 341-342; *cited,* 303-304
Bruce, Wallace, 338
Brussels International Economic Conference (1920), 96, 280-281
Bryan, William Jennings, *quoted,* 54
Bullion Report, *see* Gold Bullion Report

Bunge, Professor, 144
Bureau of Labor Statistics, *cost-of-living index,* Meeker, 67
Bureau of Labor Statistics, Wholesale Price Index, 65, 152; *adoption of* (1926 = 100), 190; *criticism of,* Snyder, 166
Bureau of Standards, 147
Burgess, W. R., *quoted,* 242-243; *cited,* 170, 249
Burtness, Congressman Olger B., 157, 184, 192
Busby, Congressman Jeff, *quoted,* 211-212; *cited,* 199, 416
Business Cycles, *expressions on,* Cassel, 99; Hawtrey, 84; Meyer, 195; League of Nations Gold Delegation, 294; *studies on, a factor in stable money movement,* 67
Business Forecasting, 386-387
Business Men, *Federal Monetary Authority and,* Rand, 209; *opposition to inflation,* 105
Business Week, 266
Butler, Nicholas Murray, 69

Canada, 302, 359
Capital Standard, Nicholson, 39
Carli, G. R., 14
Cassel, Gustav, *cited,* 102, 131, 280, 282, 289, 290, 295; *quoted,* 95-99, 182, 254
Catchings, Waddill, 105
Central Bank, *responsibility of,* Hawtrey, 82
Central Bank Cooperation, *for maintaining exchange stability,* Eisler, 101; *for reestablishment of international standard,* Bruce, 304; *for reflation,* Ottawa Report, 310; *for stabilization,* Bellerby, 86; British Trades Union Congress, 131; Cassel, 95; Genoa Resolutions, 283; Hawtrey, 81; Independent Labour Party, 134; Keynes, 89; London Chamber of Commerce, 133; Lord Vernon, 130; Mackenna, 137; Macmillan Report, 300; Ottawa Report, 312; Pethick-Lawrence, 126; Wicksell, 43, 93
Central Bank Functions, Macmillan Report, 297; Wicksell, 93
Central Bank Policy, Harrison, 229;

INDEX

DATE DUE